# Cisco Self-Study: Implementing IPv6 Networks (IPV6)

Régis Desmeules

**Cisco Press**

Cisco Press
201 West 103rd Street
Indianapolis, IN 46290 USA

# Cisco Self-Study: Implementing IPv6 Networks (IPV6)

Régis Desmeules

Published by:
Cisco Press
201 West 103rd Street
Indianapolis, IN 46290 USA

Printed in the United States of America 3 4 5 6 7 8 9 0

Third Printing September 2007

Library of Congress Cataloging-in-Publication Number: 2002100664

ISBN: 1-58705-086-2

## Warning and Disclaimer

This book is designed to provide information about implementing Cisco IPv6 networks. Every effort has been made to make this book as complete and accurate as possible, but no warranty or fitness is implied.

The information is provided on an "as is" basis. The author, Cisco Press, and Cisco Systems, Inc. shall have neither liability nor responsibility to any person or entity with respect to any loss or damages arising from the information contained in this book or from the use of the discs or programs that may accompany it.

The opinions expressed in this book belong to the author and are not necessarily those of Cisco Systems, Inc.

## Trademark Acknowledgments

All terms mentioned in this book that are known to be trademarks or service marks have been appropriately capitalized. Cisco Press or Cisco Systems, Inc. cannot attest to the accuracy of this information. Use of a term in this book should not be regarded as affecting the validity of any trademark or service mark.

## Feedback Information

At Cisco Press, our goal is to create in-depth technical books of the highest quality and value. Each book is crafted with care and precision, undergoing rigorous development that involves the unique expertise of members of the professional technical community.

Reader feedback is a natural continuation of this process. If you have any comments regarding how we could improve the quality of this book, or otherwise alter it to better suit your needs, you can contact us through e-mail at feedback@ciscopress.com. Please make sure to include the book title and ISBN in your message.

We greatly appreciate your assistance.

| | |
|---|---|
| Publisher | John Wait |
| Editor-In-Chief | John Kane |
| Cisco Systems Program Manager | Anthony Wolfenden |
| Manager, Marketing Communications, Cisco Systems | Scott Miller |
| Executive Editor | Brett Bartow |
| Acquisitions Editor | Michelle Grandin |
| Managing Editor | Patrick Kanouse |
| Development Editor | Ginny Bess |
| Project Editor | Marc Fowler |
| Copy Editor | Gayle Johnson |
| Technical Editors | Bruno Ciscato |
| | Patrick Grossetete |
| | Jun-ichiro Itojun Hagino |
| | Casimir Samanasu |
| | Saeed Bin Sarder |
| Team Coordinator | Tammi Ross |
| Book Designer | Gina Rexrode |
| Cover Designer | Louisa Adair |
| Production Team | Octal Publishing |
| Indexer | Tim Wright |

## CISCO SYSTEMS

**Corporate Headquarters**
Cisco Systems, Inc.
170 West Tasman Drive
San Jose, CA 95134-1706
USA
www.cisco.com
Tel: 408 526-4000
    800 553-NETS (6387)
Fax: 408 526-4100

**European Headquarters**
Cisco Systems International BV
Haarlerbergpark
Haarlerbergweg 13-19
1101 CH Amsterdam
The Netherlands
www-europe.cisco.com
Tel: 31 0 20 357 1000
Fax: 31 0 20 357 1100

**Americas Headquarters**
Cisco Systems, Inc.
170 West Tasman Drive
San Jose, CA 95134-1706
USA
www.cisco.com
Tel: 408 526-7660
Fax: 408 527-0883

**Asia Pacific Headquarters**
Cisco Systems, Inc.
Capital Tower
168 Robinson Road
#22-01 to #29-01
Singapore 068912
www.cisco.com
Tel: +65 6317 7777
Fax: +65 6317 7799

Cisco Systems has more than 200 offices in the following countries and regions. Addresses, phone numbers, and fax numbers are listed on the
**Cisco.com Web site at www.cisco.com/go/offices.**

Argentina • Australia • Austria • Belgium • Brazil • Bulgaria • Canada • Chile • China PRC • Colombia • Costa Rica • Croatia • Czech Republic
Denmark • Dubai, UAE • Finland • France • Germany • Greece • Hong Kong SAR • Hungary • India • Indonesia • Ireland • Israel • Italy
Japan • Korea • Luxembourg • Malaysia • Mexico • The Netherlands • New Zealand • Norway • Peru • Philippines • Poland • Portugal
Puerto Rico • Romania • Russia • Saudi Arabia • Scotland • Singapore • Slovakia • Slovenia • South Africa • Spain • Sweden
Switzerland • Taiwan • Thailand • Turkey • Ukraine • United Kingdom • United States • Venezuela • Vietnam • Zimbabwe

# About the Author

**Régis Desmeules** is an independent consultant. His specialties include IPv4, IPv6, network architecture and design, security, DNS, multimedia, Cisco routers, LAN switches, UNIX, and Microsoft implementations. He has developed and taught courses related to IPv4, IPv6, multimedia over IP, security, DNS, and MobileIP. He has taught courses in Canada and at different events such as INET, IPv6 Forum, Internet2, and Networld+ Interop. Desmeules was also a consultant for Viagénie, Inc. There he participated in IPv6 projects such as the deployment of IPv6 backbones on CA\*net2 and CA\*net3; the development and operation of Freenet6.net, one of the first tunnel servers for IPv6; the deployment of a stealth IPv6 DNS root server on the 6bone; the IPv6 Internet exchange called 6TAP and the network game Quake over IPv6. He has served as a collaborator on the IPv6 course and training that were designed for the IOS Learning Services Group at Cisco Systems, Inc. Before working for Viagénie, Desmeules worked for the largest distance education university in Canada, where he built large data, voice, and videoconference networks. He lives in the peaceful town of Quebec City in Canada.

## About the Technical Reviewers

**Bruno Ciscato** is a networking consultant focusing on IPv6. Prior to that, he worked with Cisco Systems, Inc., for six years designing service provider networks and leading the 6net Project, a large-scale IPv6 test bed for the European scientific community funded by the European Commission. He lives in Italy and loves wine and sailing.

**Patrick Grossetete** is a senior product manager at Cisco Systems. In the Internet Technology Division (ITD), he is responsible for the IPv6 strategy on Cisco IOS. Prior to that, he was Field Distinguished Engineer on the EMEA consulting team, doing network design for customers. He regularly presents on behalf of Cisco at various IPv6 events and represents Cisco at the IPv6 Forum. Before joining Cisco Systems in 1994, Grossetete worked in remedial support and as a network consultant for Digital Equipment, where he was involved with LAN products, ATM, and DECnet/OSI architecture. He lives in France with his wife and two children.

**Jun-ichiro Itojun Hagino** is a researcher at IIJ, one of the biggest ISPs in Japan. He serves as a co-chair of the IETF v6ops working group. He received a PhD from Keio University for research on object-oriented operating systems.

**Casimir Samanasu** is a Program Manager with Cisco Systems, Inc. He holds an M.S. Computer Science degree from DePaul University, Chicago, and an MBA from the University of Dallas. Casimir has developed LAN switching courses in the past and was responsible for Cisco IOS curriculum that included advanced technologies such as QoS, Multicast, Security, and VPN. As a curriculum manager, Casimir was recently responsible for the development of training for IPv6 and Mobile IP technologies, and created the "ABCs of IP Version 6" document.

**Saeed Bin Sarder** has worked in Cisco Systems' High-Speed Switching Group as a development resting engineer for more than two years. His group is responsible for testing control and data plane issues in IOS on Catalyst 6000 products, including IPv4, IPv6, MPLS, QoS, and IP multicast routing and hardware forwarding on a variety of LAN and WAN modules.

# Dedication

I would like to dedicate this book to my wife, Caroline, son, Olivier, and daughter, Sarah, for their unconditional support during the nights and weekends dedicated to this book.

A special thank-you goes to my friends Marc Blanchet, Florent Parent, and Hélène Richard at Viagénie, who provided suggestions, help, and encouragement during the writing. They all contributed to the development of tutorials and courses from which this book is inspired.

# Acknowledgments

I would like to say thank you to Bill St-Arneau and his team at Canarie in Canada, who have provided support and belief since the early development stages of the IPv6 protocol.

Thanks to the Cisco Press staff, especially Michelle, Chris, Ginny, and all the technical reviewers who contributed to this book—Patrick, Itojun, Cas, Bruno, and Saeed.

# Contents at a Glance

# Table of Contents

# Introduction

Introduced by the IETF in 1992, IPv6 appears today to be a fundamental and well-engineered solution to the IPv4 addressing space shortage. IPv6 is significantly more efficient than IPv4 because its design is based on the past 20 years experience of the IPv4 protocol.

With IPv6, we have to change our thinking, because this protocol was not only designed for computers on networks such as the current IPv4 Internet. The applicability of IPv6 is global to communication devices such as cellular, wireless, phones, PDAs, television, radio, and so on rather than being limited to computers.

One main goal of IPv6 is to make the router the key element of any network by simplifying the deployment, operation, and management of any IP-based network. Moreover, IPv6 is more advanced and scalable than IPv4 for global networks that will be made with billions of nodes, such as the 3G infrastructure. Some advantages of IPv6 are a larger address space, a simpler header, autoconfiguration, renumbering, aggregation, multihoming, transition, and coexistence with the existing IPv4 infrastructure.

In the long term, Internet gurus and high-level analysts agree that the Internet must be upgraded to IPv6. In fact, the ultimate goal of IPv6 is to completely replace IPv4. Therefore, the long-term market for IPv6 is huge, representing billions of nodes and networks all around the world.

Cisco Systems, Inc., is the world's leading supplier of internetworking hardware and software. Cisco has been involved in IETF IPv6 standardization since 1995, at the early stages of IPv6's design. Because Cisco technology carries about 80% of all Internet traffic, Cisco is obviously a key player in the worldwide deployment of IPv6.

| | |
|---|---|
| **NOTE** | Because it is difficult in this book to keep an updated list of IPv6 features that are or will by supported on the Cisco IOS Software technology for the different platforms, then, you are invited to look at the latest list of available features at www.cisco.com. You can find the latest list in the "Start Here: Cisco IOS Software Release Specifics for IPv6 Features" manual as well in the CCO Feature Navigator. |

## This Book's Objectives

Understanding the technical mechanisms of IPv6, the new IPv6 features available on Cisco IOS Software technology, and the interoperability between the Cisco routers and IPv6 implementations are fundamental to deploying scalable and reliable IPv6 networks.

Therefore, this book gives you a strong view of the Cisco IPv6 implementations, as well as an in-depth technical reference regarding designing, configuring, deploying, and debugging IPv6 on Cisco routers. You will gain expertise in IPv6 on Cisco technology through practical examples of all the IPv6 features presented in this book.

## Who Should Read This Book

This book is intended for professionals in the enterprise and provider markets such as architects, network designers, systems engineers, network managers, administrators, and any technical staff. Professionals who are planning to use Cisco technology to deploy IPv6 networks, provide IPv6 connectivity, and use IPv6 within their network backbones need this book. You will find this book valuable because it provides many examples, figures, IOS commands, and tips for using IPv6 with Cisco IOS Software technology.

You will find everything you need to describe, design, configure, support, and operate IPv6 network backbones based on Cisco routers. To get the most out of this book, you need a minimal background in IPv4 and should be able to operate Cisco routers.

# How This Book Is Organized

Although you could read this book cover-to-cover, it is designed to be flexible. You can easily move between chapters and sections to cover just the material you need more work with.

The book is divided into five parts. The first part explains the history of IPv6, the rationale behind it, and its benefits. The second part presents in detail the basic and advanced features of IPv6. Then it explains designing, enabling, configuring, and routing IPv6 networks using Cisco IOS Software technology. The third part describes the main integration and coexistence mechanisms and demonstrates integrating IPv6 on the current IPv4 infrastructure using different strategies. This part shows you examples of internetworking using Cisco IOS Software technology with different host implementations supporting IPv6. The fourth part describes the 6bone design and how this worldwide IPv6 backbone is operated. It also provides information that helps ISPs undertand the steps and rules of becoming an IPv6 provider on the IPv6 Internet. The fifth part contains the appendixes and a glossary.

The following list highlights the topics covered and the book's organization:

- **Part I: Overview of and Justification for IPv6**

  **Chapter 1, "Introduction to IPv6"** — This chapter introduces and provides an overview of the new IPv6 protocol. More specifically, it discusses the rationale of IPv6 by presenting the issues of IPv4 such as IPv4 address space exhaustion, the fast-growing global Internet routing table, and the many implications of using network address translation (NAT) mechanisms. This chapter also presents the history of IPv6 and provides an overview of IPv6 features such as larger address space, addressing hierarchy, aggregation, autoconfiguration, network renumbering, efficient headers, mobility, security, and the transition from IPv4 networks to IPv6.

- **Part II: IPv6 Design**

  **Chapter 2, "IPv6 Addressing"** — This chapter discusses the fundamentals of IPv6 and explains the application of basic IPv6 configurations on Cisco routers. More specifically, this chapter describes in detail the new IPv6 header, the IPv6 addressing architecture, the upper-layer protocols UDP and TCP, the representation of IPv6 addresses, and all types of addresses scoped in IPv6 such as link-local, site-local, and many others. This chapter also explains and provides examples of enabling IPv6 on a router, enabling and assigning IPv6 addresses to network interfaces, using the EUI-64 format to configure addresses, and verifying IPv6 configurations on interfaces.

  **Chapter 3, "IPv6 in Depth"** — This chapter is the key chapter of the book, because it describes IPv6's advanced features and mechanisms such as Neighbor Discovery Protocol (NDP), stateless autoconfiguration, prefix advertisement, duplicate address detection (DAD), the replacement of ARP, Internet Control Message Protocol for IPv6 (ICMPv6), path MTU discovery (PMTUD), the new AAAA record for the domain name system (DNS), DHCPv6, IPSec, and

Mobile IPv6. Then, to help you acquire strong practical knowledge of these advanced IPv6 features, Chapter 3 covers enabling and managing prefix advertisement on Cisco, renumbering a network, and defining IPv6 standard and extended access control lists (ACLs). It also provides examples of verifying, managing, and debugging IPv6 configurations on Cisco routers using IPv6-enabled tools and commands such as **show**, **debug**, **ping**, **traceroute**, **Telnet**, **ssh**, and **TFTP** which are EXEC commands of the IOS.

**Chapter 4, "Routing on IPv6"**—This chapter explains the differences between the EGP and IGP routing protocols for IPv6 by comparing them to their IPv4 equivalents. As in IPv4, routing protocols are fundamental for the IPv6 routing domains. Chapter 4 starts by presenting an overview of the updates and changes applied on these routing protocols to support IPv6. This chapter covers the interdomain routing protocol BGP4+ and the intradomain routing protocols RIPng, IS-IS for IPv6, and OSPFv3. This chapter also discusses and provides examples of enabling, configuring, and managing these IPv6 routing protocols on Cisco routers. More pratically, it covers configuring static and default IPv6 routes, enabling and configuring BGP4+ with IPv6, establishing multihop BGP4+ configuration, configuring BGP4+ to exchange IPv4 routes between BGP IPv6 peers, configuring prefix filtering and route maps for IPv6 with BGP4+, using link-local addresses with BGP4+, configuring RIPng, enabling and configuring IS-IS and OSPFv3 for IPv6, and redistributing IPv6 routes into BGP4+, RIPng, and IS-IS for IPv6 and OSPFv3. The last section of the chapter presents the commands used in Cisco Express Forwarding for IPv6 (CEFv6). It also describes managing some of these routing protocols using the **show** and **debug** commands.

- **Part III: IPv4 and IPv6: Coexistence and Integration**

  **Chapter 5, "IPv6 Integration and Coexistence Strategies"**—This chapter covers the main integration and coexistence strategies provided in IPv6 to maintain complete backward compatibility with IPv4 and to allow a smooth transition from IPv4 to IPv6. The integration and coexistence strategies presented in this chapter include the dual-stack approach; the multiple protocols and techniques of tunneling IPv6 packets over IPv4 networks, such as configured tunnel, tunnel broker, tunnel server, 6to4, GRE tunnel, ISATAP, and automatic IPv4-compatible tunnel; and IPv6-only-to-IPv4-only transition mechanisms such as the application-level gateway and NAT-PT. In addition, this chapter covers enabling the dual stack, enabling a configured tunnel, enabling 6to4, using a 6to4 relay, deploying IPv6 over GRE, enabling ISATAP tunnels, enabling NAT-PT, and applying static and dynamic NAT-PT configurations. This chapter also provides examples of verifying and debugging some of these transition techniques.

  **Chapter 6, "IPv6 Hosts Internetworking with Cisco"**—This chapter covers enabling and configuring IPv6 support on Microsoft Windows NT, 2000, and XP; Solaris 8; FreeBSD 4.x; Linux; and Tru64 UNIX to internetwork with Cisco IOS Software technology. You see examples of internetworking using stateless autoconfiguration, the dual-stack approach, configured tunnel, and 6to4 between the IPv6 host implementations and Cisco routers.

- **Part IV: The IPv6 Backbone**

  **Chapter 7, "Connecting to the IPv6 Internet"**—This chapter discusses how the IPv6 Internet is built and how to be connected to it. More specifically, this chapter describes the architecture, design, addressing, and routing policy of the 6Bone and how to become a pseudo-TLA on that IPv6 backbone. It also covers policy allocation and how addresses are allocated on the production IPv6 Internet by regional Internet registries (RIRs). It lists the criteria to become an IPv6 provider and describes address allocation, the reassignment of addresses to customers, and how providers may deploy IPv6 connectivity to their customers.

- **Part V: Appendixes**

  **Appendix A, "Cisco IOS Software IPv6 Commands"**—This appendix lists commands of the Cisco IOS Software technology that are available for IPv6 and that are presented in this book.

  **Appendix B, "Answers to Review Questions"**—This appendix provides the answers to each chapter's review questions. The answers to the case study questions can be found at the end of each chapter.

  **Appendix C, "RFCs Related to IPv6"**—This appendix lists IETF RFCs that explore the technical specifications of IPv6.

  **Glossary**—This element provides definitions of new technical terms introduced by IPv6.

# Icons Used in This Book

Cisco uses the following standard icons to represent different networking devices. You will encounter several of these icons within this book.

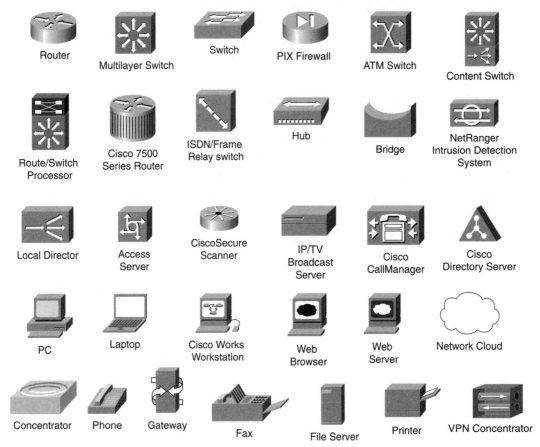

# Command Syntax Conventions

The conventions used to present command syntax in this book are the same conventions used in the *IOS Command Reference*. It describes these conventions as follows:

- Vertical bars (|) separate alternative, mutually exclusive elements.

- Square brackets ([ ]) indicate an optional element.

- Braces ({ }) indicate a required choice.

- Braces within brackets ([{ }]) indicate a required choice within an optional element.
- **Bold** indicates commands and keywords that are entered literally as shown. In configuration examples and output (not general command syntax), bold indicates commands that are manually input by the user (such as a **show** command).
- *Italic* indicates arguments for which you supply actual values.

# PART I

# Overview of and Justification for IPv6

The Internet has been growing at a very fast rate during the last ten years. The Internet runs over IP version 4 (IPv4), but this protocol was designed 20 years ago for a few hundred computers. This part of the book explains why an upgrade of the IPv4 protocol is needed. It also presents the justifications for and the main benefits of the IP version 6 (IPv6) protocol.

The following chapter comprises this part of the book:

Chapter 1    Introduction to IPv6

"Everything that can be invented has been invented."

Charles Duell, Commissioner, U.S. Patent Office, 1899

# Introduction to IPv6

Before diving into a new technology, it is critical that you understand what problems that technology is designed to solve and what new advantages it provides. When you finish this chapter, you should be able to explain the rationale for using Internet Protocol version 6 (IPv6). This chapter also presents the main features and benefits of the IPv6 protocol.

## Rationale for IPv6

You should understand that IPv6 was designed and engineered for many reasons. First and foremost, the Internet Protocol version 4 (IPv4) address scheme is limited by its 32 bits, which causes problems for the long-term growth of the Internet. Moreover, parts of the IPv4 address scheme, such as Class D and E, are reserved for special uses. This also decreases the number of globally unique unicast IPv4 addresses available. Then, very large blocks of globally unique unicast addresses were assigned to organizations in the 1980s, even though the Internet has been growing quickly, especially in Asia and Europe. But, some countries in Asia and Africa received just one Class C address for the entire country because they arrived late to the Internet.

The number of globally unique unicast IPv4 addresses still available is not enough to assign a different IP address to every new device to come. IP is considered by the market as the common denominator to converge different application layers such as data, voice, and audio. However, these new devices require many more IP addresses to interconnect all kinds of IP appliances besides just the computers currently interconnected on the Internet.

The global Internet routing table is huge and continues to grow despite mechanisms such as *classless interdomain routing* (CIDR) and *Network Address Translation* (NAT). Therefore, some studies predict the exhaustion of the current IPv4 address space between 2005 and 2011.

This exhaustion prediction prompted the Internet Engineering Task Force (IETF) to come to the general consensus that there was enough time to engineer a new IP protocol to replace IPv4 before the depletion of the address space. The history behind the development of IPv6 shows that this process has been structured and coordinated between different contributors to solve the problems of the IPv4 protocol.

The version of NAT that was developed during the early days of the web and the commercial Internet to solve critical issues was also seen by the community as a potential solution to the exhaustion of the IPv4 address space. However, a good understanding of the address translation mechanism shows how the NAT mechanism breaks the end-to-end model of the Internet, which causes more limitations to IPv4 than benefits.

# IPv4 Address Space

IPv4 is based on a 32-bit address scheme that could in theory enable a total of 4 billion hosts (exactly 4,294,967,296) on the whole Internet. However, this 32-bit scheme was originally divided into five hierarchical classes managed by the *Internet Assigned Numbers Authority* (IANA). The first three classes (A, B, and C) are available as globally unique unicast IP addresses. These classes were assigned to the requesters with a fixed prefix length using different netmask values. A *netmask* is consecutive series of bits preset to 1 designed to "mask" the network part of an IP address.

Table 1-1 shows the five classes of IPv4 addresses, along with their associated ranges and network masks.

**Table 1-1**   *Hierarchical Classes of IPv4 Addresses*

| Classes | Range | Netmask |
|---------|-------|---------|
| A | 0.0.0.0 to 127.255.255.255 | 255.0.0.0 |
| B | 128.0.0.0 to 191.255.255.255 | 255.255.0.0 |
| C | 192.0.0.0 to 223.255.255.255 | 255.255.255.0 |
| D | 224.0.0.0 to 239.255.255.255 | — |
| E | 240.0.0.0 to 255.255.255.255 | — |

The IANA is an organization dedicated to the central coordination of the Internet. The IANA is responsible for assigning numbers to protocols and blocks of IP addresses to regional Internet registries and large providers. You can find more information about IANA at www.iana.org.

In North America, where early adopters of the Internet were significant in the 1980s, almost all universities and large corporations received Class A or B addresses, even if they had a small number of computers. Today, these same organizations still have unused IPv4 addresses in their assigned blocks of IPv4 addresses, but they have not redistributed them to other organizations. Moreover, many organizations and companies that received an IPv4 address in the 1980s don't exist as such anymore. For example, Digital got bought by Compaq, which might get bought by Hewlett-Packard. Digital and Hewlett-Packard each have a Class A block of addresses.

The redistribution of unused address space is a very important issue of the Internet. In theory, it should be possible to have a global Internet routing table with 4.2 billion entries, but in real life, this represents issues of scalability, performance, and management for large network operators. How is it possible to converge a 4.2 billion-entry database in just a few milliseconds? Just the addition of hundreds of thousands of Class C addresses originating from Class B addresses into the global Internet routing table means doubling the current size of the routing table.

The number of unused IPv4 addresses within these assigned blocks of IPv4 addresses is very large.

Moreover, other large parts of the addressing scheme are not used to assign unique addresses to devices, which decreases the percentage of IPv4 addresses really available as globally unique unicast IP addresses. For example, Class D and E addresses are reserved for multicast and experimental purposes. Networks 0.0.0.0/8, 127.0.0.0/8, and 255.0.0.0/8 are reserved for protocol operations, and 10.0.0.0/8, 169.254.0.0/16, 172.16.0.0/12, 192.168.0.0/16, and 192.0.2.0/24 are special allocations for private networks (defined by RFC 1918). In fact, the sum of all already-assigned Class A and B addresses, unused address spaces, and reserved IP addresses has forced regional Internet registries and ISPs to put a hold on address assignments and distribution. Only small blocks of IPv4 addresses are assigned to organizations, which often means fewer addresses than hosts.

**NOTE**    Three regional Internet registries in the world are responsible for assigning blocks of IP addresses to providers and organizations. ARIN (American Registry for Internet Numbers) serves North America, Central America, and South America; RIPE NCC (Réseaux IP Européens Network Coordination Center) covers Europe and Africa; and APNIC (Asia Pacific Network Information Center) covers IP address assignment in Asia. All three registries have guidelines for the request of IP address spaces. You can find additional information about these registries at www.arin.net, www.ripe.net, and www.apnic.net.

The 32-bit address space of IPv4, like any other addressing scheme such the telephone numbering system, is not optimal. Christian Huitema proposes a logarithmic ratio that is applied to other address spaces, such as the one used in telephone numbers, to compare the efficiency of use.

Each addressing plan has several levels of hierarchy where some margin is provided. However, over time, the hierarchy might change due to growth and the need for mobility. Then, when an allocation is exceeded, a renumbering is needed that involves a very painful and costly operation. Renumbering of telephone area codes in North America has been done since the 1990s mainly due to the growth of new phone service.

At each level of a hierarchy, there is a loss of efficiency. When several hierarchies are present in an addressing plan, the loss of efficiency is much greater. This has a multiplicative effect on the overall efficiency.

IPv4 is not worse or better than other addressing schemes, but with the class hierarchy (A, B, C, D, and E), in which the most-significant bits of address hierarchy levels are assigned to providers and low-order bits are used for sites and subnets, the address space is less efficient. RFC 3194, *The Host-Density Ratio for Address Assignment Efficiency: An update on the H ratio,* presents detailed information about the HD ratio and the IPv4 address scheme.

The HD ratio is a percentage used to identify the pain level caused by a specific efficiency. A ratio lower than 80% is manageable, but a ratio higher than 87% is hard to sustain. RFC 3194 states that IPv4's 32-bit address space will reach the maximum pain level when 240 million globally unique unicast IP addresses are used on the Internet.

## Current IANA IP Address Space Allocation

Figure 1-1 shows the IANA allocation of IP address space in September 2002. Classes D and E, which are unavailable as globally unique unicast addresses, represent a total of 12% of the whole IPv4 address space. The 2% of unusable addresses includes 0.0.0.0/8, 127.0.0.0/8, 255.0.0.0/8, and private address spaces. The biggest slice of the graph (58%) represents the address space already assigned to organizations and regional Internet registries such ARIN, APNIC, and RIPE, meaning that 28% of the remaining IPv4 space is still unallocated.

**Figure 1-1**  *Percentage of the IPv4 Address Space Assigned in September 2002*

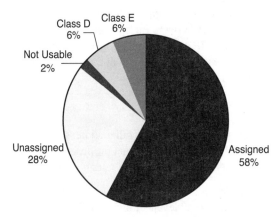

Source: Computed from information published by IANA about IPv4 address space allocation

## Future Growth of the Internet

The current situation shows that it will be much harder to get addresses in the future as they become a scarce resource and the Internet continues to grow globally. The problem is obvious in some places, but not in North America, where 75% of the IPv4 address space is allocated for less than 10% of the world population.

Moreover, temporary and semipermanent connections such as dialup are being replaced by connections such as cable-modem/xDSL, which require one permanent IP address per node instead of one temporary IP address for a pool of PPP subscribers. The ratio of subscribers per IP address changes from many:1 to 1:1. Wireless networks are emerging markets, and 802.11b devices and mobile networks are deployed everywhere. However, wireless devices frequently change physical locations, access points, and logical subnets during movement, which means that extra pools of IP addresses are requested for these devices.

Some ISPs are running out of IP addresses; therefore, they must assign private addresses to their customers through NAT. New large networks cannot get IPv4 addresses from regional Internet registries or ISPs. New technologies such PDAs, wireless devices, cellular phones, VoIP, and videoconferencing over IP applications, require globally unique unicast IP addresses. Moreover, the current generation of PCs and operating systems allows people to have their own web servers for their personal data. This also requires permanent IP addresses to be assigned on home networks.

# IPv4 Address Space Exhaustion

The work on IPv6 at the IETF started when a preliminary study in 1990 concluded that the IPv4 address space would be exhausted. More specifically, the IETF predicted that Class B would be exhausted within four years (1994). This study also identified the necessity to assign several adjacent Class C addresses instead of Class B addresses to organizations. Class C addresses are small, but there are plenty of them (2,097,152).

**NOTE**    Class C is a block that represents 255 IPv4 addresses, whereas one Class B means 65,536 IPv4 addresses. However, in reality, 254 hosts can be addressed on a Class C.

The main technical constraint of that orientation was preserving the global Internet routing table size while keeping it from exploding. With several thousand routes in the global Internet routing table, the addition of hundreds of thousands of new small routes (Class C) was an important issue to avoid. Therefore, the CIDR mechanism adopted in 1992 was put into place to summarize adjacent blocks of IPv4 addresses in one block. CIDR has helped control the growth of the Internet routing table since 1993.

Figure 1-2 shows the global Internet routing table growth since 1989 (active BGP entries). In 2001, the total number of routes was more than 100,000, then later in 2003 it was 140,000 entries (a 40% growth within 24 months) If you want real-time information about this routing table, look for a route server on the Internet. Some of these route servers are freely available for public information and debugging purposes.

**Figure 1-2** *Global Internet Routing Table Growth Since 1989*

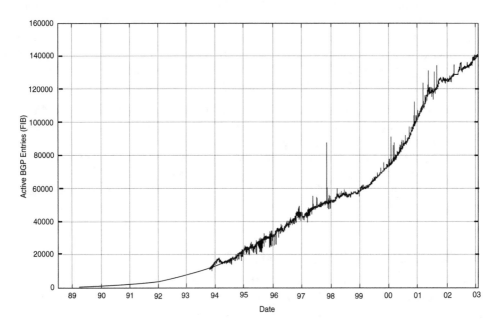

Source: BGP Table Statistics, Telstra web site, www.telstra.net/ops/bgptable.html

Example 1-1 shows the global Internet routing table on a route server.

**Example 1-1** *Looking at the Global Internet Routing Table on a Route Server*

```
#telnet route-server.ip.att.net

route-server>show ip route
show all routes of the routing table of the Internet



route-server>sh ip bgp summary

BGP router identifier 12.0.1.28, local AS number 65000
BGP table version is 665451, main routing table version 665451
117228 network entries and 2373589 paths using 116277944 bytes of memory
37354 BGP path attribute entries using 2091992 bytes of memory
24197 BGP AS-PATH entries using 630776 bytes of memory
402 BGP community entries using 15192 bytes of memory
```

**Example 1-1**  *Looking at the Global Internet Routing Table on a Route Server (Continued)*

```
24674 BGP route-map cache entries using 493480 bytes of memory
0 BGP filter-list cache entries using 0 bytes of memory
Dampening enabled. 945 history paths, 751 dampened paths
BGP activity 125101/1203692325 prefixes, 2562479/188890 paths, scan interval 60 secs
```

In Example 1-1, the highlighted line shows 117,228 network entries, which is the total number of routes, 2,373,589 paths, which is the number of BGP AS-PATH entries, and 116,277,944 bytes of memory, which is memory used on that router to handle the routing table.

Another study done by the IETF tried to predict how long it will be before the IPv4 address space is exhausted. This study projected the unavailability of new IPv4 address space between 2005 and 2011. The perception of these results was mixed and contested. Some people argued that the projection was pessimistic, and others thought it was optimistic.

# History of IPv6

Demonstration of the IP address space exhaustion led to the consensus that there was enough time to design, engineer, and test a new protocol with enhanced functionalities instead of deploying a new protocol that just adds larger addresses. This represented a unique opportunity to fix the limitations related to the IPv4 addressing scheme and to develop a protocol to ensure reliable growth of the Internet over the next decades. The process took care of requirements from various industries, including the cable and wireless industries, electric power utilities, the military, corporate networks, Internet service providers (ISPs), and many others.

In 1993, a call for proposals (RFC 1550) was issued. Three were studied in detail:

- Common Architecture for the Internet (CATNIP) proposed converging the CLNP, IP, and IPX protocols with the use of Network Service Access Point (NSAP) addresses. (Defined in RFC 1707.)

- Simple Internet Protocol Plus (SIPP) proposed increasing the IP address size to 64 bits and improving the IP header. (Defined in RFC 1752.)

- TCP/UDP Over CLNP-Addressed Networks (TUBA) suggested replacing IP (Layer 3) with Connectionless Network Protocol (CLNP), where TCP/UDP and other upper protocols could run on top of CLNP. (Defined in RFC 1347.)

The recommended proposal was SIPP, with an address size of 128 bits. The main author of SIPP was Steve Deering. IANA assigned the version number 6 to the protocol. A working group at IETF called *IP Next Generation (IPng)* was started in 1993 just before the web really led to the explosion of Internet traffic. However, the issue of IPv4 existed before the web. Then, the first specifications came in late 1995 (RFC 1883). The IPng working group was renamed *IPv6* in 2001. Figure 1-3 shows the origin and evolution of IPv6.

**Figure 1-3** *History of IPv6*

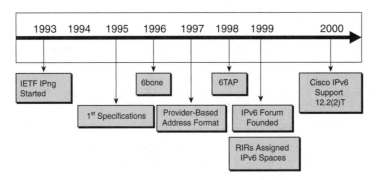

In 1996, an IPv6 test bed called the IPv6 backbone (6bone) was created over the Internet. The 6bone has used mainly a mix of Cisco IOS Software routers with IPv6 beta implementations and other router software under UNIX platforms. IPv6 prefixes within the IPv6 space 3ffe::/16 were assigned to the 6bone participants. In 1997, a first attempt was made to structure the IPv6 space as a provider-based IPv6 address format. One year later, the first IPv6 exchange, called 6TAP, was deployed at STARTAP in Chicago. In 1999, regional Internet registries (RIRs) started assigning production IPv6 prefixes using the IPv6 space 2001::/16. In the same year, the IPv6Forum, a worldwide consortium of leading Internet vendors and research and education networks, was founded to promote IPv6 in the market and to enable collaboration between vendors. In 2000, many vendors began bundling IPv6 into their mainstream products. Cisco introduced a three-phase road map for the development of IPv6 and made IPv6 support available in Cisco IOS Software Release 12.2(2)T. In 2001, Microsoft announced the availability of IPv6 in the mainstream code of its latest operating system, Windows XP.

**NOTE**     Chapter 7, "Connecting to the IPv6 Internet," provides detailed information about the 6bone and the IPv6 spaces assigned by IANA. Chapter 6, "IPv6 Hosts Internetworking with Cisco," describes the IPv6 support on Microsoft Windows XP.

# IPv5

The Internet community uses IPv4 and has used IPv6 for a couple of years. IANA is the organization that has the worldwide responsibility of assigning numbers to everything related to the Internet, which includes versions of the IP protocol. IANA assigned version 6 to the IPng protocol in 1995 following a request by the IPng working group.

What about "IP version 5"? IPv5 is an experimental resource reservation protocol intended to provide quality of service (QoS), defined as the Internet Stream Protocol (ST). It can provide real-time transport of multimedia such as voice, video, and real-time data traffic across the Internet. This protocol is based on previous work of Jim Forgie in 1979, as documented in IETF Internet Experiment Note 199. It consists of two protocols—ST for the data transport and Stream Control Message Protocol (SCMP). IPv5, also called ST2, is documented in RFC 1819 and RFC 1190.

Internet Streaming Protocol version 2 (ST2) is not a replacement for IPv4. It is designed to run and coexist with IPv4. The number 5 was assigned by IANA because this protocol works at the same link-layer framing as IPv4. A typical distributed multimedia application can use both protocols: IP for the transfer of traditional data and control information such as TCP/UDP packets, and ST2 for real-time data carriers. ST2 uses the same addressing schemes as IPv4 to identify hosts. Resource reservation over IP is now done using other protocols such as *Resource Reservation Protocol* (RSVP).

# Network Address Translation

Since 1992, CIDR has not been the only mechanism directly involved in slowing down the IPv4 address shortage. Over the years, the NAT mechanism (defined in RFC 1631), seen as a short-term solution, played a key role by allowing organizations to use few Internet globally unique unicast IP addresses for their large networks. NAT typically translates packets from a network, which uses globally unique unicast IP addresses or a private address space as defined by RFC 1918, to the Internet.

---

**NOTE**    IANA has reserved three blocks of IP addresses for private addressing. Address spaces 10.0.0.0/8, 172.16.0.0/12, and 192.168.0.0/16 are used for address translation with the Internet.

---

Figure 1-4 shows networks using private addressing. 10.0.0.0/8 and 192.168.0.0/16 are connected to the Internet through the same ISP using NAT. Because private addresses are not routed across the Internet, nodes on these private networks cannot be reached from the Internet.

**Figure 1-4**    *Networks Connected to the Internet Using NAT with Private Addressing*

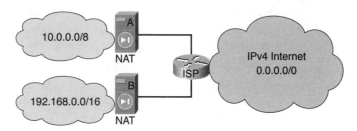

Since 1990, the combination of CIDR, NAT, and private addressing has provided benefits to the Internet by slowing the depletion of IPv4 addresses.

Moreover, one of the arguments against deploying IPv6 is the use of NAT. This is seen by some as the *permanent* solution to the shortage of IPv4 address space. However, using NAT has many implications; these were taken into consideration during the engineering of IPv6. Some of these limitations are documented in RFC 2775 and RFC 2993:

- **NAT breaks IP's end-to-end model**—IP was originally designed so that only endpoints (hosts and servers) have to handle the connection. The network itself, the underlying layers, and NAT do not have to handle connections.

- **The need to keep the state of connections**—NAT implies that the network (NAT translator) needs to keep the state of the connections and that NAT has to remember the translation of addresses and ports.

  — The need to keep the state of the connections in NAT makes fast rerouting difficult in case of a failure of the NAT device or the links near the NAT device. Networks using links and route redundancy can suffer problems.

  — Organizations deploy high-speed links (Gigabit Ethernet, 10 Gigabit Ethernet) to increase the performance of their backbones. However, address translation requires additional processing, because the state of each connection must be kept with NAT. Therefore, NAT hinders network performance.

  — For providers and organizations that must keep records of all connections made by their end users for security reasons, the recording of NAT state tables becomes mandatory to trace back to the source of problems.

- **Inhibition of end-to-end network security**—To protect the integrity of the IP header by some cryptographic functions, this header cannot be changed between the origin of the packet, which protects the header's integrity, and the final destination, which checks the integrity of the received packet.

  Any translation on the path of header parts breaks the integrity check. Although many adaptations can partly solve this issue in some cases, the fundamental problem is not easy to solve. The IPSec authentication header (AH) is an example of this problem.

  In Figure 1-5, Computer A (1), which has an IPSec implementation, sends IP packets with protocol number 51 (IPSec AH) to Computer B. NAT, before forwarding the packet (2) to network 206.123.31.0/24, changes the IP source address within the header from 10.0.0.10 to 206.123.31.1. However, the IPSec implementation in Computer B fails the integrity check because something was modified within the packet header during transport.

- **Applications that are not NAT-friendly**—More than just port and address mapping is necessary to forward the packet through the NAT device. NAT has to embed the full knowledge of all applications to do the right tricks. This is especially important in cases with dynamically allocated ports with rendezvous ports, embedded IP addresses in application protocols, security associations, and so on. The outcome is that the NAT device needs to be upgraded each time a new non-NAT-friendly application is deployed.

- **Address space collision**—When different networks and organizations use the same private address space and have to merge or connect, an address space collision results: Different hosts/servers can have the same address, and routing disables reaching the other network. However, this can be resolved by a few techniques such as renumbering or twice-NAT. But these techniques are very painful and costly and later increase NAT's complications.

- **Ratio of internal and reachable IP addresses**—NAT can be efficient when there is a large number of hosts/servers inside and very few reachable addresses outside. The ratio of internal/reachable addresses must be large to make NAT effective.

However, many servers behind NAT that must be reached from the Internet is a problem. The same protocol cannot be multiplexed on the same port using the NAT external address, such as in Network Address Port Translation (NAPT) mode. NAPT allows the sharing of one IP address using TCP and UDP ports as tokens for the translation mechanism. For example, two web servers located behind NAT that both use port TCP 80 cannot use the same external IP address without changing the port number. Because many protocols make nodes as servers, it consumes many external addresses. Consequently, NAT is not as useful.

**Figure 1-5**  *Translation Breaks the Integrity Check of IPSec AH in the End-to-End Model*

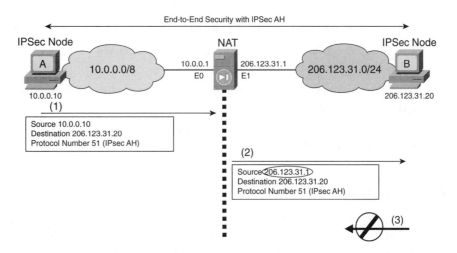

IP's original design was based on an end-to-end model. This model led to the design of thousands of Internet standards with predictable behavior for the benefit of the Internet. However, NAT, introduced as a temporary solution, breaks this end-to-end model. NAT was a patch applied to extend IPv4's lifetime for a short time. IPv6 is the long-term solution to retain the end-to-end model and the IP protocol's transparency.

# IPv6 Features

After the overview of the main problems related to the IPv4 protocol, you should see that IPv6 solves all these problems and provides new benefits. Here are the main improvements:

- The 128-bit address scheme, which provides plenty of IP addresses for the next decades.

- The larger address space provides globally unique addresses to billions of new devices such as PDAs, cellular devices, and 802.11 systems, that will be manufactured in the future.

- Multiple hierarchy levels help aggregate routes, which promotes efficient and scalable routing to the Internet.

- Multihoming with the preservation of strict route aggregation is possible.

- The autoconfiguration process allows nodes of the IPv6 network to configure their own IPv6 addresses.

- The transition between IPv6 providers is transparent to end users with the renumbering mechanism.

- ARP broadcast is replaced by multicast use on the local link.

- The IPv6 header is more efficient than IPv4. Fewer fields are present, and the header checksum is removed.

- A flow label field can provide traffic differentiation.

- New extension headers replace IPv4's Options field and provide more flexibility.

- IPv6 was designed to handle mobility and security mechanisms much more efficiently than the IPv4 protocol.

- Many transition mechanisms are designed with IPv6 to allow a smooth transition from IPv4 networks to IPv6.

The following sections examine some of these IPv6 features and discuss how they offer improvements over the IP protocol.

## Larger Address Space

IPv6 increases by a factor of 4 the number of address bits, from 32 to 128 bits. During the IPv6 design specification, there was a debate about using fixed-length 64-bit addresses versus variable-length addresses up to 160-bit. Table 1-2 compares the arguments for each.

**Table 1-2** *IPv6: 64-Bit Versus 160-Bit Proposals*

| 64-Bit Proposal | 160-Bit Proposal |
|---|---|
| Enough addressing for 10 trillion sites and $10^{15}$ nodes | Addresses compatible with NSAP addressing |
| Minimizes the increase of the header size compared to IPv4 | Autoconfiguration possible using IEEE 802.x link-layer addresses |
| — | Variable length of the addresses allows for the use of 64-bit addresses instead of fixed-length addresses. Over time, addresses can be longer. |

Finally, using fixed-length addresses of 128 bits for IPv6 was found to be the most appropriate choice.

With IPv4, the number of addressable nodes is 4,294,967,296 ($2^{32}$), which represents about two IPv4 addresses for every three people (based on a world population of 6 billion people in 2001).

By comparison, the 128-bit length of IPv6 represents $3.4 * 10^{38}$ addresses, which allows approximately $5.7 * 10^{28}$ IPv6 addresses for every person in the world. However, as in any addressing scheme, such as IPv4 and telephone systems, not all the addresses can be used, but enough are available for any kind of use. Increasing the number of bits for the address also means an increase in the IP header size. Because each IP header contains a source address and a destination address, the size of the header fields containing the addresses is 64 bits for IPv4 and 256 bits for IPv6.

Comparing the OSI reference model of IPv4 to that of IPv6 (see Figure 1-6), IPv6 represents only a change at Layer 3 (the network layer). Other layers are slightly modified. This was an important consideration during the engineering of IPv6. The other layers of the two OSI reference models are the same, which means that protocols such as TCP and UDP used with IPv4 continue to run on top of IPv6.

**Figure 1-6** *Scope of IPv6 with the OSI Reference Model*

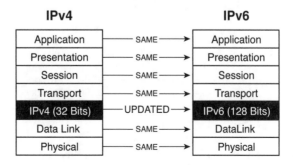

## Global Reachability

The important issue that initiated the IPv6 effort was the address space exhaustion study to give one globally unique unicast address to each device connected to the Internet. By using a much larger address space than IPv4 (4,294,967,296 addresses), IPv6 enables the use of a global and reachable address for almost every kind of device: computers, IP phones, IP faxes, TV setup boxes, cameras, pagers, wireless PDAs, 802.11b devices, cell phones, home networking, and vehicles. From now until 2006, cellular manufacturers plan to produce billions of new wireless devices that include an IP stack. These next-generation wireless devices will provide subscribers with Internet interactivity and services with their phones.

Trying to fit all these devices into the current IPv4 address space is almost impossible. Having a unique IP address for each device enables end-to-end reachability, which was lost over past years with NAT devices and private addressing. The end-to-end model is especially important for telephone call and end-to-end security. IPv6 enables the full support of application protocols without needing special processing by the network itself.

---

**NOTE**      In IPv6, NAT is undesirable between IPv6-only networks. Plenty of IPv6 addresses are available precisely to preserve the end-to-end model of the IP protocol.

---

## Levels of Addressing Hierarchy

A much larger address space enables the use of multiple levels of hierarchy inside the address space, as shown in Figure 1-7. Each level helps aggregate its IP space and enhance the allocation function. Providers and organizations may have tiered hierarchy and manage the assignment of the space below.

**Figure 1-7**   *128-bit Address Space Enables Multiple Levels of Hierarchy*

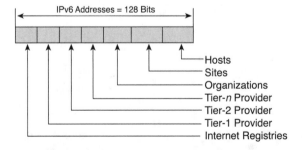

Using multiple levels in the hierarchy provides flexibility and new functionalities to the protocol.

A flexible addressing architecture is key to a network protocol. In the IPv4 world, the small 32-bit address space is an important limitation that has not led to the use of several hierarchy levels, so this affects route summarization (aggregation).

## Aggregation

A larger IPv6 address space makes room for large address allocations to ISPs and organizations. Having a large-enough prefix for an organization's entire network enables the use of only one prefix. Moreover, the ISP can summarize routes (aggregation) of all its customers' prefixes into a single prefix and announce it to the IPv6 Internet.

In Figure 1-8, ISP B advertises to the IPv6 Internet that it can route the network 2001:0420::/35, which includes IPv6 spaces assigned to customer B3 (network 2001:0420:b3::/48) and customer B10 (network 2001:0420:b10::/48). ISP A advertises to the IPv6 Internet that it can route 2001:0410::/35, including networks 2001:0410:a1::/48 and 2001:0410:a2::/48.

**Figure 1-8**    *Providers Aggregate Customer Prefixes and Then Advertise Their Prefixes to the IPv6 Internet*

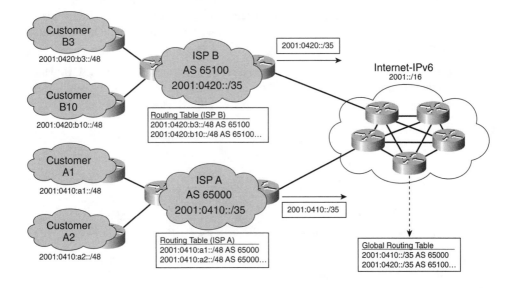

| NOTE | When a customer changes its IPv6 provider, it must change its IPv6 prefix to preserve this global aggregation. Changing providers implies network renumbering. However, autoconfiguration (discussed in a moment and presented later in detail in Chapter 3, "IPv6 in Depth") eases the renumbering of hosts within an organization. |
|------|---|

This aggregation of routes promotes an efficient and scalable routing. To connect all kinds of devices and networks on the Internet in the future, which can represent several billions of nodes, scalable routing is a requirement. However, there should be many fewer routes in the global IPv6 Internet routing table than in the current IPv4 Internet. Route aggregation in IPv6 is possible because multihomed sites can configure addresses from several upstream providers.

## Multiple Addresses

In the IPv4 world, it is not simple to connect a network to multiple providers. One way an organization can do multihoming is to get provider-independent IPv4 space from regional Internet registries. Then, an organization can conclude peering agreements with multiple providers to announce its prefix to the Internet. In the context of provider-aggregatable IPv4 space, the prefix used is part of a provider's address space. Then multihoming is possible if other ISPs used advertise the same prefix to the Internet. At the very least, it breaks any kind of aggregation in the global Internet routing table. However, multihoming is desirable for high network reliability.

Having a much larger address space with IPv6 enables the use of multiple simultaneous prefixes for an organization. An organization connected to several ISPs gets multiple prefixes that are part of these ISPs' IPv6 address spaces. This allows multihoming without breaking the global routing table, which currently is not possible in IPv4.

In Figure 1-9, the multihomed customer is connected to both ISP A and ISP B, which have assigned networks 2001:0420:b3::/48 and 2001:0410:a1::/48a to it. ISP A and ISP B advertise their /35 prefixes to the IPv6 Internet.

**Figure 1-9**   *IPv6 Enables the Use of Multiple Prefixes for Multihoming*

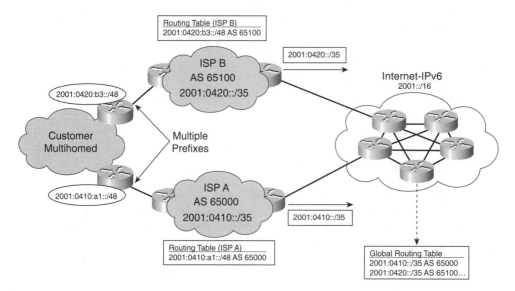

Multihoming is obviously possible with IPv4, but it has consequences for the size of the global Internet routing table, because the same network prefix may be advertised by different autonomous systems (ASs). One goal of IPv6 is to preserve the global routing table as small as possible.

The concept of multiple addresses implies that each network interface of a node might have multiple globally unique unicast IP addresses at the same time. Having multiple addresses on a network and nodes requires source address selection to choice addresses used to initiate connections. Source selection is a mechanism by which each node can select or be forced to prefer an IPv6 prefix when many are available. Moreover, if a link goes down, all routers within the multihomed network should be able to replace the current IPv6 prefix advertised by another one. The source address selection and router renumbering mechanisms are currently being discussed at the IETF. However, a mechanism called autoconfiguration is already available to allow the renumbering of all nodes on IPv6 networks.

Chapter 2, "IPv6 Addressing," presents IPv6's addressing architecture in detail.

## Autoconfiguration

Autoconfiguration is a new function enabled by IPv6. By having a much larger address space, IPv6 is designed to enable autoconfiguration of the addresses on a device while keeping the global uniqueness. As Figure 1-10 illustrates, an IPv6 router on the same local link sends network-type information such as the IPv6 prefix of the local link and the default IPv6 route. All IPv6 hosts on the local link listen to this information and then can configure by themselves their IPv6 addresses and the default router. Autoconfiguration is a mechanism by which each IPv6 host and server appends its link-layer address (for example, an Ethernet MAC address) in the EUI-64 format to the globally unique unicast IPv6 prefix advertised on the subnet.

**Figure 1-10**  *IPv6 Host Autoconfiguring Its IPv6 Address*

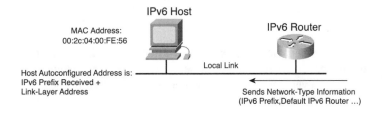

| NOTE | Autoconfiguration (defined in RFC 2462) is also called *IPv6 stateless address autoconfiguration*. |

An interface's link-layer address is based on the MAC (Media Access Control) address of the network interface converted to the EUI-64 (Extended Unique Identifier 64) format, which has a 64-bit length. The transformation of the 48-bit MAC address into EUI-64 is covered in detail in Chapter 2. An interface's link address is the lowest 64-bit part of the IPv6 address, and the IPv6 prefix is the high-order 64-bit part of the 128-bit address.

| | |
|---|---|
| **NOTE** | An IPv6 prefix assigned to a local link has a 64-bit length (/64). The low-order 64-bit part is the interface's link-layer address. Using this concept, IPv6 simplifies subnet addressing within networks by having the same prefix length instead of different netmask values, as in IPv4. |

The 128-bit address provided by autoconfiguration is guaranteed to be globally unique, because the 48-bit MAC address is a combination of a 24-bit Organizational Unique Identifier (OUI) assigned to a vendor by the IEEE with a unique 24-bit value generated for each interface built. Because it is possible under special circumstances to modify a network interface's 48-bit MAC address using software that could cause address collision, each IPv6 stack has a process enabled to detect duplicate addresses on the local link. Duplicate address detection (DAD) mechanism is explained in detail in Chapter 3.

| | |
|---|---|
| **NOTE** | Autoconfiguration is not the only way to assign an IPv6 address to a node's interface. Manually configuring a network interface can still be done in IPv6 and is mandatory for routers. IPv6 hosts can also obtain interface addresses and parameters from a DHCPv6 server. This mode (DHCPv6) is called *IPv6 stateful address configuration* (as opposed to IPv6 stateless address configuration, or autoconfiguration). Finally, another method allows a node to generate a random interface identifier that can be used as the low-order 64-bit part of the address. Random address generation was added to preserve privacy. |

Autoconfiguration enables *plug and play,* which connects devices to the network without any configuration or servers such as DHCP servers. This is a key feature to enable deployment of new devices on a very large scale on the Internet such as cell phones, wireless devices, home appliances, and home networks.

Chapter 3 covers the stateless autoconfiguration mechanism in detail.

# Renumbering

The larger address space provided by IPv6 lets organizations get IPv6 prefixes that provide IPv6 addresses for their production needs. One of the main goals of IPv6 is to keep the smallest global IPv6 routing table possible on the Internet by forcing strict aggregation. However, when an organization changes its IPv6 upstream provider, it must renumber its network.

With IPv4, renumbering is a time-consuming, error-prone task. The organization gets a new IPv4 space first, and then it must change the IPv4 addresses of all its routers, servers, hosts, and other devices on the network. Routing protocols and DNS servers must also be updated with the new IPv4 addresses at the same time. Therefore, renumbering in IPv4 incurs downtime and halts network services.

In IPv6, the renumbering process was designed to be smooth because the transition between unicast IPv6 providers can be completely transparent to end users. The combination of having multiple providers during the transition and the stateless autoconfiguration mechanism enables easy renumbering for hosts by sending the new unicast IPv6 prefix to the network. However, the renumbering of routers represents a burden for network operators, as in IPv4. A lifetime value can be assigned to advertised prefixes, allowing nodes to use the newest prefix after the expiration of the current prefix. Therefore, hosts and servers automatically pick the new global unicast IPv6 prefix and then use the new address. Figure 1-11 shows the IPv6 router on the same local link that sends network-type information such as a new IPv6 prefix and a new default IPv6 route. Hosts on this local link use these new values to autoconfigure their new IPv6 addresses.

**Figure 1-11**  *A New Unicast IPv6 Prefix Is Advertised on the Local Link During Renumbering*

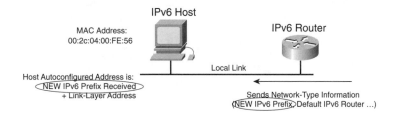

| | |
|---|---|
| **NOTE** | In IPv6, a router cannot configure its network interfaces using the autoconfiguration mechanism. IPv6 addresses on the router's interfaces must be configured manually. Moreover, router interfaces are seen by hosts and servers on the local link with another kind of IPv6 address called the *link-local address*. This guarantees that the router can be reached even while a network is renumbering. Obviously, unicast IPv6 addresses assigned to each of a router's network interfaces can change during the renumbering. Link-local address is presented in chapter 2. |

The renumbering process does not prevent hosts and servers from losing their current TCP and UDP sessions at the exact moment the transition occurs, which is only possible with a protocol such as MobileIP.

Chapter 3 presents the mechanisms of IPv6 behind network renumbering.

## Multicast Use

The ARP (Address Resolution Protocol) broadcast in IPv4, well-known by the use of the Layer 2 MAC address *ff:ff:ff:ff:ff:ff*, is inefficient for the network. Each time a broadcast request is sent to a local link, it causes at least one interrupt in every computer on the link, even though only one or two nodes are involved. The computer's network interface listens to the broadcast packet. Then it is sent to the operating system, and finally it arrives at the IP stack, where it can be used or simply ignored. In some cases, broadcasts can completely hang up a whole network; this is called a *broadcast storm*. Figure 1-12 shows a broadcast packet in IPv4 that is sent on the local link to every host from one host. This broadcast packet goes up to the IPv4 stack of all nodes on this local link.

**Figure 1-12** *ARP Broadcast Request Sent to a Local Link by Any IPv4 Host*

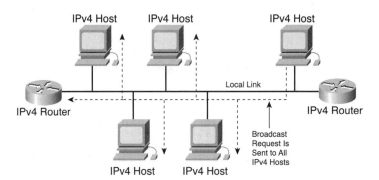

ARP broadcast is not used in IPv6. Multicasting is used instead. As illustrated in Figure 1-13, multicast group 1 defines a group of network interfaces. Network interfaces of computer A and computer D are members of multicast group 1. When a packet is sent to multicast group 1 using this group's multicast address, the packet is processed only by computers A and D, which are members of this group. Every other computer and router on this local link does not process the packet sent to multicast group 1, because they are not members.

Therefore, multicasting enables the efficient use of the network by spreading broad requests to a smaller number of possible computers by using different and specific multicast groups for the different functions. This is less costly in CPU cycles for all computers on a local link and prevents the majority of problems, such as the broadcast storms in IPv4.

Multicasting in IPv6 is used on local links to replace the ARP broadcast traffic, which means that the use of multicast routing is not required on the router infrastructure between local link subnets for that use. However, as in IPv4, this is possible to enable the multicast routing in IPv6 on routers for global use.

**Figure 1-13**  *Multicast Packet Sent to All Members of a Multicast Group on a Local Link in IPv6*

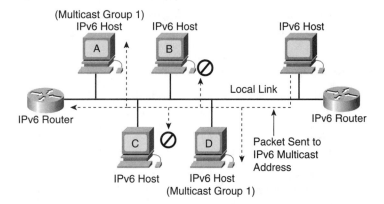

Because the range of multicast addresses in IPv6 is much larger than in IPv4, the allocation of multicast groups should not be limited. For example, a scope has been defined in the whole IPv6 addressing space for any type of multicast use.

Chapter 3 explains in detail the use of multicasting to replace ARP.

## Efficient Header

As shown in Figure 1-14, the new IPv6 header is simpler than the IPv4 packet header. Six of the IPv4 header fields are removed in the IPv6 header. The IPv4 header with the Option and Padding fields has 14 fields, and the IPv6 header has eight fields. The basic IPv6 header size is 40 octets, and the IPv4 header without the Option and Padding fields is 20 octets. The basic IPv6 header has a fixed length, and the IPv4 header when used with the Options field may have a variable length.

**Figure 1-14**  *IPv6 Header Is Simpler and Larger Than the IPv4 Header*

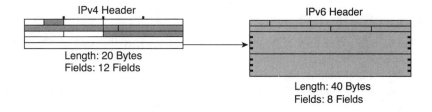

The fewer fields in the IPv6 header and its fixed length mean that it is less costly in CPU cycles for routers to forward IPv6 packets. This has direct benefits for network performance.

All fields in the IPv6 header are aligned to 64-bit, which enables direct storage and access to memory. These enhancements enable hardware-based processing, which provides scalability of the forwarding rate for the next-generation high-speed pipes. However, this remains to be seen because of the following:

- 128-bit addresses are larger than the atomic word size of the current processors, so there is more lookup to do to get the full 128-bit address.

- Performing the longest match prefix to look at 128-bit versus 32-bit before forwarding packets also has a clear impact on performance.

- Packet filtering performed at Layer 4 (TCP/UDP) results in the parsing of optional IPv6 headers (when present), which represents additional CPU cycles for routers.

Moreover, the hardware to process packets is not currently optimized to meet the performance expectations of IPv6. However, in the long term, the 64-bit alignment of IPv6 header fields should improve routing efficiency.

In IPv4, a 16-bit field is used to verify the header's integrity. The packet's sender generates the checksum and then forwards the packet to the network. Because some other fields change within the IP header, such as the TTL (Time-to-Live) value decremented at each hop, a new checksum is generated and then is filled into the IP header each time a router forwards the packet.

Another improvement to the IPv6 header is related to the *Checksum* field. This header field is simply removed to increase routing efficiency. In fact, all routers in the path do not have to make the checksum recalculation during the forwarding process. Error detection is now handled by data-link layer technologies (Layer 2) and by checksums of the end-to-end connection at the transport layer (Layer 4). The checksum done at Layers 2 and 4 is strong enough to bypass the need for Layer 3 checksum. With IPv6, checksums are required for both transport protocols TCP and UDP. UDP checksum was optional with IPv4.

Fragmentation is handled differently in IPv6. Fragmentation fields of IPv4 are either completely gone or removed and then replaced by extension headers. Chapter 2 presents details about the new way to handle fragmentation and explains the impact on the header.

# Flow Label

IPv6 includes a new *Flow Label* field in the IPv6 header, as illustrated in Figure 1-15. A source node can use this special field to request special handling for a specific sequence of packets. The Flow Label field is mainly for end-station processing, not for routers. This can be useful for streaming applications such as videoconferencing and Voice over IP that require real-time data transmission. The flow label enables per-flow processing for applications requiring QoS in routers in the path. This is better than best-effort forwarding.

**Figure 1-15**  *Flow Label Is a New Field in the IPv6 Header*

IPv6 Header

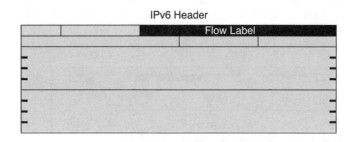

This field differentiates the traffic at the IP layer without doing other tricks to identify the flows. With this label, a router does not have to open the transport inner packet to identify the flow; it finds the information in the IP packet header. The current IETF standard does not specify the details of how to manage and process the label. Interactions with DiffServ, IntServ, RSVP, and MPLS are possible development methods.

Chapter 2 presents the IPv6 header in detail.

## Extension Header

Within an IPv4 packet, an *Options* field (RFC 791) might be present at the end of the header. This *Options* field, when present, has a variable length, depending on the optional feature used between end hosts. Routers all along the path must compute this variable field length within each packet, even though the *Options* field is only used by both end nodes. Figure 1-16 illustrates the Options field within the IPv4 header.

**Figure 1-16**  *Options Field Length Within the IPv4 Header Has a Variable Length*

IPv4 Header

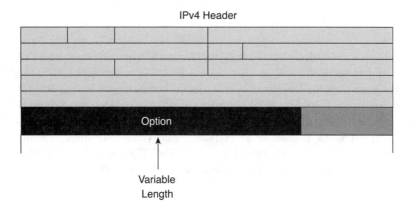

Option

Variable
Length

IPv6 uses a new approach to manage optional information in the header. Instead of using an Options field at the end of the header, IPv6 uses extension headers. Extension headers form a daisy chain of headers linked by a header field called Next Header, as shown in Figure 1-17.

**Figure 1-17** *Extension Headers Are Daisy-Chained at the End of the IPv6 Header*

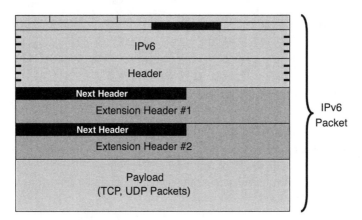

One *Next Header* field is present within every IPv6 extension header used. Many types of extension headers are defined for the different needs of IPv6 applications. This approach provides better efficiency in the option processing, because it ensures that routers and nodes compute only the headers targeted for them along a path.

Mobile IPv6 is an example of a protocol using different extension headers for its operation when a mobile node is away from its home network. Extension headers provide important improvements to the Mobile IPv6 protocol as compared to Mobile IP, used in IPv4 networks.

Chapter 2 presents extension headers in detail.

## Mobility

Mobility is a highly desirable and important feature for companies, organizations, and employees who want to access the web, e-mail, their bank accounts, and home from outside these networks, even from the car. New Layer 2 wireless technologies such as 802.11b and 3G (Third Generation) can help them fulfill these needs. 802.11b devices are cheap and can provide network connectivity with interesting bandwidth in several business locations such as offices, airports, and hotels. Billions of 3G cellular devices have an IP stack. In addition, cellular operators build IP core backbones based over IPv6. Thus, mobility with IPv6 is mandatory. Figure 1-18 illustrates the mobility provided by IPv6 networks.

**Figure 1-18**  *Many Devices Moving from IPv6 Networks to Others*

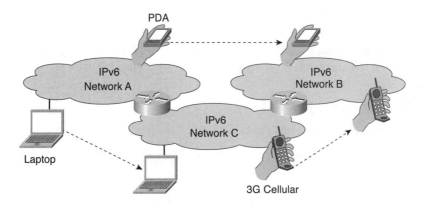

At the IP layer, the MobileIP protocol assumes that a node's IP address uniquely identifies the node's point of attachment to a network. A mobile node must be able to communicate with other nodes after changing its data link layer point of attachment without changing its IP address and breaking current connections. The MobileIP protocol lets nodes move from one IP network to another. The wireless/cellular industry uses the MobileIP protocol to grant IP mobility to wireless data.

MobileIP is available for both IPv4 and IPv6. However, with IPv6 the mobility is built into the protocol instead of being a new function added to IPv4. This means that any IPv6 node can use MobileIP as needed. MobileIPv6 uses the following IPv6 extension headers:

- A routing header for the registration

- A destination header for datagram delivery between mobile nodes and correspondent nodes

Both provide better performance for communications and enhancements to the IP protocol.

## Security

The IPSec protocol, an IETF standard for IP network security, can provide several security functions:

- Access control limits access to people who have authorization.

- Authentication certifies that the person who sends data is who the person claims to be.

- Confidentiality ensures that any data carried over a public network, including passwords, is encrypted to make it very hard for anyone to see the exchanged data.

- Integrity ensures that data has not been modified during transport.

- Replay protection keeps sessions from being recorded and then replayed later by malicious users.

Any IP protocol can be used over IPSec. IPSec is used to create encrypted tunnels over IP (virtual private networks) or simply to encrypt data exchanged between computers. Two protocols are behind IPSec:

- Authentication Header (AH)

- Encapsulating Security Payload (ESP)

AH and ESP are available for both IPv4 and IPv6 and are essentially identical for both protocols.

---

**NOTE**    As described in RFC 2460, a full implementation of IPv6 includes implementations of AH and ESP extension headers. In IPv4, AH and ESP are considered new functions added after the protocol's design.

---

Having IPSec included in every IPv6 implementation lets the IPv6 Internet have potentially more end-to-end security because of the availability of IPSec on all nodes, as shown in Figure 1-19.

**Figure 1-19**  *Mandatory IPSec in IPv6 Nodes Enables End-to-End Security on the IPv6 Internet*

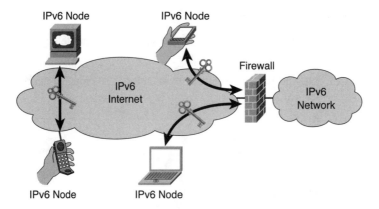

One of the downsides of IPSec, however, is that it also requires keys for each party, which means global key deployment, distribution, and management. This topic is beyond the scope of this book. If you want more information about policies and practices recommended to enable a secure PKI infrastructure, read RFC 2527, *Internet X.509 Public Key Infrastructure Certificate Policy and Certification Practices Framework.*

## Transition

The transition from an Internet made of IPv4 networks to IPv6 is another fundamental part of a new protocol. Standards bodies, the industry, and the Internet community do not want to repeat the same phenomenon as the Y2K bug, in which a major switch occurred at a specific time (December 31, 1999).

The ultimate goal of IPv6 in replacing IPv4 is well-known. However, there is no deadline for the switch from the Internet over IPv4 to IPv6. A special working group at the IETF called *Next-Generation transition from IPv4 to IPv6 (NGtrans)* was created to focus on the transition. NGtrans works in close collaboration with the IPv6 working group (formerly called IPng) to create transition strategies and mechanisms. Chapter 5, "IPv6 Integration and Coexistence Strategies," is entirely focused on these strategies and mechanisms.

---

**NOTE**    One question often asked is when will IPv6 happen? IPv6 is not like the Y2K problem, in which all the computers in the world were upgraded at the same time to smoothly enter the new millennium. No one has an answer to this question. But integration and coexistence mechanisms are in place to allow a smooth migration from IPv4 to IPv6.

---

The transition to IPv6 has been designed so that all IPv4 nodes are not required to be upgraded at the same time. Both IPv4 and IPv6 can be used concurrently on the same link-layer technologies; a smooth network transition from IPv4 to IPv6 is desired. Transition and coexistence mechanisms allow organizations to provide IPv6 connectivity to their early adopters, such as customers, research and development staff, and employees, over their current IPv4 infrastructure until there is enough demand for IPv6 or when a corporate strategy is undertaken to upgrade the infrastructure to IPv6.

Many transition and coexistence mechanisms are available and can be applied to different situations:

- Dual-stack nodes over IPv4 networks
- Islands of IPv6-only nodes over IPv4 networks
- IPv4-only nodes that can talk to IPv6 networks
- IPv6-only nodes that can talk to IPv4 networks

In Figure 1-20, a host with IPv6 and IPv4 stacks on the IPv4 network can establish an IPv6-over-IPv4 tunnel to an edge router. The router can forward IPv6 packets to native IPv6 networks. This mechanism provides IPv6 connectivity within the IPv4 network even if there is not enough demand to convert all the network infrastructure to IPv6.

**Figure 1-20** *Transition Mechanisms Allow Dual-Stack Nodes Over IPv4 Networks to Send IPv6 Packets*

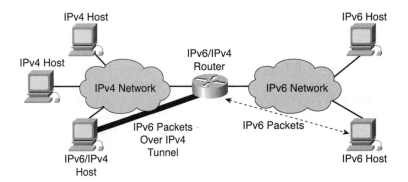

**NOTE**    A dual-stack node is a computer that runs both an IPv4 and IPv6 stack concurrently. Depending on the IP address assigned by the name resolution process (DNS), the node can use either an IPv6 or an IPv4 address to reach the destination.

Islands of IPv6-only nodes can be linked over an IPv4 network using routers with 6to4 mechanism, as shown in Figure 1-21.

**Figure 1-21** *6to4 Transition Mechanism*

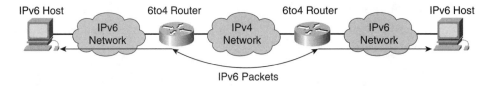

Many other transition mechanisms are available and standardized by the IETF. Chapter 5 discusses transition mechanisms. Several of them are presented using Cisco IOS Software technology.

# Summary

After reading this chapter, you should be able to explain the rationale behind IPv6 and should have a basic understanding of the main features and benefits provided by IPv6. In addition, you should remember the following information:

- Studies predict an exhaustion of the current IPv4 address space between 2005 and 2011.

- The IPv4 address space is limited by its 32-bit address scheme. Moreover, large portions of the space are already allocated, and other parts are unavailable as globally unicast addresses.

- As the Internet continues to grow, more IPv4 addresses are requested for new devices and applications.

- The combination of CIDR and NAT mechanisms has helped slow down the exhaustion of the address space. However, NAT breaks the end-to-end model of the IP protocol, so it has many limitations for protocols.

- IPv6 with its 128-bit address scheme provides plenty of IP addresses for the future.

- IPv6's larger address space provides globally unique unicast addresses to support the growth of the Internet.

- IPv6's multiple levels of hierarchy promote efficient and scalable routing to the Internet.

- Multihoming with the preservation of strict route aggregation is possible.

- The autoconfiguration mechanism allows nodes to configure their own IPv6 addresses.

- The transition between IPv6 providers is transparent to end users.

- The IPv6 header is more efficient than IPv4, fewer fields in the header are present, a new field is available, and ARP broadcast is replaced by a multicast use.

- New extension headers replace IPv4's Options field.

- Mobility and security are embedded in the protocol instead of being new functions added, as with IPv4.

- Many transition mechanisms are designed with IPv6 to allow a smooth transition from IPv4 networks to IPv6.

IPv6 is the replacement for IPv4 to ensure the growth of the Internet for future decades. There is no alternative to IPv6.

# Review Questions

Answer the following questions, and then refer to Appendix B, "Answers to Review Questions," for the answers.

1   What is the size in bits of the IPv4 address scheme?

2   Which classes of IPv4 addresses are not considered globally unique unicast IP addresses?

3   What is the main rationale behind IPv6?

4   Explain the consequences of the exhaustion of the IPv4 address space.

5   Describe the short history of IPv6 from 1993 to 2000.

6   Name some limitations of NAT.

7   Describe some of the features added by IPv6.

8   What is the size in bits of an IPv6 address?

9   Comparing the OSI reference model of IPv4 to that of IPv6, which layer is updated?

10   With plenty of IP addresses with IPv6, what is not desirable to have?

11   Define aggregation.

12   What happens when a customer changes IPv6 providers?

13   Why is multihoming more interesting with IPv6 than with IPv4?

14   Explain autoconfiguration.

15   Besides autoconfiguration, name the other methods used to configure IPv6 addresses on nodes.

16   Describe the disadvantages of ARP broadcast in IPv4.

17   List the main change in the IPv6 header compared to IPv4.

18   What is the purpose of an extension header?

19   List and define two mechanisms that are embedded in the IPv6 protocol but that are considered add-ons with IPv4.

20   How is the migration from IPv4 to IPv6 different from the Y2K bug?

# References

RFC 791, *Internet protocol, DARPA Internet Program, Protocol Specification,* USC, IETF, www.ietf.org/rfc/rfc791.txt, September 1981

RFC 1347, *CP and UDP with Bigger Addresses (TUBA), A Simple Proposal for Internet Addressing and Routing,* R. Callon, IETF, www.ietf.org/rfc/rfc1347.txt, June 1992

RFC 1517, *Applicability Statement for the Implementation of Classless Inter-Domain Routing (CIDR),* R. Hinden, IETF, www.ietf.org/rfc/rfc1517.txt, September 1993

RFC 1518, *An Architecture for IP Address Allocation with CIDR,* Y. Rekhter, T.Li, IETF, www.ietf.org/rfc/rfc1518.txt, September 1993

RFC 1519, *Classless Inter-Domain Routing (CIDR): an Address Assignment and Aggregation Strategy,* V. Fuller, et al., IETF, www.ietf.org/rfc/rfc1519.txt, September 1993

RFC 1520, *Exchanging Routing Information Across Provider Boundaries in the CIDR Environment,* Y. Rekhter, C. Topolcic, IETF, www.ietf.org/rfc/rfc1520.txt, September 1993

RFC 1550, *IP: Next Generation (IPng) White Paper Solicitation,* S. Bradner, A. Mankin, IETF, www.ietf.org/rfc/rfc1550.txt, Decembre 1993

RFC 1631, *The IP Network Address Translator (NAT),* K. Egevang, P. Francis, IETF, www.ietf.org/rfc/rfc1631.txt, May 1994

RFC 1707, *CATNIP: Common Architecture for the Internet,* M. McGovern, R. Ullmann, IETF, www.ietf.org/rfc/rfc1707.txt, October 1994

RFC 1715, *The H Ratio for Address Assignment Efficiency,* C. Huitema, IETF, www.ietf.org/rfc/rfc1715.txt, November 1994

RFC 1752, *The Recommendation for the IP Next Generation Protocol,* S. Bradner, A. Mankin, IETF, www.ietf.org/rfc/rfc1752.txt, January 1995

RFC 1918, *Address Allocation for Private Internets,* Y. Rekhter et al,. IETF, www.ietf.org/rfc/rfc1918.txt, February 1996

RFC 2002, *IP Mobility Support,* C. Perkins, IETF, www.ietf.org/rfc/rfc2002.txt, October 1996

RFC 2460, *Internet Protocol, Version 6 (IPv6) Specification*, S. Deering, R. Hinden, IETF, www.ietf.org/rfc/rfc2460.txt, December 1998

RFC 2462, *IPv6 Stateless Address Autoconfiguration*, S. Thomson, T. Narten, IETF, www.ietf.org/rfc/rfc2462.txt, December 1998

RFC 2527, *Internet X.509 Public Key Infrastructure Certificate Policy and Certification Practices Framework,* S. Chokhani, W. Ford, IETF, www.ietf.org/rfc/rfc2527.txt, March 1999

RFC 2775, *Internet Transparency*, B. Carpenter, IETF, www.ietf.org/rfc/rfc2775.txt, February 2000

RFC 2993, *Architectural Implications of NAT*, T. Hain, IETF, www.ietf.org/rfc/rfc2993.txt, November 2000

RFC 3041, *Privacy Extensions for Stateless Address Autoconfiguration in IPv6*, T. Narten, R. Draves IETF, www.ietf.org/rfc/rfc3041.txt, January 2001

*IPv6 Addressing and Routing,* PowerPoint presentation, S. Deering, www.ipv6.or.kr/ipv6summit/Download/1st-day/t-1.ppt, July 2001

*IPv6, How long can we wait?,* C. Huitema, www.huitema.net/ipv6/howlong.html

# IPv6 Design

Part II is the most fundamental part of this book because it discusses the IPv6 protocol specification and presents the main commands in the Cisco IOS Software to implement IPv6 networks. Part II begins with a description of the new IPv6 header, the IPv6 addressing architecture, and all the types of addresses that are defined in the protocol specification. This part details the Neighbor Discovery Protocol (NDP), a key protocol of IPv6 that uses Internet Control Message Protocol for IPv6 (ICMPv6) messages and multicast addresses to replace the Address Resolution Protocol (ARP). It also discusses advertising prefixes on links, stateless autoconfiguration, and the duplicate address detection (DAD) mechanism. The last chapter of this part presents an overview of the updates and changes applied on the routing protocols BGP4, RIP, IS-IS, and OSPF. The IPv6 routing protocols BGP4+, RIPng, IS-IS for IPv6, and OSPFv3 still use the longest-match prefix as the routing algorithm for route selection, as their equivalents did in IPv4.

On the practical side, Part II presents in detail the new commands added in the Cisco IOS Software technology to enable IPv6 on Cisco routers and to assign IPv6 addresses on network interfaces. Then it covers enabling and managing the advertisements of IPv6 prefixes on links, defining standard and extended IPv6 access control lists (ACLs), and using tools such as debug, ping, Telnet, and traceroute with IPv6. Finally, Part II describes in detail how to configure BGP4+, RIPng, IS-IS for IPv6, and OSPFv3 on networks with IPv6.

The following chapters comprise this part of the book:

Chapter 2      IPv6 Addressing

Chapter 3      IPv6 in Depth

Chapter 4      Routing on IPv6

"This telephone has too many shortcomings to be seriously considered as a means of communication. The device is of no value to us."

Western Union internal memo, 1876

# IPv6 Addressing

After reading this chapter, you will be able to describe the new IPv6 header format and the impact of IPv6 on User Datagram Protocol (UDP), Transport Control Protocol (TCP) datagrams, and the Maximum Transmission Unit (MTU). You will understand the addressing architecture of IPv6 with all kinds of IPv6 addresses scoped in the protocol. These addresses include link-local, site-local, aggregatable global unicast, loopback, unspecified, IPv4-compatible, multicast assigned, solicited-node multicast, and anycast. This chapter also presents IPv6 over Ethernet, multicast mapping over Ethernet, and EUI-64 format.

Throughout this chapter, you will see sample configurations using the Cisco IOS Software technology to acquire basic knowledge to configure and operate routers in an IPv6 environment. Examples show you how to enable IPv6 and IPv6 forwarding on a router. Examples also show you how to configure IPv6 addresses on network interfaces under Cisco IOS Software technology.

Finally, with the configuration exercise in the case study, you can practice commands learned in this chapter by configuring, analyzing, and displaying IPv6 using the Cisco IOS Software technology.

## IP Header

This section reviews the IPv4 header. It describes the fields and compares them to the fields in the IPv6 header.

### IPv4 Header Format

IP packets are carried over link-layer technologies such as Ethernet (10 Mbps), Fast Ethernet (100 Mbps), Gigabit Ethernet (1000 Mbps), Frame Relay, and many others. Each link-layer technology family has its own link-layer frame that carries IP packets. As shown in Figure 2-1, an IP packet is carried between the frame header and frame trailer of a link-layer frame. An IP packet has two fundamental components:

- **IP header**—The IP header contains many fields that are used by routers to forward the packet from network to network to a final destination. Fields within the IP header identify the sender, receiver, and transport protocol and define many other parameters.

- **Payload**—Represents the information (data) to be delivered to the receiver by the sender.

**Figure 2-1**   *IP Packet Carried by a Link-Layer Frame Contains a Header and a Payload*

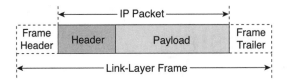

As shown in Figure 2-2, the basic IPv4 header contains 12 fields. As defined in RFC 791, *Internet Protocol DARPA Internet Program Specification,* each field of the IPv4 header has a specific use. This section summarizes the contents of the IPv4 header to help you understand the main differences between the IPv4 header and the new IPv6 header.

**Figure 2-2**   *Fields in the IPv4 Header*

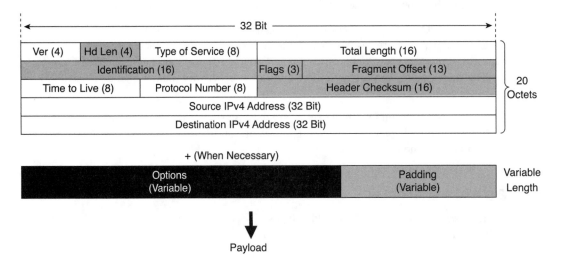

Following are the IPv4 header fields:

- **Version (4-bit)**—The version of the IP (Internet Protocol) header. The current IP version used on the Internet is 4 (IPv4). This field contains the value 4.

- **Header Length (4-bit)**—The length in octets of the header size up to the Payload field.

- **Type of Service (TOS) (8-bit)**—Specifies the treatment of the datagram during its transmission through the routers. This field can also be interpreted as Differentiated Services Code Point (DSCP).

- **Total Length (16-bit)**—The size of the IP packet in octets, including the header and the payload. This field is 16-bit, which means that the maximum size of an IPv4 packet is 65,535 octets.

- **Identification (16-bit), Flags (3-bit), and Fragment Offset (13-bit)**—Fields related to packet fragmentation by routers when the MTU along a path is smaller than the sender's MTU. The MTU is the maximum size in octets of an IP packet that can be transmitted on a specific communication medium, such as Ethernet, Fast Ethernet, and so on. For Ethernet, the MTU is 1500 octets.

- **Time to Live (8-bit)**—This field is decremented each time the packet passes through an intermediary router. When this field contains the value 0, the packet is destroyed, and an Internet Control Message Protocol for IPv4 (ICMPv4) Type 11 error message (Time Exceeded) is sent to the source node.

- **Protocol Number (8-bit)**—Specifies the upper-layer protocol used in a packet's payload, such as Transport Control Protocol (TCP), User Datagram Protocol (UDP), Internet Control Message Protocol (ICMP), or any others. Protocols supported are defined by the Internet Assigned Numbers Authority (IANA).

- **Header Checksum (16-bit)**—Represents the checksum of the IP header and is used for error checking. This field is verified and recomputed by each intermediary router along a path.

- **Source IPv4 Address (32-bit)**—The sender's IPv4 address.

- **Destination IPv4 Address (32-bit)**—The receiver's IPv4 address.

- **Options (variable)**—This optional field might appear in an IPv4 packet. The Options field is variable in size and increases the length of the header when used.

- **Padding (variable)**—Padding is used to ensure that the packet ends on a 32-bit boundary. It also increases the header's size.

- **Payload (variable)**—The payload is not a field of the basic IPv4 header. Rather, it represents the data to be delivered to a destination address. The payload includes an upper-layer header.

---

**NOTE**    Protocol numbers are assigned by IANA. A complete list of all protocol numbers assigned by IANA can be found at www.iana.org/assignments/protocol-numbers.

---

In IPv6, several fields of the IPv4 header are removed. In Figure 2-2, these fields are gray or black. The main reasons for these removals are as follows:

- **Header Length**—The basic IPv4 header is only 20 bytes long. However, the basic IPv6 header has a fixed length of 40 octets. The IPv4 header length indicates the packet's total length, including the Options field. When present, the Options field increases the length of the IPv4 header. Instead of the Options field, IPv6 uses the Extension field. The Extension field is handled differently from how IPv4 handles the Options field.

- **Identification, Flags, and Fragment Offset**—Fragmentation is handled differently in IPv6. It is no longer done by intermediate routers in the networks, but by the source node that originates the packet. Removing the Fragmentation field removes costly CPU processing at intermediate routers. The path MTU discovery (PMTUD) mechanism, discussed later in this chapter, is recommended for every IPv6 node to avoid fragmentation.

- **Header Checksum**—Link-layer technologies (Layer 2) perform their own checksum and error control. The reliability of link-layer is now good and upper-layer protocols such TCP and UDP (Layer 4) have their own checksums. UDP checksum, which was optional in IPv4, is mandatory in IPv6. Therefore, the checksum at Layer 3 is redundant, so the Header Checksum field is unnecessary in IPv6 and suppresses the recomputation process each time a packet passes through a router.

- **Options and Padding**—The Options field is radically changed in IPv6. The options are now handled by extension headers (as discussed later in this chapter). The Padding field is also removed. The removal of Options and Padding headers simplifies the IP header. Thus, the basic IPv6 header has a fixed length of 40 octets, allowing less processing by routers along the delivery path compared to IPv4. The other fields in the IPv4 header— Version, Type of Service, Total Length, Time to Live, Protocol Number, Source IPv4 Address, and Destination IPv4 Address—either were not changed or were modified only slightly (as described in the next section).

## Basic IPv6 Header Format

As defined in RFC 2460, *Internet Protocol, Version 6 (IPv6) Specification,* the basic IPv6 header contains eight fields, in comparison with 12 fields in IPv4 (without the Options and Padding fields), for a total length of 40 octets. Moreover, the basic IPv6 header might have one too many extension headers daisy-chained following the 40 octets. This section summarizes the fields of the basic IPv6 header.

The IPv6 protocol represents an upgrade of the IPv4 protocol. As shown in Figure 2-3, the Flow Label field and the extension headers with their variable length are new in IPv6. Here are the descriptions of the fields in the basic IPv6 header:

- **Version (4-bit)**—The IP version. This field contains the value 6 rather than the value 4 contained in an IPv4 packet.

- **Traffic Class (8-bit)**—This field and its functions are similar to the Type of Service field in IPv4. This field tags an IPv6 packet with a Differentiated Services Code Point (DSCP) that specifies how the packet should be handled.

- **Flow Label (20-bit)**—This field is used to tag a flow for IPv6 packets. This is new in the IPv6 protocol. The current IETF standard does not specify the details about how to manage and process the Flow Label.

**NOTE**    Refer to the IETF draft "IPv6 Flow Label Specification" (www.ietf.org/internet-drafts/draft-ietf-ipv6-flow-label-06.txt) for detailed information on the specification and the possible usage of the Flow Label field with IPv6.

- **Payload Length (16-bit)**—This field represents the payload's length. The payload is the remaining part of the packet following the IPv6 header.

- **Next Header (8-bit)**—As shown in Figure 2-4, this field defines the type of information following the basic IPv6 header. The type of information can be an upper-layer protocol such as TCP or UDP, or it can be one of the new optional extension headers. The Next Header field is similar to the Protocol Number field in IPv4. Supported protocols are defined by the IANA.

- **Hop Limit (8-bit)**—This field defines the maximum number of hops (intermediate routers) that the IP packet can pass through. Each hop decreases this value by 1. As in IPv4, when this field contains the value 0, the packet is destroyed and an Internet Control Message Protocol for IPv6 (ICMPv6) Type 3 message (Time Exceeded) is sent to the source node. See Chapter 3, "IPv6 in Depth," for information about ICMPv6.

- **Source Address (128-bit)**—This field identifies the IPv6 source address of the sender.

- **Destination Address (128-bit)**—This field identifies the packet's IPv6 destination address.

**Figure 2-3**    *Fields Within the Basic IPv6 Header*

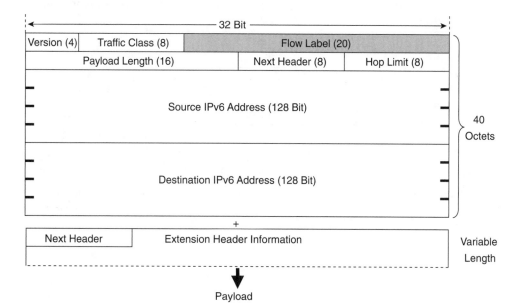

**Figure 2-4** *Next Header Field Specifies the Type of Information Following the Basic IPv6 Header*

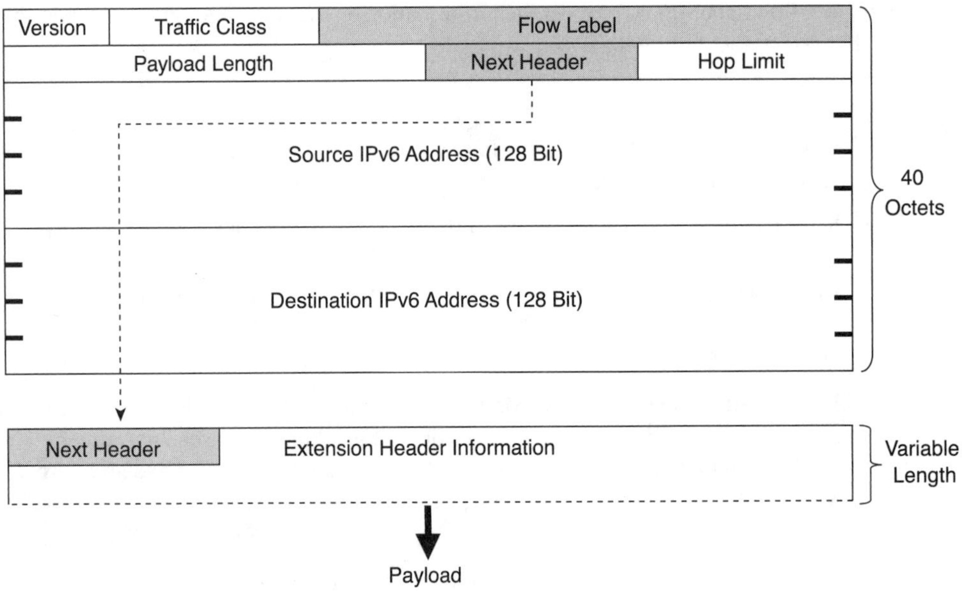

Table 2-1 compares IPv4 and IPv6 headers.

**Table 2-1** *Comparison of IPv4 and IPv6 Headers*

| Fields of the IPv4 Header | Fields of the IPv6 Header | Comparison of IPv4 and IPv6 Headers |
| --- | --- | --- |
| Version (4-bit) | Version (4-bit) | Same function but the IPv6 header contains a new value. |
| Header length (4-bit) | — | Removed in IPv6. The basic IPv6 header always has 40 octets. |
| Type of service (8-bit) | Traffic class (8-bit) | Same function for both headers. |
| — | Flow label (20-bit) | New field added to tag a flow for IPv6 packets. |
| Total length (16-bit) | Payload length (16-bit) | Same function for both headers. |
| Identification (16-bit) | — | Removed in IPv6 because fragmentation is handled differently in IPv6. |

**Table 2-1**    *Comparison of IPv4 and IPv6 Headers (Continued)*

| Fields of the IPv4 Header | Fields of the IPv6 Header | Comparison of IPv4 and IPv6 Headers |
|---|---|---|
| Flags (3-bit) | — | Removed in IPv6 because fragmentation is handled differently in IPv6. |
| Fragment offset (13-bit) | — | Removed in IPv6 because fragmentation is handled differently in IPv6. |
| Time to live (8-bit) | Hop limit (8-bit) | Same function for both headers. |
| Protocol number (8-bit) | Next header (8-bit) | Same function for both headers. |
| Header checksum (16-bit) | — | Removed in IPv6. Link-layer technologies and upper-layer protocols handle checksum and error control. |
| Source address (32-bit) | Source address (128-bit) | Source address is expanded in IPv6. |
| Destination address (32-bit) | Destination address (128-bit) | Destination address is expanded in IPv6. |
| Options (variable) | — | Removed in IPv6. The way to handle this option is different in IPv4. |
| Padding (variable) | — | Removed in IPv6. The way to handle this option is different in IPv4. |
| — | Extension headers | New way in IPv6 to handle Options fields, fragmentation, security, mobility, Loose Source Routing, Record Route, and so on. The following section presents IPv6's extension headers. |

## IPv6 Extension Headers

IPv6 extension headers are optional headers that may follow the basic IPv6 header. Several types of extension headers are defined in RFC 2460, *Internet Protocol, Version 6 (IPv6) Specification*. One IPv6 packet may include zero, one, or multiple extension headers. As shown in Figure 2-5, when multiple extension headers are used in an IPv6 packet, they form a chained list of headers identified by the Next Header field of the previous header.

**Figure 2-5**   *Multiple Extension Headers May Form a Chained List of Headers All Linked to the Next Header Field*

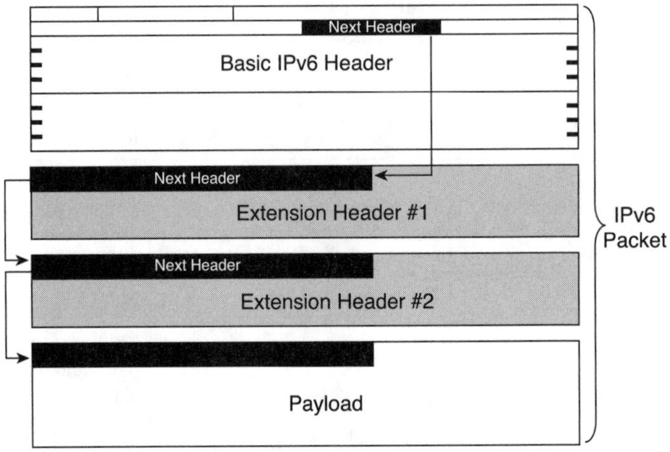

For typical IPv6 applications, the last header of a chain is the upper-layer protocol carrying the packet's payload. The upper-layer protocol may be TCP, UDP, or an ICMPv6 packet, for example.

Here are IPv6's defined extension headers:

- **Hop-by-Hop Options header (protocol 0)**—This field is read and processed by every node and router along the delivery path. The Hop-by-Hop Options header is used for Jumbo-gram packets and the Router Alert. An example of applying the Hop-by-Hop Options header is Resource Reservation Protocol (RSVP) because each router needs to look at it.

---

**NOTE**   IPv6 can send packets greater than 65,535 octets, especially on a network with a very large MTU value. As defined in RFC 2675, *IPv6 Jumbograms,* these packets are called *Jumbograms.* IPv4 cannot send packets greater than 65,535 octets because the Total Length field is a 16-bit value. Basically, the IPv6 header has the same limitation of 65,535 octets related to the field Payload Length. However, by using a 32-bit field within the Hop-by-Hop Options header, a Jumbogram packet may have a maximum length of 4,294,967,295 octets.

---

**NOTE**   When a source node sends an IPv6 packet to a destination node using extension headers, intermediate routers along the delivery path must not scan and process extension headers. However, as defined in RFC 2711, *IPv6 Router Alert Option,* the Router Alert feature within the Hop-by-Hop Options header may be used when a packet that is sent to a particular destination requires special processing by intermediate routers along the delivery path.

---

- **Destination Options header (protocol 60)** — This header carries optional information that is specifically targeted to a packet's destination address. The Mobile IPv6 protocol specification, which is a draft status at IETF, proposes to use the Destination Options header to exchange registration messages between mobile nodes and the home agent. Mobile IP is a protocol allowing mobile nodes to keep permanent IP addresses even if they change point of attachment.

- **Routing header (protocol 43)** — This header can be used by an IPv6 source node to force a packet to pass through specific routers on the way to its destination. A list of intermediary routers may be specified within the Routing header when the Routing Type field is set to 0. This function is similar to the Loose Source Routing option in IPv4.

## Routing Header in Detail

Compared to IPv4, the way of handling Loose Source Routing is different in IPv6. As soon as the list of intermediary IPv6 routers is done, before sending the IPv6 packet, the source node executes the following operations in this order:

**Step 1**  Makes the first router of the intermediary routers list the destination address in the basic IPv6 header rather than the original IPv6 destination.

**Step 2**  Makes the original IPv6 destination the final destination of the intermediary list of routers.

**Step 3**  Decrements by 1 the Segments Left field of the Routing header as the packet travels along each router. This field acts as a pointer to contain the remaining number of router segments to the original destination.

Then, at each intermediary router of the list, the following steps occur:

(a) The intermediary router changes the destination address of the basic IPv6 header to target the next router on the intermediary list.

(b) The router decrements by 1 the Segments Left field of the Routing header.

(c) The router puts its own address to the intermediary list of routers in the Routing header just before the next router (the way to record route).

(d) If the router is the last of the intermediary routers list, it changes the IPv6 destination address of the basic IPv6 header to the final destination node, which is in fact the packet's original destination.

The destination node, after having received the packet with the Routing header, can see the list of intermediary routers recorded in the Routing header. Then, the destination node can also send reply packets to the source node using a Routing header and can specify the same router list but in the inverse order.

As illustrated in Figure 2-6, source node A wants to deliver a packet to destination node B by forcing the packet to pass through a list of intermediary routers specified within a Routing header. Router R2 and then router R4 are identified in the list of intermediary routers to deliver the packet to destination node B. Node A first sends the packet to router R2. The packet uses router R2 as the destination address within the basic IPv6 header. The next address of the intermediary list of routers is router R4, and the last address of the list is destination node B. After receiving the packet, router R2 sends the packet to router R4. The packet uses router R4 as the destination address within the basic IPv6 header. The next address of the router's intermediary list is now destination node B, which is the packet's original destination node. Finally, after receiving the packet, router R4 sends its packet to destination node B through router R6 instead of router R7 (the shortest path to reach destination node B). Because router R6 is not on the list of intermediary routers, the packet is forwarded normally by router R4. The packet uses destination node B as the destination address, and the Routing header contains the list of intermediary routers (R2, R6) that belong to this path.

**Figure 2-6**    *Packet Passing Through the List of Intermediary Routers Along the Delivery Path*

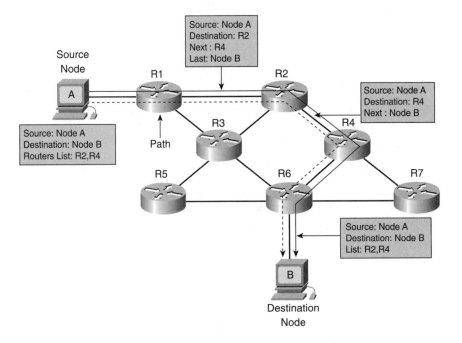

Only a few applications exist for using the Routing header in IPv6. Mobile IPv6 is an example of a protocol that uses the Routing header when a node is away from its home network. The Routing header provides efficiency to the protocol compared to Mobile IPv4. Chapter 3 presents an overview of the Mobile IPv6 protocol.

See RFC 2460, *Internet Protocol, Version 6 (IPv6) Specification,* for additional information about the Routing header specification and fields.

Now that you have read about the Routing header in detail, the following list presents other extension headers defined in the IPv6 protocol:

- **Fragment header (protocol 44)** — In IPv6, the PMTUD mechanism is recommended to all IPv6 nodes. PMTUD is discussed in detail in Chapter 3. When an IPv6 node does not support PMTUD and it must send a packet larger than the greatest MTU along the delivery path, the Fragment header is used. When this happens, the node fragments the packets and sends each fragment using Fragment headers. Then the destination node reassembles the original packet by concatenating all the fragments.

---

**NOTE**    In IPv6, fragmentation is undesirable. When necessary, fragmentation is performed by source nodes, not by routers along a packet's delivery path. In IPv4, fragmentation is done at the originating nodes as well as at the intermediate routers.

---

- **Authentication header (protocol 51)** — This header is used in IPSec to provide authentication, data integrity, and replay protection. It also ensures protection of some fields of the basic IPv6 header. This header is identical in both IPv4 and IPv6. It is well-known as the IPSec authentication header (AH).

- **Encapsulating Security Payload header (protocol 50)** — This header is also used in IPSec to provide authentication, data integrity, replay protection, and confidentiality of the IPv6 packet. Similar to the authentication header, this header is identical in both IPv4 and IPv6. It is well-known as IPSec Encapsulating Security Payload (ESP).

## Multiple Extension Headers

When multiple extension headers are used in an IPv6 packet, their order must be as follows:

1 Basic IPv6 header

2 Hop-by-Hop Options

3 Destination Options (if the Routing header is used)

4 Routing

5 Fragment

6 Authentication

7 Encapsulating Security Payload

8 Destination Options

9 Upper-layer (TCP, UDP, ICMPv6, ...)

Packets including several extension headers must be processed strictly by the destination nodes in the order they appear in the IPv6 packet. The node that receives packets must not, for example, scan through a packet looking for a particular kind of extension header and process that header before processing all the preceding ones.

## User Datagram Protocol (UDP) and IPv6

UDP (protocol 17) is considered an upper-layer protocol by IPv4 and IPv6. UDP has not been changed for IPv6 and continues to run on top of both IPv6 and IPv4 headers. However, as shown in Figure 2-7, the Checksum field in the UDP packet is mandatory with IPv6. This field was optional in IPv4. Therefore, the UDP Checksum field must be computed by IPv6 source nodes before an IPv6 packet is sent.

**Figure 2-7**    *UDP Checksum Field in the UDP Packet Is Mandatory with IPv6*

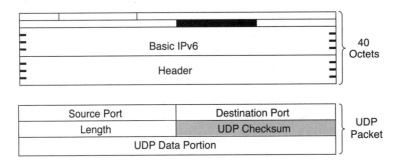

The UDP checksum is necessary because the Checksum field of the IPv4 header was removed. This field was used to verify the integrity of the inner packet.

## Transport Control Protocol (TCP) and IPv6

TCP (protocol 6) is also considered an upper-layer protocol by IPv4 and IPv6. The Checksum field within the TCP header is mandatory in IPv4. Because TCP is a very complex protocol, no change was proposed to this protocol for IPv6. It was decided during the engineering of IPv6 to continue to run TCP and UDP protocols on top of IPv6 without structural modifications.

## Maximum Transmission Unit (MTU) for IPv6

In IPv4, a link's minimum MTU length is 68 octets. Every Internet module in IPv4 must be able to forward IPv4 packets of 68 bytes without further fragmentation. The maximum length of an IPv4 header is 60 octets. The minimum fragment size is eight octets.

As shown in Figure 2-8, an IPv6 link's minimum MTU length is 1280 octets, compared to 68 octets in IPv4.

**Figure 2-8**    *IPv6's Minimum MTU Size Is 1280 Octets*

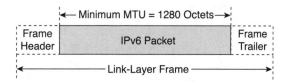

Moreover, in IPv6 every link in the Internet, including PPP links, tunnels, and so on, has an MTU size of 1280 octets or greater. However, in IPv6 the minimum supported datagram length is 1500 octets. The minimum supported datagram is the size of the datagram after the IP-layer reassembly (accept pieces and put them back together) by the IP implementation. In IPv4, the minimum supported datagram size is 576 octets.

## Path MTU Discovery (PMTUD) for IPv6

To avoid packet fragmentation in IPv6, which is harmful and costly to the CPU cycle for nodes and intermediary routers, RFC 2460 strongly recommends that IPv6 nodes implement PMTUD for IPv6 (defined in RFC 1981). PMTUD is initiated by source nodes and allows them to find the smallest MTU value on the delivery path. PMTUD is covered in detail in Chapter 3.

## Very Large MTU

The maximum packet size supported by the basic IPv6 header is 65,536 octets, which is limited by the 16-bit length of the Payload Length field. As covered earlier in the Hop-by-Hop exten-sion header description, larger packets called Jumbograms are possible in IPv6. In comparison with the maximum size of a Jumbogram (4,294,967,295 octets), note that the MTU size of the 10-GB Ethernet technology is 9216 octets.

# Addressing

IPv6 addresses are four times the size of IPv4 addresses. The representation of IPv6 addresses is also very different. This section covers the new representations, syntaxes, and compressed forms of IPv6 addresses.

# Representation of IPv6 Addresses

As defined in RFC 2373, *IP Version 6 Addressing Architecture,* three formats represent IPv6 addresses. The preferred format is the longest method. It represents all 32 hexadecimal characters that form an IPv6 address. The preferred format may also be seen as the representation that matches a computer's "thinking."

The next method is the compressed representation of an IPv6 address. To simplify the typing of IPv6 addresses by humans, it is possible to compress the address when zero values are present in the IPv6 address. This means that preferred and compressed formats are different representations of the same IPv6 addresses, a new concept in comparison with IPv4.

Finally, the third method to represent an address is related to transition mechanisms where an IPv4 address is embedded in an IPv6 address. This last representation is less important than the preferred and the compressed format, because it is useful only if you're using specific transition mechanisms such as automatic IPv4-compatible tunnels and dynamic Network Address Translation Protocol Translation (NAT-PT). Automatic IPv4-compatible tunnels and dynamic NAT-PT mechanisms are discussed in detail in Chapter 5, "IPv6 Integration and Coexistence Strategies."

## Preferred IPv6 Address Representation

As shown in Figure 2-9, the preferred representation, also known as the complete form of an IPv6 address, has a series of eight 16-bit hexadecimal fields separated by colons (:). Each 16-bit field is textually represented by four hexadecimal characters, meaning that the value of each 16-bit field may have hexadecimal values 0x0000 through 0xFFFF. Alphanumeric characters used in hexadecimal are case-insensitive.

**Figure 2-9** *IPv6 Addresses Have Eight Fields of 16-Bit Hexadecimal Values Separated by Colons*

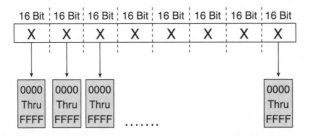

The preferred format is the longest representation of an IPv6 address. A total of 32 hexadecimal characters may be represented in this preferred form (eight fields of four hexadecimal characters). In comparison, an IPv4 address has four 8-bit decimal fields separated by dots (.) for a possible total of 12 decimal characters.

Table 2-2 shows examples of IPv6 addresses in the preferred representation.

**Table 2-2**    *Examples of IPv6 Addresses in the Preferred Format*

| Preferred Format of IPv6 Addresses |
| --- |
| 0000:0000:0000:0000:0000:0000:0000:0000 |
| 0000:0000:0000:0000:0000:0000:0000:0001 |
| 2001:0410:0000:1234:FB00:1400:5000:45FF |
| 3ffe:0000:0000:0000:1010:2a2a:0000:0001 |
| 3FFE:0B00:0C18:0001:0000:1234:AB34:0002 |
| FE80:0000:0000:0000:0000:0000:0000:0009 |
| FFFF:FFFF:FFFF:FFFF:FFFF:FFFF:FFFF:FFFF |

## Compressed Representation

In IPv6, it is common to use addresses that contain long strings of 0s. To make writing addresses containing 0 bits easier for humans, a special syntax compresses consecutive 0 values in two situations—successive 16-bit fields made of 0s and leading 0s in 16-bit fields of an IPv6 address.

### Successive 16-Bit Fields Made up of 0s

To simplify the length of an IPv6 address when one to multiple successive 16-bit fields of 0 characters are present, it is legal to represent these fields of 0s as :: (a double colon). However, only one :: is permitted in an IPv6 address. This method makes many IPv6 addresses very small. The compressed representation of an IPv6 address also means that the same address can have several representations.

**NOTE**    When the :: is present in an IPv6 address, an address parser can identify the number of missing 0s. Then, the parser fills 0 characters between the two parts of the address until the 128-bit address is complete. If more than one :: is present in a compressed IPv6 address, there is no way for the parser to identify the size of each field of 0s. Therefore, only one :: is permitted per IPv6 address.

Table 2-3 presents examples of IPv6 addresses in the preferred format that have been compressed because they have one or more successive 16-bit fields of 0 characters. Bold characters in the preferred format addresses represent values to be removed to compress the addresses.

**Table 2-3** *Examples of IPv6 Addresses in the Preferred Format That Are Formatted in the Compressed Format*

| Preferred Format | Compressed Format Using :: |
|---|---|
| **0000:0000:0000:0000:0000:0000:0000:0000** | :: |
| **0000:0000:0000:0000:0000:0000:0000:**0001 | ::0001 |
| 2001:0410:**0000**:1234:FB00:1400:5000:45FF | 2001:0410::1234:FB00:1400:5000:45FF |
| 3ffe:**0000:0000:0000:**1010:2a2a:0000:0001 | 3ffe::1010:2a2a:0000:0001 |
| 3FFE:0B00:0C18:0001:**0000**:1234:AB34:0002 | 3FFE:0B00:0C18:0001::1234:AB34:0002 |
| FE80:**0000:0000:0000:0000:0000:0000:**0009 | FE80::0009 |
| FFFF:FFFF:FFFF:FFFF:FFFF:FFFF:FFFF:FFFF | FFFF:FFFF:FFFF:FFFF:FFFF:FFFF:FFFF:FFFF |

The address FFFF:FFFF:FFFF:FFFF:FFFF:FFFF:FFFF:FFFF is an example of an address in which all bits are set to 1. Therefore, this address cannot be compressed. Compressed form using the :: is available only when multiple successive 16-bit fields of 0 characters are present.

Table 2-4 presents *illegal* examples of compressed addresses. The compressed addresses represented use the :: more than once, which is an *illegal* IPv6 compressed address representation.

**Table 2-4** *Examples of Illegal IPv6 Compressed Address Representations*

| Preferred Format | Compressed Format Using :: |
|---|---|
| 0000:0000:AAAA:0000:0000:0000:0000:0001 | ::AAAA::0001 |
| 3ffe:0000:0000:0000:1010:2a2a:0000:0001 | 3ffe::1010:2a2a::0001 |

## Leading 0s in 16-Bit Fields of an IPv6 Address

The second method to compress addresses is applicable to each 16-bit hexadecimal field of an IPv6 address when one or more leading 0s are present. Leading 0s of each field can simply be removed to simplify the length of an IPv6 address. However, if every hexadecimal character of a 16-bit field is set to 0, at least one 0 character must be kept. Table 2-5 shows examples of addresses compressed when leading 0s are present. In these examples, all leading 0s of each 16-bit field are removed and all the following values are kept. Bold characters in the preferred format addresses represent values to be removed to compress the addresses.

## Combining Both Compression Methods

Compression of successive 16-bit fields made of 0 characters and compression of leading 0 characters within 16-bit fields can be mixed to simplify the length of IPv6 addresses. Table 2-6 presents examples in which both compression methods are applied. Bold characters in the preferred format addresses represent values to be removed to compress the addresses.

**Table 2-5**     *ExamplesofIPv6AddressesinWhichLeading0sof16-BitFieldsAreRemovedtoCompresstheAddress*

| Preferred Format | Compressed Format |
|---|---|
| 0000:0000:0000:0000:0000:0000:0000:0000 | 0:0:0:0:0:0:0:0 |
| 0000:0000:0000:0000:0000:0000:0000:0001 | 0:0:0:0:0:0:0:1 |
| 2001:0410:0000:1234:FB00:1400:5000:45FF | 2001:410:0:1234:FB00:1400:5000:45FF |
| 3ffe:0000:0000:0000:1010:2a2a:0000:0001 | 3ffe:0:0:0:1010:2a2a:0:1 |
| 3FFE:0B00:0C18:0001:0000:1234:AB34:0002 | 3FFE:B00:C18:1:0:1234:AB34:2 |
| FE80:0000:0000:0000:0000:0000:0000:0009 | FE80:0:0:0:0:0:0:9 |
| FFFF:FFFF:FFFF:FFFF:FFFF:FFFF:FFFF:FFFF | FFFF:FFFF:FFFF:FFFF:FFFF:FFFF:FFFF:FFFF |

**Table 2-6**     *Examples of IPv6 Addresses Formatted in the Compressed Representation*

| Preferred Format | Compressed Format |
|---|---|
| 0000:0000:0000:0000:0000:0000:0000:0000 | :: |
| 0000:0000:0000:0000:0000:0000:0000:0001 | ::1 |
| 2001:0410:0000:1234:FB00:1400:5000:45FF | 2001:410::1234:FB00:1400:5000:45FF |
| 3ffe:0000:0000:0000:1010:2a2a:0000:0001 | 3ffe::1010:2a2a:0:1 |
| 3FFE:0B00:0C18:0001:0000:1234:AB34:0002 | 3FFE:B00:C18:1::1234:AB34:2 |
| FE80:0000:0000:0000:0000:0000:0000:0009 | FE80::9 |

## IPv6 Address with an Embedded IPv4 Address

The third representation of an IPv6 address is to use an embedded IPv4 address within the IPv6 address.

The first part of the IPv6 address uses the hexadecimal representation, and the IPv4 address part is in decimal format. This is a specific representation of an IPv6 address used by transition mechanisms.

**NOTE**     The low-order 32-bit of the address may also be represented in hexadecimal on the implementation supporting the automatic IPv4-compatible tunnel mechanism. Thus, the decimal values are converted into hex.

**NOTE**        As mentioned at the beginning of this section, this form of IPv6 address is used by only two transition mechanisms. The transition mechanisms using this format are supported in the Cisco IOS Software technology, but the automatic IPv4-compatible tunnel mechanism is being deprecated in favor of more-efficient mechanisms. However, the transition mechanism called dynamic NAT-PT still embeds an IPv4 address within an IPv6 address for its operation. Thus, it uses this form of address.

Figure 2-10 shows the format of an IPv6 address using an embedded IPv4 address. This kind of address is made up of six high-order fields of 16-bit hexadecimal values, represented by X characters, followed by four low-order fields of 8-bit decimal values (IPv4 address), represented by d characters (for a total of 32 bits).

**Figure 2-10**   *IPv6 Address with an Embedded IPv4 Address*

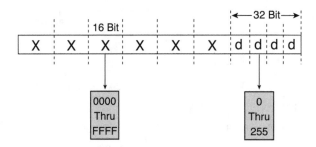

Two kinds of IPv6 addresses have an embedded IPv4 address:

- **IPv4-compatible IPv6 address**—Used to establish an automatic tunnel to carry IPv6 packets over IPv4 networks. This address is related to a transition mechanism of the IPv6 protocol.

- **IPv4-mapped IPv6 address**—Used only on the local scope of nodes having both IPv4 and IPv6 stacks. Nodes use IPv4-mapped IPv6 addresses internally only. These addresses are never known outside the node itself and should not go on the wire as IPv6 addresses.

Although they both use the same address representation of an IPv4 address embedded in an IPv6 address, a different IPv6 prefix is defined for each kind of embedded IPv4 address. The IPv6 prefix for the IPv4-compatible IPv6 address is represented by the high-order 96-bit set to 0 followed by the 32-bit of the IPv4 address. The prefix for the IPv4-mapped IPv6 address is represented by the high-order 80-bit set to 0, then the next 16-bit set to 1, and finally followed by the 32-bit of the IPv4 address of the local node. The next section presents in detail the format of the IPv6 address with an embedded an IPv4 address.

Table 2-7 shows examples of each kind of IPv4 address embedded in IPv6 addresses and also demonstrates that both addresses can be represented in compressed format. The first address presented is the IPv4-compatible IPv6 address and the second is an IPv4-mapped IPv6 address. Bold characters in the preferred format addresses represent values to be removed to compress the addresses.

**Table 2-7**    *Examples of IPv4-Compatible IPv6 Addresses and IPv4-Mapped IPv6 Addresses*

| Preferred Format | Compressed Format |
|---|---|
| **0000:0000:0000:0000:0000:0000**:206.123.31.2 | 0:0:0:0:0:0:206.123.31.2 or ::206.123.31.2 |
| **0000:0000:0000:0000:0000:0000**:ce7b:1f01 | 0:0:0:0:0:0:ce7b:1f01 or ::ce7b:1f01 |
| **0000:0000:0000:0000:0000:**FFFF:206.123.31.2 | 0:0:0:0:0:FFFF:206.123.31.2 or ::FFFF:206.123.31.2 |
| **0000:0000:0000:0000:0000:**FFFF:ce7b:1f01 | 0:0:0:0:0:FFFF:ce7b:1f01 or ::FFFF:ce7b:1f01 |

**NOTE**    Although the dynamic NAT-PT mechanism is based on the IPv4-compatible IPv6 address format, it does not use the IPv6 prefix presented here. Refer to Chapter 5 for more details about the prefix used by the dynamic NAT-PT mechanism.

## IPv6 Address Representation for URL

In Uniform Resource Locator (URL) format, the colon (:) character is already defined to specify an optional port number. Here are examples of URLs using the colon character to specify a port number:

www.example.net:8080/index.html

https://www.example.com:8443/abc.html

In IPv6, the URL parser of Internet browsers must be able to differentiate between the colon of a port number and the colon in an IPv6 address. However, this is impossible because the compressed representation of an IPv6 address may include the double colon anywhere in the IPv6 address.

Therefore, to identify the IPv6 address while still keeping the colon character for URL format (port number), the IPv6 address must be enclosed in brackets, as defined in RFC 2732, *Format for Literal IPv6 Addresses in URL's*. Then, after the brackets, the port number may be added, followed by the directory and filename. Here are examples of URLs with IPv6 addresses between brackets:

[3ffe:b80:c18:1::50]:8080/index.html

https://[2001:410:0:1:250:fcee:e450:33ab]:8443/abc.html

However, using IPv6 addresses inside brackets should normally be used for diagnostic purposes only or when the naming service (DNS) is unavailable. Because IPv6 addresses are longer than IPv4 addresses, users tend to use the DNS and the fully qualified domain name (FQDN) format instead of the IPv6 address in hexadecimal representation.

## IPv6 and Subnetting

In IPv4, there are two ways to represent a network prefix:

- **Decimal representation**—A network mask is specified in d.d.d.d format. The network mask value represents the number of consecutive bits in binary that are set to 1.

- **Classless interdomain routing (CIDR) notation**—The network prefix mask may also be specified with a decimal number representing the number of consecutive bits in binary set to 1. The slash character is used between the prefix and the network mask value.

Both representations mean the same number of network mask bits for nodes. For example, the network prefix 192.168.1.0 with the network mask value of 255.255.255.0 is the same as 192.168.1.0/24 in CIDR notation. The range of IP addresses available for nodes in this network varies from 192.168.1.1 to 192.168.1.254.

In IPv6, the network mask representation using the long form, such as d.d.d.d, is gone because of the new length of the IPv6 address. The only acceptable form to represent a network mask in IPv6 is CIDR notation. Although IPv6 addresses are in hexadecimal format, the network mask value is still a decimal value. Table 2-8 shows examples of IPv6 addresses and network prefixes using the network value in CIDR notation.

**Table 2-8**    *Examples of IPv6 Prefixes with Network Masks*

| IPv6 Prefix | Description |
|---|---|
| 2001:410:0:1:0:0:0:45FF/128 | Represents a subnet with only one IPv6 address. |
| 2001:410:0:1::/64 | Network prefix 2001:410:0:1::/64 can handle $2^{64}$ nodes. This is the default prefix length for a subnet. |
| 2001:410:0::/48 | Network prefix 2001:410:0::/48 can handle $2^{16}$ network prefixes of 64-bit. This is the default prefix length for a site. |

For both IPv4 and IPv6, the number of bits set to 1 in the network mask defines the length of the network prefix; the remaining part is for node addressing. This information is fundamental to IP. It tells each node when packets must be sent to the default router or to a specific node on the same link-layer subnet.

Another difference in IPv6 is the absence of reserved addresses in a network prefix range. In IPv4, the first and last addresses of the prefix range are reserved addresses. A range's first address is the network address and the last one is the broadcast address. This means that the total number of IPv4 addresses available in a range equals $n^2-2$, where $n$ is the number of bits for the host addressing. For example, with the network prefix 192.168.1.0/24, addresses 192.168.1.0 and 192.168.1.255 must not be assigned to nodes because they are reserved. In IPv4, it is also common to use different network mask values within a site. One subnet can use a network mask value, and the next subnet may use a different value.

IPv6 has no broadcast or network reserved addresses. Moreover, the number of bits for node addressing within a site prefix (48-bit) in IPv6 is so large that it is not necessary to make an addressing plan for a site using different network mask values. Therefore, network mask calculation for each subnet and the use of Variable-Length Subnet Masks (VLSMs) are not required. In IPv6, the subnetting allocation is much simpler than in IPv4.

## IPv6 Address Types

Independent of representation and subnetting, different kinds of addresses are defined for IPv6, as described in RFC 2373, *IP Version 6 Addressing Architecture*. This section presents the types of IPv6 addresses defined in the protocol. In IPv6, addresses are assigned to network interfaces, not to nodes. Moreover, each interface owns and uses multiple IPv6 addresses simultaneously.

As shown in Figure 2-11, the three types of addresses are unicast, anycast, and multicast. Under the scope of each kind of address are one or more types of addresses. Unicast has link-local, site-local, aggregatable global, loopback, unspecified, and IPv4-compatible addresses. Anycast has aggregatable global, site-local, and link-local. Multicast has assigned and solicited-node. Specific scopes of IPv6's 128-bit addressing scheme are already assigned to each type of address.

**Figure 2-11**  *Types of Addresses in the IPv6 Addressing Architecture*

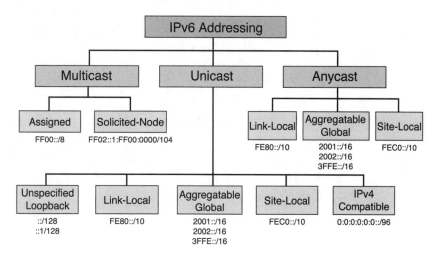

## Link-Local Address

IPv6 introduces scoped unicast addresses, which can be used only in a restricted context. The unicast link-local address is scoped and is used only between nodes connected on the same local link. The link-local address is used by several IPv6 mechanisms, such as Neighbor Discovery Protocol (NDP), described in detail in Chapter 3.

When an IPv6 stack is enabled on a node, one link-local address is automatically assigned to each interface of the node at boot time. As shown in Figure 2-12, the IPv6 link-local prefix FE80::/10 is used and the interface identifier in Extended Unique Identifier 64 (EUI-64) format is appended as the address's low-order 64-bit. Bits 11 through 64 are set to 0 (54-bit). Link-local addresses are only for local-link scope and must never be routed between subnets within a site.

**Figure 2-12**  *Link-Local Address*

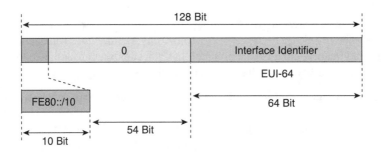

**NOTE**      The IEEE defined an extended unique identifier based on 64-bit—EUI-64. EUI-64 format is a combination of the public 24-bit manufacturer ID assigned by the IEEE and a 40-bit value assigned by the manufacturer to its products. EUI-64 is related to the interface link-layer address. This chapter provides detailed information about the conversion of a link-layer address into EUI-64 format.

Because the low-order 64-bit of the link-local address is the interface identifier itself, the length of the link-local prefix is based on a 64-bit length (/64).

As shown in Table 2-9, the link-local address is represented by the IPv6 prefix FE80:0000:0000:0000:0000:0000:0000:0000/10 in the preferred format and by FE80::/10 in the compressed representation.

**Table 2-9**    *Link-Local Address Representations*

| Representation | Value |
|---|---|
| Preferred format | FE80:0000:0000:0000:0000:0000:0000:0000/10 |
| Compressed format[1] | FE80:0:0:0:0:0:0:0/10 |
| Compressed format | FE80::/10 |
| Binary format | High-order 10-bit is set to 1111 1110 10 |

[1]   This is an intermediary compressed representation of the same address. This address is valid, but the shortened format of an IPv6 address should be used.

In IPv6, a node having an aggregatable global unicast address on a local link uses the link-local address of its default IPv6 router rather than the router's aggregatable global unicast address. If network renumbering must occur, meaning that the unicast aggregatable global prefix is changed to a new one, the default router can always be reached using the link-local address. Link-local addresses of nodes and routers do not change during network renumbering. Chapter 3 presents an example of prefix renumbering on a local link.

## Site-Local Address

A *site-local address* is another unicast scoped address to be used only within a site. Site-local addresses are not enabled by default on nodes like link-local addresses, meaning that they must be assigned.

A site-local address is similar to private address spaces in IPv4, such as 10.0.0.0/8, 172.16.0.0/12, and 192.168.0.0/16, as defined in RFC 1918, *Address Allocation for Private Internets*. Site-local addresses may be used by any organization that has not received aggregatable global unicast IPv6 spaces from a provider. A site-local prefix and address may be assigned to any nodes and routers within a site. However, site-local addresses must never be routed on the global IPv6 Internet.

**NOTE**    Although site-local addresses are similar to the private addressing in IPv4, Network Address Translation (NAT) with IPv6 is undesirable between IPv6-only networks. Huge numbers of IPv6 addresses are available within the IPv6 address space to preserve the end-to-end model of the IP protocol.

As shown in Figure 2-13, the site-local address consists of the prefix FEC0::/10, a 54-bit field called Subnet-ID, and an interface identifier in EUI-64 format used as the low-order 64-bit.

**Figure 2-13** *Site-Local Address*

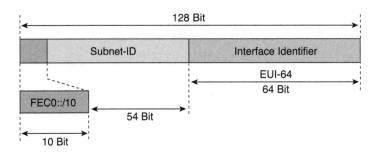

The 54-bit Subnet-ID is available for site subnetting. This field allows a site to create up to $2^{54}$ different IPv6 subnets (/64 prefix). Each subnet can use a different IPv6 prefix.

| NOTE | The old Subnet-ID length for site-local addresses was based on 16-bit, allowing a site to create up to 65,535 different IPv6 subnets. |
|------|---|

For example, a site with ten subnets may assign site-local prefixes such as the following:

- Subnet 1 — FEC0:0:0:0001::/64
- Subnet 2 — FEC0:0:0:0002::/64
- Subnet 3 — FEC0:0:0:0003::/64
- Subnet 4 — FEC0:0:0:0004::/64
- Subnet 5 — FEC0:0:0:0005::/64
- Subnet 6 — FEC0:0:0:0006::/64
- Subnet 7 — FEC0:0:0:0007::/64
- Subnet 8 — FEC0:0:0:0008::/64
- Subnet 9 — FEC0:0:0:0009::/64
- Subnet 10 — FEC0:0:0:000A::/64

As shown in Table 2-10, the site-local address is represented by the IPv6 prefix FEC0:0000:0000:0000:0000:0000:0000:0000/10 in the preferred format and by FEC0::/10 in the compressed representation.

**Table 2-10**  *Site-Local Address Representations*

| Representation | Value |
|---|---|
| Preferred format | FEC0:0000:0000:0000:0000:0000:0000:0000/10 |
| Compressed format[1] | FEC0:0:0:0:0:0:0:0/10 |
| Compressed format | FEC0::/10 |
| Binary format | High-order 10-bit is set to 1111 1110 11 |

[1]  This is an intermediary compressed representation of the same address. This address is valid, but the shortened format of an IPv6 address should be used.

Site-local addresses are designed for devices that will never communicate with the global IPv6 Internet. Site-local addresses may have the following uses within a site:

- Printers

- Intranet servers

- Network switches, bridges, gateways, wireless access points, and so on

- Any servers and routers that must only be reached internally for management purposes

For now, site-local addresses are recommended to organizations that have plans to deploy the IPv6 protocol on their networks before getting aggregatable global unicast IPv6 spaces from providers. Site-local addressing is also recommended for experimental scenarios of network renumbering.

It is important to note that an IPv6 node may have several unicast IPv6 addresses, so site-local addresses can be used at the same time as aggregatable global unicast addresses. In this case, DNS is the tie-breaker. Moreover, it is expected that the site will use the same subnet ID for the site-local and aggregatable global unicast prefixes.

## Aggregatable Global Unicast Address

*Aggregatable global unicast addresses* are IPv6 addresses used for the generic IPv6 traffic on the IPv6 Internet. Aggregatable global unicast addresses are similar to the unicast addresses used to communicate across the IPv4 Internet.

Aggregatable global unicast addresses represent the most important part of the IPv6 addressing architecture. The structure of aggregatable global unicast enables a strict aggregation of routing prefixes to limit the size of the global Internet routing table.

Each aggregatable global unicast IPv6 address has three parts:

- **Prefix received from a provider**—The prefix assigned to an organization (leaf site) by a provider should be at least a /48 prefix, as recommended in RFC 3177, *IAB/IESG Recommendations on IPv6 Address Allocations to Sites*. The /48 prefix represents the high-order 48-bit of the network prefix. Moreover, the prefix assigned to the organization is part of the provider's prefix.

- **Site**—With one /48 prefix allocated to an organization by a provider, it is possible for that organization to enable up to 65,535 subnets (assignment of 64-bit's prefix to subnets). The organization can use bits 49 to 64 (16-bit) of the prefix received for subnetting.

- **Host**—The host part uses each node's interface identifier. This part of the IPv6 address, which represents the address's low-order 64-bit, is called the *interface ID*.

As shown in Figure 2-14, the prefix 2001:0410:0110::/48 is assigned by a provider to an organization. Then, within this organization, the prefix 2001:0410:0110:0002::/64 is enabled on a network subnet. Finally, a node on this subnet owns the IPv6 address 2001:0410:0110:0002:0200:CBCF:1234:4402.

**Figure 2-14**  *Aggregatable Global Unicast Address*

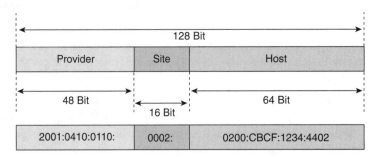

This is a simple example of an aggregatable global unicast prefix assigned to a leaf site by a provider. Chapter 7, "Connecting to the IPv6 Internet," provides detailed information about aggregatable global unicast assignments between multiple sites, providers, and leaf sites.

## IANA Assignments of Aggregatable Global Unicast Prefixes

The IANA assigned one IPv6 address prefix range in the whole IPv6 addressing space for aggregatable global unicast addresses. As shown in Table 2-11, this aggregatable global unicast address space is characterized by the IPv6 prefix 2000::/3.

**Table 2-11**    *Aggregatable Global Unicast Address Space*

| Representation | Values |
|---|---|
| Range | 2xxx:xxxx:xxxx:xxxx:xxxx:xxxx:xxxx:xxxx/3 |
| First address of the range | 2000:0000:0000:0000:0000:0000:0000:0000 |
| Last address of the range | 3FFF:FFFF:FFFF:FFFF:FFFF:FFFF:FFFF:FFFF |
| Binary format | High-order 3-bit is set to 001 |

From the 2000::/3 prefix, three smaller prefixes (/16) were assigned for public use. As shown in Table 2-12, the prefix 2001::/16 is available for the production of the IPv6 Internet. Prefix 2002::/16 is reserved for nodes using the 6to4 transition mechanism. 3FFE::/16 is the prefix used on the 6bone for testing purposes.

**Table 2-12**    */16 Prefixes of the IPv6 Address Space 2000::/3 Assigned as Aggregatable Global Unicast Addresses*

| Prefixes | Binary Representation | Description |
|---|---|---|
| 2001::/16 | 0010 0000 0000 0001 | IPv6 Internet |
| 2002::/16 | 0010 0000 0000 0010 | 6to4 transition mechanism |
| 2003::/16 through 3FFD::/16 | 0010 xxxx xxxx xxxx | Unassigned (available) |
| 3FFE::/16 | 0010 1111 1111 1110 | 6bone |

Note that prefixes 2003::/16 through 3FFD::/16 are still unassigned by the IANA. This represents about 8196 prefixes (/16). Within one /16 prefix, the whole IPv4 Internet can enter billions of times. This is an example of IPv6's huge addressing space. Getting many more IP addresses is not a problem with IPv6.

**NOTE**    Refer to Chapter 5 for detailed information on the 6to4 mechanism that is based on the 2002::/16 prefix.

## Multicast Address

*Multicast* is a technique in which a source node sends a single packet to multiple destinations simultaneously (one-to-many). In contrast, *unicast* is a way for a source node to send a single packet to one destination (one-to-one).

Multicast implies the concept of a group:

- Any node can be a member of a multicast group
- A source node may send packets to a multicast group
- All members of a multicast group get packets that are sent to the group

The main goal of multicasting is having an efficient network to save bandwidth on links by optimizing the number of packets exchanged between nodes. However, nodes and routers on networks must use specific ranges of IP addresses to get the benefits of multicasting. In IPv4, this range is 224.0.0.0/3, where the high-order 3-bit of the IPv4 address is set to 111.

As shown in Table 2-13, the multicast address in IPv6 is defined by the IPv6 prefix FF00:0000:0000:0000:0000:0000:0000:0000/8 in the preferred format and by FF00::/8 in the compressed representation.

**Table 2-13**    *Multicast Address Representations*

| Representation | Value |
|---|---|
| Preferred format | FF00:0000:0000:0000:0000:0000:0000:0000/8 |
| Compressed format[1] | FF00:0:0:0:0:0:0:0/8 |
| Compressed format | FF00::/8 |
| Binary format | High-order 8-bit is set to 1111 1111 |

[1]    This is an intermediary compressed representation of the same address. This address is valid, but the shortened format of an IPv6 address should be used.

In IPv4, the time-to-live (TTL) is used to scope multicast traffic. IPv6 multicast has no TTL, because the scoping is defined within the multicast address.

IPv6 makes heavy use of multicast addresses in the mechanisms of the protocol such as the replacement of Address Resolution Protocol (ARP) in IPv4, prefix advertisement, duplicate address detection (DAD), and prefix renumbering. All these mechanisms are presented in detail in Chapter 3.

In IPv6, all nodes on the local link listen to multicast and may send multicast packets to exchange information. Therefore, IPv6 nodes can know all their neighbor nodes and neighbor routers just by listening to multicast packets on the local link. This is a different technique than ARP in IPv4 in terms of getting information about the network neighborhood.

In multicast, the scope is a mandatory parameter that restricts the sending of multicast packets to a determined sector or part of the network.

As shown in Figure 2-15, the format of the multicast address defines several scopes and types of addresses using the 4-bit fields Flag and Scope. These fields are located after the FF::/8 prefix. Finally, the low-order 112-bit of the multicast address is the multicast group ID.

The Flag field indicates the type of multicast address. Two types of multicast addresses are defined:

- **Permanent**—An address assigned by the IANA
- **Temporary**—Not permanently assigned

**Figure 2-15**   *Format of the Multicast Address with the Flag and Scope Fields*

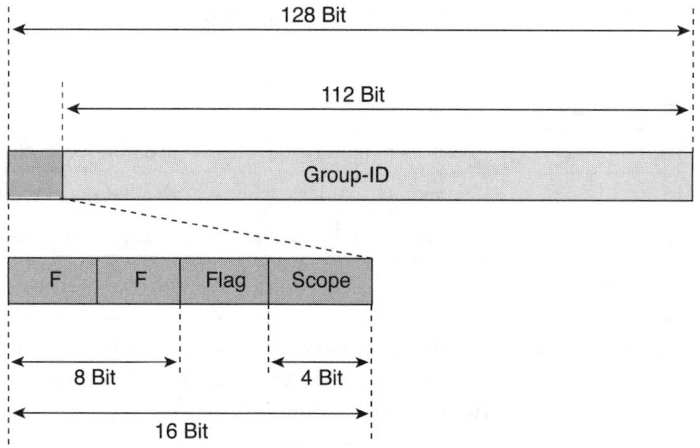

As shown in Table 2-14, the high-order 3-bit of the Flag field is reserved and must be initialized using 0 values. However, the remaining bit indicates the type of multicast address.

**Table 2-14**   *Values and Meanings of the Flag Field (4-Bit)*

| Binary Representation | Hexadecimal Value | Type of Multicast Address |
|---|---|---|
| 0000 | 0 | Permanent Multicast Address |
| 0001 | 1 | Temporary Multicast Address |

The next 4-bit field, called Scope, defines the scope of the multicast address. Table 2-15 shows the possible values and types of the Scope field defined for multicasting. Other values not represented here are either reserved or unassigned.

**Table 2-15**   *Values and Meanings of the Scope Field (4-Bit)*

| Binary Representation | Hexadecimal Value | Type of Scope |
|---|---|---|
| 0001 | 1 | Interface-local scope |
| 0010 | 2 | Link-local scope |
| 0011 | 3 | Subnet-local scope |
| 0100 | 4 | Admin-local scope |
| 0110 | 5 | Site-local scope |
| 1000 | 8 | Organization scope |
| 1110 | E | Global scope |

Table 2-16 presents examples of multicast addresses in different scopes. FF02::/16 is a permanent address used only on a local-link scope. FF12::/16 has a similar scope but is considered a temporary address. FF05::/16 is a permanent address with a site-local scope.

**Table 2-16** *Examples of Multicast Addresses with Different Scopes*

| Multicast addresses | Description |
|---|---|
| FF02::/16 | Permanent multicast address with a link-local scope |
| FF12::/16 | Temporary multicast address with a link-local scope |
| FF05::/16 | Permanent multicast address with a site-local scope |

**NOTE**    When an IPv6 node sends a multicast packet to a multicast address, the source address within the packet cannot be a multicast address. Moreover, multicast addresses cannot be used as source addresses in any IPv6 extension routing header.

## Multicast Assigned Address

RFC 2373 defines and reserves several IPv6 addresses within the multicast scope for the operation of the IPv6 protocol. These reserved addresses are called *multicast assigned addresses*. Table 2-17 presents all multicast assigned addresses in IPv6.

**Table 2-17** *Multicast Assigned Addresses*

| Multicast Address | Scope | Meaning | Description |
|---|---|---|---|
| FF01::1 | Node | All nodes | All nodes on the interface-local scope |
| FF01::2 | Node | All routers | All routers on the interface-local scope |
| FF02::1 | Link local | All nodes | All nodes on the local-link scope |
| FF02::2 | Link local | All routers | All routers on the link-local scope |
| FF05::2 | Site | All routers | All routers in a site scope |

Assigned multicast addresses are used in the context of specific mechanisms of the protocol. For example, a router on a subnet that needs to send a message to all nodes on the same subnet uses the FF02::1 multicast address. One node on a subnet that has to send a message to all nodes on the same subnet also uses the same multicast address. All IPv6 nodes and routers are instructed in their IPv6 stack to recognize these multicast assigned addresses.

## Solicited-Node Multicast Address

The second type of multicast addressing is *solicited-node multicast addressing*. For each unicast and anycast address configured on an interface of a node or router, a corresponding solicited-node multicast address is automatically enabled. The solicited-node multicast address is scoped to the local link.

A solicited-node multicast address is a specific type of address used by two fundamental IPv6 mechanisms:

- **Replacement of ARP in IPv4**—Because ARP is not used in IPv6, the solicited-node multicast address is used by nodes and routers to learn the link-layer addresses of neighbor nodes and routers on the same local link. As with ARP in IPv4, knowledge of link-layer addresses of neighbor nodes is mandatory to make link-layer frames to deliver IPv6 packets.

- **Duplicate Address Detection (DAD)**—DAD is part of NDP. It allows a node to verify whether an IPv6 address is already in use on its local link before using that address to configure its own IPv6 address with stateless autoconfiguration. The solicited-node multicast address is used to probe the local link in search of a specific unicast or anycast address already configured on another node.

| | |
|---|---|
| **NOTE** | DAD and NDP are described in detail in Chapter 3. |

As shown in Table 2-18, the solicited-node multicast address is defined by the IPv6 prefix FF02:0000:0000:0000:0000:0001:FF00:0000/104 in the preferred format and by FF02::1:FF00:0000/104 in the compressed representation.

**Table 2-18**    *Solicited-Node Multicast Address Representations*

| Representation | Value |
|---|---|
| Preferred format | FF02:0000:0000:0000:0000:0001:FF00:0000/104 |
| Compressed format[1] | FF02:0:0:0:0:1:FF00:0000/104 |
| Compressed format | FF02::1:FF00:0000/104 |

[1]  This is an intermediary compressed representation of the same address. This address is valid, but the shortened format of an IPv6 address should be used.

The solicited-node multicast address consists of the prefix FF02::1:FF00:0000/104 and the low-order 24-bit of the unicast or anycast address. As shown in Figure 2-16, the low-order 24-bit of the unicast or anycast address is appended to the prefix FF02::1:FF.

**Figure 2-16**  *Solicited-Node Multicast Address*

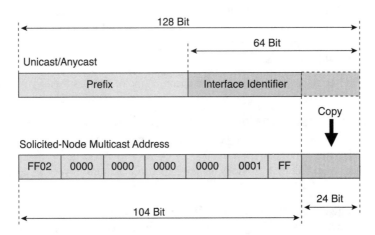

Table 2-19 presents examples of solicited-node multicast addresses made from unicast addresses.

**Table 2-19**  *Examples of Solicited-Node Multicast Addresses Made from Unicast Addresses*

| Unicast Addresses | Solicited-Node Multicast Address |
|---|---|
| 2001:410:0:1:0:0:0:45FF | **FF02::1:FF**00:45FF |
| 2001:420:0:1:250:3434:0100:1234 | **FF02::1:FF**00:1234 |
| FEC0:0:0:1:1:1:1:999 | **FF02::1:FF**01:0999 |
| 3FFE:B00:C18:1:2:2:45:410 | **FF02::1:FF**45:0410 |

## Anycast Address

Unicast is a method used by a source node to send a packet to one destination (one-to-one), multicast is used for one-to-many communication, and anycast is used for one-to-nearest communication. *Anycast* is a mechanism that delivers a packet sent to an anycast address of the nearest node member of the anycast group. Anycast enables a type of discovery mechanism to the nearest point. The network itself plays the key role in anycast by routing the packet to the nearest destination by measuring network distance.

Anycast is available in both IPv4 and IPv6. In IPv4, organizations that receive a portable IPv4 space from a regional Internet registry such ARIN, RIPE NCC, or APNIC may announce their IPv4 prefix to the global Internet using Border Gateway Protocol (BGP). Routing announcements are done by BGP from several sites on the Internet using the same Autonomous System Number (ASN). Servers using an anycast prefix within these sites can share the same IP address. Packets sent to this anycast prefix by nodes on the global Internet are routed by the BGP routers to the best path in terms of AS-Path. Therefore, the packet is delivered to the nearest destination using the anycast mechanism.

**NOTE**    Chapter 5 presents a practical example in which an IPv4 anycast prefix is announced on the global Internet. The Internet has several 6to4 relays, and it is difficult to find the IPv4 addresses to use them. The IPv4 anycast prefix in this case allows any 6to4 router connected to the Internet to automatically find the nearest 6to4 relay. Chapter 5 also provides details about the 6to4 mechanism and 6to4 routers.

Anycast addresses use aggregatable global unicast addresses. They can also use site-local or link-local addresses. Note that it is impossible to distinguish an anycast address from a unicast address.

## Reserved Anycast Address

One anycast address is reserved for special use. As shown in Table 2-20, this address is formed with the subnet's /64 unicast prefix and then bits 65 through 128 are set to 0.

**Table 2-20**    *Reserved Anycast Address Representations*

| Representation | Reserved anycast address |
|---|---|
| Preferred format | *UNICAST_PREFIX*  :0000:0000:0000:0000,where*UNICAST_PREFIX* is a 64-bit value |
| Binary format | Bits 65 through 128 are set to 0 |

This reserved anycast address is also called the *subnet-router anycast address*. All IPv6 routers are required to support subnet-router anycast addresses for each of their subnet interfaces.

Only a few applications use anycast addresses in IPv6. Mobile IPv6 is an example of a protocol designed to use anycasting. When a mobile node is away from its home network and wants to discover its home agent IPv6 address, it can use anycasting. The mobile node can send an ICMPv6 "Home Agent Address Discovery Request" message to the Mobile IPv6 home agent anycast address of its home subnet prefix. Then, the mobile node waits until one home agent returns an ICMPv6 "Home Agent Address Discovery Reply" message containing a list of home agents.

However, Mobile IPv6 is a recent protocol. More work has to be done on anycast in general to get real benefits from this kind of address.

## Loopback Address

Similar to the IPv4 protocol, each device has one loopback address, which is used by the node itself. As shown in Table 2-21, the loopback address is represented by the prefix 000:0000:0000: 0000:0000:0000:0000:0001 in the preferred format and by ::1 in the compressed representation. In comparison, the loopback address in IPv4 is 127.0.0.1.

**Table 2-21** *Loopback Address Representations*

| Representation | Value |
|---|---|
| Preferred format | 0000:0000:0000:0000:0000:0000:0000:0001 |
| Compressed format[1] | 0:0:0:0:0:0:0:1 |
| Compressed format | ::1 |
| Binary format | All bits are set to 0 except the 128th bit, which is set to 1 |

[1] This is an intermediary compressed representation of the same address. This address is valid, but the shortened format of an IPv6 address should be used.

## Unspecified Address

An unspecified address is a unicast address not assigned to any interface. It indicates the absence of an address and is used for special purposes. For example, when a host requests an IPv6 address from a Dynamic Host Configuration Protocol for IPv6 (DHCPv6) server or a packet is sent by DAD, this type of address is used. As shown in Table 2-22, the unspecified address is represented by the prefix 0000:0000:0000:0000:0000:0000:0000:0000 in the preferred format and by :: in the compressed representation.

**Table 2-22** *Unspecified Address Representations*

| Representation | Value |
|---|---|
| Preferred format | 0000:0000:0000:0000:0000:0000:0000:0000 |
| Compressed format[1] | 0:0:0:0:0:0:0:0 |
| Compressed format | :: |
| Binary format | All bits are set to 0 |

[1] This is an intermediary compressed representation of the same address. This address is valid, but the shortened format of an IPv6 address should be used.

## IPv4-Compatible IPv6 Address

As mentioned earlier, an IPv4-compatible IPv6 address is a special unicast IPv6 address used by transition mechanisms on hosts and routers to automatically create IPv4 tunnels to deliver IPv6 packets over IPv4 networks.

Figure 2-17 shows the format of the IPv4-compatible IPv6 address. The prefix is made with the high-order 96-bit set to 0. The remaining 32-bit (low-order) represents the IPv4 address in decimal form.

**Figure 2-17**  *IPv4-Compatible IPv6 Address*

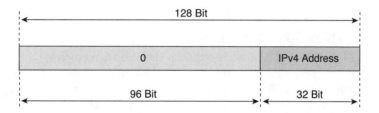

The IPv4-compatible IPv6 address is used by transition mechanisms for routers and hosts to automatically create tunnels over IPv4 networks. This mechanism automatically establishes an IPv6-over-IPv4 tunnel between two nodes over IPv4 using the IPv4 destination address inside the destination IPv6 address. With dynamic NAT-PT, destination IPv4 addresses are mapped into IPv6 addresses.

| NOTE | The automatic tunneling transition mechanism using IPv4-compatible IPv6 addresses is being deprecated in favor of other more-enhanced transition mechanisms. Chapter 5 presents both automatic tunneling and dynamic NAT-PT. |
| --- | --- |

As shown in Table 2-23, the IPv4-compatible IPv6 address is represented by the IPv6 prefix 0000:0000:0000:0000:0000:0000::/96 in the preferred format and by ::/96 in the compressed representation.

**Table 2-23**  *IPv4-Compatible IPv6 Address Representation*

| Representation | Value |
| --- | --- |
| Preferred format | 0000:0000:0000:0000:0000:0000::/96 |
| Compressed format[1] | 0:0:0:0:0:0:0::/96 |
| Compressed format | ::/96 |
| Binary format | High-order 96-bit is set to 0 |

[1]  This is an intermediary compressed representation of the same address. This address is valid, but the shortened format of an IPv6 address should be used.

## Required IPv6 Addresses

As discussed in this chapter, IPv6 nodes and routers have several IPv6 addresses at the same time. However, these IPv6 addresses are used in different contexts. IPv6's 128-bit address space enables efficient use of addresses for the protocol design. Therefore, as described in RFC 2373, nodes and routers must support several IPv6 addresses.

### Required IPv6 Addresses for Nodes

Table 2-24 lists required IPv6 addresses for nodes in IPv6. As soon as the node is IPv6-enabled, it has one link-local address per interface, one loopback address, and all-nodes multicast addresses FF01::1 and FF02::1. Also, it may have one-to-many assigned aggregatable global unicast addresses and the corresponding solicited-node multicast addresses. If the node is a member of another multicast group, it may have other multicast addresses.

**Table 2-24**    *Required IPv6 Addresses for Nodes*

| Required Addresses | Representations of These Addresses |
|---|---|
| Link-local address for each network interface | FE80::/10 |
| Loopback address | ::1 |
| All-nodes multicast addresses | FF01::1, FF02::1 |
| Assigned aggregatable global unicast address | 2000::/3 |
| Solicited-node multicast address for each unicast and anycast address used | FF02::1:FF*xx*:*xxxx* , where *xx*:*xxxx* is the low-order 24-bit of each unicast or anycast address |
| Multicast addresses of all groups to which the host belongs | FF00::/8 |

### Required IPv6 Addresses for Routers

Table 2-25 presents the required IPv6 addresses for routers in IPv6. Basically, routers have all required IPv6 addresses for nodes. Then, routers have all-routers multicast addresses FF01::2, FF02::2, and FF05::2. One subnet-router anycast address and other anycast configured addresses are required addresses for routers.

**Table 2-25**    *Required IPv6 Addresses for Routers*

| Required Addresses | Representations of These Addresses |
|---|---|
| All required IPv6 addresses for a node | FE80::/10, ::1, FF01::1, FF02::1, 2000::/3, FF02::1:FF*xx*:*xxxx*,  FF00::/8 |
| All-routers multicast addresses | FF01::2, FF02::2, FF05::2 |
| Subnet-router anycast address | *UNICAST_PREFIX*  :0:0:0:0 |
| Other anycast configured addresses | 2000::/3 |

# Addressing Architecture of IPv6

IPv6 has a large address space because of its 128-bit address scheme. As discussed in this chapter, several parts of this address space are used for the functions of the protocol itself such link-local, site-local, multicast address, multicast assigned address, solicited-node multicast address, loopback, unspecified, and IPv4-compatible IPv6 address. Although several parts of the 128-bit address are used, only a small percentage (less than 2%) of the whole space is reserved for those functions.

Table 2-26 presents an overview of spaces allocated compared to IPv6's entire addressing space. The first column, Prefix in Binary, represents the high-order 16-bit of each allocation. The character *x* means that these bits may have any binary value. The second column is the range in hexadecimal values for the allocation. The next two columns show the ratio and percentage per allocation compared to the whole IPv6 space. The last column describes the specific use of the allocation.

**Table 2-26**     *IPv6 Spaces Allocated for the Whole IPv6 Space*

| Prefix in Binary (High-Order 16-Bit) | Range in Hexadecimal | Size (Ratio) | % | Description of the Allocation |
|---|---|---|---|---|
| 0000 0000 *xxxx xxxx* | 0000 to 00FF | 1/256 | 0.38% | Unspecified, loopback, IPv4-compatible address |
| 0000 0001 *xxxx xxxx* | 0100 to 01FF | 1/256 | 0.38% | Unassigned |
| 0000 001*x xxxx xxxx* | 0200 to 03FF | 1/128 | 0.77% | NSAP |
| 0000 010*x xxxx xxxx* | 0400 to 05FF | 1/128 | 0.77% | Unassigned |
| 0000 011*x xxxx xxxx* | 0600 to 07FF | 1/128 | 0.77% | Unassigned |
| 0000 1*xxx xxxx xxxx* | 0800 to 0FFF | 1/32 | 3.13% | Unassigned |
| 0001 *xxxx xxxx xxxx* | 1000 to 1FFF | 1/16 | 6.26% | Unassigned |
| 001*x xxxx xxxx xxxx* | 2000 to 3FFF | 1/8 | 12.5% | Aggregatable global unicast addresses (IANA) |
| 010*x xxxx xxxx xxxx* | 4000 to 5FFF | 1/8 | 12.5% | Unassigned |
| 011*x xxxx xxxx xxxx* | 6000 to 7FFF | 1/8 | 12.5% | Unassigned |
| 100*x xxxx xxxx xxxx* | 8000 to 9FFF | 1/8 | 12.5% | Unassigned |
| 101*x xxxx xxxx xxxx* | A000 to BFFF | 1/8 | 12.5% | Unassigned |
| 110*x xxxx xxxx xxxx* | C000 to DFFF | 1/8 | 12.5% | Unassigned |
| 1110 *xxxx xxxx xxxx* | E000 to EFFF | 1/16 | 6.26% | Unassigned |
| 1111 0*xxx xxxx xxxx* | F000 to F7FF | 1/32 | 3.13% | Unassigned |

*continues*

**Table 2-26** *IPv6 Spaces Allocated for the Whole IPv6 Space (Continued)*

| Prefix in Binary (High-Order 16-Bit) | Range in Hexadecimal | Size (Ratio) | % | Description of the Allocation |
|---|---|---|---|---|
| 1111 10xx xxxx xxxx | F800 to FBFF | 1/64 | 1.6% | Unassigned |
| 1111 110x xxxx xxxx | FC00 to FDFF | 1/128 | 0.77% | Unassigned |
| 1111 1110 0xxx xxxx | FE00 to FE7F | 1/512 | 0.2% | Unassigned |
| 1111 1110 10xx xxxx | FE80 to FEBF | 1/1024 | 0.1% | Link-local |
| 1111 1110 11xx xxxx | FEC0 to FEFF | 1/1024 | 0.1% | Site-local |
| 1111 1111 xxxx xxxx | FF00 to FFFF | 1/256 | 0.38% | Multicast |

Here are the highlights of the IPv6 address space allocations:

- 00::/8 or ::/8 is the range reserved for unspecified (::), loopback (::1), and IPv4-compatible addresses (::/96). This allocation uses about 0.38% (1/256) of the address space.

- 200::/7 is reserved for Network Service Access Point (NSAP) allocation, which uses 0.77% (1/128) of the space. There is no current use of this reserved space for NSAP. NSAP addresses are mainly used in ATM technologies. In the past, another address range was reserved for the IPX (Internetwork Packet Exchange) protocol. However, the reserved range for IPX was deprecated.

- 2000::/3 is the aggregatable global unicast address allocation, which uses 12.5% (1/8) of the address space. Aggregatable global unicast addresses are production IPv6 addresses for the IPv6 Internet. However, this range contains a total of 8192 /16 prefixes, and the IANA has started the assignment of public addresses only with prefixes 2001::/16, 2002::/16, and 3FFE::/16 (3 out of 8192). Note that one /16 prefix can handle several times the whole IPv4 Internet address space.

- FE80::/10 is the link-local address space, which uses 0.1% (1/1024) of the whole space. Each network interface has one link-local address automatically assigned.

- FEC0::/10 is the site-local address space, which uses 0.1% (1/1024) of the whole space. Site-local addresses can be used internally within any network.

- FF00::/8 is the multicast address space, which uses 0.38% (1/256) of the space. Multicast addresses are used in the basic operation of the IPv6 protocol.

- Less than 2% of the whole addressing is reserved or assigned for real use.

Table 2-26 demonstrates that IPv6's 128-bit address scheme provides enough addresses for the next decades.

# Configuring IPv6 on Cisco IOS Software Technology

The Cisco IOS Software technology available on routers supports most features of the IPv6 protocol required to deploy and manage IPv6 networks. This part of the chapter examines IPv6 features implemented on Cisco IOS Software technology. These features are necessary to enable IPv6, activate IPv6 on network interfaces, and configure mechanisms within NDP (Neighbor Discovery Protocol) such as the replacement of ARP, stateless autoconfiguration, prefix advertisement, DAD (Duplicate Address Detection), and prefix renumbering. NDP, stateless autoconfiguration, prefix advertisement, DAD, and prefix renumbering are saved for Chapter 3.

This section focuses on the configuration and operation of the IPv6 addresses in Cisco IOS Software technology. It also assumes that you have successfully installed Cisco IOS software, including IPv6 support, on your router. You can download the Cisco IOS Software with IPv6 support from Cisco.com. Basic information about IPv6 for Cisco technology is available at www.cisco.com/ipv6/.

---

**NOTE**    To learn how to install the Cisco IOS Software with IPv6 support on your router, refer to Task 1 of the case study near the end of this chapter.

---

## Enabling IPv6 on Cisco IOS Software Technology

The first step of enabling IPv6 on a Cisco router is the activation of IPv6 traffic forwarding to forward unicast IPv6 packets between network interfaces. By default, IPv6 traffic forwarding is disabled on Cisco routers.

The **ipv6 unicast-routing** command is used to enable the forwarding of IPv6 packets between interfaces on the router. The syntax for this command is as follows:

```
Router(config)#ipv6 unicast-routing
```

The **ipv6 unicast-routing** command is enabled on a global basis.

The next step after the completion of this command is the activation of IPv6 on network interfaces.

### Enabling CEFv6 on Cisco

Cisco Express Forwarding (CEF) is also available for IPv6 on Cisco. The behavior of CEFv6 is the same as CEF for IPv4. However, there are new configuration commands for CEFv6 and common commands for both CEFv6 and CEF for IPv4.

The **ipv6 cef** command enables the central CEFv6 mode. IPv4 CEF must be enabled using the **ip cef** command. Similarly, IPv4 dCEF must be enabled before dCEFv6. The **ipv6 cef** command is enabled on a global basis.

Chapter 4, "Routing on IPv6," presents in detail current and new commands used to configure and manage CEF for IPv6.

# IPv6 Over Data-Link Technologies

IPv6 is defined to run on almost all data-link technologies such as Ethernet, FDDI, Token Ring, ATM, PPP, Frame Relay, nonbroadcast multiaccess (NBMA), and ARCnet. The following RFCs describe the behavior of the IPv6 protocol on each of these data-link technologies:

- **Ethernet**—RFC 2464, *Transmission of IPv6 Packets over Ethernet Networks*

- **FDDI**—RFC 2467, *Transmission of IPv6 Packets over FDDI Networks*

- **Token Ring**—RFC 2470, *Transmission of IPv6 Packets over Token Ring Networks*

- **ATM**—RFC 2492, *IPv6 over ATM Networks*

- **PPP**—RFC 2472, *IP Version 6 over PPP*

- **Frame Relay**—RFC 2590, *Transmission of IPv6 Packets over Frame Relay Networks*

- **NBMA**—RFC 2491, *IPv6 over Non-Broadcast Multiple Access (NBMA) networks*

- **ARCnet**—RFC 2497, *Transmission of IPv6 Packets over ARCnet Networks*

- **Generic packet tunneling**—RFC 2473, *Generic Packet Tunneling in IPv6 Specification*

- **IEEE-1394**—RFC 3146, *Transmission of IPv6 Packets over IEEE 1394 Networks*

Cisco IOS Software technology with IPv6 supports several interface types such as Ethernet, Fast Ethernet, Gigabit Ethernet, Cisco HDLC, PPP, Frame Relay PVC, ATM PVC, tunnels, and loopback. Configuration examples presented in this book are mostly focused on Ethernet technology because this is the most popular data-link technology used in networks.

## IPv6 Over Ethernet

Similar to IPv4, IPv6 runs over any Ethernet technology. However, the protocol ID value specified in Ethernet frames that carry IPv6 packets is different from the protocol ID in IPv4. The protocol ID value within Ethernet frames identifies the Layer 3 protocol used such as IPv4, IPv6, or even other protocols such as IPX, DECnet, AppleTalk, and so on.

As shown in Table 2-27, the protocol ID is 0x0800 with IPv4 and 0x86DD with IPv6.

**Table 2-27** *Protocol ID Values for IPv4 and IPv6*

| Protocol | Protocol ID in Ethernet Frames |
|----------|-------------------------------|
| IPv4 | 0x0800 |
| IPv6 | 0x86DD |

Thus, routers, servers, and nodes can differentiate protocols circulating simultaneously on networks with the protocol ID value of Ethernet frames.

## IPv6 Over Popular Data Link Layers Used on Cisco

For the PPP link, one IPv6 Control Protocol (IPv6CP) packet is encapsulated in the Information field of the PPP data link layer. For IPv6 packets over the PPP link, the protocol ID indicates 0x8057 for IPv6CP.

Cisco-High-level Data Link Control (HDLC), the default serial protocol on a Cisco router, is a synchronous data link layer protocol developed by ISO. It specifies a data encapsulation method on synchronous serial links. For IPv6 packets over Cisco-HDLC, the protocol ID is 0x86 I 0xDD.

Finally, for IPv6 on the ATM AAL5 SNAP, the protocol ID is 0x86DD as well as on Ethernet.

## Multicast Mapping Over Ethernet

As mentioned earlier, the IPv6 protocol makes heavy use of multicasting in several mechanisms used on a local-link scope such the replacement of ARP, stateless autoconfiguration, prefix advertisement, DAD, and prefix renumbering.

Therefore, IPv6 has a special mapping of multicast addresses to Ethernet link-layer addresses (Ethernet MAC addresses). The mapping is made by appending the low-order 32-bit of a multicast address to the prefix 33:33, which is defined as the multicast Ethernet prefix for IPv6. As shown in Figure 2-18, the low-order 32-bit of the 00:00:00:01 all-nodes multicast address (FF02::1) is appended to the Multicast Ethernet prefix 33:33.

**Figure 2-18**  *Multicast Mapping Over an Ethernet Address Using an All-Nodes Multicast Address*

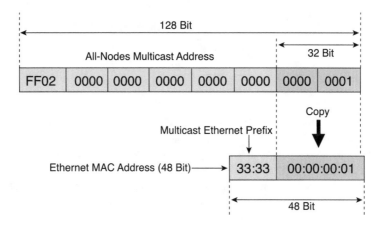

The 48-bit address 33:33:00:00:00:01 represents the Ethernet MAC address (link-layer address) that is used as destination in the Ethernet frame to send a packet to the IPv6 destination FF02::1 (all-nodes multicast address). By default, all nodes that are IPv6-enabled on this local link listen and get any IPv6 packets using 33:33:00:00:00:01 as the destination in the Ethernet MAC address. This is an example of the all-nodes multicast address, but all other multicast assigned addresses presented in the "Multicast Address" section are used in the same way.

## EUI-64 Format of an IPv6 Address

Link-local, site-local, and the stateless autoconfiguration mechanism as defined in RFC 2462 use EUI-64 format to make their IPv6 addresses. Stateless autoconfiguration is a mechanism that allows nodes on a network to configure their IPv6 addresses themselves without any intermediary device, such as a DHCP server.

The link-local address and stateless autoconfiguration are functions of IPv6 that automatically expand the Ethernet MAC address based on a 48-bit format into a 64-bit format (EUI-64). The conversion from 48-bit to 64-bit is a two-step operation.

As shown in Figure 2-19, the first step consists of inserting the value FFFE in the middle of the 48-bit link-layer address between the OUI section (vendor code) and the ID section (similar to a serial number). The original Ethernet MAC address presented here based on 48-bit is 00:50:3E:E4:4C:00.

**Figure 2-19** *First Step of the 48-Bit MAC Address Conversion into EUI-64 Format*

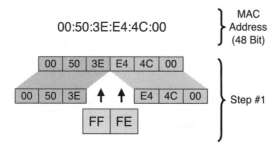

As shown in Figure 2-20, the second and last step consists of setting the seventh bit of the 64-bit address. This bit identifies the 48-bit address's uniqueness or lack thereof. An Ethernet address may have two significances. The address can be globally or locally managed. Globally managed means that you use the vendor MAC address, such as 08-00-2B-xx-xx-xx (a DEC example). Locally means that you can rewrite the MAC address with your own value (a Sun example). In this case, the seventh bit indicates 1 for local and 0 for global. However, in EUI-64 format, the value is reversed: 0 for local and 1 for global. In summary, for IPv6 addresses using EUI-64 format, if the seventh bit is set to 1, the address is globally unique. Otherwise, it is local.

**Figure 2-20** *Second Step of the 48-Bit MAC Address Conversion into EUI-64 Format*

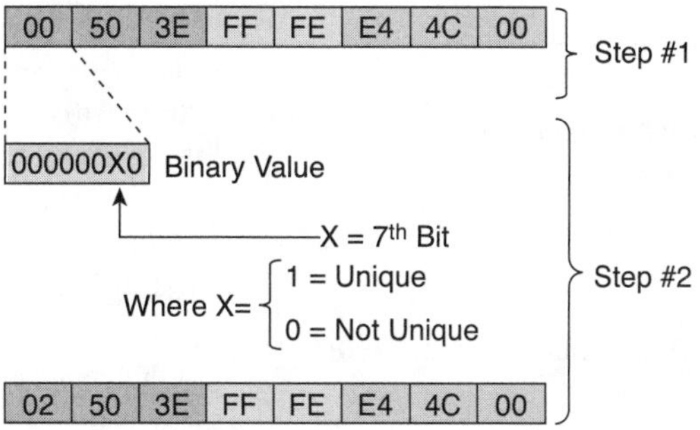

# Enabling IPv6 on Network Interfaces

After IPv6 forwarding is enabled on the router, the next step is assigning an IPv6 address to an interface. There are different methods to configure IPv6 addresses under a Cisco router. This section teaches you different ways to configure IPv6 addresses on Cisco IOS Software technology.

## Static Address Configuration

As shown in Table 2-28, the command **ipv6 address** may be used to configure the link-local address (FE80::/10), the site-local (FEC0::/10) address, or an aggregatable global unicast address (2000::/3) on network interface. This method is similar to the static address configuration, thus, the entire IPv6 address must be specified and must have a legal representation as presented earlier in this chapter.

**Table 2-28**    **ipv6 address** *Command*

| Command | Description |
|---------|-------------|
| **Step 1** <br><br> Router(config)#**interface** *interface-type interface-number* | Specifies an interface type and interface number. |
| **Example** <br><br> RouterA(config)#**interface FastEthernet 0/0** | Interface FastEthernet 0/0 is selected. |
| **Step 2** <br><br> Router(config-if)#**ipv6 address** *ipv6-address/ prefix-length*  [**link-local**] | Specifies an IPv6 address and prefix length to be assigned to the network interface. By default, when a site-local or aggregatable global unicast address is specified with this command, the link-local address is automatically configured. The default prefix length is 64-bit. |

*continues*

**Table 2-28**   **ipv6 address** *Command (Continued)*

| Command | Description |
|---|---|
| **Example**<br><br>RouterA(config-if)#**ipv6 address 2001:0410:0:1:0:0:0:1/64** | The aggregatable global unicast address 2001:0410:0:1:0:0:0:1/64 is configured on the interface. After the completion of this command, the link-local address is automatically configured. |
| **Example**<br><br>RouterA(config-if)#**ipv6 address FEC0:0:0:1::1/64** | The site-local address FEC0:0:0:1::1/64 is configured on the interface. After the completion of this command, the link-local address is automatically configured. |
| **Example**<br><br>RouterA(config-if)#**ipv6 address FE80:0:0:0:0123:0456:0789:0abc link-local** | The link-local address FE80:0:0:0:0123:0456:0789:0abc is configured here. This command with the **link-local** argument can be used to override the default link-local address assigned by the router. |

**NOTE**   As soon as you have assigned a site-local or aggregatable global unicast IPv6 address with a prefix length to a network interface on a Cisco router, the result is an advertisement of the specified prefix on the router's local interface. Refer to Chapter 3 for detailed information about prefix advertisement and stateless autoconfiguration.

**NOTE**   You can assign multiple site-local and aggregatable global unicast IPv6 addresses to each interface, but only one link-local address is permitted. Moreover, in the current Cisco IOS Software release, a site-local address is treated as an aggregatable global unicast address.

**NOTE**   As described in RFC 2373, the recommended length of an IPv6 prefix assigned to a subnet is 64-bit.

## Configuring the Loopback Interface

You can configure site-local or aggregatable global unicast addresses on the loopback interface using the **ipv6 address** command. In the following example, the interface loopback0 is selected:

```
RouterA(config)#interface loopback0
```

In the following example, the address fec0:0:0:9::1/128 is assigned to the loopback0 interface:

```
RouterA(config-if)#ipv6 address fec0:0:0:9::1/128
```

## Static Address Configuration Using EUI-64 Format

With this method, using the **ipv6 address** command, you can configure addresses on interfaces using EUI-64 format, as discussed earlier in this chapter. It is important to specify the address's high-order 64-bit (IPv6 prefix). Then the router automatically completes the low-order 64-bit using EUI-64 format.

The following example specifies the prefix and prefix length to assign to the interface:

```
Router(config-if)#ipv6 address ipv6-prefix/prefix-length eui-64
```

The router completes the low-order 64-bit using EUI-64 format. After this command is completed, the link-local address is automatically configured.

In the following example, the aggregatable global unicast prefix 2001:0410:0:1::/64 is used to configure the address. The aggregatable global unicast and link-local addresses are automatically configured:

```
RouterA(config-if)#ipv6 address 2001:0410:0:1::/64 eui-64
```

In the following example, the site-local prefix FEC0:0:0:1::/64 is used to configure the address. The site-local and link-local addresses are automatically configured:

```
RouterA(config-if)#ipv6 address FEC0:0:0:1::/64 eui-64
```

---

**NOTE**   You can assign multiple site-local and aggregatable global unicast IPv6 addresses using this command.

---

## Enabling Only IPv6 on a Network Interface

You can also enable just IPv6 on an interface without specifying an aggregatable global unicast or site-local address by using the **ipv6 enable** command, as shown here:

```
Router(config-if)#ipv6 enable
```

This command also automatically configures the link-local address on the interface. By default, this command is disabled.

## Configuring an Unnumbered Interface

You can use the command **ipv6 unnumbered** to instruct an interface to use another interface's aggregatable global unicast address as a source address for packets originating from the unnumbered interface, as shown here:

```
Router(config-if)#ipv6 unnumbered interface
```

## Configuring the MTU on an Interface

On Cisco routers, the default MTU value on the Ethernet (10 Mbps) and Fast Ethernet (100
Mbps) interfaces is preset to 1500 octets. However, this value can be modified using the **ipv6
mtu** command:

```
Router(config-if)#ipv6 mtu bytes
```

The following is an example of configuring the MTU value 1492 on the network interface:

```
RouterA(config-if)#ipv6 mtu 1492
```

## Verifying an Interface's IPv6 Configuration

Figure 2-21 shows an example of a basic IPv6 network topology in which Router A with one
Fast Ethernet interface is connected to a local link. In this example, the network administrator
assigns two prefixes to this local link:

- 2001:410:0:1::/64 as an aggregatable global unicast prefix
- FEC0:0:0:1::/64 as a site-local prefix

**Figure 2-21**  *Router with One Interface Connected to a Link*

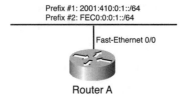

Prefix #1: 2001:410:0:1::/64
Prefix #2: FEC0:0:0:1::/64

Fast-Ethernet 0/0

Router A

Before enabling IPv6 on Router A, you can use the **show interface** command to display the
link-layer address (Ethernet MAC address) and MTU value of the FastEthernet 0/0 interface.
Example 2-1 shows that the FastEthernet 0/0 interface owns 00:50:3E:E4:4C:00 as the link-
layer address and uses 1500 bytes as the MTU value.

**Example 2-1**  *Displaying an Interface's Link-Layer Address and MTU Value Using the*    **show interface** *Command*

```
RouterA#show interface fastEthernet 0/0

FastEthernet0/0 is up, line protocol is up
  Hardware is AmdFE, address is 0050.3ee4.4c00 (bia 0050.3ee4.4c00)
  MTU 1500 bytes, BW 10000 Kbit, DLY 1000 usec,
<output omitted>
```

Then you can enable IPv6 on Router A and configure an address on interface FastEthernet 0/0. As shown in Example 2-2, the command **ipv6 address 2001:410:0:1::/64 eui-64** forces the router to complete the address's low-order 64-bit by using the interface's link-layer address (Ethernet MAC address). The Ethernet MAC address used in this example is 00:50:3E:E4:4C:00.

**Example 2-2**  *Enabling IPv6 on the Router and Configuring Two Addresses on Interface FastEthernet 0/0 Using the*    **ipv6 address** *Command*

```
RouterA#configure terminal
RouterA(config)#ipv6 unicast-routing
RouterA(config)#int fastethernet 0/0
RouterA(config-if)#ipv6 address 2001:410:0:1::/64 eui-64
RouterA(config-if)#ipv6 address FEC0::1:0:0:1:1/64
RouterA(config-if)#exit
RouterA(config)#exit
```

Finally, the **show ipv6 interface** command allows you to display parameters related to the IPv6 configuration applied to a specific interface.

In Example 2-3, as soon as IPv6 is enabled on this interface, the link-local address FE80::250:3EFF:FEE4:4C00 is automatically enabled. The EUI-64 option specified with the **ipv6 address** command instructs the router to append the low-order 64-bit 250:3EFF:FEE4:4C00 to the aggregatable prefix 2001:410:0:1::/64. However, the site-local address FEC0::1:0:0:1:1 was statically configured. Note that only one link-local address is enabled, although there are two unicast addresses.

**Example 2-3**  **show ipv6 interface** *Displays Parameters Related to Interface FastEthernet 0/0*

```
RouterA#show ipv6 interface fastEthernet 0/0
FastEthernet0/0 is up, line protocol is up
  IPv6 is enabled, link-local address is FE80::250:3EFF:FEE4:4C00
  Global unicast address(es):
    2001:410:0:1:250:3EFF:FEE4:4C00, subnet is 2001:410:0:1::/64
    FEC0::1:0:0:1:1, subnet is FEC0:0:0:1::/64
  Joined group address(es):
    FF02::1
    FF02::2
```

*continues*

**Example 2-3** **show ipv6 interface** *Displays Parameters Related to Interface FastEthernet 0/0 (Continued)*

```
      FF02::1:FF01:1
      FF02::1:FFE4:4C00
  MTU is 1500 bytes
<output omitted>
```

As shown in Example 2-3, the interface automatically joins several multicast assigned addresses. Here is the meaning of each multicast assigned address:

- **FF02::1**—Represents all nodes and routers on the link-local.

- **FF02::2**—Represents all routers on the link-local.

- **FF02::1:FF01:1**—Solicited-node multicast address used for the mechanisms that replace ARP. This address is also used by DAD. One solicited-node multicast address is enabled for each unicast address configured on the interface. Therefore, this address is the solicited-node multicast address related to the unicast address FEC0::1:0:0:1:1.

- **FF02::1:FFE4:4C00**—Solicited-node multicast address related to the unicast address 2001:410:0:1:250:3EFF:FEE4:4C00.

**NOTE**    Mechanisms that replace ARP is covered in detail in Chapter 3.

# Summary

In this chapter, you learned about the new IPv6 header format and the impact of IPv6 on User Datagram Protocol (UDP), Transport Control Protocol (TCP), and Maximum Transmission Unit (MTU). You also learned about IPv6's addressing architecture, with its different kinds of IPv6 addresses such as link-local, site-local, aggregatable global unicast, loopback, unspecified, IPv4-compatible, multicast assigned, solicited-node multicast, and anycast. This chapter also covered IPv6 over Ethernet, multicast mapping over Ethernet, and EUI-64 format.

You learned how to configure and operate Cisco routers with IPv6. You saw examples of how to enable IPv6 on a router and configure static IPv6 addresses on network interfaces such as aggregatable global unicast, site-local, and link-local. Then you configured IPv6 addresses using EUI-64 format and defined the MTU on the interface. Finally, you verified aggregatable global unicast, site-local, link-local, multicast assigned, and solicited-node multicast addresses enabled on the router's network interfaces.

# Configuration Exercise: Configuring an IPv6 Network Using Cisco Routers

Complete the following exercise to configure IPv6 on a network to practice skills learned in this chapter.

---

**NOTE**    Configuration Exercises allow you to practice your skills and knowledge by configuring IPv6 on a Cisco router using commands presented in this chapter. In the exercise presented here, only one router with multiple Fast Ethernet interfaces provides IPv6 connectivity to nodes on a network. This exercise assumes that you have minimal experience with the command-line interface (CLI) and that you can download a new Cisco IOS Software from the Cisco website.

---

## Objectives

In the following exercise, you will complete the following tasks:

1   Install a new Cisco IOS Software with IPv6 support on a Cisco router. The filename of the new image is c2600-is-mz.2001120.

2   Enable IPv6 on the Cisco router.

3   Assign IPv6 addresses to interfaces.

4   Verify interfaces and addresses assigned.

## Network Architecture for Tasks 1 and 2

Figure 2-22 shows a basic network architecture used for Tasks 1 and 2.

**Figure 2-22**  *Network Architecture for Enabling IPv6 on a Router*

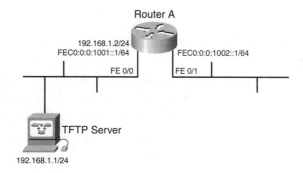

## Command List

In this configuration exercise, you will use the commands shown in Table 2-29. Refer to this list during the exercise.

**Table 2-29**    *Configuration Exercise Command List*

| Command | Description |
|---|---|
| **copy running-config startup-config** | Saves a current configuration to NVRAM. |
| **copy tftp flash** | Installs a new IOS on a router using a TFTP server. |
| **hostname** *name* | Configures the router's name. |
| **interface** *interface-type interface-number* | Specifies an interface type and interface number. |
| **ip address** *ip-address network-mask* | Configures an IPv4 address to an interface. |
| **ip cef** | Enables CEF for IPv4. |
| **ipv6 cef** | Enables CEF for IPv6. |
| **ipv6 unicast-routing** | Enables IPv6 traffic forwarding. |
| **ipv6 address** *ipv6-address/prefix-length* | Configures an IPv6 static address with a prefix length. |
| **no ip address** *ip-address network-mask* | Disables an IPv4 address. |
| **show interface** *interface-type interface-number* | Displays general information about the interface. |
| **show ipv6** | Displays general information about IPv6 support on a router. |
| **show ipv6 interface** *interface-type interface-number* | Displays the IPv6 configuration applied to an interface type and interface number. |

## Task 1: Basic Router Setup and Installing New Cisco IOS Software with IPv6 Support

Configure a basic setup on Router A to install the new IOS on the router with IPv6 support. The TFTP server is connected to the same link-layer network as the Fast Ethernet (FE) 0/0 interface. The TFTP server can only be reached over IPv4 using 192.168.1.1 as the IPv4 address.

**Step 1**    The name of your router is Router A. Set the host name on your router. Which command is used to perform this task?

The following shows how to configure the host name on Router A:

```
Router#conf t
Router(config)#hostname RouterA
Router(config)#exit
RouterA#
```

**Step 2**    Assign an IPv4 address with the netmask value shown in the following table to the router's interface FE 0/0. Other interfaces are not used in the basic router setup task. What command used on the Cisco router configures an IPv4 address on a network interface?

| Router's Interface | IPv4 Address | Netmask |
|---|---|---|
| Fast Ethernet 0/0 | 192.168.1.2 | 255.255.255.0 |

The following shows how to configure an IPv4 address on interface FE 0/1 of Router A:

```
RouterA(config)#interface fastEthernet 0/0
RouterA(config-if)#ip address 192.168.1.2 255.255.255.0
RouterA(config-if)#exit
RouterA(config)#exit
```

**Step 3**    On the router, enter the command to download and install a new IOS with IPv6 support using a TFTP server. What command installs an IOS from a TFTP server?

The following command shows how to install a new IOS on a router using a TFTP server:

```
RouterA#copy tftp flash
Address or name of remote host []? 192.168.1.1
Source filename []? c2600-is-mz.20011207
Destination filename [c2600-is-mz.20011207]?
Do you want to over write? [confirm] ENTER
Accessing tftp://192.168.1.1/c2600-is-mz.20011207...
Erase flash: before copying? [confirm] ENTER
Erasing the flash filesystem will remove all files! Continue? [confirm]
Erasing device...
eeeeeeeeeeeeeeeeeeeeeeeeeeeeeeeeeeeeeeeeeeeeeeeeeeeeeeeeeeeeeeeee ...erased
Erase of flash: complete
Loading c2600-is-mz.20011207 from 192.168.1.1 (via FastEthernet0/0):
<output omitted>
[OK - 12460516/24920064 bytes]
Verifying checksum... OK (0xE9F1)
12460516 bytes copied in 106.92 secs (117552 bytes/sec)
```

**Step 4**    As soon as the new image is successfully downloaded, reboot the router, log into enable mode, and verify that the IPv6-enabled image is fully installed in the router. What command verifies IPv6 support in the IOS?

The following command can be used to verify whether IPv6 support is enabled:

```
RouterA#show ipv6 ?
  access-list  Summary of access lists
  cef          Cisco Express Forwarding for IPv6
  interface    IPv6 interface status and configuration
  mtu          MTU per destination cache
  neighbors    Show IPv6 neighbor cache entries
  prefix-list  List IPv6 prefix lists
  protocols    IPv6 Routing Protocols
  rip          RIP routing protocol status
  route        Show IPv6 route table entries
  routers      Show local IPv6 routers
  traffic      IPv6 traffic statistics
  tunnel       Summary of IPv6 tunnels
RouterA#show ipv6
```

**NOTE**   If a syntax error occurs here, it indicates that the router is not running an IOS with IPv6 support.

**Step 5**   You may remove the IPv4 address on interface FE 0/1, because this configuration exercise is entirely focused on IPv6. What command used on the Cisco router removes an IPv4 address on a network interface?

The following removes the IPv4 address on interface FE 0/0 of Router A:

```
RouterA(config)#interface fastEthernet 0/0
RouterA(config-if)#no ip address 192.168.1.2 255.255.255.0
RouterA(config-if)#exit
RouterA(config)#exit
```

**Step 6**   Save the current configuration to NVRAM:

```
RouterA#copy running-config startup-config
Destination filename [startup-config]?
Building configuration...
[OK]
```

# Task 2: Enable IPv6 on the Router and Configure Static Addresses

Complete the following steps:

**Step 1**   Enter the command to enable IPv6 traffic forwarding on the router to forward unicast IPv6 packets between interfaces. Then enable CEFv6 in the router. What commands will you use?

```
RouterA#conf t
RouterA(config)#ipv6 unicast-routing
RouterA(config)#ip cef
RouterA(config)#ipv6 cef
RouterA(config)#exit
```

**Step 2**    Verify the hardware address (Ethernet MAC address) of all interfaces on Router A, and calculate the link-local address of each interface. Fill in the following table. What command gets the hardware address of each interface?

| Interface | Hardware Address | Link-Local Address |
|---|---|---|
| Fast Ethernet 0/0 | | |
| Fast Ethernet 0/1 | | |

```
RouterA#show interface fastEthernet 0/0
FastEthernet0/0 is up, line protocol is up
  Hardware is AmdFE, address is 0050.3ee4.4c00 (bia 0050.3ee4.4c00)
  MTU 1500 bytes, BW 10000 Kbit, DLY 1000 usec,
     reliability 255/255, txload 1/255, rxload 1/255
  Encapsulation ARPA, loopback not set
  Keepalive set (10 sec)
  Half-duplex, 10Mb/s, 100BaseTX/FX
  ARP type: ARPA, ARP Timeout 04:00:00
  Last input 00:03:01, output 00:00:07, output hang never
  Last clearing of "show interface" counters never
  Queueing strategy: fifo
  <data omitted>
  ..
RouterA#show interface fastEthernet 0/1
FastEthernet0/1 is administratively down, line protocol is down
  Hardware is AmdFE, address is 0050.3ee4.4c01 (bia 0050.3ee4.4c01)
  MTU 1500 bytes, BW 100000 Kbit, DLY 100 usec,
     reliability 255/255, txload 1/255, rxload 1/255
  Encapsulation ARPA, loopback not set
  Keepalive set (10 sec)
  Auto-duplex, Auto Speed, 100BaseTX/FX
  ARP type: ARPA, ARP Timeout 04:00:00
  Last input never, output never, output hang never
  Last clearing of "show interface" counters never
  Queueing strategy: fifo
```

**Step 3**    Suppose that the router acts as an IPv6 host. Configure one static unicast IPv6 address per interface. Use the addresses in the following table to configure the router's interfaces. What command assigns one IPv6 address per interface?

| Interfaces | IPv6 Addresses |
|---|---|
| Fast Ethernet 0/0 | FEC0:0:0:1001::1/128 |
| Fast Ethernet 0/1 | FEC0:0:0:1002::1/128 |

```
RouterA#conf t
Enter configuration commands, one per line.  End with CNTL/Z.
RouterA(config)#interface fastEthernet 0/0
RouterA(config-if)#ipv6 address fec0:0:0:1001::1/128
RouterA(config-if)#interface fastEthernet 0/1
RouterA(config-if)#ipv6 address fec0:0:0:1002::1/128
RouterA(config)#exit
```

**Step 4**    Verify the static and link-local addresses of each interface. What command
displays IPv6 addresses used on an interface? Then compare the link-local
addresses with those calculated in Step 2. Are they similar?

```
RouterA#show ipv6 interface fastEthernet 0/0
FastEthernet0/0 is up, line protocol is up
  IPv6 is enabled, link-local address is FE80::250:3EFF:FEE4:4C00
  Global unicast address(es):
    FEC0:0:0:1001::1, subnet is FEC0:0:0:1001::/128
  Joined group address(es):
    FF02::1
    FF02::2
    FF02::1:FF00:1
    FF02::1:FFE4:4C00
  MTU is 1500 bytes
  ICMP error messages limited to one every 100 milliseconds
  ICMP redirects are enabled
  ND DAD is enabled, number of DAD attempts: 1
  ND reachable time is 30000 milliseconds
  ND advertised reachable time is 0 milliseconds
  ND advertised retransmit interval is 0 milliseconds
  ND router advertisements are sent every 200 seconds
  ND router advertisements live for 1800 seconds
  Hosts use stateless autoconfig for addresses.

RouterA#show ipv6 interface fastEthernet 0/1
FastEthernet0/1 is administratively down, line protocol is up
  IPv6 is enabled, link-local address is FE80::250:3EFF:FEE4:4C01
  Global unicast address(es):
    FEC0:0:0:1002::1, subnet is FEC0:0:0:1002::/128
  Joined group address(es):
    FF02::1
    FF02::2
    FF02::1:FF00:1
    FF02::1:FFE4:4C01
  MTU is 1500 bytes
  ICMP error messages limited to one every 100 milliseconds
  ICMP redirects are enabled
  ND DAD is enabled, number of DAD attempts: 1
  ND reachable time is 30000 milliseconds
  ND advertised reachable time is 0 milliseconds
  ND advertised retransmit interval is 0 milliseconds
  ND router advertisements are sent every 200 seconds
  ND router advertisements live for 1800 seconds
  Hosts use stateless autoconfig for addresses.
```

**Step 5**    Save the current configuration to NVRAM:

```
RouterA#copy running-config startup-config
Destination filename [startup-config]?
Building configuration...
```

# Review Questions

Answer the following questions, and then refer to Appendix B, "Answers to Review Questions," for the answers.

1  For each of the fields in the following table, give the field's length and indicate whether it is used in the IPv4 header or IPv6 header.

| Field | Length in Bits | IPv4 Header | IPv6 Header |
|---|---|---|---|
| Type of Service | | | |
| Identification | | | |
| Version | | | |
| Time to live | | | |
| Header checksum | | | |
| Header length | | | |
| Traffic Class | | | |
| Total Length | | | |
| Flow Label | | | |
| Flags | | | |
| Padding | | | |
| Extension header | | | |
| Payload Length | | | |
| Protocol Number | | | |
| Hop Limit | | | |
| Source Address | | | |
| Destination Address | | | |
| Options | | | |
| Next Header | | | |
| Fragment Offset | | | |

2  List the fields removed from the IPv4 header.

**3**  What new field is added in the IPv6 header?

**4**  Describe the use of the Next Header field in the IPv6 header.

**5**  List the extension headers that may be placed after the basic IPv6 header, and place them in the order they must appear.

**6**  What is mandatory with UDP when used over IPv6?

**7**  What is recommended as a mechanism for nodes in IPv6 to avoid fragmentation?

**8**  What are IPv6's minimum MTU and recommended minimum MTU?

**9**  What are the three representations of IPv6 addresses?

**10**  Compress the following IPv6 addresses into the shortest form possible.

| Preferred Representation | Compressed Representation |
|---|---|
| A0B0:10F0:A110:1001:5000:0000:0000:0001 | |
| 0000:0000:0000:0000:0000:0000:0000:0001 | |
| 2001:0000:0000:1234:0000:0000:0000:45FF | |
| 3ffe:0000:0010:0000:1010:2a2a:0000:1001 | |
| 3FFE:0B00:0C18:0001:0000:1234:AB34:0002 | |
| FEC0:0000:0000:1000:1000:0000:0000:0009 | |
| FF80:0000:0000:0000:0250:FFFF:FFFF:FFFF | |

**11**  Describe the IPv6 address representation for URL.

**12**  List the three kinds of addresses in the IPv6 addressing architecture.

**13**  For each of the following address types, find the IPv6 prefix and write the address in the compressed representation.

Unspecified

Loopback

IPv4-compatible IPv6

Link-local

Site-local

Multicast

Solicited-node multicast

Aggregatable global unicast

**14**  What is a link-local address?

**15**  What is similar to the site-local address in IPv4?

**16**  In the following table, list the solicited-node multicast address that corresponds to each unicast address.

| Unicast Address | Solicited-Node Multicast Address |
|---|---|
| A0B0:10F0:A110:1001:5000:0000:0000:0001 | |
| 2001:0000:0000:1234:0000:0000:0000:45FF | |
| 3ffe:0000:0010:0000:1010:2a2a:0000:1001 | |
| 3FFE:0B00:0C18:0001:0000:1234:AB34:0002 | |
| FEC0:0000:0000:1000:1000:0000:0000:0009 | |

**17**  Give the length in bits of the host and site parts of an aggregatable global unicast IPv6 address.

**18**  What three prefixes are assigned by IANA and are available as public addresses in IPv6?

**19**  What is the Cisco IOS Software command to enable IPv6 on a Cisco router?

**20**  What protocol ID is used for IPv6 in Ethernet frames?

**21**  Explain how IPv6 multicast addresses are mapped over Ethernet.

**22**  Generate IPv6 interface IDs (in EUI-64 format) from the following Ethernet link-layer addresses.

| Ethernet Link-Layer Address | IPv6 Interface ID |
|---|---|
| 00:90:27:3a:9e:9a | |
| 00:90:27:3a:8d:c3 | |
| 00:00:86:4b:fe:ce | |

**23**  What command assigns one IPv6 address to an interface using EUI-64 format?

**24**  What is the goal of the path MTU discovery mechanism?

# References

RFC 768, *User Datagram Protocol,* J. Postel, IETF, www.ietf.org/rfc/lrfc768.txt, August 1980

RFC 791, *Internet Protocol, DARPA Internet Program, Protocol Specification,* USC, IETF, www.ietf.org/rfc/rfc791.txt, September 1981

RFC 792, *Internet Control Message Protocol,* J. Postel, IETF, www.ietf.org/ietf/rfc/rfc792.txt, September 1981

RFC 793, *Transmission Control Protocol,* DARPA Internet Program, IETF, www.ietf.org/rfc/rfc793.txt, September 1981

RFC 1191, *Path MTU Discovery,* J. Mogul, S. Deering, IETF, www.ietf.org/ietf/rfc/rfc1191.txt, November 1990

RFC 1981, *Path MTU Discovery for IP version 6,* J. McCann et al., IETF, www.ietf.org/rfc/rfc1981.txt, August 1996

RFC 2373, *IP Version 6 Addressing Architecture,* R. Hinden, S. Deering, IETF, www.ietf.org/rfc/rfc2373.txt, July 1998

RFC 2374, *An IPv6 Aggregatable Global Unicast Address Format,* R. Hinden, S. Deering, M. O'Dell, IETF, www.ietf.org/rfc/rfc2374.txt, July 1998

RFC 2460, *Internet Protocol, Version 6 (IPv6) Specification,* S. Deering, R. Hinden, IETF, www.ietf.org/rfc/rfc2460.txt, December 1998

RFC 2461, *Neighbor Discovery for IP Version 6 (IPv6),* T. Narten, E. Normark, W. Simpson, IETF, www.ietf.org/rfc/rfc2461.txt, December 1998

RFC 2462, *IPv6 Stateless Address Autoconfiguration,* S. Thomson, T. Narten, IETF, www.ietf.org/rfc/rfc2462.txt, December 1998

RFC 2463, *Internet Control Message Protocol (ICMPv6) for the Internet Protocol version 6 (IPv6),* A. Conta, S. Deering, IETF, www.ietf.org/rfc/rfc2463.txt, December 1998

RFC 2464, *Transmission of IPv6 Packets over Ethernet Networks,* M. Crawford, IETF, www.ietf.org/rfc/rfc2464.txt, December 1998

RFC 2467, *Transmission of IPv6 Packets over FDDI Networks,* M. Crawford, IETF, www.ietf.org/rfc/rfc2467.txt, December 1998

RFC 2470, *Transmission of IPv6 Packets over Token Ring Networks,* M. Crawford, T. Narten, S. Thomas, IETF, www.ietf.org/rfc/rfc2470.txt, December 1998

RFC 2472, *IP Version 6 over PPP,* D. Haskin, E. Allen, IETF, www.ietf.org/rfc/rfc2472.txt, December 1998

RFC 2473, *Generic Packet Tunneling in IPv6 Specification,* A. Conta, S. Deering, IETF, www.ietf.org/rfc/rfc2473.txt, December 1998

RFC 2491, *IPv6 over Non-Broadcast Multiple Access (NBMA) Networks,* G. Armitage et al., IETF, www.ietf.org/rfc/rfc2491.txt, January 1999

RFC 2492, *IPv6 over ATM Networks,* G. Armitage, P. Schulter, M. Jork, IETF, www.ietf.org/rfc/rfc2492.txt, January 1999

RFC 2497, *Transmission of IPv6 Packets over ARCnet Networks,* I. Souvatzis, IETF, www.ietf.org/rfc/rfc2497.txt, January 1999

RFC 2529, *Transmission of IPv6 over IPv4 Domains without Explicit Tunnels,* B. Carpenter, C. Jung, IETF, www.ietf.org/rfc/rfc2529.txt, March 1999

RFC 2590, *Transmission of IPv6 Packets over Frame Relay Networks Specification,* A. Conta, A. Malis, M. Mueller, IETF, www.ietf.org/rfc/rfc2590.txt, May 1999

RFC 2675, *IPv6 Jumbograms,* D. Borman, S. Deering, R. Hinden, IETF, www.ietf.org/rfc/rfc2675.txt, August 1999

RFC 2711, *IPv6 Router Alert Option,* C. Partridge, A. Jackson, IETF, www.ietf.org/rfc/rfc2711.txt, October 1999

RFC 2732, *Format for Literal IPv6 Addresses in URL's,* R. Hinden, B. Carpenter, L. Masinter, IETF, www.ietf.org/rfc/rfc2732.txt, December 1999

RFC 3146, *Transmission of IPv6 Packets over IEEE 1394 Networks,* K. Fujisawa, A. Onoe, IETF, www.ietf.org/rfc/rfc3146.txt, October 2001

RFC 3177, *IAB/IESG Recommendations on IPv6 Address Allocations to Sites,* IAB, IETF, www.ietf.org/rfc/rfc3177.txt, September 2001

"I think there is a world market for maybe five computers."

Thomas Watson, CEO of IBM, 1943

# CHAPTER 3

# IPv6 in Depth

This chapter examines in detail Internet Control Message Protocol (ICMP) for IPv6 and path MTU discovery (PMTUD) for IPv6. It also examines in depth the mechanisms in Neighbor Discovery Protocol (NDP) such as the replacement of the Address Resolution Protocol (ARP) in IPv4, stateless autoconfiguration, prefix advertisement, duplicate address detection (DAD), and prefix renumbering. Then you will be able to describe the use of Domain Name System (DNS), Dynamic Host Configuration Protocol (DHCP), IPSec, and Mobile IP with IPv6.

After Chapter 2, "IPv6 Addressing," which covered enabling IPv6 on the Cisco router and having configured IPv6 addresses on network interfaces, this chapter focuses on the following:

- Managing neighbor entries in the router's neighbor discovery table

- Tuning neighbor discovery messages

- Enabling and tuning prefix advertisement on the interface

- Disabling router advertisements on the router when needed

- Renumbering the prefix advertised on the network interface

- Creating the hosts table (DNS) in the router for IPv6 addresses

- Defining standard and extended IPv6 access control lists (ACLs) with reflexive ACL

- Enabling standard and extended IPv6 ACLs on the network interface

- Using tools such ping, Telnet, traceroute, SSH (Secure Shell), and Trivial File Transfer Protocol (TFTP) with IPv6 on the router for diagnostic and debugging purposes

Finally, with the configuration exercise, you will practice commands learned in this chapter by configuring, analyzing, showing, testing, and debugging IPv6 on the Cisco IOS Software technology.

# Internet Control Message Protocol for IPv6 (ICMPv6)

*Internet Control Message Protocol (ICMP)* reports errors and information to the source nodes regarding the delivery of IP packets to the destination. In IPv4 and IPv6, ICMP defines messages for diagnostic, information, and management purposes. ICMP for IPv6 (ICMPv6), as defined in RFC 2463, handles messages supported by ICMP for IPv4 (ICMPv4) and has additional messages for the specific operation of the IPv6 protocol. As illustrated in Table 3-1, ICMPv6 handles the same basic errors and informational messages as ICMPv4 such as Destination Unreachable, Packet Too Big, Time Exceeded, Echo Request, and Echo Reply.

**Table 3-1** *Errors and Informational Messages Used for Both ICMPv4 and ICMPv6*

| Message | Type Number | Type of Message | Definition |
|---|---|---|---|
| Destination Unreachable | 1 | Error | The IP address or port is not active in the destination host. |
| Packet Too Big | 2 | Error | The packet is larger than the Maximum Transmission Unit (MTU) of the outgoing link. |
| Time Exceeded | 3 | Error | When the time-to-live (TTL) field is 0, the packet is discarded, and an intermediary router notifies the source. |
| Echo Request | 128 | Informational | A message sent to a destination to request a reply message. |
| Echo Reply | 129 | Informational | A message used as response to the Echo Request message. |

ICMPv6 is defined as protocol 58 by the Internet Assigned Numbers Authority (IANA). As shown in Figure 3-1, this protocol number is used in the Next Header field of the basic IPv6 header to specify an ICMPv6 packet. IPv6 considers an ICMPv6 packet to be an upper-layer protocol, like TCP and UDP, meaning that it must be placed after all possible extension headers in the IPv6 packet.

As shown in Figure 3-1, the fields within an ICMPv6 packet are as follows:

- **ICMPv6 Type**—This field identifies the type of ICMPv6 message. Error and informational messages listed in Table 3-1 are examples of these types of messages.

- **ICMPv6 Code**—This field provides specific details related to the type of message sent to a node. It ensures an additional level of message granularity.

- **Checksum**—Computed value used to detect data corruption in ICMPv6 during transport.

- **ICMPv6 Data**—This field might or might not be used, depending on the type of message. When used, this field provides information to the destination node.

**Figure 3-1**    *ICMPv6 Packet with Its Fields Used Next to the IPv6 Header*

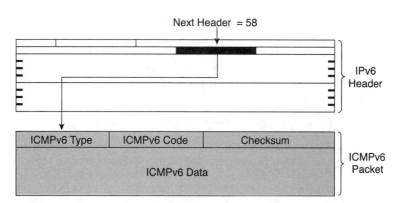

In IPv6, several mechanisms and functionalities of the protocol use ICMPv6 messages:

- **Replacement of the Address Resolution Protocol (ARP)**—A mechanism used on local-link scope to replace ARP in IPv4. Nodes and routers keep track of their neighbors. New ICMPv6 messages are defined in IPv6 for that specific use.

- **Stateless autoconfiguration**—The autoconfiguration functionality allows nodes to configure their IPv6 addresses by themselves using the prefixes advertised on the local links by routers. Prefix advertisement and stateless autoconfiguration use new ICMPv6 messages.

- **Duplicate Address Detection (DAD)**—At the boot and during the stateless autoconfiguration process, each node verifies the existence of a tentative IPv6 address before using it. This function is also performed using new ICMPv6 messages.

- **Prefix renumbering**—Prefix renumbering is a mechanism used when an IPv6 prefix on a network is changed to new one. Like prefix advertisement, prefix renumbering uses new ICMPv6 messages.

- **Path MTU discovery (PMTUD)**—A mechanism by which a source node detects the largest MTU value along a delivery path to a destination host. ICMPv6 messages are also used to perform this task.

All these IPv6 mechanisms and functionalities are presented in detail in this chapter.

Because ICMPv6 messages are used by several mechanisms in IPv6, a **debug** command is available in the Cisco IOS Software technology for ICMPv6 messages. However, the **debug ipv6 icmp** command enables debugging mode for ICMPv6 messages except those related to Neighbor Discovery Protocol (NDP). Logs can be printed on the console port or sent to a syslog server. The syntax for this command is as follows:

```
Router#debug ipv6 icmp
```

**undebug ipv6 icmp** deactivates debugging mode for ICMPv6 messages. The syntax for this command is as follows:

```
Router#undebug ipv6 icmp
```

Example 3-1 displays logs on the console after the activation of the **debug ipv6 icmp** command on Router A. The first two lines show the ICMPv6 type 128 echo request message received from the host 2001:410:0:1:200:86FF:FE4B:F9CE. The next line shows the router replies to this node with an ICMPv6 type 129 echo reply message.

**Example 3-1** *Show ICMPv6 Messages Using the* **debug ipv6 icmp** *Command*

```
RouterA#debug ipv6 icmp
ICMPv6: Received ICMPv6 packet from 2001:410:0:1:200:86FF:FE4B:F9CE, type 128
ICMPv6: Received echo request from 2001:410:0:1:200:86FF:FE4B:F9CE
ICMPv6: Sending echo reply to 2001:410:0:1:200:86FF:FE4B:F9CE
ICMPv6: Received ICMPv6 packet from 2001:410:0:1:200:86FF:FE4B:F9CE, type 128
<output omitted>
```

# Path MTU Discovery (PMTUD) for IPv6

As described in RFC 1191, the path MTU discovery (PMTUD) mechanism was defined for IPv4 in 1990; it is not new to the IPv6 protocol. However, in IPv4 PMTUD is optional and is not commonly used by nodes.

The main goal of PMTUD is finding out the MTU value along a path when a packet is sent to a destination to avoid fragmentation. Then the source node can use the maximum MTU size found to communicate with the destination node. Fragmentation may occur in intermediary routers when the packet is larger than the link layer's MTU. Fragmentation is a harmful and costly operation in terms of CPU cycles for routers. Moreover, in some circumstances, fragmentation over fragmentation might occur in several intermediate routers along a delivery path, causing a decrease in performance.

Fragmentation in IPv6 is not performed by intermediary routers. The source node may fragment packets by itself only when the path MTU is smaller than the packets to deliver. As described in RFC 2460, *Internet Protocol, Version 6 (IPv6) Specification,* it is strongly recommended that IPv6 nodes implement PMTUD for IPv6 to avoid fragmentation.

As defined in RFC 1981, *Path MTU Discovery for IP version 6,* PMTUD for IPv6 uses ICMPv6 error message Type 2, Packet Too Big, for its operation. Figure 3-2 shows an example of PMTUD for IPv6 used by a source node. First, the source node that sends the first IPv6 packet to a destination node uses 1500 bytes as the MTU value (1). Then, the intermediary Router A replies to the source node using an ICMPv6 message Type 2, Packet Too Big, and specifies 1400 bytes as the lower MTU value in the ICMPv6 packet (2). The source node then sends the packet but instead uses 1400 bytes as the MTU value; the packet passes through Router A (3). However, along the path, intermediary Router B replies to the source node using an ICMPv6 message Type 2 and specifies 1300 bytes as the MTU value (4). Finally, the source node resends the packet using 1300 bytes as the MTU value. The packet passes through both intermediary routers and is delivered to the destination node (5). The session is now established between source and destination nodes, and all packets sent between them use 1300 bytes as the MTU value (6).

**Figure 3-2**    *PMTUD Uses ICMPv6 Type 2 Messages*

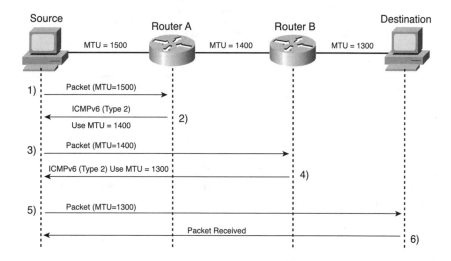

The MTU values found by PMTUD for IPv6 are cached by source nodes. With Cisco IOS Software technology, you can display the PMTUD values cached per destination using the command **show ipv6 mtu**. The syntax of this command follows:

```
Router#show ipv6 mtu
```

# Neighbor Discovery Protocol (NDP)

Neighbor Discovery Protocol (NDP), as defined in RFC 2461, *Neighbor Discovery for IP Version 6 (IPv6)*, is a key protocol of IPv6. Moreover, Figure 3-3 illustrates that NDP is an umbrella that defines these mechanisms:

- **Replacement of ARP**—Because ARP has been removed in IPv6, IPv6 provides a new way to determine link-layer addresses of nodes on the local link. This new mechanism uses a mix of ICMPv6 messages and multicast addresses.

- **Stateless autoconfiguration**—This mechanism allows nodes on the local link to configure their IPv6 addresses by themselves by using a mix of ICMPv6 messages and multicast addresses.

- **Router redirection**—The router sends ICMPv6 messages to an IPv6 node to inform it of the presence of a better router address on the same local link to reach a destination network.

**Figure 3-3** *NDP Is an Umbrella for Mechanisms*

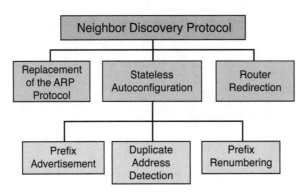

New ICMPv6 messages are defined for NDP's specific scope. As shown in Table 3-2, these ICMPv6 messages are labeled in the context of NDP. These new ICMPv6 messages are Router Solicitation, Router Advertisement, Neighbor Solicitation, Neighbor Advertisement, and Redirect Message.

**Table 3-2** *ICMPv6 Messages Defined for NDP*

| ICMPv6 Type | Name of Message |
|-------------|-----------------|
| Type 133 | Router solicitation (RS) |
| Type 134 | Router advertisement (RA) |
| Type 135 | Neighbor solicitation (NS) |
| Type 136 | Neighbor advertisement (NA) |
| Type 137 | Redirect message |

Table 3-3 shows the ICMPv6 messages that are used by NDP mechanisms. ARP replacement uses neighbor solicitation (ICMPv6 Type 135) and neighbor advertisement (ICMPv6 Type 136) messages. Prefix advertisement and prefix renumbering use router solicitation (ICMPv6 Type 133) and router advertisement (ICMPv6 Type 134) messages. DAD uses neighbor solicitation. Router redirection uses redirection message (ICMPv6 Type 137).

On Cisco equipment, parameters of NDP and the mechanisms under its umbrella are controlled using the **ipv6 nd** command. The following sections describe in detail each mechanism under the scope of NDP.

**Table 3-3**    *ICMPv6 Messages Used by NDP Mechanisms*

| Mechanism | ICMPv6 Type 133 | ICMPv6 Type 134 | ICMPv6 Type 135 | ICMPv6 Type 136 | ICMPv6 Type 137 |
|---|---|---|---|---|---|
| Replacement of ARP | | | X | X | |
| Prefix advertisement | X | X | | | |
| Prefix renumbering | X | X | | | |
| DAD | | | X | | |
| Router redirection | | | | | X |

# Replacement of ARP by Neighbor Solicitation and Neighbor Advertisement Messages

In IPv4, ARP is used by nodes on the local link to determine link-layer addresses of other nodes. Each node handles an ARP cache, which contains link-layer addresses of nodes learned with ARP. In IPv6, the determination of nodes' link-layer addresses uses a combination of neighbor solicitation messages (ICMPv6 Type 135), neighbor advertisement messages (ICMPv6 Type 136), and the solicited-node multicast address (FF02::1:FF*xx:xxxx*), as discussed in Chapter 2.

As explained in the following list, the NDP used in IPv6 is much more efficient than ARP in IPv4:

- In IPv6, only neighbor nodes concerned with this mechanism compute neighbor solicitation and neighbor advertisement messages in their stack. In IPv4, ARP broadcast messages are used to find a node's link-layer addresses. However, ARP broadcast forces all nodes on the local link to push all ARP broadcast messages toward the IPv4 stack.

- In IPv6, nodes communicate their link-layer addresses to each other in the same request. In IPv4, two ARP broadcast messages are needed to obtain the same result.

- Reachability of IPv6 addresses and link-layer addresses in the neighbor cache is verified. With ARP in IPv4, entries are removed after expiration (timeout).

## How Neighbor Solicitation and Neighbor Advertisement Work

This section describes in detail how neighbor solicitation messages, neighbor advertisement messages, and solicited-node multicast addresses are used in IPv6 to replace ARP. Then, Cisco IOS Software commands related to neighbor solicitation and neighbor advertisement are explained.

The following steps occur, as shown in Figure 3-4:

**Step 1**   Using the address FEC0::1:0:0:1:A, node A wants to deliver packets to destination node B using the IPv6 address FEC0::1:0:0:1:B on the same local link. However, node A does not know node B's link-layer address. Node A sends an ICMPv6 Type 135 message (neighbor solicitation) on the local link using its site-local address FEC0::1:0:0:1:A as the IPv6 source address, the solicited-node multicast address FF02::1:FF01:B corresponding to the target address FEC0::1:0:0:1:B as the destination IPv6 address, and the source link-layer address 00:50:3e:e4:4c:00 of the sender, node A, as data of the ICMPv6 message.

The source link-layer address of this frame is the link-layer address 00:50:3e:e4:4c:00 of node A. The destination link-layer address 33:33:FF:01:00:0B of this frame uses multicast mapping of the destination IPv6 address FF02::1:FF01:B.

**NOTE**   Note that the local link in this example is an Ethernet link. Refer to Chapter 2 for additional details on the multicast mapping for Ethernet defined for IPv6.

**Step 2**   Node B, which is listening to the local link for multicast addresses, intercepts the neighbor solicitation message because the destination IPv6 address FF02::1:FF01:B represents the solicited-node multicast address corresponding to its IPv6 address FEC0::1:0:0:1:B.

**Step 3**   Node B replies by sending a neighbor advertisement message using its site-local address FEC0::1:0:0:1:B as the IPv6 source address and the site-local address FEC0::1:0:0:1:A as the destination IPv6 address. It also includes its link-layer address 00:50:3e:e4:4b:01 in the ICMPv6 message.

After receiving neighbor solicitation and neighbor advertisement messages, node A and node B know each other's link-layer addresses. Learned link-layer addresses are kept in a neighbor discovery table (neighbor cache). Therefore, the nodes can communicate on the local link.

The neighbor solicitation message is also used by nodes to verify the reachability of neighbor nodes in the neighbor discovery table (neighbor cache). However, the unicast addresses of the neighbor nodes are used as destination IPv6 addresses in ICMPv6 messages instead of solicited-node multicast addresses in this situation.

It is possible for a node that changes its link-layer address to inform all other neighbor nodes on the local link by sending a neighbor advertisement message using the all-nodes multicast address FF02::1. The neighbor discovery table of the nodes on the local link is updated with the new link-layer address.

**Figure 3-4**    *NeighborSolicitationandNeighborSolicitationMessagesUsedtoFindtheNode'sLink-LayerAddresses on the Local Link*

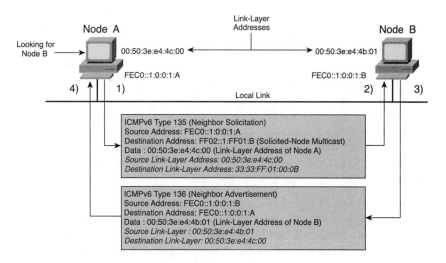

Table 3-4 summarizes the types of multicast addresses and ICMPv6 messages involved in the mechanism that replaces ARP.

**Table 3-4**    *Multicast Addresses and ICMPv6 Messages Used by the Mechanism That Replaces ARP*

| Mechanism | Multicast Address | ICMPv6 Message |
|---|---|---|
| Replacement of ARP | Solicited-node multicast address (FF02::1:FF*xx*:*xxxx* ) | ICMPv6 Type 135 (neighbor solicitation) <br> ICMPv6 Type 136 (neighbor advertisement) |

## Displaying the Neighbor Discovery Table's Neighbor Adjacency Entries

You can display neighbor adjacency entries of the neighbor discovery table using the following command:

```
Router#show ipv6 neighbors [ipv6-address-or-name | interface_type interface_number]
```

As shown in Example 3-2, the **show ipv6 neighbors** command displays IPv6 addresses of neighbors, the lifetime (in minutes), the link-layer address, the state, and the network interface of the router where the neighbor is known. The REACH state means that the neighbor can be reached. The STALE state means that these neighbors have not been reached within the last 30 minutes (this is the default value).

**Example 3-2** **show ipv6 neighbors** *Command*

```
RouterA#show ipv6 neighbors
IPv6 Address               Age Link-layer Addr State Interface
FEC0::1:200:86FF:FE4B:F9CE   0 0000.864b.f9ce   REACH FastEthernet0/0
<waiting of 10 minutes>
RouterA#show ipv6 neighbors
IPv6 Address               Age Link-layer Addr State Interface
FEC0::1:200:86FF:FE4B:F9CE   2 0000.864b.f9ce   STALE FastEthernet0/0
FE80::200:86FF:FE4B:F9CE    10 0000.864b.f9ce   STALE FastEthernet0/0
```

## Adding a Static Neighbor Entry to the Neighbor Discovery Table

On the Cisco router, you can add a static neighbor entry to the neighbor discovery table.

**NOTE**    Cisco implemented the adding of a static neighbor entry because most IPv6 traffic generator devices do not correctly support IPv6's NDP. Thus, it is not possible to send IPv6 traffic through a router because the neighbor entry does not get created in the neighbor discovery table. By adding the static entry command, Cisco IOS Software technology allows for the testing of devices to be used even without proper NDP support.

The **ipv6 neighbor** command allows you to add a static entry to the neighbor discovery table. The unicast IPv6 address, the network interface of the router where the neighbor is present, and the link-layer address are mandatory parameters of this command:

```
Router(config)#ipv6 neighbor ipv6-address interface hw-address
```

This command is enabled on a global basis.

**NOTE**    If a neighbor entry is already in the neighbor discovery table before the addition, the existing neighbor entry is converted to a static entry.

Example 3-3 shows the addition of a static neighbor entry to the neighbor discovery table. The IPv6 address FEC0::1:0:0:1:B, related to the link-layer address 0080.12ff.6633, is added to Router A's neighbor discovery table.

**Example 3-3** *Adding a Static Neighbor Entry to the Neighbor Discovery Table*

```
RouterA(config)#ipv6 unicast-routing
RouterA(config)#ipv6 neighbor fec0::1:0:0:1:b fastEthernet 0/0 0080.12ff.6633
RouterA(config)#exit
RouterA#show ipv6 neighbors
IPv6 Address                   Age Link-layer Addr State Interface
FEC0::1:200:86FF:FE4B:F9CE      15 0000.864b.f9ce  STALE FastEthernet0/0
FEC0::1:0:0:1:B                  - 0080.12ff.6633   REACH FastEthernet0/0
FE80::200:86FF:FE4B:F9CE        15 0000.864b.f9ce  STALE FastEthernet0/0
```

## Removing Neighbor Entries from the Neighbor Discovery Table

You can remove all entries from the neighbor discovery table using the **clear ipv6 neighbors** command:

```
Router#clear ipv6 neighbors
```

## Tuning Parameters of Neighbor Discovery Messages

Using a Cisco IOS Software command, you can tune neighbor discovery messages for a time interval and the reachability of neighbors.

The **ipv6 nd ns-interval** command sets the time interval between neighbor solicitation messages. For normal operation, Cisco does not recommend very short time intervals. The syntax of the **ipv6 nd ns-interval** command is as follows:

```
Router(config-if)#ipv6 nd ns-interval milliseconds
```

This command is enabled on an interface basis. By default, this value is adjusted to 1000 milliseconds (1 second).

The **ipv6 nd reachable-time** command configures the amount of time that a neighbor is considered reachable after an event confirms its reachability. A shorter value discovers dead neighbors more quickly, but it is more expensive in bandwidth consumption and processing. Cisco does not recommend very short reachable-time intervals in normal operation. The syntax of the **ipv6 nd reachable-time** command is as follows:

```
Router(config-if)#ipv6 nd reachable-time milliseconds
```

This command is enabled on an interface basis.

By default, this value is adjusted to 30 minutes (1,800,000 milliseconds).

# Stateless Autoconfiguration

As defined in RFC 2462, *IPv6 Stateless Address Autoconfiguration,* stateless autoconfiguration is one of the most interesting and useful new feature of IPv6. It allows nodes on the local link to configure their unicast IPv6 addresses by themselves from the information advertised on a link by a router.

This section describes the mechanisms involved in stateless autoconfiguration. As shown in Figure 3-3, these mechanisms are as follows:

- **Prefix advertisement**—Advertises prefixes and parameters on a local link. The prefix advertisement information is used by IPv6 nodes to configure their IPv6 addresses.

- **DAD**—Ensures that each IPv6 address configured on an interface using stateless autoconfiguration is unique on the link local scope.

- **Prefix renumbering**—Advertises modified prefixes or new prefixes and parameters on the local link to renumber a prefix already advertised.

For each mechanism presented, the following sections cover the commands and parameters used on Cisco equipment to configure stateless autoconfiguration.

| NOTE | Routers cannot assign their IPv6 addresses to interfaces using stateless autoconfiguration. Stateless autoconfiguration is designed for nodes only. |
|------|---|

## Prefix Advertisement

Prefix advertisement is the initial mechanism involved in stateless autoconfiguration. The prefix advertisement mechanism uses router advertisement messages (ICMPv6 Type 134) and all-nodes multicast address FF02::1. Router advertisement messages are sent periodically on the local link to the all-nodes multicast address.

| NOTE | With stateless autoconfiguration, IPv6 routers are the only kind of devices allowed to advertise prefixes on local links. It is prohibited for the node to advertise prefixes. The prefix length used in stateless autoconfiguration is 64-bit. |
|------|---|

## Advertising an IPv6 Prefix on a Cisco Router

As described in Chapter 2, the advertisement of an IPv6 prefix on a Cisco router is enabled as soon as a site-local or aggregatable global unicast IPv6 address with a prefix length is configured on a network interface. The **ipv6 address** command, as described in Chapter 2, is used for that purpose. If you assign several IPv6 addresses using different prefixes to the same network interface, the different prefixes are advertised to hosts on the local link.

Router advertisement messages contain parameters used by nodes during and after the autoconfiguration process:

- **IPv6 prefix**—One to several IPv6 prefixes may be advertised per local link. By default, the prefix length advertised for stateless autoconfiguration is 64 bits. Nodes get the IPv6 prefix, and then they append their link-layer addresses in EUI-64 format to the prefix received. The combination of this information provides a 128-bit address to the nodes.

- **Lifetime**—A lifetime value for each prefix advertised is provided to nodes. This value may vary from 0 to infinite. Nodes verify this value to cease the use of a prefix after it has expired, such as when the value equals 0. There are two types of lifetime values per prefix:

  - **Valid lifetime**—How long the node's address remains in the valid state. When this value expires, the node's address becomes invalid.

  - **Preferred lifetime**—How long the address configured by a node through stateless autoconfiguration remains preferred. The preferred lifetime must be less than or equal to the valid lifetime. When this value expires, all addresses received by stateless autoconfiguration and using this prefix are deprecated. Therefore, nodes cannot use deprecated addresses to establish new connections. But nodes still accept connections while the valid time is not expired. This parameter is used for prefix renumbering.

- **Default router information**—Provides information about the existence and lifetime of the default router's IPv6 address. In IPv6, the default router address used by node is the router's link-local address (FE80::/10). Therefore, even if the prefix is renumbered, the router can always be reached.

- **Flags/options**—Specific flags and options for nodes. You can use a flag to instruct nodes to use stateful autoconfiguration rather than stateless autoconfiguration. The flags and options available on Cisco IOS Software are defined in detail in a moment, when the **ipv6 nd prefix** command is described.

---

**NOTE**    Stateful autoconfiguration allows nodes to get their addresses and configuration parameters manually or from a server. The server maintains a database that keeps track of addresses already assigned to nodes. DHCPv6 is an example of stateful autoconfiguration in IPv6.

---

## How Prefix Advertisement Works

This section describes how router advertisement messages and multicast addresses are used to advertise prefixes in IPv6. The Cisco IOS Software commands related to prefix advertisement are presented later.

As shown in Figure 3-5, Router A sends periodic router advertisement messages (ICMPv6 Type 134) using its link-local address FE80::250:3EFF:FEE4:4C00 as the source IPv6 address and the all-nodes multicast address FF02::1 as the destination IPv6 address. The prefix advertised by the router advertisement messages is FEC0:0:0:1::/64 with infinite values as valid and preferred lifetimes. Then, nodes A and B, which listen to the multicast address FF02::1 on the local link, get router advertisement messages and can configure their IPv6 addresses by themselves.

**Figure 3-5** *StatelessAutoconfigurationUsesaRouterAdvertisementMessagetoAllowNodesontheLocalLinkto Configure Their IPv6 Addresses*

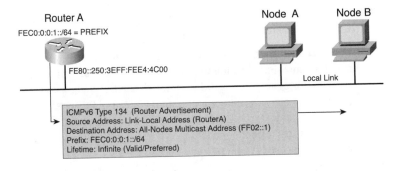

## Displaying Prefix Advertisement Parameters

As shown in Example 3-4, the command **show ipv6 interface** *interface* **prefix** displays parameters of the prefix advertised on an interface. In this example, the prefix 2001:410:0:1::/64 is advertised with a valid lifetime of 2,592,000 seconds and a preferred lifetime of 604,800 seconds. As you can see from the value [LA], the L-bit and A-bit flags are enabled for the specified prefix. L-bit and A-bit flags are discussed in the next section.

**Example 3-4** **show ipv6 interface** *interface* **prefix** *Command*

```
RouterA#show ipv6 interface fastEthernet 0/0 prefix
IPv6 Prefix Advertisements FastEthernet0/0
Codes: A - Address, P - Prefix-Advertisement, O - Pool
       X - Proxy RA, U - Per-user prefix, D - Default
       N - Not advertised, C - Calendar

AD  2001:410:0:1::/64 [LA] valid lifetime 2592000 preferred lifetime 604800
```

**NOTE**    On Cisco equipment, the valid lifetime is set to 30 days (2,592,000 seconds), and the preferred lifetime is adjusted to seven days (604,800 seconds) by default.

## Overriding Default Parameters of Prefix Advertisement

The **ipv6 nd prefix** command overrides parameters of prefixes advertised by a router. This command controls individual parameters of any prefix advertised (enabled on a per-interface basis):

```
Router(config-if)#ipv6 nd prefix ipv6-prefix/prefix-length | default
  [[valid-lifetime preferred-lifetime] | [at valid-date preferred-date] [off-link]
  [no-autoconfig] [no-advertise]]
```

The following describes the parameters and keywords that may be used with the **ipv6 nd prefix** command:

- *ipv6-prefix/prefix-length*—Defines the prefix length to be managed. The prefix length in stateless autoconfiguration is 64-bit.

- **default**—This keyword may be used to set default parameters for all prefixes advertised for each interface. Default values such as valid and preferred lifetimes are configured.

- *valid-lifetime*—How long in seconds the IPv6 address of a node received by stateless autoconfiguration remains in the valid state. After that valid time period, the address is considered invalid.

- *preferred-lifetime*—How long in seconds an IPv6 address remains preferred.

- **at** *valid-date*—A date may be set for the prefix's expiration. After a specific date, the prefix is no longer advertised on the local link. This option is available with Cisco IOS Software technology only.

- **at** *preferred-date*—A date may be set for the prefix's preferred date. This option is available with Cisco IOS Software technology only.

- **off-link**—This flag is related to the L-bit, as defined in RFC 2461, *Neighbor Discovery for IP Version 6 (IPv6)*. When the optional off-link keyword is used in Cisco IOS Software technology, the L-bit flag is turned off. However, when the L-bit is turned on (the default setting), it indicates in the router advertisement messages that the specified prefix is assigned to the local link. Therefore, nodes sending traffic to addresses that contain the specified prefix consider the destination to be locally reachable on the link. By default, the L-bit flag is enabled in Cisco IOS Software technology.

- **no-autoconfig**—This flag is related to the A-bit, as defined in RFC 2461. The A-bit is also known as the autonomous address-configuration flag. When the optional keyword **no-autoconfig** is used in Cisco IOS Software technology, the A-bit flag is turned off. However, when the A-bit is turned on (the default setting), it indicates to hosts on the local link that the specified prefix can be used for stateless autoconfiguration. Therefore, the prefix is advertised with lifetime values indicating how long addresses created from the specified prefix remain preferred and valid. By default, the A-bit flag is enabled in Cisco IOS Software technology.

- **no-advertise**—When a prefix is flagged with the optional **no-advertise** keyword, it indicates to hosts on the local link that the specified prefix cannot be used for stateless autoconfiguration (the prefix is not included in the router advertisement messages). By default, this flag is turned off in Cisco IOS Software technology; therefore, prefixes are advertised on the local link. With the optional **no-advertise** keyword, it is possible to not advertise a specific prefix even though you configured an IPv6 address with a prefix length on a network interface.

To remove an advertised prefix, use the **no** form of this command:

```
Router(config-if)#no ipv6 nd prefix ipv6-prefix
```

Figure 3-6 shows a typical scenario, in which Router A advertises the prefix 2001:410:0:1::/64 using router advertisement messages. Nodes on the local link can configure their addresses using this prefix.

**Figure 3-6**   *Router A Advertises a Prefix by Sending Router Advertisement Messages on the Local Link*

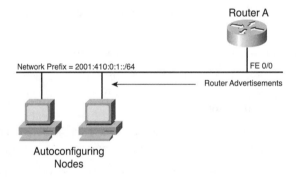

Example 3-5 shows a configuration that overrides default parameters of the prefix 2001:0410:0:0::/64 advertised on the network interface FastEthernet 0/0. The **ipv6 address 2001:0410:0:1::/64 eui-64** command is used not only to assign an IPv6 address to this interface, but also to enable prefix advertisement on that interface using 2001:0410:0:1::/64 as the prefix. The command **ipv6 nd prefix** specifies 43,200 seconds (12 hours) as the valid and preferred lifetimes.

**Example 3-5**   *Enabling and Controlling Prefix Advertisement on Interface Fast-Ethernet 0/0*

```
RouterA#configure terminal
RouterA(config)#int fastethernet 0/0
RouterA(config-if)#ipv6 address 2001:0410:0:1::/64 eui-64
RouterA(config-if)#ipv6 nd prefix 2001:410:0:1::/64 43200 43200
RouterA(config-if)#exit
RouterA(config)#exit
```

Another scenario is shown in Figure 3-7. Both Router A and Router B send router advertisement messages on an adjacent local link. Router A advertises prefix 2001:410:0:1::/64 on interface FastEthernet0/0, and Router B advertises the same prefix on its FastEthernet0/1 interface. Router B also advertises the other prefix, 2001:410:0:2::/64, on interface FastEthernet 0/0.

**Figure 3-7**  *Router A and Router B Advertise Prefixes 2001:410:0:1::/64 and 2001:410:0:2::/64 on Different Local Links*

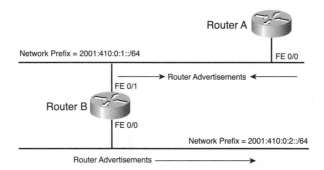

Example 3-6 shows configurations applied on both Router A and Router B according to Figure 3-7. The command **ipv6 address** is used in this example to enable prefix advertisement on the interfaces.

**Example 3-6**  *Configuring Router A and Router B to Advertise Prefixes*

```
RouterA#configure terminal
RouterA(config)#int fastethernet 0/0
RouterA(config-if)#ipv6 address 2001:0410:0:1::/64 eui-64
RouterA(config-if)#exit
RouterA(config)#exit

RouterB#configure terminal
RouterB(config)#int fastethernet 0/1
RouterB(config-if)#ipv6 address 2001:0410:0:1::/64 eui-64
RouterB(config-if)#interface fastethernet 0/0
RouterB(config-if)#ipv6 address 2001:0410:0:2::/64 eui-64
RouterB(config)#exit
```

## Disabling Router Advertisements on the Interface

You can turn off router advertisement on the interface. By default, router advertisement is available on Ethernet (10, 100, 1000 Mbps) FDDI and Token Ring interfaces on Cisco equipment when the global command **ipv6 unicast-routing** is enabled.

The command **ipv6 nd suppress-ra** turns off router advertisements on an interface basis:

```
Router(config-if)#ipv6 nd suppress-ra
```

The following command cancels the suppression of router advertisements:

```
Router(config-if)#no ipv6 nd suppress-ra
```

The **ipv6 nd suppress-ra** command is enabled on a per-interface basis.

The suppression of router advertisements is useful on a link in which adjacency routers are connected. When two routers advertise the same prefix on an adjacent link, the nodes might see different lifetime values and default routers.

To force nodes on a link where multiple adjacency routers are present to select one default router, the suppression of router advertisements on every router except one using the command **ipv6 nd suppress-ra** is recommended.

As shown in Figure 3-8, Router A and Router B are adjacent on a link. Router advertisement can be turned off on Router B. Therefore, nodes use parameters and Router A's default address.

**Figure 3-8**  *Router B with Router Advertisement Turned off on Interface FastEthernet 0/1*

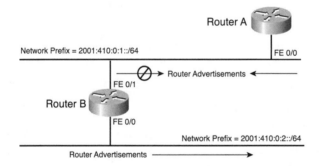

Example 3-7 shows the command **ipv6 nd suppress-ra** applied on interface FastEthernet 0/1 of Router B to turn off router advertisement.

**Example 3-7**  *Turning off Router Advertisement on an Interface*

```
RouterA#configure terminal
RouterA(config)#int fastethernet 0/0
RouterA(config-if)#ipv6 address 2001:0410:0:1::/64 eui-64
RouterA(config-if)#exit
RouterA(config)#exit

RouterB#configure terminal
RouterB(config)#int fastethernet 0/1
```

**Example 3-7**  *Turning off Router Advertisement on an Interface (Continued)*

```
RouterB(config-if)#ipv6 address 2001:0410:0:1::/64 eui-64
RouterB(config-if)#ipv6 nd suppress-ra
RouterB(config-if)#interface fastethernet 0/0
RouterB(config-if)#ipv6 address 2001:0410:0:2::/64 eui-64
RouterB(config)#exit
```

When multiple routers are connected on the same link, you can display prefixes and parameters advertised by the other routers using the Cisco IOS Software commands.

As shown in Example 3-8, the **show ipv6 routers** command displays router advertisement information received from other routers. This example shows information about the prefix 2001:410:0:2::/64 advertised on the link where the interface FastEthernet 0/0 is physically connected.

**Example 3-8**  *Displaying Router Advertisement Information Received on Interface FastEthernet 0/0*

```
RouterA#show ipv6 routers
Router FE80::260:8FF:FE37:BF6 on FastEthernet0/0, last update 3 min
  Hops 64, Lifetime 1800 sec, AddrFlag=0, OtherFlag=0, MTU=1500
  Reachable time 0 msec, Retransmit time 0 msec
  Prefix 2001:410:0:2::/64 onlink autoconfig
    Valid lifetime 2592000, preferred lifetime 604800
```

## Tuning Prefix Advertisement Parameters

On Cisco routers, you can modify prefix advertisement parameters. These parameters are related to router advertisement messages and stateless autoconfiguration, as described in the following:

- **Router advertisement lifetime**—The lifetime of a router advertisement message (ICMPv6 Type 134). This parameter defines how long in seconds each message is considered valid after it is sent. This value is included in all router advertisement messages that are sent. By default, this parameter is set to 1800 seconds (30 minutes) on Cisco routers. The **ipv6 nd ra-lifetime** command modifies this parameter:

  ```
  Router(config-if)# ipv6 nd ra-lifetime seconds
  ```

  This command is enabled on a per-interface basis.

- **Router advertisement interval**—The amount of time in seconds between consecutive router advertisement messages. This value may be less than or equal to the router advertisement lifetime. By default, this parameter is set to 200 seconds on Cisco routers. This parameter has a direct effect on how long a booting node has to wait for the next router advertisement message to configure its address. If the node cannot wait for the next router advertisement message, it can send a router solicitation message to force a router on the local link to send a new router advertisement message. (Router solicitation is discussed in the next section.) The **ipv6 nd ra-interval** command defines this parameter:

```
Router(config-if)# ipv6 nd ra-interval seconds
```

This command is enabled on a per-interface basis.

- **managed-config-flag**—When this parameter is not set, the nodes are allowed to use stateless autoconfiguration (but not stateful autoconfiguration) to configure their IPv6 addresses by themselves. By default on Cisco routers, this value is not set, meaning that stateless autoconfiguration is enabled. Otherwise, when this flag is set, the nodes should use a stateful autoconfiguration mechanism (but not stateless autoconfiguration) such as a DHCPv6 server to get their IPv6 addresses. Therefore, the **ipv6 nd managed-config-flag** command enables stateful autoconfiguration:

```
Router(config-if)# ipv6 nd managed-config-flag
```

On the opposite side, the **no ipv6 nd managed-config-flag** command disables stateful autoconfiguration:

```
Router(config-if)# no ipv6 nd managed-config-flag
```

These commands are enabled on a per-interface basis.

- **other-config-flag**—This flag is also related to stateful autoconfiguration. When it is turned off, the nodes should not use a stateful autoconfiguration mechanism to configure parameters other than the IPv6 address. By default, this value is set to off. The **ipv6 nd other-config-flag** command enables this flag:

```
Router(config-if)# ipv6 nd other-config-flag
```

This command is enabled on a per-interface basis.

## Requesting Router Advertisement Using Router Solicitation

Router advertisement messages are sent periodically on local links by routers. However, when nodes boot, it might be a long time before the next router advertisement message. In this situation, any node can send a router solicitation message (ICMPv6 Type 133) to the all-routers multicast address FF02::2 on the local link. When the router solicitation message is received, a router on the local link responds with a router advertisement message (ICMP Type 134) using the all-nodes multicast address FF02::1.

Figure 3-9 illustrates this mechanism. Node A sends a router solicitation message using the link-local address (FE80::/10) as the IPv6 source address to the all-routers multicast address FF02::2. Router A listens for multicast packets corresponding to groups it belongs to and gets the router solicitation message. Then Router A responds with a router advertisement message (ICMP Type 134) using its link-local address as a source IPv6 address to the all-nodes multicast address FF02::1.

**Figure 3-9**    *RouterSolicitationMessageIsSenttoAsktheRoutertoRespondwithaRouterAdvertisementMessage*

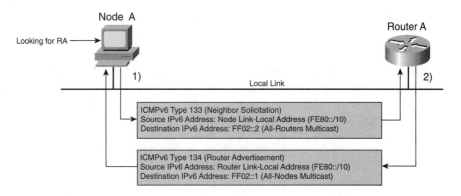

**NOTE**    To avoid the flooding of router solicitation messages on the link, each node can send only three router solicitation messages at boot time. In the absence of an IPv6 router on the link, this rule keeps links from being flooded by router solicitation messages.

Table 3-5 summarizes the types of multicast addresses and ICMPv6 messages that are used the most in prefix advertisement.

**Table 3-5**    *Multicast Addresses and ICMPv6 Messages Used by Prefix Advertisement*

| Mechanism | Multicast Address | ICMPv6 Message |
|---|---|---|
| Prefix advertisement | All-nodes multicast (FF02::1) | ICMPv6 Type 134 (router advertisement) |
| | All-routers multicast (FF02::2) | ICMPv6 Type 133 (router solicitation) |

# How Duplicate Address Detection (DAD) Works

DAD is an NDP mechanism involved in stateless autoconfiguration and at the boot of a node. Before a node can configure its IPv6 unicast address using stateless autoconfiguration, it must verify on the local link that the tentative address it wants to use is unique and not already in use by another node.

DAD uses neighbor solicitation messages (ICMPv6 Type 135) and solicited-node multicast addresses to perform this task. This operation requires the node to send a neighbor solicitation message on the local link using the unspecified address (::) as its source IPv6 address and the solicited-node multicast address of the tentative unicast address as the destination IPv6 address. If a duplicate address is discovered during the procedure, the tentative address cannot be assigned to the interface. Otherwise, the tentative address is configured to the interface.

Figure 3-10 illustrates this mechanism. First, node A initiates DAD. Node A intends to configure the tentative IPv6 unicast address 2001:410:0:1::1:a on its interface. Therefore, node A sends a neighbor solicitation message using the unspecified address (::) as the IPv6 source address and the solicited-node multicast address FF02::1:FF01:000A of the tentative unicast address 2001:410:0:1::1:a as the destination address.

As soon as the neighbor solicitation has been sent on the local link, if a node responds to that request, it means that the tentative unicast IPv6 address is in use by another node. In the absence of a reply (as shown in Figure 3-10), node A considers the tentative unicast address 2002:410:0:1::1:a to be unique on the local link and can assign it to its interface.

**Figure 3-10** *Node A Sends a Neighbor Solicitation Message on the Local Link to Perform DAD*

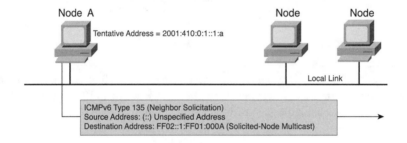

## Tuning DAD

By default, DAD is enabled on Cisco routers. The number of neighbor solicitation messages to send on the local link before considering an address's uniqueness is set to 1. However, as described in Table 3-6, the command **ipv6 nd dad attempts** may be used to modify this number of neighbor solicitation messages. The acceptable range is between 0 and 600 messages. This command used with the value 0 disables DAD.

**Table 3-6** **ipv6 nd dad attempts** *Command*

| Command | Description |
|---------|-------------|
| Router(config-if)# **ipv6 nd dad attempts** *number* | Defines the number of router solicitation messages for DAD to send on the link before considering an IPv6 address unique. |
| **Example** <br> RouterA(config-if)# **ipv6 nd dad attempts 3** | DAD sends three neighbor solicitation messages on the link before considering the IPv6 address unique. |
| **Example** <br> RouterA(config-if)# **ipv6 nd dad attempts 0** | The value 0 disables DAD on an interface. |

This command is enabled on a per-interface basis.

Table 3-7 summarizes the types of multicast addresses and ICMPv6 messages that are used the most in DAD.

**Table 3-7**   *Multicast Addresses and ICMPv6 Messages Used by DAD*

| Mechanism | Multicast Address | ICMPv6 Message |
|---|---|---|
| DAD | Solicited-node multicast address (FF02::1:FF*xx*:*xxxx* ) | ICMPv6 Type 135 (neighbor solicitation) |

# How Prefix Renumbering Works

A key benefit of the IPv6 protocol is its capability to provide transparent renumbering of the network to end users when the prefix must be changed for a new one. Because of the strict aggregation of the IPv6 protocol, prefix renumbering is necessary when an organization decides to change its IPv6 provider.

Prefix renumbering allows a smooth transition from a prior network prefix to a new prefix. Getting the benefits of transparent renumbering implies the use of stateless autoconfiguration for all of a site's nodes. Other network renumbering methods may be used, but they are less transparent than prefix renumbering in the context of stateless autoconfiguration.

Prefix renumbering is performed by routers already advertising prefixes on local links. This mechanism uses the same ICMPv6 messages and multicast addresses as the prefix advertisement mechanism. In fact, prefix renumbering is a new concept using time parameters contained in router advertisement messages to perform the task.

First, all routers in the site continue to advertise the current prefix, but the valid and preferred lifetimes are decreased to a value close to 0. Then routers begin to advertise the new prefixes on local links. Therefore, at least two prefixes coexist on every local link. This means that router advertisement messages contain one old and one new IPv6 prefix.

By receiving these router advertisement messages, nodes are discover the deprecation of the current prefix with a short life, but they also obtain the new prefix. During this transition time, all nodes use two unicast addresses:

- **Old unicast address**—The old address is based on the old prefix. Current connections using the old address are still handled.

- **New unicast address**—New connections are established using the new address.

When the old prefix is completely deprecated (its lifetime has expired), router advertisement messages include the new prefix only. A prefix is deprecated when the valid/preferred lifetime values are set to 0.

---

**NOTE**   During prefix renumbering, features such as IPv6 ACLs or QoS set with the old prefix must be updated to reflect the new prefix as well on the IPv6 router.

---

## Configuring Prefix Renumbering

Cisco IOS Software technology introduces proprietary parameters in router advertisement messages to help with prefix renumbering. By using the command **ipv6 nd prefix**, you can specify an exact date and time when a prefix must be considered deprecated rather than manually decreasing prefixes' lifetimes. The new keywords for this purpose are **at** *valid-date* and **at** *preferred-date*. The following is the syntax for the **ipv6 nd prefix** command:

```
Router(config-if)#ipv6 nd prefix ipv6-prefix/prefix-length | default
  [[valid-lifetime preferred-lifetime] | [at valid-date preferred-date]
  [off-link] [no-autoconfig] [no-advertise]]
```

When a date and time are specified using these parameters, the router performs a time countdown, meaning that each new router advertisement message includes decreased lifetime values until 0.

---

**NOTE**   To use parameters related to date and time with the **ipv6 nd prefix** command, you must adjust the date and time on the router. You can do this using the **clock set** command or by specifying a Network Time Protocol (NTP) server through the **ntp server** command.

---

Example 3-9 shows the command **ipv6 nd prefix** used to perform prefix renumbering on interface FastEthernet 0/0 based on the *valid-date* and *preferred-date* keywords. The initial date/time on the router is set to February 10, 2003 at 16:35:00 using the **clock set** command. The command **ipv6 nd prefix** determines that the prefix 2001:410:0:1::/64 is deprecated by February 10, 2003 at 17:00:00 (25 minutes later). However, the other prefix, 2001:420:0:2::/64, continues to be advertised using default values. In this example, the router advertisement interval is set to 60 seconds.

**Example 3-9**   *PrefixDeprecatedUsingthe* **ipv6ndprefix***CommandandtheParametersvalid-dateandpreferred-date*

```
RouterA#clock set 16:35:00 10 February 2003
RouterA(config)#interface Fast-Ethernet 0/0
RouterA(config-if)#ipv6 address 2001:410:0:1::/64 eui-64
RouterA(config-if)#ipv6 address 2001:420:0:2::/64 eui-64
RouterA(config-if)#ipv6 nd ra-interval 60
RouterA(config-if)#ipv6 nd prefix 2001:410:0:1::/64 at Feb 10 2003 17:00
  Feb 10 2003 17:00
RouterA(config-if)#exit
```

## Debugging Prefix Advertisement and Prefix Renumbering

The command **debug ipv6 nd** may be used to display information related to neighbor discovery messages (prefix advertisement and prefix renumbering). Example 3-10 shows debugging information when a prefix is deprecated using the **ipv6 nd prefix** command and the date and time as keywords. In this example, remaining valid/preferred lifetimes for the prefix

2001:410:0:1::/64 are decreased each time the router sends a new router advertisement message. Finally, when the prefix is deprecated, router advertisement messages are empty, because no new prefix is advertised.

**Example 3-10** debug ipv6 nd *Command*

```
RouterA#debug ipv6 nd
RouterA#ICMP Neighbor Discovery events debugging is on
01:51:14: ICMPv6-ND: Sending RA to FF02::1 on FastEthernet0/0
01:51:14: ICMPv6-ND:     prefix = 2001:410:0:1::/64 onlink autoconfig
01:51:14: ICMPv6-ND:         1138/1138 (valid/preferred)
01:52:09: ICMPv6-ND: Sending RA to FF02::1 on FastEthernet0/0
01:52:09: ICMPv6-ND:     prefix = 2001:410:0:1::/64 onlink autoconfig
01:52:09: ICMPv6-ND:         1084/1084 (valid/preferred)
<Data omitted>
02:09:15: ICMPv6-ND: Sending RA to FF02::1 on FastEthernet0/0
02:09:15: ICMPv6-ND:     prefix = 2001:410:0:1::/64 onlink autoconfig
02:09:15: ICMPv6-ND:         58/58 (valid/preferred)
02:10:10: ICMPv6-ND: Sending RA to FF02::1 on FastEthernet0/0
02:10:10: ICMPv6-ND:     prefix = 2001:410:0:1::/64 onlink autoconfig
02:10:10: ICMPv6-ND:         2/2 (valid/preferred)
02:11:02: ICMPv6-ND: Sending RA to FF02::1 on FastEthernet0/0
02:12:02: ICMPv6-ND: Sending RA to FF02::1 on FastEthernet0/0
02:12:57: ICMPv6-ND: Sending RA to FF02::1 on FastEthernet0/0
```

**NOTE**    The default router is always seen in the routing tables of nodes on the local link with its link-local addresses (FE80::/10). This guarantees that all routers can be reached even when network renumbering occurs. During renumbering, unicast IPv6 addresses assigned to router interfaces change, but not link-local addresses.

# Router Redirection

Router redirection is an NDP mechanism in IPv6. Routers use ICMPv6 redirection messages to inform nodes on the link that a better router exists on the link to forward packets. Then the node that receives the ICMPv6 redirect message may modify its local routing table according to the new router address in the ICMPv6 redirection message. The router redirection mechanism in IPv6 uses redirect messages (ICMPv6 Type 137). This mechanism is the equivalent of the redirect message in IPv4.

As shown in Figure 3-11, node A wants to send packets to LAN ZZ. First, node A delivers the first packet to its default router (Router A). However, after forwarding this packet to LAN ZZ, Router A knows that Router C is a better path for nodes on this local link to forward packets to LAN ZZ. Therefore, in the second step, Router A sends node A an ICMPv6 redirect message that contains Router C's IPv6 address. Finally, node A sends the next packets to be sent to LAN ZZ to Router C.

**Figure 3-11** *ICMPv6 Redirect Messages*

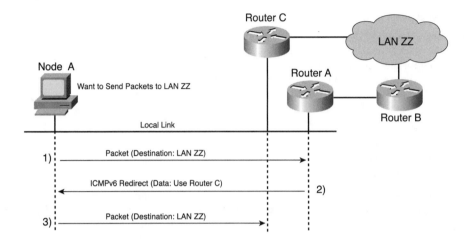

ICMPv6 redirect is enabled by default on Cisco interfaces. The command **ipv6 redirects** may be used to disable or enable the sending of ICMPv6 redirect messages. Here is an example of disabling the sending of messages:

```
Router(config-if)# no ipv6 redirects
```

The following example shows the command to enable the sending of messages. By default, ICMPv6 redirect is enabled on all interfaces.

```
Router(config-if)# ipv6 redirects
```

The **ipv6 redirects** command is enabled on a per-interface basis.

The command **ipv6 icmp error-interval** may be used to limit the minimum rate at which the router can generate ICMPv6 error messages. By default, this parameter is set to 500 milliseconds. Here is the syntax of the **ipv6 icmp error-interval** command:

```
Router(config)# ipv6 icmp error-interval msec
```

This command is enabled on a global basis.

## NDP Summary

As described throughout this section, NDP mechanisms are fundamental components of the IPv6 protocol. You have learned about the following:

- Replacement of ARP by neighbor solicitation and neighbor advertisement messages

- Stateless autoconfiguration uses prefix advertisement, DAD, and prefix renumbering mechanisms.

- Router redirection is similar to redirection in IPv4.

Table 3-8 summarizes the ICMPv6 messages and multicast addresses involved in each mechanism described.

**Table 3-8**    *ICMPv6 Messages, Multicast, and Other Addresses Used by All NDP Mechanisms*

| Mechanism | ICMPv6 Message | Multicast Address |
|---|---|---|
| Replacement of ARP | Type 135 (neighbor solicitation) | All-nodes multicast (FF02::1) |
| | Type 136 (neighbor advertisement) | Solicited-node multicast (FF02::1:FF*xx*:*xxxx*) |
| Prefix advertisement | Type 133 (router solicitation) | All-nodes multicast (FF02::1) |
| | Type 134 (router advertisement) | All-routers multicast (FF02::2) |
| DAD | Type 135 (neighbor solicitation) | Solicited-node multicast (FF02::1:FF*xx*:*xxxx*) |
| Prefix renumbering | Type 133 (router solicitation) | All-nodes multicast (FF02::1) |
| | Type 134 (router advertisement) | All-routers multicast (FF02::2) |
| Router redirection | Type 137 (router redirection) | — |

You should be able to deploy, manage, and support IPv6 on local links, networks, and routers.

# Domain Name System (DNS)

The IETF has defined new Domain Name System (DNS) resource record types for IPv6 addresses. This section discusses AAAA and PTR records, which are used for IPv6 addresses in DNS servers.

## AAAA Records

In IPv4, the A resource record maps a host name to an IPv4 address. Similarly, the AAAA resource record maps a host name to an IPv6 address. Table 3-9 shows two examples of different resource records using the same fully qualified domain name (FQDN).

**Table 3-9**    *DNS Resource Records for IPv4 and IPv6*

| Protocol | Record | DNS Mapping |
|---|---|---|
| IPv4 | A | www.example.org A 206.123.31.200 |
| IPv6 | AAAA | www.example.org AAAA 2001:410:1:1:250:3EFF:FEE4:1 |

The AAAA record has been available since release 4.9.4 of the ISC Berkeley Internet Name Domain (BIND) software. BIND is the DNS server software used by most DNS root server operators; generic Top-Level Domains (gTLDs) such as .com, .net, .org, and so on; and country code Top-Level Domains (ccTLDs).

As with a DNS server that has IPv6 support, it is possible on a limited scale to configure static host names for IPv6 addresses using the command ipv6 host on Cisco routers. Table 3-10 presents examples of the command ipv6 host.

**Table 3-10**    **ipv6 host** *Command*

| Command | Description |
| --- | --- |
| Router(config)#**ipv6 host** *name* [*port*] *ipv6-address1* [*ipv6-address2 ...*] | Defines a static host name-to-IPv6 address mapping. |
| **Example**<br>RouterA(config)#**ipv6 host RouterA 2001:410:0:1:250:3EFF:FEE4:4C00** | Assigns the IPv6 address 2001:410:0:1:250:3EFF:FEE4:4C00 to the host name RouterA. |
| **Example**<br>RouterA(config)#**ipv6 host RouterB FEC0::1:0:0:1:1** | Assigns the IPv6 address FEC0::1:0:0:1:1 to the host name RouterB. |

This command is enabled on a global basis.

The resolver DNS using Cisco IOS Software technology accepts either an IPv6 address or an IPv4 address as a name server. By using the command **ip name-server**, as shown in Table 3-11, you can specify a DNS server's IPv6 address. Therefore, the router queries this name server using IPv6 as the transport for the name resolution.

**Table 3-11**    **ip name-server** *Command*

| Command | Description |
| --- | --- |
| Router(config)# **ip name-server** *ipv6-address* | Configures the IP address of a DNS server that the router can query. The address may be an IPv4 or IPv6 address. It may accept up to six different name servers. |
| **Example**<br>RouterA(config)# **ip name-server FEC0::1:0:0:1ff:10** | Configures the router to query the name server that can be reached using the IPv6 address FEC0::1:0:0:1ff:10 for name resolution. |

This command is enabled on a global basis.

---

**NOTE**    You must enable domain lookup on the router using the command **ip domain lookup**.

---

During the resolution of any host name values, the router queries all name servers specified in an attempt to resolve the name into an IPv6 address. If no AAAA record (IPv6 address) is found, the router queries the same name servers to resolve the name into an A record (IPv4 address). Therefore, if the same FQDN is recorded in a zone file using both A and AAAA records, the router always resolves the IPv6 address first and communicates using IPv6 as transport.

## Resource Record PTR for IPv6

For IPv6 reverse addressing, which is the mapping of an IPv6 address to a host name, the PTR (pointer) record is used, as in IPv4. However, as defined in RFC 3152, *Delegation of IP6.ARPA,* a special top-level domain (TLD) called ip6.arpa is defined. In the early days of the IPv6 protocol, the TLD was ip6.int. Although this TLD is still used, it is being deprecated.

The PTR record is represented using a sequence of nibbles separated by dots with the suffix ip6.arpa. The sequence of nibbles is encoded in reverse order: The low-order nibble is encoded first, followed by the next low-order nibble, and so on. Each nibble is represented by a hexadecimal value. The preferred form is the only acceptable form to use for the PTR record.

Here's an example of a PTR record made from valid IPv6 addresses:

IPv6 address = 2001:0410:0000:1234:FB00:1400:5000:45FF

PTR = f.f.5.4.0.0.0.5.0.0.4.1.0.0.b.f.4.3.2.1.0.0.0.0.0.0.1.4.0.1.0.0.2.ip6.arpa

Here's an example of the PTR record in the DNS zone file:

f.f.5.4.0.0.0.5.0.0.4.1.0.0.b.f.4.3.2.1.0.0.0.0.0.0.1.4.0.1.0.0.2.ip6.arpa. IN PTR www.example.org

## Other Resource Records Defined for IPv6

Other resource record types such as A6, DNAME, and BITSLABEL, were defined specifically for IPv6, but were moved by the IETF community to experimental status in August 2001.

If you want more information about A6, DNAME, and BITSLABEL, read RFC 2874, *DNS Extensions to Support IPv6 Address Aggregation and Renumbering,* RFC 2672, *Non-Terminal DNS Name Redirection,* and RFC 2673, *Binary Labels in the Domain Name System.*

# Securing the Network Using IPv6 Access Control Lists (ACLs)

Packet filtering helps restrict, limit, and control traffic entering or exiting the network. As in IPv4, on IPv6 routers you can define and enable standard and extended IPv6 ACLs to control IPv6 traffic. This section presents commands and examples of IPv6 ACLs.

## Creating IPv6 ACLs

To create an IPv6 ACL, you must first assign a unique name to each ACL using the command **ipv6 access-list**. The steps are presented in Table 3-12. This command enables both standard and extended IPv6 ACLs. Cisco recommends writing IPv6 ACLs using the submode configuration. After the name of the ACL has been defined, the system enters submode configuration and displays the prompt (config-ipv6-acl)#.

**Table 3-12**   ipv6 access-list *Command*

| Command | Description |
|---|---|
| Router(config)# **ipv6 access-list** *access-list-name* | Defines the name of an IPv6 standard or extended ACL. |
| **Example**<br>RouterA(config)# **ipv6 access-list blocksitelocal**<br>RouterA(config-ipv6-acl)# | Defines the name blocksitelocal for the IPv6 ACL. |

This command is enabled on a global basis.

As in IPv4, an ACL for IPv6 is made up of one or several statements using **permit** or **deny**. Each ACL statement must define at least the type of protocol, the source, and/or the destination address to match. In IPv6, if all the ACL statements are unmatched, the implicit statement **deny ipv6 any any** is imposed. The meaning of **any** address in IPv6 is equivalent to **::/0**. You do not see the implicit statement, and it is in the last line of an IPv6 ACL.

---

**NOTE**    The order of the statements is important in the ACL configuration. The order is from specific to general.

---

## Applying IPv6 ACLs on the Interface

The final step after you've defined an IPv6 ACL is to apply the ACL to the router's interfaces. The command to apply an IPv6 ACL to an interface in IPv6 is **ipv6 traffic-filter**. The IPv6 ACL may be used to filter incoming or outgoing traffic. The syntax for this command is as follows:

```
Router(config-if)#ipv6 traffic-filter access-list-name {in | out}
```

This command is enabled on a per-interface basis.

## Defining Standard IPv6 ACLs

Standard IPv6 ACLs permit or deny packets based only on the source and/or destination address. After you've defined the unique name of the standard IPv6 ACL, the next step is writing the statements. You may write the statements using the submode configuration or by entering the ACL *access-list-name* for each new statement. Cisco recommends writing IPv6 ACLs using the submode configuration.

The syntax for the **ipv6 access-list** command used to define standard IPv6 ACLs is as follows:

```
Router(config)#ipv6 access-list access-list-name {permit | deny}
    {source-ipv6-prefix/prefix-length | any | host host-ipv6-address}
    {destination-ipv6-prefix/prefix-length | any | host host-ipv6-address}
    [log | log-input]
```

The following describes the parameters and keywords that may be used with the **ipv6 access-list** command:

- *access-list-name*—Specifies the name of the IPv6 ACL.

- **permit**—Permits conditions for the IPv6 ACL.

- **deny**—Denies conditions for the IPv6 ACL.

- *source-ipv6-prefix/prefix-length*—The source IPv6 prefix with the length of the prefix from which the packet is being sent.

- **any**—Any IPv6 address that is equivalent to ::/0.

- **host** *host-ipv6-address*—A single IPv6 address. *This keyword must be used in the submode configuration only.*

- *destination-ipv6-prefix/prefix-length*—The destination IPv6 prefix with the length of the prefix to which the packet is being sent.

- **log**—The log keyword for the IPv6 access list logging.

- **log-input**—The log keyword for the IPv6 access list logging. With this keyword, the logging includes the input interface and the source MAC address where applicable.

This command is enabled on a global basis.

---

**NOTE**      To remove an entire IPv6 ACL, use the **no ipv6 access-list** *ipv6-access-name* command.

---

Table 3-13 defines the standard IPv6 ACL named INTRANET.

Figure 3-12 shows a network in which prefixes 2001:410:0:1::/64 and FEC0:0:0:1::/64 are used on interface FastEthernet 0/0 of Router A. On this subnet, site-local FEC0::/10 and aggregatable global unicast addresses within the prefix 2001::/16 are assigned to nodes. Router A acts as a border router between this network and the IPv6 provider. However, because site-local addresses (FEC0::/10) are not routed on the IPv6 Internet, the local policy of this network does not allow packets using the site-local prefix FEC0::/16 to exit the network. Of course, packets using other IPv6 source addresses, such as the prefix 2001:410:0:1::/64, are allowed to exit the network.

**Table 3-13**  ipv6 access-list *Command*

| Command | Description |
|---|---|
| **Statement 1**<br><br>RouterA(config)# **ipv6 access-list INTRANET permit 2001:410:0:1::/64 2001::/16** | Permits all packets from the source network 2001:410:0:1::/64 to the destination network 2001::/16. |
| **Statement 2**<br><br>RouterA(config)# **ipv6 access-list INTRANET deny FEC0::/16 2001::/16** | Denies all packets from the source network FEC0::/16 to the destination network 2001::/16. |

**Figure 3-12**  *Filtering Does Not Allow Packets from Site-Local Prefix FEC0::/16 to Be Sent to the IPv6 Provider*

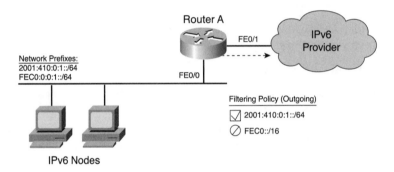

Therefore, a standard IPv6 ACL should be applied on Router A to manage the traffic. Example 3-11 shows a typical standard IPv6 ACL configuration applied to Router A in Figure 3-12. The first statement, **ipv6 access-list blocksitelocal deny FEC0::/16 any**, denies all IPv6 packets using FEC0::/16 as a source address to any destination network. The next statement, **ipv6 access-list blocksitelocal permit any any**, permits IPv6 packets using any other IPv6 addresses as source addresses to exit the network. The command **ipv6 traffic-filter blocksitelocal out** is applied to the interface FastEthernet 0/1 to filter outgoing traffic.

**Example 3-11**  *Configuring and Applying a Standard IPv6 ACL on a Cisco Router*

```
RouterA#configure terminal
RouterA(config)#ipv6 access-list blocksitelocal deny FEC0::/16 any
RouterA(config)#ipv6 access-list blocksitelocal permit any any
RouterA(config)#interface FastEthernet 0/1
RouterA(config-if)#ipv6 traffic-filter blocksitelocal out
RouterA(config)#exit
RouterA#show running-config
<output omitted>
```

**Example 3-11**  *Configuring and Applying a Standard IPv6 ACL on a Cisco Router (Continued)*

```
!
interface FastEthernet0/1
 ipv6 traffic-filter blocksitelocal out
...
!
<output omitted>
!
ipv6 access-list blocksitelocal
 deny ipv6 FEC0::/16 any
 permit ipv6 any any
!
<output omitted>
```

**NOTE**    For prefix filtering related to routing protocols such as Border Gateway Protocol (BGP), the command **ipv6 prefix-list** is used instead. Chapter 4, "Routing on IPv6," presents examples of prefix filtering using this command.

## Defining Extended IPv6 ACLs

As in IPv4, extended IPv6 ACLs permit or deny packets based on a combination of source address, destination address, transport layer protocol, source port, destination port, and other features of IP. The behavior of the extended IPv6 ACL is similar to the extended IPv4 ACL.

However, the extended IPv6 ACL is adapted to specific and new features of the IPv6 protocol:

- **New optional keywords added**—IPv6 packets can be matched against Traffic Class and Flow Label fields of the basic IPv6 header. Packets can also be matched against the presence of a routing extension header, the presence of a noninitial fragment extension header, or missing or undetermined transport (Layer 4) information. The new optional keywords are **dscp**, **flow-label**, **fragments**, **routing**, and **undetermined-transport**.

- **New ICMPv6 message types supported**—Because new ICMPv6 message types are defined for IPv6, such as neighbor advertisement, neighbor solicitation, router advertisement, and router solicitation, the new keywords added are **nd-na**, **nd-ns**, **router-advertisement**, and **router-solicitation**.

- **New implicit IPv6 rules added for NDP**—New implicit rules allowing neighbor solicitation and neighbor advertisement messages from any to any are imposed to bring the functionality into line with IPv4 ACLs, which do not block ARP. These rules were added before the default implicit **deny ipv6 any any** rule in the last matching condition. The new implicit rules for extended IPv6 ACLs are

    — **permit icmp any any nd-ns**

       — **permit icmp any any nd-na**

       — **deny ipv6 any any**

---

**NOTE**     You can overrule the implicit rules by specifying earlier IPv6 ACL entries. Implicit rules are not displayed by the **show ipv6 access-list** command.

---

The syntax for the **ipv6 access-list** command used to define extended IPv6 ACLs is as follows:

```
Router(config)#ipv6 access-list access-list-name{permit | deny}[protocol]
  {source-ipv6-prefix/prefix-length | any | host host-ipv6-address}
  [eq | neq | lt | gt | range source-port(s)]
  {destination-ipv6-prefix/prefix-length | any | host host-ipv6-address}
  [eq | neq | lt | gt | range destination-port(s)][dscp value][flow-label value]
  [fragments][routing][undetermined-transport][[reflect reflexive-access-list-name]
  [timeout value]][time-range time-range-name][log | log-input][sequence value]
```

Here are the descriptions of this command's keywords and parameters:

- *access-list-name*—Specifies the name of the IPv6 ACL.

- **permit**—Permits conditions for the IPv6 ACL.

- **deny**—Denies conditions for the IPv6 ACL.

- *protocol*—Layer 4 protocols supported are basically the same as in IPv4, such as **TCP**, **UDP**, **ICMP**, and so on. Here are the new keywords added for ICMPv6:

  - **nd-na**—Neighbor advertisement message. Neighbor advertisement is ICMPv6 Type 136.

  - **nd-ns**—Neighbor solicitation message. Neighbor solicitation is an ICMPv6 Type 135.

  - **router-advertisement**—Router advertisement is ICMPv6 Type 134.

  - **router-solicitation**—Router solicitation is ICMPv6 Type 133.

- *source-ipv6-prefix/prefix-length*—The source IPv6 prefix with the length of the prefix from which the packet is being sent.

- **any**—Any IPv6 address that is equivalent to ::/0.

- **host** *host-ipv6-address*—The source IPv6 address (a single IPv6 address) from which the packet is being sent. This keyword must be used in the submode configuration only.

- *destination-ipv6-prefix/prefix-length*—The destination IPv6 prefix with the length of the prefix to which the packet is being sent.

- **eq**—The Layer 4 operator *equal*.

- **neq**—The Layer 4 operator *not equal*.

- **lt**—The Layer 4 operator *less than*.

- **gt**—The Layer 4 operator *greater than*.

- **range** *source-port(s)*—The Layer 4 operator for inclusive range of source port(s).

- **range** *destination-ports(s)*—The Layer 4 operator for inclusive range of destination port(s).

- **dscp** *value*—Differentiated Services Code Point (DSCP) defines a value to match against the Traffic Class field in the basic IPv6 header. The high-order 6 bits of the Traffic Class field (8-bit) are called the DiffServ bits, as defined in RFC 2474, *Definition of the Differentiated Service Field (DS Field) in the IPv4 and IPv6 Headers*. The DSCP value can be specified as a decimal value in the range from 0 to 63 or as predefined name.

- **flow-label** *value*—Defines a value to match against the Flow Label field (20-bit) in the basic IPv6 header. The *value* may vary from 0 to 1,048,575.

- **fragments**—Matches the presence of a noninitial fragment extension header following the basic IPv6 header. This keyword can be used to permit or deny such datagrams.

- **routing**—Matches the presence of a routing extension header following the basic IPv6 header. This keyword can be used to permit or deny such datagrams.

- **undetermined-transport**—Matches any IPv6 datagram in which the upper-layer protocol (Layer 4) cannot be determined. This includes any unknown extension headers, which cannot be traversed.

- **reflect** *reflexive-access-list-name*—Specifies a reflexive IPv6 ACL.

- **timeout** *value*—The timeout value for the specified reflexive IPv6 ACL.

- **time-range** *time-range-name*—Specifies a time-based IPv6 ACL.

- **log**—The log keyword for IPv6 access list logging.

- **log-input**—The log keyword for IPv6 access list logging. With this keyword, the logging includes the input interface and the source MAC address where applicable.

- **sequence** *value*—Defines a number that can be incremented for each entry. Useful for ordering ACL entries.

This command is enabled on a global basis.

| CAUTION | With extended IPv6 ACLs, there is no default implicit rule for PMTUD. As discussed earlier, the source node uses the PMTUD mechanism to detect the largest MTU value along a delivery path to a destination host. Be sure to define a statement allowing ICMPv6 Type 2, Packet Too Big, from any to any in your extended IPv6 ACL to avoid an issue with big datagrams. However, it should be simpler to permit ICMP from any to any for IPv6's other needs such as echo-request and echo-reply messages. |
|---|---|

Table 3-14 presents examples of extended IPv6 ACL statements using the new keywords.

**Table 3-14**  *Examples of Extended IPv6 ACL Statements*

| Command | Description |
|---|---|
| Router(config)# **ipv6 access-list TEST** | Defines the extended IPv6 ACL called TEST. The system enters the IPv6 ACL submode configuration. |
| Router(config-ipv6-acl)# **permit icmp any any router-advertisement** | Permits *router advertisement* messages from any IPv6 source address to reach any IPv6 destination address. |
| Router(config-ipv6-acl)# **permit icmp any any router-solicitation** | Permits router solicitation messages from any IPv6 source address to reach any IPv6 destination address. |
| Router(config-ipv6-acl)# **permit udp any host 3ffe:b00:0:1::1 eq domain** | Permits UDP packets from any IPv6 source address to reach the IPv6 destination host 3ffe:b00:0:1::1 on port 53 (DNS). |
| Router(config-ipv6-acl)# **permit tcp 3ffe:b00:0:1::/64 any reflect OUTGOING** | Permits TCP packets from the source network 3ffe:b00:0:1::/64 to reach any destination IPv6 network on any TCP port. This statement adds a reflexive ACL entry to OUTGOING when matched. |
| Router(config-ipv6-acl)# **deny any 2001:410:0:1::/64 routing** | Denies packets from any IPv6 source address from reaching the destination network 2001:410:0:1::/64 when a routing extension header is present. |
| Router(config-ipv6-acl)# **deny any 2001:410:0:1::/64 fragments** | Denies packets from any IPv6 source address from reaching the destination network 2001:410:0:1::/64 when a fragment extension header is present. |
| Router(config-ipv6-acl)# **permit any 2001:410:0:1::/64 flow-label 100** | Permits packets from any IPv6 source address to reach the destination network 2001:410:0:1::/64 when the Flow Label field equals 100. |
| Router(config-ipv6-acl)# **deny any any log** | Denies packets from any source IPv6 address from reaching any destination address and logs them. This rule overrules the implicit rule **deny any any** using the submode configuration. |

Figure 3-13 illustrates the use of extended IPv6 ACLs for traffic filtering. This network is connected to the IPv6 Internet through border router B. This network hosts a web server on port 80 at address 2001:410:0:1::1 and a DNS server on port 53 at address 2001:410:0:1::2. The web and DNS services can be reached by any node on the IPv6 Internet. However, any other incoming traffic from the IPv6 Internet except ICMPv6 packets is prohibited. ICMPv6 traffic is allowed for PMTUD.

**Figure 3-13**    *Filtering Allows Packets from the IPv6 Internet to the Web and DNS Servers Within the Network 2001:410:0:1::/64*

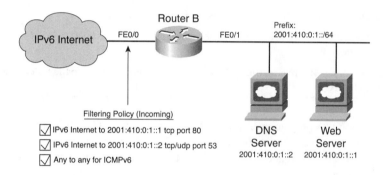

Table 3-15 presents the extended IPv6 ACL applied on border router B, as illustrated in Figure 3-13.

**Table 3-15**    *Extended IPv6 ACL Applied on Router B in Figure 3-13*

| Command | Description |
|---|---|
| RouterB(config)# **ipv6 access-list PUBLIC** | Defines the extended IPv6 ACL called PUBLIC. The system enters the IPv6 ACL submode configuration. |
| RouterB(config-ipv6-acl)# **permit tcp any host 2001:410:0:1::1 eq www** | Permits any TCP packets from any IPv6 source address to reach the host destination 2001:410:0:1::1 on destination port 80. This statement allows any host on the IPv6 Internet to reach the web server 2001:410:0:1::1. |
| RouterB(config-ipv6-acl)# **permit udp any host 2001:410:0:1::2 eq domain** | Permits any UDP packet from any IPv6 source address to reach the host IPv6 destination 2001:410:0:1::2 on destination port 53. This statement allows any host on the IPv6 Internet to reach the DNS server 2001:410:0:1::2 (DNS query). |
| RouterB(config-ipv6-acl)# **permit tcp any host 2001:410:0:1::2 eq domain** | Permits any TCP packet from any IPv6 source address to reach the host IPv6 destination 2001:410:0:1::2 on destination port 53. DNS zone transfers and responses to a DNS query greater than 572 octets use TCP. |

*continues*

**Table 3-15** *Extended IPv6 ACL Applied on Router B in Figure 3-13 (Continued)*

| Command | Description |
|---|---|
| RouterB(config-ipv6-acl)#**permit icmp any any** | Permits all ICMPv6 messages from any IPv6 source address to reach any destination IPv6 address. This rule is added for PMTUD and for IPv6's other needs. |
| RouterB(config-ipv6-acl)# **deny any any log** | Denies packets from reaching any source IPv6 address to any destination address and logs them. This rule overrules the implicit rule **deny any any** using the submode configuration. |
| RouterB(config-ipv6-acl)# **exit** | Exits the submode configuration. |
| RouterB(config)# **interface fastethernet 0/0** | Interface fastethernet 0/0 is selected. |
| RouterB(config-if)# **ipv6 traffic-filter PUBLIC in** | Applies the extended IPv6 ACL to the fastethernet 0/0 interface to filter incoming traffic. |

This section was only an overview of the extended IPv6 ACL. Except for the new keywords added for IPv6, the behavior of the extended IPv6 ACL is identical to IPv4. For more information about extended ACLs, refer to the documentation on the Cisco website at www.cisco.com.

## Reflexive and Time-Based IPv6 ACLs

As in IPv4, reflexive and time-based ACLs are supported in IPv6. The preceding section presented the keywords **reflect** and **time-range**, which are used for that purpose. Their syntax and the behavior are identical to the extended IPv4 ACL:

- **Reflexive ACL**—When an outgoing or incoming session is allowed by an ACL entry, a temporary entry is created in a reflexive ACL. That temporary entry is used to match the return traffic of the allowed session. The **evaluate** keyword applies the specified reflexive ACL within a separate ACL. If no match is made, the next ACL entry following **evaluate** is tried in turn. Multiple **evaluate** keywords are permitted within an ACL.

- **Time-based ACL**—Defines a time period during which the ACL entry is valid.

If a reflexive ACL is defined in IPv6, it is embedded in an extended IPv6 ACL using the **evaluate** command. The syntax is as follows:

```
Router(config-ipv6-acl)#evaluate reflexive-access-control-list
```

Figure 3-14 illustrates the use of extended IPv6 ACLs with reflexive filtering. This network uses prefixes 2001:410:0:2::/64 and FEC0:410:0:2::/64, which are connected to the IPv6 Internet through border router C. The IPv6 hosts inside this network are allowed to reach any IPv6 destination on the IPv6 Internet using any TCP and UDP service. The extended IPv6 ACL applied on border router C is defined to allow outbound traffic using the aggregatable global unicast prefix 2001:410:0:2::/64. However, the extended IPv6 ACL denies the sending of packets using the site-local prefix as the source address to the IPv6 Internet. Finally, any ICMPv6 traffic is allowed for PMTUD.

**Figure 3-14**  *Filtering Allows Packets from 201:410:0:2::/64 to the IPv6 Internet Using Reflexive for TCP/UDP Sessions*

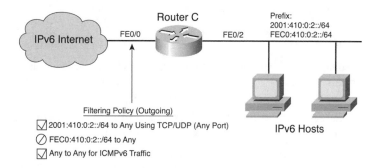

Table 3-16 presents the extended IPv6 ACL with reflexive applied on border router C, as illustrated in Figure 3-14.

**Table 3-16**  *Extended IPv6 ACL with Reflexive Applied on Router C in Figure 3-14*

| Command | Description |
|---|---|
| RouterC(config)# **ipv6 access-list OUTGOING** | Defines the extended IPv6 ACL called OUTGOING. The system enters the IPv6 ACL submode configuration. |
| RouterC(config-ipv6-acl)#**permit tcp 2001:410:0:2::/64 any reflect REFLECTOUT** | Permits any TCP packets from the source network 2001:410:0:2::/64 to reach any destination network. This statement adds a reflexive ACL entry in REFLECTOUT when matched. |
| RouterC(config-ipv6-acl)#**permit udp 2001:410:0:2::/64 any reflect REFLECTOUT** | Permits any UDP packets from the source network 2001:410:0:2::/64 to reach any destination network. This statement adds a reflexive ACL entry in REFLECTOUT when matched. |
| RouterC(config-ipv6-acl)#**deny fec0::/10 any** | Denies all outgoing IPv6 packets from using the site-local prefix as the IPv6 source address. |
| RouterC(config-ipv6-acl)# **permit icmp any any** | Permits all ICMPv6 messages from any IPv6 source address to reach any destination IPv6 address. This rule is added for PMTUD and for IPv6's other needs. |

*continues*

**Table 3-16**    *Extended IPv6 ACL with Reflexive Applied on Router C in Figure 3-14 (Continued)*

| Command | Description |
|---|---|
| RouterC(config-ipv6-acl)# **deny any any log** | Denies packets from any source IPv6 address to reach any destination address and logs them. This rule overrules the implicit rule **deny any any** using the submode configuration. |
| RouterC(config-ipv6-acl)# **exit** | Exits the submode configuration. |
| RouterC(config)# **ipv6 access-list INCOMING** | Defines the extended IPv6 ACL called INCOMING. The system enters the IPv6 ACL submode configuration. |
| RouterC(config-ipv6-acl)# **permit icmp any any** | Permits all ICMPv6 messages from any IPv6 source address to reach any destination IPv6 address. This rule is added for PMTUD and for IPv6's other needs. |
| RouterC(config-ipv6-acl)# **evaluate REFLECTOUT** | Defines the reflexive ACL called REFLECTOUT in the INCOMING extended IPv6 ACL. |
| RouterC(config-ipv6-acl)# **deny any any log** | Denies packets from any source IPv6 address to reach any destination address and logs them. This rule overrules the implicit rule **deny any any** using the submode configuration. |
| RouterC(config)# **interface fastethernet 0/0** | Interface fastethernet 0/0 is selected. |
| RouterC(config-if)# **ipv6 traffic-filter OUTGOING out** | Applies the extended IPv6 ACL OUTGOING to the fastethernet 0/0 interface to filter outbound traffic. |
| RouterC(config-if)# **ipv6 traffic-filter INCOMING in** | Applies the extended IPv6 ACL INCOMING to the fastethernet 0/0 interface to filter inbound traffic. |

This section was only an overview of the reflexive ACL. Its behavior is identical in IPv4. For more information about the reflexive ACL, refer to the documentation on the Cisco website at www.cisco.com.

# Managing IPv6 ACLs

This section presents commands to display, clear, and debug traffic related to IPv6 ACLs.

## Displaying IPv6 ACLs

You can display IPv6 ACLs defined on the router by using the command **show ipv6 access-list**. Here is the syntax:

```
Router# show ipv6 access-list [access-list-name]
```

The number of matches against each statement is displayed. The entries can be cleared using the **clear ipv6 access-list** command. Its syntax is as follows:

```
Router# clear ipv6 access-list [access-list-name]
```

### Debugging IPv6 Using ACLs

On Cisco routers, the **debug ipv6 packet** command displays packets matching an IPv6 ACL. This command shows only packets matching IPv6 ACL permit entries. The syntax for this command is as follows:

```
Router# debug ipv6 packet [access-list access-list-name] [detail]
```

The optional keywords **log** and **log-input** can be used inside any IPv6 ACL. These keywords are useful to debug the IPv6 traffic being matched by the ACL. The **ipv6 access-list log-update threshold** *value* command defines a hit threshold when the **log** or **log-input** entries are logged.

# Cisco IOS Software IPv6 Tools

This section covers the ping and traceroute tools, used as helpful diagnostic commands to basically validate connectivity with IPv6 destinations. This section also covers other tools used to manage the router, such as Telnet, SSH, TFTP, and the HTTP server on Cisco.

## Using the Cisco IOS Software IPv6 ping Command

Troubleshooting support for IPv6 is available with the **ping** command. This command allows the sending of ICMPv6 echo request messages to an IPv6 destination node. For each ICMPv6 echo request message received, the destination responds using an ICMPv6 echo reply message. The absence of an ICMPv6 echo reply message can indicate a problem between sender and receiver nodes.

This command accepts a destination address or the host name as an argument. However, the address family IPv6 must be specified. Example 3-12 shows the use of the **ping ipv6** command with a destination IPv6 address.

**Example 3-12** **ping ipv6** *Command Sends ICMPv6 Echo Request Messages to an IPv6 Destination*

```
RouterA#ping ?
  WORD  Ping destination address or hostname
  ip    IP echo
  ipv6  IPv6 echo
  srb   srb echo
  tag   Tag encapsulated IP echo
  <cr>
RouterA#ping ipv6 2001:410:0:1:200:86ff:fe4b:f9ce
Type escape sequence to abort.
Sending 5, 100-byte ICMP Echos to 2001:410:0:1:200:86FF:FE4B:F9CE, timeout is 2
  seconds:
!!!!!
Success rate is 100 percent (5/5), round-trip min/avg/max = 1/1/1 ms
```

## Using the Cisco IOS Software IPv6 traceroute Command

Troubleshooting support for IPv6 is also available with the **traceroute** command. It lets you trace the route to reach an IPv6 destination node. This command displays the list of intermediary routers up to the final destination.

This command accepts a destination address or the host name as an argument. However, the address family ipv6 must be specified. Example 3-13 shows the use of the **traceroute ipv6** command with a destination IPv6 address.

**Example 3-13** **traceroute ipv6** *Command Traces the Route to an IPv6 Destination*

```
RouterA#traceroute ?
  WORD       Trace route to destination address or hostname
  appletalk  AppleTalk Trace
  clns       ISO CLNS Trace
  ip         IP Trace
  ipv6       IPv6 Trace
  ipx        IPX Trace
  oldvines   Vines Trace (Cisco)
  vines      Vines Trace (Banyan)
  <cr>
RouterA#traceroute ipv6 2001:410:0:1:200:86FF:FE4B:F9CE
Type escape sequence to abort.
Tracing the route to 2001:410:0:1:200:86FF:FE4B:F9CE
  1 2001:410:0:1:200:86FF:FE4B:F9CE 0 msec *  0 msec
```

## Using Cisco IOS Software IPv6 Telnet

The Telnet application is mainly used to get connected to a system that can be reached remotely over an IP network. By default, a Telnet server is enabled on Cisco routers.

Telnet clients and servers both support IPv6 on the router. Therefore, it is possible to establish a Telnet session to a Cisco router using its IPv6 address. The command **telnet** accepts a destination address or the host name as an argument. However, when the host name is used, the IPv6 address is tried first, and then the IPv4 address, to make the connection. Example 3-14 shows Router A using Telnet to reach another router with its IPv6 address.

**Example 3-14** *Telnetting to a Router Using Its IPv6 Address*

```
RouterA#telnet 2001:410:0:1:250:3EFF:FEE4:4C00
Trying 2001:410:0:1:250:3EFF:FEE4:4C00 ... Open
User Access Verification
Password:
```

# Using Cisco IOS Software IPv6 Secure Shell (SSH)

SSH (Secure Shell) may be used in place of Telnet to access a remote system over an IP network. With Telnet, malicious users can sniff logins, passwords, and the content of a whole session on the network. SSH provides secure authentication and sessions.

Support for IPv6 has been added to the SSH client and server. SSH is available on Cisco IOS Software for both IPv4 and IPv6 with 3DES cryptographic software.

## SSH Client with IPv6 Support

As with Telnet, the command **ssh** accepts a destination IPv6 address or the host name as an argument. The syntax is the same as the IPv4 command. However, when the host name is used, the IPv6 address is tried first, and then the IPv4 address, to make the connection. Following is the syntax of the **ssh** command:

```
Router#ssh [-l userid][-c {des | 3des}] [-o numberofpasswdprompts n] [-p portnum]
    {ipv6-address | hostname} [command]
```

## SSH Server with IPv6 Support

The commands for the SSH server on Cisco IOS Software have been extended to support IPv6. The SSH server is supported on platforms using Cisco IOS Software with 3DES software. The command **ip ssh** {[**timeout** *seconds*] | [**authentication-retries** *integer*]} configures SSH control variables on the router.

**show ip ssh** displays the SSH server's version and configuration. **show ssh** displays the status of the connections on the SSH server.

# Using Cisco IOS Software IPv6 TFTP

You may download and upload files between the router and a TFTP server over IPv6. The command **tftp** accepts a destination IPv6 address or the host name as an argument. However, when the host name is used, the IPv6 address is tried first, and then the IPv4 address, to make the connection.

Example 3-15 presents an example of a router using **tftp** with an IPv6 address to copy the configuration to the TFTP server 2001:410:0:1::10.

**Example 3-15** *TFTP to a TFTP Server Using an IPv6 Address*

```
Router#copy running-config tftp
Address or name of remote host []? 2001:410:0:1::10
Destination filename [router-config]?
```

## Enabling the HTTP Server with IPv6 Support on Cisco IOS Software

The **ip http server** command has been updated to accept both IPv4 and IPv6 addresses on the router. However, when the HTTP server is enabled, it is for both IPv4 and IPv6, because the Cisco IOS Software with IPv6 does not provide the configuration of a single protocol.

When enabling the HTTP server using **ip http server**, it is highly recommended to restrict access to the router by defining an IPv6 ACL.

# Dynamic Host Configuration Protocol for IPv6 (DHCPv6)

Dynamic Host Configuration Protocol (DHCP) has been updated to support IPv6. DHCPv6 can provide stateful autoconfiguration to IPv6 hosts. DHCPv6 handles the addressing architecture and new features of the IPv6 protocol as follows:

- It enables more control on nodes than stateless autoconfiguration.

- It can be used concurrently on networks where stateless autoconfiguration is available.

- It can provide IPv6 addresses to hosts in the absence of routers on a network.

- It can be used for network renumbering.

- It can be used to delegate /48 or /64 prefixes to Customer Premises Equipment (CPE) routers such as a home gateway.

The process of getting IPv6 configuration data with DHCPv6 for an IPv6 host is similar to that in IPv4, but with a few exceptions. For example, the IPv6 host first detects the presence of IPv6 router(s) on the local link. One of two things occurs:

- If an IPv6 router is found, the IPv6 host examines the router advertisement messages to determine if DHCPv6 (stateful autoconfiguration) can be used:

  — If DHCPv6 can be used, the IPv6 host (a node with DHCPv6 client support only) sends a DHCPv6 solicit message to the all-DHCPv6-agents multicast address (FF02::1:2) on the local link using its link-local address (FE80::/10) as the source address.

  — If DHCPv6 cannot be used, the IPv6 host uses stateless autoconfiguration to configure its IPv6 address using the prefix advertised in the router advertisement messages.

- If the local link has no IPv6 router, the IPv6 host (a node with DHCPv6 client support only) sends a DHCPv6 solicit message to the all-DHCPv6-agents multicast address (FF02::1:2) on the local link using its link-local address (FE80::/10) as the source address.

# IPv6 Security

Security within the IPv6 protocol is based on the IPSec protocol. IPSec is available in both IPv4 and IPv6. As described in RFC 2460, a full implementation of IPv6 includes insertions of Authentication Headers (AH) and Encapsulating Security Payload (ESP) extension headers. Having IPSec on any IPv6 node should allow end-to-end security sessions.

For routers with IPv6 support, IPSec can be used in different areas:

- **OSPFv3**—The Open Shortest Path First version 3 protocol (OSPFv3) uses AH and ESP extension headers as an authentication mechanism instead of the variety of authentication schemes and procedures defined in OSPFv2.

- **Mobile IPv6**—This protocol specification is an IETF draft status proposed to use IPSec for binding update authentication.

- **Tunnels**—IPSec tunnels can be configured between sites (IPv6 routers) instead of having every host use IPSec.

- **Network management**—IPSec can be used to secure router access for network management.

IPSec is defined in two separate IPv6 extension headers that can be chained together within the same IPv6 packet. This section presents an overview of the IPv6 Authentication Header and the Encapsulating Security Payload extension header.

## IPSec Authentication Header (AH)

The first IPSec header is the Authentication Header (AH). It provides integrity, authentication of the source node, and protection against replay. IPSec AH protects the integrity of most of the IPv6 header fields, except those that change over the path, such as the Hop Limit field. Moreover, IPSec AH authenticates the source through a signature-based algorithm.

The key difference between IPv4 and IPv6 security is the fact that IPSec is mandatory for IPv6, as described in RFC 2460. This means that all end-to-end IP communications could be secured if there is enough keying infrastructure to do on a large-scale basis.

## IPSec Encapsulating Security Payload (ESP)

The second IPSec header is the Encapsulating Security Payload (ESP) header. This header provides confidentiality, authentication of the source node, integrity of the inner packet, and protection against replay.

# Mobile IP

The *Mobile IP protocol* is designed to allow network nodes to maintain their IP connectivity with remote nodes while moving from one point of attachment to another. The Mobile IP protocol is mostly designed for wireless devices, although it can be used with any wired technology.

## Mobile IPv6

The Mobile IPv6 protocol has important design changes compared to Mobile IPv4:

- **Foreign agent**—Mobile IPv6 has no foreign agent, because each mobile IPv6 node can handle the mobility. However, the home agent is still mandatory in IPv6.

- **Internet nodes**—Any compliant IPv6 node has mobility support built in. This is not the case in IPv4, because the Mobile IPv4 support is an addition to the IPv4 protocol.

- **Registration**—UDP on port 434, used in IPv4 to exchange messages between the mobile nodes and the agents, is replaced by the use of the Destination extension header in IPv6.

- **Packet delivery**—The first packet delivered to the mobile node by its home agent is sent through an IPv6-in-IPv6 tunnel. But subsequent packets exchanged between the mobile node and any Internet nodes use the Routing extension header. This is much more efficient for the exchange of packets between the mobile and correspondent nodes than passing all packets through the home agent, such with Mobile IPv4.

In conclusion, Mobile IPv6 is much more efficient than Mobile IPv4 in many aspects.

---

**NOTE**     The Mobile IPv6 specification work is not yet complete at the IETF.

---

# Summary

In this chapter, you learned about the new Internet Control Message Protocol for IPv6 (ICMPv6) messages; the use of path Maximum Transmission Unit discovery (PMTUD) with IPv6; and the mechanisms within Neighbor Discovery Protocol (NDP), such as the replacement of Address Resolution Protocol (ARP) in IPv4, stateless autoconfiguration, prefix advertisement, duplicate address detection (DAD), and prefix renumbering. You now understand the impact of IPv6 on popular protocols such as Domain Name System (DNS), Dynamic Host Configuration Protocol (DHCP), IPSec Authentication Header (AH), IPSec Encapsulating Security Payload (ESP), and Mobile IP.

Then you read about managing neighbor entries in the router's neighbor discovery table, tuning NDP messages, enabling and tuning prefix advertisements on the router's network interface,

disabling router advertisements on the interface when necessary, and renumbering an advertised IPv6 prefix. You also learned about creating a host table for IPv6 access, defining standard
and extended IPv6 ACLs, and enabling them on a router's interfaces. Finally, you saw diagnostic and management tools with IPv6 support such as ping, Telnet, traceroute, SSH, and TFTP
on the Cisco router.

# Configuration Exercise: Managing Prefixes on the IPv6 Network Using Cisco Routers

Complete the following exercises to advertise IPv6 prefixes on a network to practice the skills
you learned in this chapter.

## Objectives

In the following exercises, you will complete these tasks:

**1**  Enable prefix advertisement with a site-local prefix.

**2**  Verify prefix advertisement parameters.

**3**  Change the default prefix advertisement parameters.

**4**  Display NDP debug messages.

**5**  Renumber a site-local prefix with a global unicast prefix.

**6**  Deprecate a prefix.

## Network Architecture for Task 1

Figure 3-15 shows the network topology used for Task 1. The router must be configured to
advertise site-local prefixes on network interfaces FastEthernet 0/0 and FastEthernet 0/1.

**Figure 3-15**  *NetworkTopologyforAdvertisingSite-LocalPrefixesonFastEthernet0/0andFastEthernet0/1Interfaces*

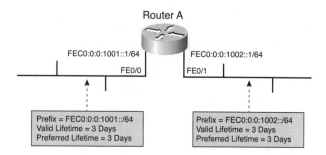

Router A

FEC0:0:0:1001::1/64          FEC0:0:0:1002::1/64

FE0/0          FE0/1

Prefix = FEC0:0:0:1001::/64
Valid Lifetime = 3 Days
Preferred Lifetime = 3 Days

Prefix = FEC0:0:0:1002::/64
Valid Lifetime = 3 Days
Preferred Lifetime = 3 Days

## Command List

In this configuration exercise you will use the commands shown in Table 3-17. Refer to this list during the exercise.

**Table 3-17** *Configuration Exercise Command List*

| Command | Description |
|---------|-------------|
| **clock** *set hh:mm:ss day month year* | Sets the date. |
| **copy running-config startup-config** | Saves the current configuration to NVRAM. |
| **copy tftp flash** | Installs a new IOS on a router using a TFTP server. |
| **debug ipv6 nd** | Enables debug mode for neighbor discovery messages. |
| **interface** *interface-type interface-number* | Specifies an interface type and interface number. |
| **ipv6 address** *ipv6-address/prefix-length* | Configures an IPv6 static address with a prefix length. |
| **ipv6 nd prefix** ipv6-*prefix/prefix-length* [**at** *valid-date preferred-date* ] | Automatically decreases the valid and preferred dates of a specified prefix. |
| **ipv6 nd prefix** ipv6-*prefix/prefix-length* [*valid-lifetime preferred-lifetime* ] | Changes the valid and preferred lifetimes of a specified prefix. |
| **ipv6 nd suppress-ra** | Suppresses router advertisement on a specific interface. |
| **ipv6 nd ra-interval** *number* | Defines the router advertisement interval. |
| **show ipv6** | Displays general information about IPv6 support on a router. |
| **show ipv6 interface** *interface-type interface-number* **prefix** | Displays parameters of the prefix advertised to an interface. |
| **undebug ipv6 nd** | Disables debug mode for neighbor discovery messages. |

## Task 1: Enable Router Advertisement with Site-Local Prefixes

Complete the following steps:

**Step 1**  Enter the command to enable prefix advertisement on interface FastEthernet 0/0 of Router A using the prefix FEC0:0:0:1001::/64. To perform this task, you need to configure the IPv6 address FEC0:0:1001::1 with the prefix length /64 on FastEthernet 0/0. What command will you use?

```
RouterA#conf t
RouterA(config)#int fastEthernet 0/0
RouterA(config-if)#ipv6 address fec0:0:0:1001::1/64
RouterA(config-if)#exit
```

**Step 2**    Enter the command to enable prefix advertisement on interface FastEthernet
0/1 of Router A using the prefix FEC0:0:0:1002::/64. To perform this task,
you need to configure the IPv6 address FEC0:0:1002::1 with the prefix length
/64 on the FastEthernet 0/1. What command will you use?

```
RouterA#conf t
RouterA(config)#int fastEthernet 0/1
RouterA(config-if)#ipv6 address fec0:0:0:1002::1/64
RouterA(config-if)#exit
```

**Step 3**    Display the prefix advertisement parameters for both interfaces. What
command is used to get parameters of the prefix advertised by the router?

```
RouterA#show ipv6 interface fastEthernet 0/0 prefix
IPv6 Prefix Advertisements FastEthernet0/0
Codes: A - Address, P - Prefix-Advertisement, O - Pool
       X - Proxy RA, U - Per-user prefix, D - Default
       N - Not advertised, C - Calendar

AD  FEC0:0:0:1001::/64 [LA] valid lifetime 2592000 preferred lifetime 604800
RouterA#show ipv6 interface fastEthernet 0/1 prefix
IPv6 Prefix Advertisements FastEthernet0/1
Codes: A - Address, P - Prefix-Advertisement, O - Pool
       X - Proxy RA, U - Per-user prefix, D - Default
       N - Not advertised, C - Calendar

AD  FEC0:0:0:1002::/64 [LA] valid lifetime 2592000 preferred lifetime 604800
```

**Step 4**    Change the valid and preferred lifetimes to a value of three days. What
command will you use to change these parameters on each interface?

```
RouterA(config)#int fast
RouterA(config)#int fastEthernet 0/0
RouterA(config-if)#ipv6 nd prefix fec0:0:0:1001::/64 259200 259200
RouterA(config-if)#int fast
RouterA(config-if)#int fastethernet 0/1
RouterA(config-if)#ipv6 nd prefix fec0:0:0:1002::/64 259200 259200
RouterA(config-if)#exit
```

**Step 5**    Display the new prefix advertisement parameters on each interface.

```
RouterA#show ipv6 interface fastethernet 0/0 prefix
IPv6 Prefix Advertisements FastEthernet0/0
Codes: A - Address, P - Prefix-Advertisement, O - Pool
       X - Proxy RA, U - Per-user prefix, D - Default
       N - Not advertised, C - Calendar

AP  FEC0:0:0:1001::/64 [LA] valid lifetime 259200 preferred lifetime 259200
RouterA#show ipv6 interface fastethernet 0/1 prefix
IPv6 Prefix Advertisements FastEthernet0/1
Codes: A - Address, P - Prefix-Advertisement, O - Pool
```

```
          X - Proxy RA, U - Per-user prefix, D - Default
          N - Not advertised, C - Calendar

AP  FEC0:0:0:1002::/64 [LA] valid lifetime 259200 preferred lifetime 259200
```

**Step 6** Enable debugging mode for NDP to display router advertisement messages on interface FastEthernet 0/1.

```
RouterA#debug ipv6 nd
ICMP Neighbor Discovery events debugging is on
RouterA#
02:29:33: ICMPv6-ND: Sending RA to FF02::1 on FastEthernet0/0
02:29:33: ICMPv6-ND:     prefix = FEC0:0:0:1001::/64 onlink autoconfig
02:29:33: ICMPv6-ND:         259200/259200 (valid/preferred)
02:32:53: ICMPv6-ND: Sending RA to FF02::1 on FastEthernet0/0
02:32:53: ICMPv6-ND:     prefix = FEC0:0:0:1001::/64 onlink autoconfig
02:32:53: ICMPv6-ND:         259200/259200 (valid/preferred)
RouterA#undebug ipv6 nd
ICMP Neighbor Discovery events debugging is off
RouterA#
```

**Step 7** Change the default router advertisement interval to 5 seconds. The default router advertisement interval is 200 seconds. What is the command to change the router advertisement interval?

```
RouterA#conf t
RouterA(config)#int fastEthernet 0/0
RouterA(config-if)#ipv6 nd ra-interval 5
RouterA(config-if)#exit
RouterA(config)#exit
RouterA#debug ipv6 nd
ICMP Neighbor Discovery events debugging is on
RouterA#
02:37:21: ICMPv6-ND: Sending RA to FF02::1 on FastEthernet0/0
02:37:21: ICMPv6-ND:     prefix = FEC0:0:0:1001::/64 onlink autoconfig
02:37:21: ICMPv6-ND:         259200/259200 (valid/preferred)
02:37:25: ICMPv6-ND: Sending RA to FF02::1 on FastEthernet0/0
02:37:25: ICMPv6-ND:     prefix = FEC0:0:0:1001::/64 onlink autoconfig
02:37:25: ICMPv6-ND:         259200/259200 (valid/preferred)
02:37:30: ICMPv6-ND: Sending RA to FF02::1 on FastEthernet0/0
02:37:30: ICMPv6-ND:     prefix = FEC0:0:0:1001::/64 onlink autoconfig
02:37:30: ICMPv6-ND:         259200/259200 (valid/preferred)undebug ip
02:37:34: ICMPv6-ND: Sending RA to FF02::1 on FastEthernet0/0
02:37:34: ICMPv6-ND:     prefix = FEC0:0:0:1001::/64 onlink autoconfig
02:37:34: ICMPv6-ND:         259200/259200 (valid/preferred)v6 nd
ICMP Neighbor Discovery events debugging is off
```

**Step 8** Save the current configuration to NVRAM.

```
RouterA#copy run start
Destination filename [startup-config]?
Building configuration...
```

## Network Architecture for Task 2

Figure 3-16 presents the network topology used for Task 2. This site received an aggregatable global unicast prefix from its provider. The site should use this prefix instead of the site-local prefix. Therefore, Router A must be configured to deprecate the prefix FEC0:0:0:1001::1/64 within 30 minutes and advertise the new prefix 2001:420:0:1::/64 on interface FastEthernet 0/0. However, on interface FastEthernet 0/1, the prefix FEC0:0:0:1002::1/64 must be completely suppressed.

**Figure 3-16**  *Advertising, Depreciating, and Suppressing Prefixes on a Router*

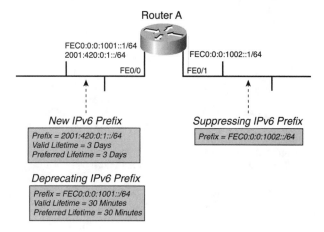

## Task 2: Renumber Site-Local Prefixes with Aggregatable Global Unicast Prefixes

Complete the following steps:

**Step 1**    Enter the command to deprecate the prefix FEC0:0:0:1001::/64 on interface FastEthernet 0/0. Begin by setting valid and preferred lifetimes to the value of 30 minutes. What command will you use?

```
RouterA#conf t
RouterA(config)#int fastEthernet 0/0
RouterA(config-if)#ipv6 nd prefix fec0:0:0:1001::/64 1800 1800
RouterA(config-if)#exit
RouterA(config)#exit
```

**Step 2**    Display the prefix advertisement parameters of the FastEthernet 0/0 interface to be sure that the valid and preferred lifetimes are set to 30 minutes. What command is used to get parameters of the prefix advertised on that interface?

```
RouterA#show ipv6 interface fastethernet 0/0 prefix
IPv6 Prefix Advertisements FastEthernet0/0
Codes: A - Address, P - Prefix-Advertisement, O - Pool
```

```
         X - Proxy RA, U - Per-user prefix, D - Default
         N - Not advertised, C - Calendar
AP  FEC0:0:0:1001::/64 [LA] valid lifetime 1800 preferred lifetime 1800
```

**Step 3**   Enter the command to advertise the new prefix 2001:420:0:1::/64 on
         interface FastEthernet 0/0 with valid and preferred lifetimes of three days.
         What commands will you use to accomplish this?

```
RouterA#conf t
RouterA(config)#int fastEthernet 0/0
RouterA(config-if)#ipv6 address 2001:0:420:1::/64
RouterA(config-if)#ipv6 nd prefix 2001:0:420:1::/64 259200 259200
RouterA(config-if)#exit
RouterA(config)#exit
```

**Step 4**   Display the prefix advertisement parameters of the FastEthernet 0/0
         interface.

```
RouterA#show ipv6 interface fastethernet 0/0 prefix
IPv6 Prefix Advertisements FastEthernet0/0
Codes: A - Address, P - Prefix-Advertisement, O - Pool
       X - Proxy RA, U - Per-user prefix, D - Default
       N - Not advertised, C - Calendar
AP  2001:0:420:1::/64 [LA] valid lifetime 259200 preferred lifetime 259200
AP  FEC0:0:0:1001::/64 [LA] valid lifetime 1800 preferred lifetime 1800
```

**Step 5**   Enter the command to suppress the advertisement of the prefix
         FEC0:0:0:1002::/64 on interface FastEthernet 0/1. What command will you
         use?

```
RouterA#conf t
RouterA(config)#int fastEthernet 0/1
RouterA(config-if)#ipv6 nd suppress-ra
RouterA(config-if)#exit
RouterA(config)#exit
```

**Step 6**   Enable debugging mode for NDP to display router advertisement messages
         of both IPv6 prefixes.

```
RouterA#debug ipv6 nd
ICMP Neighbor Discovery events debugging is on
01:30:36: ICMPv6-ND: Sending RA to FF02::1 on FastEthernet0/0
01:30:36: ICMPv6-ND:     prefix = 2001:0:420:1::/64 onlink autoconfig
01:30:36: ICMPv6-ND:         259200/259200 (valid/preferred)
01:30:36: ICMPv6-ND:     prefix = FEC0:0:0:1001::/64 onlink autoconfig
01:30:36: ICMPv6-ND:         1800/1800 (valid/preferred)
01:30:41: ICMPv6-ND: Sending RA to FF02::1 on FastEthernet0/0
01:30:41: ICMPv6-ND:     prefix = 2001:0:420:1::/64 onlink autoconfig
01:30:41: ICMPv6-ND:         259200/259200 (valid/preferred)
01:30:41: ICMPv6-ND:     prefix = FEC0:0:0:1001::/64 onlink autoconfig
```

**Step 7**   Set the date in your router and deprecate the advertisement of the site-local prefix FEC0:0:0:1001::/64 on the interface FastEthernet 0/0 at a specific date. Deprecate the site-local prefix 5 hours after the current date, and use the same valid date and preferred date. What command will you use?

```
RouterA#clock set 12:00:00 15 March 2003
RouterA(config)#interface FastEthernet 0/0
RouterA(config-if)#ipv6 nd prefix fec0:0:0:1001::/64 at Mar 15 2003 17:00
   Mar 15 17:00
RouterA(config-if)#exit
```

**Step 8**   Save the current configuration to NVRAM.

```
RouterA#copy run start
Destination filename [startup-config]?
Building configuration...
```

# Review Questions

Answer the following questions, and then refer to Appendix B, "Answers to Review Questions," for the answers.

**1**   Complete the following table by specifying the name of each ICMPv6 message type.

| ICMPv6 Type | Name of Message |
| --- | --- |
| Type 133 | |
| Type 134 | |
| Type 135 | |
| Type 136 | |
| Type 137 | |

**2**   Fill in the following table by specifying which ICMPv6 message types are used for each NDP mechanism.

| Mechanism | Type 133 | Type 134 | Type 135 | Type 136 | Type 137 |
| --- | --- | --- | --- | --- | --- |
| Replacement of ARP | | | | | |
| Prefix advertisement | | | | | |
| DAD | | | | | |
| Prefix renumbering | | | | | |
| Router redirection | | | | | |

**3** What is the goal of stateless autoconfiguration?

**4** List the main information carried by the router advertisement message when a prefix is advertised.

**5** What command displays the prefix advertisement parameters on an interface?

**6** What command overrides the default prefix advertisement parameters on an interface?

**7** What is duplicate address detection (DAD)?

**8** Fill in the following table with the type of multicast address used for each NDP mechanism listed.

| Mechanism | Multicast Address |
|---|---|
| Replacement of ARP | |
| Prefix advertisement | |
| DAD | |
| Prefix renumbering | |
| Router redirection | |

**9** What new DNS record was added for IPv6?

**10** What are the implicit rules in an extended IPv6 ACL?

**11** What commands and tools are available in IOS IPv6 to diagnose problems and manage a router?

# References

RFC 768, *User Datagram Protocol,* J. Postel, IETF, www.ietf.org/rfc/rfc768.txt, August 1980

RFC 791, *Internet Protocol, DARPA Internet Program, Protocol Specification,* USC, IETF, www.ietf.org/rfc/rfc791.txt, September 1981

RFC 792, *Internet Control Message Protocol,* J. Postel, IETF, www.ietf.org/rfc/rfc792.txt, September 1981

RFC 793, *Transmission Control Protocol,* DARPA Internet Program, IETF, www.ietf.org/rfc/rfc793.txt, September 1981

RFC 1191, *Path MTU Discovery,* J. Mogul, S. Deering, IETF, www.ietf.org/rfc/rfc1191.txt, November 1990

RFC 1981, *Path MTU Discovery for IP version 6,* J. McCann et al., IETF, www.ietf.org/rfc/rfc1981.txt, August 1996

RFC 2002, *IP Mobility Support,* C. Perkins, IETF, www.ietf.org/rfc/rfc2002.txt, October 1996

RFC 2373, *IP Version 6 Addressing Architecture,* R. Hinden, S. Deering, IETF, www.ietf.org/rfc/rfc2373.txt, July 1998

RFC 2374, *An IPv6 Aggregatable Global Unicast Address Format,* R. Hinden, S. Deering, M. O'Dell, IETF, www.ietf.org/rfc/rfc2374.txt, July 1998

RFC 2460, *Internet Protocol, Version 6 (IPv6) Specification,* S. Deering, R. Hinden, IETF, www.ietf.org/rfc/rfc2460.txt, December 1998

RFC 2461, *Neighbor Discovery for IP Version 6 (IPv6),* T. Narten, E. Normark, W. Simpson, IETF, www.ietf.org/rfc/rfc2461.txt, December 1998

RFC 2462, *IPv6 Stateless Address Autoconfiguration,* S. Thomson, T. Narten, IETF, www.ietf.org/rfc/rfc2462.txt, December 1998

RFC 2463, *Internet Control Message Protocol (ICMPv6) for the Internet Protocol version 6 (IPv6),* A. Conta, S. Deering, IETF, www.ietf.org/rfc/rfc2463.txt, December 1998

RFC 2474, *Definition of the Differentiated Services Field (DS Field) in the IPv4 and IPv6 Headers,* K. Nichols, S. Blake et al., IETF, www.ietf.org/rfc/rfc2474.txt, December 1998

RFC 2672, *Non-Terminal DNS Name Redirection,* M. Crawford, IETF, www.ietf.org/rfc/rfc2672.txt, August 1999

RFC 2673, *Binary Labels in the Domain Name System,* M. Crawford, IETF, www.ietf.org/rfc/rfc2673.txt, August 1999

RFC 2675, *IPv6 Jumbograms,* D. Borman, S. Deering, R. Hinden, IETF, www.ietf.org/rfc/rfc2675.txt, August 1999

RFC 2711, *IPv6 Router Alert Option,* C. Partridge, A. Jackson, IETF, www.ietf.org/rfc/rfc2711.txt, October 1999

RFC 2874, *DNS Extensions to Support IPv6 Address Aggregation and Renumbering*, M. Crawford, C. Huitema, www.ietf.org/rfc/rfc2874.txt, July 2000

RFC 2894, *Router Renumbering for IPv6*, M. Crawford, IETF, www.ietf.org/rfc/rfc2894.txt, August 2000

RFC 3152, *Delegation of IP6.ARPA,* R. Bush, IETF, www.ietf.org/rfc/rfc3152.txt, August 2002

RFC 3177, *IAB/IESG Recommendations on IPv6 Address Allocations to Sites,* IAB, IETF, www.ietf.org/rfc/rfc3177.txt, September 2001

"Computers in the future may weigh no more than one and one half tons."

*Popular Mechanics,* 1949

# CHAPTER 4

# Routing on IPv6

After reading this chapter, you will understand the main differences between the routing protocols that are deployed over IPv6 networks. The IPv6 version of the interdomain routing protocol Border Gateway Protocol (BGP-4) and intradomain routing protocols such as Routing Information Protocol (RIP), integrated Intermediate System-to-Intermediate System (IS-IS), and Open Shortest Path First (OSPF) are similar to their equivalents in IPv4.

This chapter's main goal is to present an overview of the updates and changes applied on these routing protocols to support IPv6 rather than describe in detail each routing protocol's complete specifications, mechanisms, and applicability.

Throughout this chapter are configurations and examples of IPv6-supported routing protocols using the Cisco IOS Software technology to show you how to deploy them in your networks. More specifically, the examples show you how to configure, enable, and manage BGP, RIP, IS-IS, and OSPF with IPv6 support using Cisco IOS Software technology.

Finally, with the configuration exercise, you can practice the commands you learn in this chapter and configure some of the routing protocols that are supported by IPv6.

## Introduction to Routing with IPv6

The IPv6 routing protocols still use the longest-match prefix as the routing algorithm for route selection, as their equivalents did in IPv4. However, because the IPv6 protocols are defined as a new family of protocols, the IPv6 routing table is handled and managed separately from the IPv4 routing table when both protocols are enabled simultaneously on a router.

The following sections cover these topics:

- **IPv6 routing table on the router**—This section briefly describes the commands used to display the IPv6 routing table in the Cisco IOS Software technology.

- **Administrative distances of the routing protocols**—The administrative distances of the IPv6-supported routing protocols remain unchanged in comparison with their equivalents in IPv4.

## Displaying the IPv6 Routing Table

The most important task of any intermediary router in a network receiving IP datagrams is determining the best path to the destination. Then the intermediary router forwards each IP packet on the next network segment to reach another intermediary router that repeats the same process up to the final destination. To determine the best path during the forwarding process, the routers use a routing table that points out the next network segment to use. The routing table contains entries either defined dynamically through routing protocols or statically configured by network administrators.

As soon as the **ipv6 unicast-routing** command is enabled in the Cisco IOS Software, as discussed in Chapter 2, "IPv6 Addressing," the router can forward IPv6 packets between its interfaces using the IPv6 routing table.

**show ipv6 route** is a new command that displays the IPv6 routing table in the Cisco IOS Software that contains the list of destination network routes with the mask, the output interface, the type of route (C for connected, S for static, and so on), and each route's administrative distance. This command is equivalent to the well-known **show ip route** command in IPv4.

Example 4-1 shows the **show ipv6 route** command. This example shows that several aggregatable global unicast routes, such as 2001:410:ffff:1::/64, 2002:410:ffff:2::/64, and 3ffe:b00:ffff:1::/64, are pointing out the router's interfaces. The routes are related to the link-local prefix FE80::/10 and the multicast prefix FF00::/10, which also appear in the routing table. These routes are automatically included by the router in the IPv6 routing table. Finally, the last entry in the routing table displays a default IPv6 route (::/0) added statically by the network administrator.

**Example 4-1** *Displaying IPv6 Routes Using the* **show ipv6 route** *Command*

```
RouterA#show ipv6 route
IPv6 Routing Table - 11 entries
Codes: C - Connected, L - Local, S - Static, R - RIP, B - BGP
       U - Per-user Static route
       I1 - ISIS L1, I2 - ISIS L2, IA - ISIS interarea
L   2001:410:FFFF:1::1/128 [0/0]
     via ::, Ethernet1
C   2001:410:FFFF:1::/64 [0/0]
     via ::, Ethernet1
L   2001:410:FFFF:2::1/128 [0/0]
     via ::, Ethernet0
C   2001:410:FFFF:2::/64 [0/0]
     via ::, Ethernet0
L   3FFE:B00:FFFF:1::1/128 [0/0]
     via ::, Ethernet1
C   3FFE:B00:FFFF:1::/64 [0/0]
     via ::, Ethernet1
L   FE80::/10 [0/0]
     via ::, Null0
L   FF00::/8 [0/0]
     via ::, Null0
S   ::/0 [1/0]
     via fe80::250:3eff:fee4:4c01 , Ethernet1
```

## Administrative Distances

*Administrative distance* is a value representing a routing protocol's reliability. Over time, routing protocols were prioritized from the most-reliable to the least-reliable using the administrative distance values. During the forwarding process, the routers use the administrative distance to select the best path when several routes using different routing protocols point to the same destination network. The lower the administrative distance value, the more prioritized the route for the router. The administrative distances of IPv6-supported routing protocols are unchanged from the equivalent protocols in IPv4. Table 4-1 shows the administrative distances of each IPv6 routing protocol supported in the Cisco IOS Software technology.

**Table 4-1**    *Administrative Distances of IPv6 Routing Protocols*

| Routing Protocol | Administrative Distance (Default) |
|---|---|
| Connected interface | 0 |
| Static route (toward the interface) | 0 |
| Static route (toward the next hop) | 1 |
| External BGP (eBGP) | 20 |
| OSPF | 110 |
| IS-IS | 115 |
| RIP | 120 |
| Internal BGP (iBGP) | 200 |

**NOTE**    Table 4-1 shows the routing protocols with IPv6 support that currently are supported in the Cisco IOS Software. Other IPv4 routing protocols such as Interior Gateway Routing Protocol (IGRP), internal Enhanced Interior Gateway Routing Protocol (EIGRP), external Exterior Gateway Protocol (EGP), and External EIGRP, are not listed in this table. Only EIGRP is considered by Cisco as a potential candidate for an IPv6 implementation.

# Static IPv6 Routes

This section describes the commands used to configure static IPv6 routes. As with IPv4, the static IPv6 routes are added manually in the router's configuration. The syntax for IPv6 static configurations differs from the equivalent commands in IPv4.

## Configuring Static IPv6 Routes

The **ipv6 route** command adds static IPv6 routes. This command is equivalent to the **ip route** command in IPv4. As soon as the destination IPv6 network has been specified, the route must point to either a *next-hop* IPv6 address or a router's *interface*, as shown in the following:

```
Router(config)#ipv6 route ipv6-prefix/prefix-length {next-hop | interface}
   [distance]
```

The *ipv6-prefix* parameter is the destination IPv6 network. The *prefix-length* is the length of the IPv6 prefix given. The *next-hop* is an IPv6 address used to reach the destination IPv6 network. The *interface* can be used to direct the static route out of the interface such as serial links or tunnels. The *distance* is an optional parameter that sets the administrative distance. By default, the administrative distance of a static route is 1.

| | |
|---|---|
| **NOTE** | It is not recommended in the IPv6 specifications to use an aggregatable global unicast or site-local address as a next-hop address. If you do, Internet Control Message Protocol for IPv6 (ICMPv6) redirection messages (Type 137) will not work. Router redirection is discussed in detail in Chapter 3, "IPv6 in Depth." The next-hop address has to be a link-local address. However, when you configure a link-local address as the next hop, you must identify in the configuration the corresponding network interface on the router. In the Cisco IOS Software technology, the recommended syntax for the **ipv6 route** command in this situation is **ipv6 route** *ipv6-prefix/prefix-length interface link-local-address*. |

The destination IPv6 network 2001:410:ffff::/48 is reached through the next-hop address fe80::250:3eff:fee4:4c01 using the corresponding network interface ethernet0, as shown in the following:

```
Router(config)#ipv6 route 2001:410:ffff::/48 ethernet0 fe80::250:3eff:fee4:4c01
```

The destination IPv6 network 3ffe::/16 is reached through the Tunnel0 interface:

```
Router(config)#ipv6 route 3ffe::/16 Tunnel0
```

The following is a default IPv6 route configuration that points to the next-hop address fe80::250:3eff:fee4:4c01 using the corresponding network interface ethernet1:

```
Router(config)#ipv6 route ::/0 ethernet1 fe80::250:3eff:fee4:4c01
```

| | |
|---|---|
| **NOTE** | The **ipv6 route ::/0** *interface next-hop* command is equivalent to the **ip route 0.0.0.0 0.0.0.0** *next-hop* command in IPv4. The destination ::/0 means any IPv6 address. |

The **ipv6 route** command is enabled on a global basis.

## Displaying IPv6 Routes

The command **show ipv6 route** displays the current IPv6 routing table in the router. This command is equivalent to the **show ip route** command in IPv4. As in IPv4, it is possible to display a specific type of IPv6 route such as **connected**, **local**, **static**, **rip**, **bgp**, **isis**, or **ospf**. However, when an IPv6 prefix is specified with the **show ipv6 route** command, a single IPv6 route is displayed. The syntax for this command is as follows:

```
Router#show ipv6 route [connected | local | static | rip | bgp | isis | ospf] |
  [ipv6-prefix/prefix-length | ipv6-address]
```

If the *ipv6-prefix/prefix-length* parameter is specified, a single route is displayed. The *ipv6-address* is optional and can display routing information for a specific IPv6 address.

---

**NOTE**     When you configure an IPv6 address on an interface using the **ipv6 address** command, as discussed in Chapter 2, two entries are inserted into the IPv6 routing table. The first entry is the full 128-bit interface address itself, so this first entry is marked with an L for a local route. The second entry is the prefix entry with the appropriate mask, so this second entry is marked with a C for a connected route. However, if you configure an IPv6 address with 128-bit as the *prefix-length,* you get only a single entry, flagged as both L for local route and C for connected route. The local route simply indicates an interface address.

---

# EGP Protocols for IPv6

The first family of routing protocols presented in this chapter is related to the EGPs. EGPs are used for peering between autonomous systems (ASs). This section presents only one EGP, the well-known Border Gateway Protocol 4 (BGP-4). BGP-4 is the *de facto* EGP used in interdomains by providers and organizations to exchange routing information between ASs.

---

**NOTE**     The content of this chapter is organized in order from the most-prominent routing protocols to the least-prominent. BGP-4 with IPv6 support has been available in the Cisco IOS Software technology since 1995, and it has been used on the 6bone for six years. Thus, BGP-4 is considered the most prominent IPv6 routing protocol used on the 6bone and on the IPv6 Internet today.

---

## Introduction to BGP-4

BGP-4 is a path vector routing protocol that uses TCP (Transmission Control Protocol) on port 179 to establish connections with other BGP-4 routers called *BGP neighbors*. The path vector information carried by BGP-4 between neighbors is called *attributes*.

BGP-4 exchanges network reachability information with BGP neighbors using update messages. These messages are incremental: Only updates are exchanged between BGP neighbors. If a route is added or removed, an update message is sent to inform the BGP neighbors.

During their operation on a wide network, BGP-4 routers have multiple AS paths for reaching a particular network destination. Thus, the BGP-4 algorithm is designed to determine the best AS path needed to reach a particular network among lists of feasible AS paths. BGP AS path determination is based on a list of attributes. BGP-4 was designed to be a highly scalable routing protocol for huge networks such as the global Internet.

---

**NOTE**    This chapter provides only an overview of the routing protocols. If you want to learn more about BGP-4, read a reference book such as *Internet Routing Architectures* by Bassam Halabi (Cisco Press). The Cisco website also provides plenty of information regarding BGP-4 and how to manage it over wide deployments of IP networks.

---

# BGP4+ for IPv6

RFC 1771, *A Border Gateway Protocol 4 (BGP-4),* defines the BGP-4 standard. BGP-4 is mainly implemented and used today in Cisco router implementations, but it can carry routing information only for the IPv4 protocol.

An enhanced version called BGP4+, also known as *multiprotocol BGP,* extends the BGP-4 specifications to include multiple protocol extensions for new address families such as IPv6, IPX, and VPN. Therefore, BGP4+ can carry routing information for IPv6 and other protocols, including IPv4. RFC 2858, *Multiprotocol Extensions for BGP-4,* and RFC 2545, *Use of BGP-4 Multiprotocol Extensions for IPv6 Inter-Domain Routing,* define the attributes that were updated to handle IPv6 addresses with BGP4+.

Here are the attributes that are updated in the BGP-4 specifications to support IPv6:

- **NEXT_HOP**—This multiprotocol attribute defines the IP address of the border router that should be used as the next hop to the destinations listed. The NEXT_HOP attribute in BGP4+ is expressed as an IPv6 address. This attribute can contain either one aggregatable global unicast IPv6 address or an aggregatable global unicast IPv6 address *and* the next hop's link-local IPv6 address.

    — **Aggregatable global unicast IPv6 address**—As mentioned in Chapter 2, aggregatable global unicast addresses are based on the prefix 2000::/3. For example, a NEXT_HOP value would be 2001:410:ffff:1::1 for an aggregatable global unicast IPv6 address.

    — **Link-local IPv6 address**—As discussed in Chapter 2, link-local addresses are based on the unicast prefix fe80::/10. A link-local address may be used as a NEXT_HOP value with BGP4+ if there is local reachability with the BGP neighbor (adjacency routers). For example, for a NEXT_HOP value to reach an adjacent BGP4+ router using its link-local address, the link-local address would be something such as fe80::200:abcd:af56:fefc. Detailed information on using a link-local address with BGP4+ is presented later in this chapter.

- **NLRI**—NLRI (network layer reachability information) is a set of destinations. A *destination* is defined in BGP-4 as a network prefix with a prefix length value. This attribute can now be expressed as an IPv6 prefix with BGP4+. For example, the NLRI for the network prefix 2001:410:ffff::/48 is 2001:410:ffff::/48.

---

**NOTE**    The complete specification of BGP-4 is beyond the scope of this book. As noted earlier, these specifications are the updates added to the BGP-4 specifications for IPv6. Refer to RFC 1771, *A Border Gateway Protocol 4 (BGP-4),* for the complete BGP-4 specification.

---

## Enabling BGP4+ for IPv6 on Cisco

Since 1995, the 6bone has been using the BGP4+ routing protocol to exchange IPv6 routing information between pseudo-TLA (Top-Level Aggregator) providers for testing purposes. Moreover, almost all IPv6 router vendors and developers, including the Cisco IOS Software technology, now support a BGP4+ version with IPv6 support.

---

**NOTE**    Refer to Chapter 7, "Connecting to the IPv6 Internet," for detailed information on the 6bone and pseudo-TLA.

---

### Configuring BGP4+ for IPv6

The following steps define and configure a BGP4+ routing process on a router. After you configure the routing process, establish a BGP peer using IPv6 addresses. Follow these steps to configure BGP4+ for IPv6:

**Step 1**    Enable a BGP process on the router. To do this, specify the local autonomous system:

```
Router(config)#router bgp autonomous-system
```

For example, enable a BGP process on the router for the local AS65001:

```
Router(config)#router bgp 65001
```

**Step 2**  By default, the advertisement of routing information for the IPv4 address family is activated automatically for each session using the **neighbor [..] remote-as** command. If you use the **no bgp default ipv4-unicast** command, only the IPv6 address family is advertised in BGP updates:

```
Router(config-router)#no bgp default ipv4-unicast
```

**Step 3**  In IPv4, the local router ID parameter is automatically assigned using the highest IPv4 address configured on the router, with preference given to addresses on the loopback interface. Although IPv6 addresses are longer than IPv4 addresses, the local router ID parameter for BGP has the same size and format for both IPv4 and IPv6. The local router ID is a 32-bit number written as four octets separated by periods (dotted-decimal format). When no IPv4 is set on the router (IPv6-only router), the local router ID parameter must be defined in the BGP configuration as an IPv4 address using the **bgp router-id** *ipv4-address* command. You can use any IPv4 address as a value for the local router ID parameter:

```
Router(config-router)#bgp router-id 172.16.1.10
```

**Step 4**  Define a BGP neighbor. The *ipv6-address* is the BGP neighbor's next-hop IPv6 address. This command defines either an iBGP or eBGP neighbor:

```
Router(config-router)#neighbor ipv6-address remote-as autonomous-system
```

For example, the following command defines an eBGP neighbor using 2001:410:ffff:1::1 as the next-hop aggregatable global unicast IPv6 address and AS65002 as the AS:

```
Router(config-router)#neighbor 2001:410:ffff:1::1 remote-as 65002
```

**Step 5**  You can assign a BGP neighbor's IPv6 address to a peer group using **neighbor** *ipv6-address* **peer-group** *peer-group-name*. For example, this command assigns the 2001:410:ffff:2::1 IPv6 address of the BGP neighbor to the peer group cisco99:

```
Router(config-router)#neighbor 2001:410:ffff:2::1 peer-group cisco99
```

**Step 6**  Place the router in the address-family ipv6 configuration submode:

```
Router(config-router)#address-family ipv6 [unicast]
```

The **unicast** keyword is optional. By default, the router is placed in the unicast address family IPv6.

**Step 7**  Enable the exchange of information with the BGP neighbor. The BGP neighbor can be an IPv4 address, the name of a BGP peer group, or an IPv6 address. By default, the exchange of information with BGP neighbors is enabled for the IPv4 address family only. When the neighbor is an IPv6 address, the **neighbor [..] activate** command must be used to activate the BGP peer:

```
Router(config-router-af)#neighbor {ip-address | peer-group-name | ipv6-address}
    activate
```

For example, the following command enables the exchange of IPv6 routing information with the BGP neighbor 2001:410:ffff:1::1:

```
Router(config-router-af)#neighbor 2001:410:ffff:1::1 activate
```

**Step 8**   Specify an IPv6 prefix to announce via BGP4+ for this AS. The IPv6 prefix is entered into the BGP4+ routing table using the **network** statement:

```
Router(config-router-af)#network ipv6-prefix/prefix length
```

For example, here the prefix 2001:420:ffff::/48 is entered into the BGP table:

```
Router(config-router-af)#network 2001:420:ffff::/48
```

**Step 9**   Leave address-family ipv6 configuration mode and return to BGP router configuration mode:

```
Router(config-router-af)#exit-address-family
```

The **router bgp** command is enabled on a global basis.

---

**NOTE**   Refer to the Cisco IOS Software BGP command documentation for a complete description of the BGP configuration commands not covered in this section.

---

Figure 4-1 shows a network architecture over a native IPv6 infrastructure that uses BGP4+ as the routing protocol. Router R1 from AS65001 establishes external BGP peering (multihop eBGP configuration) with Router R3 from AS65002 through an IPv6 provider. The network prefix within AS65001 is 2001:410:ffff::/48, and AS65002 owns the prefix 3ffe:b00:ffff::/48. Router R1 is connected to the IPv6 provider using the Ethernet0 interface. It has the aggregatable global unicast IPv6 address 2001:410:ffff:1::1 assigned to this interface. A default IPv6 route points to the link-local address of the provider's router fe80::250:3eff:fea4:5f12. Router R3 is connected to the same provider on the Ethernet1 interface. It uses 3ffe:b00:ffff:2::2 as an aggregatable global unicast IPv6 address, and its default IPv6 route points to fe80::250:3eff:feb5:6023.

In this example, both aggregatable global unicast IPv6 addresses assigned to these interfaces establish multihop eBGP peering.

**Figure 4-1** *eBGP Peering Established Between Routers R1 and R3*

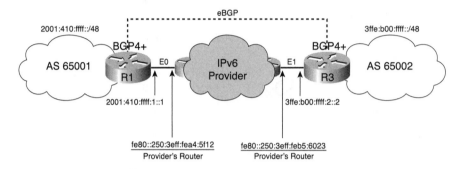

Example 4-2 reflects how multihop eBGP peering with IPv6 is established via BGP4+ configuration on Router R1 in Figure 4-1. The **ipv6 address 2001:410:ffff:1::1/64** command assigns the static IPv6 address to the interface Ethernet0. Because there is no need for router advertisement on the Ethernet0 interface, the **ipv6 nd suppress-ra** command disables advertisement on the Ethernet0 interface. For this multihop eBGP configuration, a default IPv6 route that points to the link-local address fe80::250:3eff:fea4:5f12 of the provider's router through the Ethernet0 interface is configured using the **ipv6 route ::/0** command.

**Example 4-2** *Enabling eBGP Peering in Router R1*

```
RouterR1#configure terminal
RouterR1(config)#interface e0
RouterR1(config-if)#ipv6 address 2001:410:ffff:1::1/64
RouterR1(config-if)#ipv6 nd suppress-ra
RouterR1(config-if)#exit
RouterR1(config)#ipv6 route ::/0 ethernet0 fe80::250:3eff:fea4:5f12
RouterR1(config)#router bgp 65001
RouterR1(config-router)#no bgp default ipv4-unicast
RouterR1(config-router)#bgp router-id 1.1.1.1
RouterR1(config-router)#neighbor 3ffe:b00:ffff:2::2 remote-as 65002
RouterR1(config-router)#address-family ipv6
RouterR1(config-router-af)#neighbor 3ffe:b00:ffff:2::2 activate
RouterR1(config-router-af)#exit-address-family
RouterR1(config-router)#exit
```

**NOTE**     Before establishing a multihop BGP configuration over IPv4 or IPv6, BGP routers must be able to reach each other. Therefore, Interior Gateway Protocol (IGP) routing information must be provided to the routers for this purpose. This is a simple scenario, but Examples 4-2 and 4-3 use a default IPv6 route instead of IGP to provide routing information to both routers. Detailed information about IGP with IPv6 support is presented later in this chapter.

As discussed earlier, the BGP process on Router R1 is enabled using **router bgp 65001**. Then the **no bgp default ipv4-unicast** command disables the default protocol IPv4 for this BGP configuration because the infrastructure is based only on IPv6. Next, the **bgp router-id 1.1.1.1** command defines this router's local router ID parameter. BGP peering to Router R3 is defined using the **neighbor 3ffe:b00:ffff:2::2 remote-as 65002** command. This command identifies the BGP neighbor with its next-hop IPv6 address and AS number 65002. However, to be enabled, this peering must be activated in address-family ipv6 subcommand mode using the **neighbor 3ffe:b00:ffff:2::2 activate** command.

Example 4-3 shows the BGP4+ configuration applied on Router R3. The same commands used in Example 4-2 are used in this example, except for the next-hop link-local address, the corresponding network interface of the link-local address, and the AS number. This BGP4+ configuration refers to Router R3 in Figure 4-1.

**Example 4-3**    *Enabling eBGP Peering in Router R3*

```
RouterR3#configure terminal
RouterR3(config)#interface e1
RouterR3(config-if)#ipv6 address 3ffe:b00:ffff:2::2/64
RouterR3(config-if)#ipv6 nd suppress-ra
RouterR3(config-if)#exit
RouterR3(config)#ipv6 route ::/0 ethernet1 fe80::250:3eff:feb5:6023

RouterR3(config)#router bgp 65002
RouterR3(config-router)#no bgp default ipv4-unicast
RouterR3(config-router)#bgp router-id 2.2.2.2
RouterR3(config-router)#neighbor 2001:410:ffff:1::1 remote-as 65001
RouterR3(config-router)#address-family ipv6
RouterR3(config-router-af)#neighbor 2001:410:ffff:1::1 activate
RouterR3(config-router-af)#exit-address-family
RouterR3(config-router)#exit
```

## Configuring BGP4+ for IPv6 with Prefix Filtering

Now that you know how to enable BGP peering between routers and networks based on IPv6, this section shows you how prefix lists can be used to filter BGP update messages that include IPv6 information. Since Cisco IOS Software version 12.0, prefix lists are available as an alternative to access lists for BGP-4 filtering. Prefix lists are more flexible and user-friendly than standard and extended access lists.

Configuring BGP4+ for IPv6 with prefix filtering is a two-step task:

- Defining the prefix list itself by naming the prefix list, determining the order of the statements, and configuring the actions and parameters to filter the prefixes

- Applying the prefix list within the BGP4+ configuration

The following sections discuss in detail defining and applying prefix lists for IPv6 with BGP4+.

## Defining Prefix Lists for IPv6

Prefix lists are available for the IPv6 protocol and can be used with BGP4+ to filter BGP update messages. The **ipv6 prefix-list** command defines a prefix list for IPv6. The **ipv6 prefix-list** command is equivalent to the **ip prefix-list** command in IPv4. The syntax for this command is as follows:

```
Router(config)#ipv6 prefix-list name [seq seq-value] permit | deny
   ipv6-prefix/prefix-length [ge min-value] [le max-value]
```

The *name* argument is the name of the prefix list. The parameter *seq-value* is a sequence number used with the keyword **seq** to determine the order in which the statements are used during filtering. **deny** and **permit** are the action parameters. *ipv6-prefix/prefix-length* is the IPv6 prefix and the length of the prefix to be matched. *min-value* and *max-value* define ranges of prefix length to be matched for prefixes that are more specific than the *ipv6-prefix/prefix-length* values. The operator **ge** means greater than or equal to, and the operator **le** means less than or equal to.

You permit IPv6 routes in the fec0::/10 prefix with a prefix length of up to 48 bits with the following:

```
Router(config)#ipv6 prefix-list bgpfilterin seq 5 permit FEC0::/10 le 48
```

You permit IPv6 routes in the 3ffe::/16 prefix with a prefix length of up to 32 bits with the following:

```
Router(config)#ipv6 prefix-list bgpfilterin seq 10 permit 3ffe::/16 le 32
```

The **ipv6 prefix-list** command is configured on a global basis.

## Applying Prefix Lists with BGP4+

After the IPv6 prefix list has been defined, you can apply it in the BGP4+ configuration. The IPv6 prefix list must be applied to a BGP neighbor in the address-family ipv6 subcommand mode. The syntax for this command is as follows:

```
Router(config-router)#address-family ipv6
```

This places the router in the address-family ipv6 configuration submode.

You apply an IPv6 prefix list to a BGP neighbor to filter input or output route announcements with the following:

```
Router(config-router-af)#neighbor {peer-group-name | ipv6-address} prefix-list
   prefix-list-name {in | out}
```

The *ipv6-address* argument is the neighbor's next-hop IPv6 address. Optionally, the IPv6 address can be a *peer-group-name* instead. The *prefix-list-name* argument is the name of the IPv6 prefix list defined earlier. The **in** and **out** arguments applied on the prefix list are to inbound or outbound update messages. For example, you can apply the IPv6 prefix list bgpfilterin, defined in the preceding section, to the BGP neighbor 2001:410:ffff:1::1 to inbound BGP4+ route announcements:

```
Router(config-router-af)#neighbor 2001:410:ffff:1::1 prefix-list bgpfilterin in
```

Then leave the address-family ipv6 configuration mode and return to the global BGP router configuration mode:

```
Router(config-router-af)#exit-address-family
```

The **neighbor** *ipv6-address* **prefix-list** command is applied in the address-family ipv6 subcommand mode.

Figure 4-2 shows a BGP4+ configuration using an IPv6 prefix list applied in Router R1 from AS65001. Router R1 has established eBGP peering with Router R3 from AS65002. However, the manager of AS65001 wants to advertise the prefix 2001:410::/32 to AS65002. Because AS65002 is connected to the 6bone and has potentially multiple BGP neighbors with other ASs, the network administrator wants to filter incoming BGP route announcements received from AS65002. The network administrator wants to receive prefixes of the 6bone 3ffe::/16 based on a prefix length between 16 and 24 bits. Therefore, an IPv6 prefix list is created and then applied in the BGP4+ configuration of Router R1 to enforce this filtering policy for BGP.

**Figure 4-2**    *Prefix Filtering Applied in Router R1's BGP4+ Configuration*

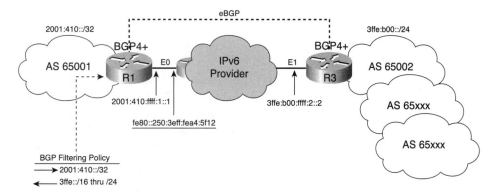

Example 4-4 shows the IPv6 prefix list configuration applied in the BGP4+ configuration of Router R1, as shown in Figure 4-2. The command **ipv6 prefix-list outbound seq 5 permit 2001:410::/32** defines the prefix of AS65001 as permitted. Then, the command **ipv6 prefix-list inbound seq 5 permit 3ffe::/16 le 24** defines the prefixes within the range 3ffe::/16 to 3ffe::/24 as permitted. In Example 4-4, these two IPv6 prefix lists are applied in the BGP4+ configuration in Router R1's address-family ipv6 subcommand mode using the **neighbor 3ffe:b00:ffff:2::2 prefix-list** command.

**Example 4-4**    *Applying IPv6 Prefix Filtering in Router R1*

```
RouterR1#configure terminal
RouterR1(config)#ipv6 prefix-list outbound seq 5 permit 2001:410::/32
RouterR1(config)#ipv6 prefix-list inbound seq 5 permit 3ffe::/16 le 24
RouterR1(config)#interface e0
```

*continues*

**Example 4-4** *Applying IPv6 Prefix Filtering in Router R1 (Continued)*

```
RouterR1(config-if)#ipv6 address 2001:410:ffff:1::1/64
RouterR1(config-if)#ipv6 nd suppress-ra
RouterR1(config-if)#exit
RouterR1(config)#ipv6 route ::/0 ethernet0 fe80::250:3eff:fea4:5f12
RouterR1(config)#router bgp 65001
RouterR1(config-router)#no bgp default ipv4-unicast
RouterR1(config-router)#bgp router-id 1.1.1.1
RouterR1(config-router)#neighbor 3ffe:b00:ffff:2::2 remote-as 65002
RouterR1(config-router)#address-family ipv6
RouterR1(config-router-af)#neighbor 3ffe:b00:ffff:2::2 activate
RouterR1(config-router-af)#neighbor 3ffe:b00:ffff:2::2 prefix-list outbound out
RouterR1(config-router-af)#neighbor 3ffe:b00:ffff:2::2 prefix-list inbound in
RouterR1(config-router-af)#exit-address-family
RouterR1(config-router)#exit
```

**NOTE**    The IPv6 prefix lists in Example 4-4 are applied only to BGP4+ updates received and sent with the BGP neighbor 3ffe:b00:ffff:2::2.

## Configuring BGP4+ for IPv6 with a Route Map

Support for IPv6 with the **route-map** command is available in the Cisco IOS Software. A route map is a kind of advanced access list that can be used in BGP-4 to modify the BGP attributes of network prefixes (routes received from a BGP neighbor and routes announced to another BGP neighbor). In a route map configuration with IPv6 for BGP4+, a **prefix list** is used with the **route-map** command to match the IPv6 network prefix on which you modify the BGP attributes.

Configuring BGP4+ for IPv6 with **route-map** consists of defining a prefix list (as discussed in the preceding section), defining the route map for IPv6, and applying the route map in the BGP4+ configuration. The following sections discuss defining a route map for IPv6 and applying it to a BGP4+ configuration.

### Defining Route Maps for IPv6

The same **route-map** command used in IPv4 creates a route map for IPv6. However, the **match** and **set** commands were enhanced to be specific to the IPv6 protocol. Moreover, this section presents only the updates added to the **route-map** command for IPv6. Refer to the Cisco website for the other commands supported with **route-map**. The syntax of the **route-map** command is as follows:

```
Router(config)#route-map map-tag [permit | deny] [sequence-number]
```

This command defines the conditions for the policy routing. *map-tag* is the route map name. **permit** and **deny** are optional action keywords to be performed if the route-map match conditions are met. *sequence-number* is another optional argument that defines the position of a new route map statement. This is the same command as in IPv4.

The following command defines filter-messages as a new route map statement and enters the route map subcommand mode:

```
Router(config)#route-map filter-messages
```

The next command defines the conditions to match with IPv6. The conditions can be a route's matching IPv6 address, next-hop IPv6 address, or advertised IPv6 source address. A prefix list name must be specified in the matching condition:

```
Router(config-route-map)#match ipv6 {ipv6-address | next-hop | route-source}
    prefix-list [prefix-list-name]
```

The conditions to match are defined in the prefix list name filter-traffic:

```
Router(config-route-map)#match ipv6 address prefix-list filter-traffic
```

The **set ipv6** command defines the action to be performed on a match condition:

```
Router(config-route-map)#set ipv6 next-hop [ipv6-address] [link-local-address]
```

The action allowed is the specification of a route's **next-hop** aggregatable global unicast IPv6 address. Optionally, the **next-hop** argument in IPv6 can be the link-local address of an adjacent BGP4+ neighbor. A later section shows you how the **set ipv6 next-hop** command is applied in the BGP4+ configuration.

This command defines the next-hop IPv6 address as 3ffe:b00:ffff:1::1:

```
Router(config-route-map)#set ipv6 next-hop 3ffe:b00:ffff:1::1
```

The **route-map** command is configured on a global basis.

## Applying a Route Map with BGP4+

After the route map configuration is complete, you can apply the route map in the BGP4+ configuration. The route map must be applied to a BGP neighbor in the address-family ipv6 subcommand mode. The syntax for this command is as follows:

```
Router(config-router)#address-family ipv6
```

This places the router in the address-family ipv6 configuration submode.

Apply the route map to a BGP neighbor to modify the input or output route attributes with the following:

```
Router(config-router-af)#neighbor {peer-group-name | ipv6-address} route-map
    map-tag {in | out}
```

For example, you can apply the route map change-policy to the incoming route announcements from the BGP neighbor 2001:410:ffff:1::1:

```
Router(config-router-af)#neighbor 2001:410:ffff:1::1 route-map change-policy in
```

Leave the address-family ipv6 configuration submode and return to the BGP router configuration mode:

```
Router(config-router-af)#exit-address-family
```

Figure 4-3 shows a BGP4+ configuration in which you can tune the BGP path selection by modifying the local preference attribute using route map statements on routes received from a BGP neighbor. Router R1 from AS65001 has established multihop eBGP peerings to AS65100 and AS65200. However, the network administrator of the AS65001 domain prefers the path to AS65100 for outgoing packets if the same routes are received from both AS65100 and AS65200. Therefore, a route map statement is configured and applied in Router R1's BGP4+ configuration to prefer the path to AS65100.

**Figure 4-3**   *Preferring a Route in Router R1's BGP4+ Configuration Using*   **route-map**

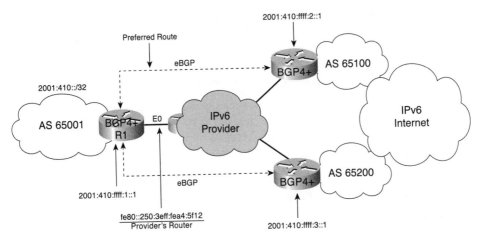

Example 4-5 reflects the route map configuration applied in Router R1's BGP4+ configuration shown in Figure 4-3. The command **route-map PreferAS65100 permit 10** defines the route map statement. Then the command **set local-preference 120** defines the value 120 as the local preference attribute. The default value of the local preference attribute with BGP is 100. The BGP algorithm prefers the highest local preference value when two routes point out the same destination network. The route map is applied in the BGP4+ configuration in the address-family ipv6 subcommand mode using the **neighbor 2001:410:ffff:2::1 route-map PreferAS65100 in** command. The route map forces the routes received from AS65100 to have a local preference of 120 rather than 100.

**Example 4-5**   *Applying a Route Map in Router R1's BGP4+ Configuration*

```
RouterR1#configure terminal
RouterR1(config)#route-map PreferAS65100 permit 10
RouterR1(config-route-map)#set local-preference 120
RouterR1(config-route-map)#exit
RouterR1(config)#interface e0
RouterR1(config-if)#ipv6 address 2001:410:ffff:1::1/64
RouterR1(config-if)#ipv6 nd suppress-ra
RouterR1(config-if)#exit
```

**Example 4-5** *Applying a Route Map in Router R1's BGP4+ Configuration (Continued)*

```
RouterR1(config)#ipv6 route ::/0 ethernet0 fe80::250:3eff:fea4:5f12
RouterR1(config)#router bgp 65001
RouterR1(config-router)#no bgp default ipv4-unicast
RouterR1(config-router)#bgp router-id 1.1.1.1
RouterR1(config-router)#neighbor 2001:410:ffff:2::1 remote-as 65100
RouterR1(config-router)#neighbor 2001:410:ffff:3::1 remote-as 65200
RouterR1(config-router)#address-family ipv6
RouterR1(config-router-af)#neighbor 2001:410:ffff:2::1 activate
RouterR1(config-router-af)#neighbor 2001:410:ffff:3::1 activate
RouterR1(config-router-af)#neighbor 2001:410:ffff:2::1 route-map PreferAS65100 in
RouterR1(config-router-af)#exit-address-family
RouterR1(config-router)#exit
```

**NOTE**    The route map shown in Example 4-5 and applied to the eBGP neighbor 2001:410:ffff:2::1 only indicates in AS65001 the path preference to exit the AS. However, this local configuration does not force all incoming packets to pass through AS65100.

## Configuring BGP4+ for IPv6 Using Link-Local Addresses

As mentioned earlier, the NEXT_HOP attribute is expressed as an IPv6 address and can now contain a neighbor's link-local address rather than just one aggregatable global unicast IPv6 address. Using link-local addresses of the adjacent BGP neighbors can be useful because this does not require the allocation of aggregatable global unicast IPv6 addresses on links.

Using link-local addresses with BGP might also be interesting when an IPv6 exchange point (IPv6 IX) is built. Some ISP participants might not want to use the IPv6 prefix from other ISPs to configure on their router's interfaces in the IPv6 IX. By configuring an IPv6 link-local address in the BGP configuration, this scenario appears neutral.

However, the use of a link-local address in BGP mandates a specific configuration. Configuring BGP4+ with a link-local address in the Cisco IOS Software consists of identifying the physical interface of the router corresponding to the destination of the link-local address and then defining a route map to modify the NEXT_HOP attribute to inform the neighbor of the physical interface's aggregatable global unicast address.

### Identifying the Router's Physical Interface

When specifying a link-local address for the BGP peering configuration, the physical interface associated with the link-local address must be identified in the BGP configuration using the **neighbor** *link-local-address* **update-source** *interface* command. Because a link-local address is tied to a single link, the router must specify the interface to be made unambiguous.

### Defining a Route Map to Advertise the Aggregatable Global Unicast Address to the Neighbor

To advertise the router's aggregatable global unicast IPv6 address to the neighbor, a route map statement must be defined to set the NEXT_HOP attribute on outbound BGP4+ updates sent. The NEXT_HOP attribute must contain both the link-local address and the aggregatable global unicast IPv6 address of the identified interface. Because the link-local address defines the BGP neighbor, the link-local address is already contained in the NEXT_HOP attribute. Therefore, the **set ipv6 next-hop** command in a route map statement is required to add the aggregatable global unicast IPv6 address of the identified interface in the NEXT_HOP attribute.

---

**NOTE**  If the BGP peering using link-local addresses is established without a route map statement advertising the router's aggregatable global unicast address, BGP updates sent to the BGP neighbor are defined as the unspecified address (::). Therefore, the BGP updates are ignored and are dropped by the BGP neighbor.

---

Table 4-2 presents the steps used to define BGP peering on a router using the link-local address of an adjacent BGP neighbor.

**Table 4-2**  *Defining a BGP Peer Using a Link-Local Address*

| Command | Description |
|---|---|
| **Step 1**<br><br>Router(config)#**route-map** *map-tag* | Defines a route map name for a BGP4+ configuration. |
| **Example**<br><br>Router(config)#**route-map linklocalAS65002** | Defines linklocalAS65002 as the name of a route map statement. |
| **Step 2**<br><br>Router(config-route-map)#**set ipv6 next-hop** *ipv6-address* | Specifies the aggregatable global unicast IPv6 address advertised as the next-hop attribute. |
| **Example**<br><br>Router(config-route-map)#**set ipv6 next-hop 2001:410:ffff:1::1** | Defines the aggregatable global unicast IPv6 address 2001:410:ffff:1::1 as the next-hop attribute. |
| **Step 3**<br><br>Router(config)#**router bgp** *autonomous-system* | Enables a BGP process on the router. Specifies the local AS. |
| **Step 4**<br><br>Router(config-router)#**no bgp default ipv4-unicast** | Only the IPv6 address family is advertised. |

**Table 4-2**    *Defining a BGP Peer Using a Link-Local Address (Continued)*

| Command | Description |
|---|---|
| **Step 5**<br><br>Router(config-router)#**neighbor** *link-local-ipv6-address* **remote-as** *autonomous-system* | Defines a BGP neighbor. The *ipv6-address* is the IPv6 address of the adjacent BGP neighbor. This command defines either iBGP or eBGP. |
| **Example**<br><br>Router(config-router)#**neighbor fe80::260:3eff:fe47:1533 remote-as 65002** | Defines the eBGP neighbor using fe80::260:3eff:fe47:1533 as the link-local address and 65002 as the AS. |
| **Step 6**<br><br>Router(config-router)#**neighbor** *link-local-address* **update-source** *interface* | Identifies the interface associated with the neighbor's link-local address. |
| **Example**<br><br>Router(config-router)#**neighbor fe80::260:3eff:fe47:1533 update-source ethernet0** | Defines the interface ethernet0 as the interface associated with the neighbor's link-local address. |
| **Step 7**<br><br>Router(config-router)#**address-family ipv6** | Places the router in the address-family ipv6 configuration submode. |
| **Step 8**<br><br>Router(config-router-af)#**neighbor** {*ip-address* \| *peer-group-name* \| *ipv6-address*} **activate** | Enables the exchange of information with the BGP neighbor. |
| **Example**<br><br>Router(config-router-af)#**neighbor fe80::260:3eff:fe47:1533 activate** | Enables the exchange of BGP4+ IPv6 routing information with the link-local address of the neighbor fe80::260:3eff:fe47:1533. |
| **Step 9**<br><br>Router(config-router-af)#**neighbor** {*peer-group-name* \| *ipv6-address*} **route-map** *map-tag* {**in** \| **out**} | Applies a route map to input or output route announcements as specified in the route map statement. The route map configuration must set the aggregatable global unicast IPv6 address on the router as the next-hop argument using the **set ipv6 next-hop** command. |

*continues*

**Table 4-2** *Defining a BGP Peer Using a Link-Local Address (Continued)*

| Command | Description |
|---|---|
| **Example**<br><br>Router(config-router-af)#**neighbor fe80::260:3eff:fe47:1533 route-map linklocalAS65002 out** | Applies the route map linklocalAS65002 to the outgoing route announcements toward the BGP neighbor fe80::260:3eff:fe47:1533. |
| **Step 10**<br><br>Router(config-router-af)#**exit-address-family** | Leaves the address-family configuration mode and returns to the BGP router configuration mode. |

**NOTE**     Having the link-local address enabled automatically on the interfaces by the router using EUI-64 format might affect your BGP4+ operation if you must replace your router's interface. To avoid reconfiguring BGP4+ with your BGP neighbors in this situation, it is recommended that you manually assign the link-local address to the router's interfaces instead. Refer to Chapter 2 to learn how to manually assign the link-local address to interfaces.

Figure 4-4 shows Router R1 from AS65001 establishing external BGP peering with Router R3 from AS65002 using the link-local address. The network prefix within AS65001 is 2001:410:ffff::/48, and AS65002 owns the prefix 3ffe:b00:ffff::/48. Router R1's interface Ethernet0 is connected on the same link as Router R3's interface Ethernet1. On Router R1, the aggregatable global unicast IPv6 address 2001:410:ffff:1::1 is assigned to the Ethernet2 interface, and the link-local address fe80::260:3eff:fe47:1533 is configured on the Ethernet0 interface. On Router R3, the aggregatable global unicast IPv6 address 3ffe:b00:ffff:2::2 is assigned to the Ethernet3 interface, and the link-local address fe80::260:3eff:fe78:3351 is configured on the Ethernet1 interface. In this example, the link-local addresses assigned to Router R1's Ethernet0 interface and Router R3's Ethernet1 interface establish the eBGP peer.

**Figure 4-4**    *eBGP Peering Established Between Routers R1 and R3 Using Link-Local Addresses*

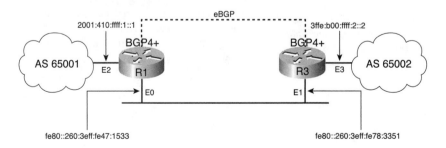

Example 4-6 shows the BGP4+ configuration applied on Router R1 to establish the eBGP peer to Router R3 using link-local addresses, as shown in Figure 4-4. The **route-map linklocalAS65002** and **set ipv6 next-hop 2001:410:ffff:1::1** commands define the next-hop attribute to the aggregatable global unicast IPv6 address 2001:410:ffff:1::1. Then the **neighbor fe80::260:3eff:fe78:3351 remote-as 65002** command configures the eBGP peers using the link-local address of Router R3's Ethernet1 interface in AS65002. The **neighbor fe80::260:3eff:fe78:3351 update-source ethernet0** command specifies that the source address used for this peering is the link-local address assigned to Router R1's Ethernet0 interface. BGP peering is enabled in the address-family ipv6 subcommand mode using the **neighbor fe80::260:3eff:fe78:3351 activate** command. Finally, the route map statement used to set the next-hop attribute is applied using the command **neighbor fe80::260:3eff:fe78:3351 route-map linklocalAS65002 out**.

**Example 4-6** *Enabling eBGP Peering Using Link-Local Addresses in Router R1*

```
RouterR1#configure terminal
RouterR1(config)#interface e2
RouterR1(config-if)#ipv6 address 2001:410:ffff:1::1/64
RouterR1(config-if)#ipv6 nd suppress-ra
RouterR1(config-if)#exit
RouterR1(config)#route-map linklocalAS65002
RouterR1(config-route-map)#set ipv6 next-hop 2001:410:ffff:1::1
RouterR1(config-route-map)#exit
RouterR1(config)#router bgp 65001
RouterR1(config-router)#no bgp default ipv4-unicast
RouterR1(config-router)#bgp router-id 1.1.1.1
RouterR1(config-router)#neighbor fe80::260:3eff:fe78:3351 remote-as 65002
RouterR1(config-router)#neighbor fe80::260:3eff:fe78:3351 update-source ethernet0
RouterR1(config-router)#address-family ipv6
RouterR1(config-router-af)#neighbor fe80::260:3eff:fe78:3351 activate
RouterR1(config-router-af)#neighbor fe80::260:3eff:fe78:3351 route-map
   linklocalAS65002 out
RouterR1(config-router-af)#exit-address-family
RouterR1(config-router)#exit
```

## Exchanging IPv4 Routes Between BGP IPv6 Peers

As discussed in Chapter 5, "IPv6 Integration and Coexistence Strategies," the IPv4 and IPv6 protocols will have to coexist on the same network infrastructure for an undetermined period of time. A situation might occur in which two separate IPv4 networks linked via a native IPv6 provider have to exchange their IPv4 routes through BGP IPv6 peers. Because BGP4+ supports the two address families, this is possible with a multiprotocol BGP peer group, the **neighbor [..] soft-reconfiguration** command, and a route map configuration to exchange IPv4 routes between BGP IPv6 peers.

Figure 4-5 illustrates Router R1 from AS65100 establishing a multihop eBGP peering over IPv6 with Router R3 from AS65200. On domain A, which is based on both IPv6 and IPv4, network prefixes within AS65100 are 2001:410:ffff::/48 for IPv6 and 133.220.0.0/16 for IPv4.

On domain B (AS65200), the network prefixes are 3ffe:b00:ffff::/48 for IPv6 and 132.214.0.0/16 and 133.210.0.0/16 for IPv4. The link-local addresses fe80::1001 and fe80::2090 are the default gateway IPv6 addresses of the IPv6-only network between the two dual-stacked domains. A multihop eBGP over IPv6 is configured between Router R1 of AS65100 and Router R3 of AS65200. In this network design, the IPv4 network prefixes 132.214.0.0/16 and 133.210.0.0/16 within AS65200 are advertised to AS65100 through the multihop eBGP IPv6 peer.

**Figure 4-5**   *IPv4 Routes Exchanged Between eBGP IPv6 Peers*

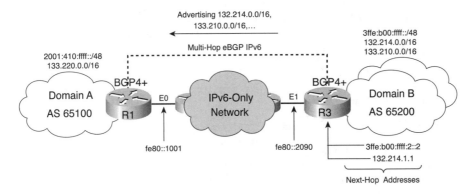

Example 4-7 shows the multiprotocol BGP configuration applied on Router R1 within AS65100 that allows IPv4 routes to be exchanged between the BGP IPv6 peers. Router R3 advertises the IPv4 routes 132.214.0.0/16 and 133.210.0.0/16. However, Example 4-7 describes the specific configuration applied in Router R1 to perform this task.

First, the **ipv6 route ::/0 ethernet0 fe80::1001** command is the default IPv6 route that points out the router of the IPv6-only network. Then the **router bgp 65100** command places the router in the configuration mode for BGP. The command **neighbor ipv6-only-peer peer-group** creates a multiprotocol BGP peer group. The **neighbor 3ffe:b00:fff:2::2 remote-as 65200** command defines the external BGP neighbor using 3ffe:b00:fff:2::2 as the next-hop aggregatable global unicast IPv6 address in AS65200. Then the rest of the configuration is performed in the address-family ipv4 submode instead of the address-family ipv6 subcommand mode to exchange IPv4 prefixes between the two BGP IPv6 peers. The **neighbor ipv6-only-peer activate** command lets the neighbor exchange prefixes for the IPv4 address family with the local Router R1. Then the **neighbor ipv6-only-peer soft-reconfiguration inbound** command asks the local Router R1 to store the BGP updates received from the members of the BGP peer group without modifying them. The **neighbor 3ffe:b00:ffff:2::2 peer-group ipv6-only-peer** command assigns the IPv6 address of the eBGP IPv6 peer (Router R3) to the peer group ipv6-only-peer. Finally, the route-map IPv4-AS65200 is applied to incoming IPv4 routes for the BGP IPv6 neighbor 3ffe:b00:ffff:2::2. Because IPv4 routes are advertised between the two BGP IPv6 peers, it is mandatory in the Router R1 configuration to define the next-hop IPv4 address for the IPv4 routes advertised by Router R3. The **set ip next-hop 132.214.1.1** command in the **route-map IPv4-AS65200** configuration realizes this operation.

**Example 4-7**  *Configuring eBGP IPv6 Peering to Exchange IPv4 Routes*

```
RouterR1#configure terminal
RouterR1(config)#ipv6 route ::/0 ethernet0 fe80::1001
RouterR1(config)#router bgp 65100
RouterR1(config-router)#neighbor ipv6-only-peer peer-group
RouterR1(config-router)#neighbor 3ffe:b00:ffff:2::2 remote-as 65200
RouterR1(config-router)#address-family ipv4
RouterR1(config-router-af)#neighbor ipv6-only-peer activate
RouterR1(config-router-af)#neighbor ipv6-only-peer soft-reconfiguration inbound
RouterR1(config-router-af)#neighbor 3ffe:b00:ffff:2::2 peer-group ipv6-only-peer
RouterR1(config-router-af)#neighbor 3ffe:b00:ffff:2::2 route-map IPv4-AS65200 in
RouterR1(config-router-af)#exit-address-family
RouterR1(config-router)#exit
RouterR1(config)#route-map IPv4-AS65200 permit 10
RouterR1(config-route-map)#set ip next-hop 132.214.1.1
RouterR1(config-route-map)#exit
```

**NOTE**     The main goal of this BGP configuration is to allow Router R1 to receive the IPv4 network prefixes 132.214.0.0/16 and 133.210.0.0/16. In the IPv4 routing table, the next-hop address of these network prefixes is 132.214.1.1. This BGP configuration is used only to exchange the IPv6 routing information from Router R3 of AS65200 to Router R1 of AS65100. A similar configuration must be applied in Router R3 to advertise the IPv4 network prefix 133.220.0.0/16 to Router R1.

**NOTE**     It is important to understand that IPv4 connectivity must be available between domains A and B to establish IPv4 sessions between the domains' nodes. See Chapter 5 for detailed information on strategies and mechanisms to carry IPv4 packets over IPv6-only networks and vice versa.

**NOTE**     You also can exchange IPv6 routes between two BGP IPv4 peers using the same model.

## MD5 Authentication with BGP4+

As defined in RFC 2385, *Protection of BGP Sessions Via TCP MD5 Signature Option*, BGP can protect itself from the introduction of spoofed TCP segments into the connection stream (of particular concern are TCP resets) using a TCP option that carries an MD5 digest. RFC 2385 does not distinguish between IPv4 and IPv6 pseudo-headers, but it appears to refer to IPv4 headers.

This feature has been adapted to IPv6 in the Cisco IOS Software. Thus, authentication between BGP IPv6 peers is now possible. MD5 authentication, when used between BGP IPv6 peers, must be configured in the address-family ipv6 subcommand mode. The command is used in the same manner as the IPv4 **neighbor [..] password** command, but in the address-family ipv6 subcommand mode. The syntax for the **neighbor [..] password** command is as follows:

```
Router(config-router-af)#neighbor {ipv6-address | peer-group-name} password 5
   password-string
```

The *ipv6-address* argument is the IPv6 address of the BGP neighbor. The *peer-group-name* is the name of the BGP peer group. The **password** keyword enables authentication on the TCP connection between BGP neighbors. The number **5** stands for MD5. Finally, the *password-string* is the shared secret used on both BGP peers.

Example 4-8 is a BGP4+ configuration. It shows an example of MD5 authentication between BGP IPv6 peers using the **neighbor [..] password** command in the address-family ipv6 subcommand mode.

**Example 4-8** *Redistributing Static IPv6 Routes into BGP4+*

```
RouterR1#configure terminal
RouterR1(config)#router bgp 65001
RouterR1(config-router)#no bgp default ipv4-unicast
RouterR1(config-router)#bgp router-id 1.1.1.1
RouterR1(config-router)#neighbor 2001:410:ffff:2::1 remote-as 65100
RouterR1(config-router)#address-family ipv6
RouterR1(config-router-af)#neighbor 2001:410:ffff:2::1 password 5
   secured-bgp-session
RouterR1(config-router-af)#neighbor 2001:410:ffff:2::1 activate
```

**NOTE**    The same secret password must be used on both BGP peers. Otherwise, the TCP connection will fail.

## Redistributing IPv6 Routes into BGP4+

The redistribution of routes into BGP4+ is similar to this task in IPv4. As in IPv4, there are several ways to advertise IPv6 prefixes into the BGP4+ protocol:

- Configuring the **network** command in the address-family ipv6 subcommand mode, as discussed earlier

- Redistributing static IPv6 routes configured manually on the router into BGP4+ (this way is an alternative to using the **network** command)

- Redistributing IPv6 routes learned dynamically through IGPs such as RIPng, IS-IS for IPv6, and OSPFv3 into BGP4+

Redistributing IPv6 routes with BGP4+ from either static routes or IGP is realized in the address-family ipv6 subcommand mode of BGP4+ using the **redistribute** command. This command is used in the same manner as the IPv4 **redistribute** command. The syntax for the **redistribute** command in the address-family ipv6 subcommand mode is as follows:

```
Router(config-router-af)#redistribute {bgp | connected | isis | ospf | rip |
    static}
```

### Redistributing Static IPv6 Routes into BGP4+

Optional parameters such as **metric** and **route-map** may be supplied with the **redistribute static** command. A new **metric** value may be forced for the static IPv6 routes redistributed into BGP4+. Then, a **route-map** may be used to filter routes against a routing policy. The syntax for the **redistribute static** command in BGP4+ is as follows:

```
Router(config-router-af)#redistribute static [metric metric-value] [route-map
    map-tag]
```

---

**NOTE**    After the redistribution of IPv6 routes is performed, you can validate the redistribution between any routing protocols using the **show ipv6 protocols** command. This command is equivalent to the **show ip protocols** command in IPv4.

---

The BGP4+ configuration in Example 4-9 shows an example of static IPv6 route redistribution in BGP4+. The routes 2001:410:ffff::/48 and 2001:410:ffff::/48 are added to Router R1's IPv6 routing table. Then, both routes are redistributed into BGP4+ using the **redistribute static** command in the address-family ipv6 subcommand mode.

**Example 4-9**    *Redistributing Static IPv6 Routes into BGP4+*

```
RouterR1#configure terminal
RouterR1(config)#ipv6 route 2001:410:ffff::/48 null 0
RouterR1(config)#ipv6 route 2001:420:ffff::/48 null 0
RouterR1(config)#router bgp 65001
<OUTPUT OMITTED>
RouterR1(config-router)#address-family ipv6
RouterR1(config-router-af)#redistribute static
```

| NOTE | As in IPv4, IPv6 routes redistributed into BGP4+ must already be available in the IPv6 routing table. However, if your routing table has no route and you want to place static routes in the IPv6 routing table only to redistribute them into BGP4+, you must define **null 0** as the destination network interface with the **ipv6 route** command. This configuration is similar to the **ip route** *ipv4-prefix mask* **null 0** command in IPv4. |
|------|---|

### Redistributing IGP into BGP4+

As in IPv4, you can redistribute routes from IGP into BGP4+. However, this is not recommended because it might cause route instability in the BGP4+ routing table (it might generate several BGP update messages to BGP peers). Although redistributing IGP into BGP4+ is not recommended, the following section presents commands for redistributing RIPng and IS-IS for IPv6 routes into BGP4+.

### Redistributing RIPng into BGP4+

The **redistribute rip** command is used in BGP4+'s address-family ipv6 subcommand mode to define the redistribution of RIPng into BGP4+. The *process* argument is the RIPng process on the router that must be redistributed. The optional **metric** parameter identifies a new metric value associated with RIPng routes advertised into BGP4+. Finally, a **route-map** may be used optionally to filter incoming IPv6 routes from the source protocol RIPng to BGP4+. The syntax for the **redistribute rip** command in BGP4+ is as follows:

```
Router(config-router-af)#redistribute rip process [metric metric-value] [route-map
    map-tag]
```

| NOTE | RIPng is discussed in detail later in this chapter. |
|------|---|

### Redistributing IS-IS for IPv6 into BGP4+

The **redistribute isis** command defines the redistribution of IS-IS for IPv6 routes into BGP4+. The *process* argument is the IS-IS process. The **level-1**, **level-2**, and **level-1-2** keywords specify the level of IS-IS routes that is injected into BGP4+ from IS-IS. The **metric-type** argument identifies the IS-IS metric associated with routes advertised into IS-IS: **internal** means an IS-IS metric less than 63 (the default), and **external** is an IS-IS metric less than 128 but greater than 64. As with RIPng, the optional **metric** parameter may be used to identify a new metric value associated with IS-IS routes advertised into BGP4+. Finally, a **route-map** may be used optionally to filter incoming IPv6 routes from the source protocol IS-IS to BGP4+. The syntax for the **redistribute isis** command is as follows:

```
Router(config-router-af)#redistribute isis process {level-1 | level-2 | level-1-2}
    [metric-type {external | internal}] [metric metric-value] [route-map map-tag]
```

**NOTE**    IS-IS for IPv6 is discussed in detail later in this chapter.

## Verifying and Managing BGP4+ for IPv6

You can display information, IPv6 BGP neighbors, and statistics using the **show bgp ipv6** command, which displays the IPv6 BGP table. This command is equivalent to the **show ip bgp** command in IPv4:

```
Router#show bgp ipv6 [ipv6-prefix/0-128 | community | community-list | dampened-paths |
    filter-list | flap-statistics | inconsistent-as | neighbors | quote-regexp |
    regexp | summary]
```

Table 4-3 describes the command options and parameters you can use with the **show bgp ipv6** command.

**Table 4-3**    **show bgp ipv6** *Command Parameters*

| Command Parameter | Description |
| --- | --- |
| *ipv6-prefix/0-128* | Displays all the path information related to the IPv6 prefix and prefix length given as arguments. |
| **community** | Displays information on the routes matching IPv6 BGP communities. |
| **community-list** | Displays information on the routes matching the IPv6 BGP community list. |
| **dampened-paths** | Displays information on the IPv6 paths suppressed due to dampening. |
| **filter-list** | Displays routes conforming to the filter list. |
| **flap-statistics** | Displays information on the flap statistics of IPv6 BGP neighbors. |
| **inconsistent-as** | Displays information on routes that have inconsistent origin autonomous systems. |
| **neighbors** | Displays information on the state of IPv6 BGP neighbors. |
| **quote-regexp** | Displays IPv6 BGP routes that match the AS path regular expression as a quoted string of characters. |
| **regexp** | Displays IPv6 BGP routes that match the AS path regular expression. |
| **summary** | Displays summary information regarding the state of IPv6 BGP neighbors. |

You can reset IPv6 BGP neighbors, TCP connections, and flap dampening using the **clear bgp ipv6** command. This command is equivalent to the **clear bgp** command in IPv4. The syntax for this command is as follows:

```
Router#clear bgp ipv6 {* | autonomous-system | ipv6-address | dampening | external |
    flap-statistics | peer-group}
```

Table 4-4 presents the options and parameters of the **clear bgp ipv6** command.

**Table 4-4**     **clear bgp ipv6** *Command Parameters*

| Command Parameter | Description |
|---|---|
| * | Resets all IPv6 BGP neighbors. |
| *autonomous-system* | Resets all IPv6 BGP neighbors with the AS number given as an argument. |
| *ipv6-address* | Resets the TCP connection to the specified BGP neighbor and removes from the BGP table all routes that have been learned from this session. |
| **dampening** | Resets all flap-dampening information related to IPv6 BGP neighbors. |
| **external** | Resets all external IPv6 peers. |
| **flap-statistics** | Clears all route flap statistics related to IPv6 BGP neighbors. |
| *peer-group* | Resets the TCP connection to this peer group and removes from the BGP table all routes that have been learned from this session. |

The command **debug bgp ipv6** displays debug information related to the BGP4+ routing protocol. Table 4-5 lists the arguments that can be specified with this command. This command is equivalent to the **debug bgp** command in IPv4.

**Table 4-5**     **debug bgp ipv6** *Command Parameters*

| Command Parameter | Description |
|---|---|
| *dampening* | Enables BGP routing protocol debugging for IPv6. Displays messages related to dampening. |
| *updates* | Enables BGP routing protocol debugging for IPv6. Displays BGP4+ update messages. |

### Verifying Prefix Lists with IPv6

The command **show ipv6 prefix-list** may be used to display summary or specific detailed information related to the IPv6 prefix lists configured in the router. This command is equivalent to the **show ip prefix-list** command in IPv4. The syntax for this command is as follows:

```
Router#show ipv6 prefix-list [summary | detail] name
```

# IGP Protocols for IPv6

The second family of routing protocols presented in this chapter are the Interior Gateway Protocols (IGPs). IGPs are used inside ASs and domains. The most common IPv4 routing protocols used inside domains are Routing Information Protocol (RIP), Intermediate System-to-Intermediate System (IS-IS), Open Shortest Path First (OSPF), and Enhanced Interior Gateway Routing Protocol (EIGRP).

The following is a short overview of IGP's properties:

- **RIP**—Version 1 of this routing protocol was one of the first IGPs used inside IPv4 domains. RIP is a distance vector routing protocol based on the Bellman-Ford algorithm. It uses User Datagram Protocol (UDP) on port 520 to advertise routing information to other RIP routers. RIP was designed to work with IPv4 and IPX on small networks. However, the scalability of this routing protocol is limited to a radius of 15 hops maximum. RIP provides hop count information to calculate the best paths to reach destination networks. RIP's convergence speed is considered slow compared to link-state routing protocols such as OSPF and IS-IS. The RIP version with IPv6 support is called RIPng. RIPng evolved from RIP version 2. RIPng is discussed in detail in the following sections.

- **IS-IS**—This protocol uses the Open System Interconnection (OSI) terminology with IPv4. IS-IS was primarily designed as the OSI routing protocol (ISO 10589), and then extensions were designed to add IPv4 support (RFC 1195), well-known as *integrated*. This routing protocol uses International Organization for Standardization (ISO) network service access point (NSAP) addresses and OSI packets to advertise messages between adjacent IS-IS routers. IS-IS is a link-state protocol based on Dijkstra's SPF (shortest path first) algorithm. It has very large scalability, and it is hierarchical. IS-IS routers must be members of IS-IS areas. IS-IS provides cost information for links (the default interface cost is 10) to calculate the best paths to reach destination networks. IS-IS's convergence time is considered fast in comparison to RIP. IS-IS with IPv6 support is covered in detail in the following sections.

- **OSPF**—OSPF was inspired by one of the first drafts of the IS-IS protocol. OSPF is another link-state protocol based on Dijkstra's SPF algorithm. OSPF advertises routing information to OSPF routers using IPv4 packets based on protocol 89. Like IS-IS, OSPF has large scalability and is hierarchical: OSPF routers must be members of areas. OSPF provides link cost information, like IS-IS, except that the cost is calculated on the interfaces' bandwidth characteristics. OSPF's convergence speed is considered fast compared to RIP. OSPF version 3 supports IPv6. OSPFv3 is covered in detail in the following sections.

- **EIGRP**—This is an advanced version of the proprietary routing protocol IGRP, developed by Cisco years ago. EIGRP is an advanced distance vector protocol with the addition of link-state protocol properties. EIGRP is based on the Diffusion Update Algorithm (DUAL) and has large scalability. EIGRP was designed to work with IPv4, IPX, and AppleTalk. EIGRP advertises routing information to EIGRP routers using IPv4 packets based on protocol 88. EIGRP provides link cost information based on a composite metric using the bandwidth and a delay value to calculate the best paths to reach destination networks. EIGRP's convergence time is considered very fast.

| NOTE | As mentioned at the beginning of this chapter, this chapter provides only an overview of the routing protocols. If you need more information on RIP, IS-IS, OSPF, and EIGRP, you should read *IP Routing Fundamentals, Cisco OSPF Command and Configuration Handbook,* or *Building Scalable Networks with Cisco,* all published by Cisco Press. Otherwise, the Cisco website provides plenty of information on and examples of these routing protocols when deployed over IPv4 networks. |
|---|---|

IPv6 support for IGP in the Cisco IOS Software currently is limited to RIP, IS-IS, and OSPF. In the following sections, these protocols are discussed in the order in which they became available for IPv6.

# RIPng for IPv6

RFC 1058, *Routing Information Protocol,* and RFC 1723, *RIP Version 2,* define RIPv1 and RIPv2. RIPv2 is the most advanced version of RIP implemented, available, and used today in Cisco router implementations.

| NOTE | The Cisco IOS Software supports both RIPv1 and RIPv2. However, configuring RIPv1 or RIPv2 with IPv4 on Cisco is beyond the scope of this book. |
|---|---|

Routing Information Protocol next generation (RIPng) is the counterpart of RIPv2, but for IPv6. As defined in RFC 2080, *RIPng for IPv6,* RIPng has most of the same capabilities of RIPv2:

- **Distance vector**—RIPng is a distance vector protocol based on the Bellman-Ford algorithm.

- **Radius of operation**—Like RIP, RIPng is limited to a radius of 15 hops.

- **UDP-based protocol**—RIPng uses UDP datagrams to send and receive routing information.

- **Broadcast information**—Periodic broadcasts can be sent using multicast addresses to reduce traffic on nodes that are not listening to RIP messages.

Because IPv6 represents a new protocol to support, RIPng has been updated to handle it. Here are the main updates added in RIPng:

- **Destination prefix**—Destination prefixes are based on 128-bit instead of 32-bit (as in IPv4).

- **Next-hop address**—Next-hop addresses are based on 128-bit instead of 32-bit (as in IPv4).

- **Transport**—RIPng messages are sent over IPv6 packets.

- **UDP port number**—The standard UDP port number for IPv6 is 521 instead of 520, as in IPv4. This UDP port sends and receives routing information between RIPng routers.

- **Link-local address**—RIPng updates are sent to adjacent RIPng routers using the link-local address FE80::/10 as the source address.

- **Multicast address**—The standard multicast address used with RIPng is FF02::9, instead of 224.0.0.9 in IPv4. The FF02::9 represents the all-RIP-routers multicast address on the link-local scope.

## Enabling RIPng on Cisco

RIPng was the first IGP supported in the Cisco IOS Software technology. The Cisco IOS Software technology supports up to four RIPng processes simultaneously. The **ipv6 router rip** command defines a RIPng process on the router and is the first step used to enable a RIPng process. The *tag* argument refers to a short string that identifies a unique RIPng process. The **ipv6 router rip** command is equivalent to the **router rip** command in IPv4. The syntax for this command is as follows:

```
Router(config)#ipv6 router rip tag
```

The **ipv6 router rip** command is used on a global basis.

## Configuring RIPng

As soon as the RIPng process is defined on the router, you have to enable RIPng on the interfaces using the command **ipv6 rip** *tag* **enable**, as shown in Table 4-6. Table 4-6 lists the other subcommands used to generate a default IPv6 route in RIPng and shows how to summarize routes.

**Table 4-6**    **ipv6 rip tag** *Subcommands*

| Command | Description |
|---------|-------------|
| **enable** | Enables RIPng on an interface. |
| **default-information originate** | Generates a default IPv6 route (::/0) in RIPng and sends it in RIP updates. |

*continues*

**Table 4-6** ipv6 rip tag *Subcommands (Continued)*

| Command | Description |
|---|---|
| **default-information only** | Generates a default IPv6 route (::/0) in RIP. This suppresses the sending of any other IPv6 routes except the default IPv6 route. |
| **summary-address** *ipv6-prefix/prefix-length* | Summarizes the IPv6 routes. When the first *length* bits of a route match the statement, the statement's prefix is advertised instead. In this case, multiple routes are replaced by a single route whose metric is the lowest metric of the multiple routes. This command may be used multiple times. |

These parameters are used on an interface basis.

**NOTE**     It is possible to enable RIPng on one of the router's unnumbered tunnel interfaces. However, RIPng must be enabled on both the tunnel and the physical interfaces using **ipv6 rip** *tag* **enable**. In this context, the tunnel interface uses the source IPv6 address of the physical interface.

Figure 4-6 illustrates a network with four routers using RIPng as the routing protocol. The RIPng protocol, like any IGP, is used in the network topology to propagate the prefixes of all subnets. Router R3 is connected to the Internet-IPv6. On Router R3's FastEthernet 0/0 and FastEthernet 0/1 interfaces, the default IPv6 route is advertised by RIPng with the origin of Router R3.

**Figure 4-6**     *Router R3 Advertising the Default IPv6 Route with the Origin of Router R3*

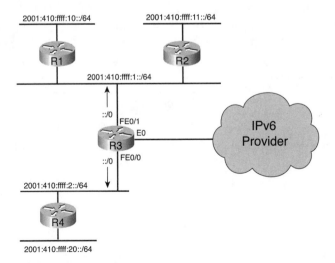

Example 4-10 presents the configuration applied on Router R3 in Figure 4-6. First, the **ipv6 router rip RIPNGR3** command defines the RIPng process. The unicast IPv6 addresses 2001:410:ffff:1::1/64 and 2001:410:ffff:2::1/64 are assigned to interface fastethernet0/1 and fastethernet0/0. Then, the command **ipv6 rip RIPNGR3 enable** is applied on both interfaces, which enables RIPng. Finally, the command **ipv6 rip default-information originate** advertises the default IPv6 route with the origin of Router R3.

**Example 4-10** *Enabling RIPng in Router R3 with the Advertisement of the Default Route*

```
RouterR3#configure terminal
RouterR3(config)#ipv6 router rip RIPNGR3
RouterR3(config-rtr)#int fastethernet0/1
RouterR3(config-if)#ipv6 address 2001:410:ffff:1::1/64
RouterR3(config-if)#ipv6 rip RIPNGR3 enable
RouterR3(config-if)#ipv6 rip default-information originate
RouterR3(config-if)#int fastethernet0/0
RouterR3(config-if)#ipv6 address 2001:410:ffff:2::1/64
RouterR3(config-if)#ipv6 rip RIPNGR3 enable
RouterR3(config-if)#ipv6 rip default-information originate
RouterR3(config-if)#exit
RouterR3(config)#ipv6 route ::/0 ethernet0
```

## Tuning the RIPng Process

This section covers the parameters you can use to tune the RIPng process. The parameters listed in Table 4-7 are available in the router subcommand mode using the **ipv6 router rip** command. After you enter the **ipv6 router rip** command, you should see the router prompt (router-rtr). These parameters are the same as the ones available in the router rip subcommand mode in IPv4.

**Table 4-7**    *RIPng Router Commands*

| Command | Description |
|---------|-------------|
| Router(config-rtr)#**distance** *distance* | Defines the administrative distance for a RIPng process. If two RIP processes attempt to insert the same IPv6 route into the same routing table, the route with the lower administrative distance takes precedence. The default value is 120. |
| Router(config-rtr)#**distribute-list prefix-list** *pfx-name* {*in* | *out*} [*interface* ] | Applies an IPv6 access list to RIPng routing updates received or sent on an interface. If no interface is specified, the IPv6 access list is applied to all interfaces on the router. |
| Router(config-rtr)#**metric-offset** *number* | Sets the increment to a new value between 1 and 16. By default, the RIPng metric is incremented by 1 before being entered in the routing table. |

*continues*

**Table 4-7**    *RIPng Router Commands (Continued)*

| Command | Description |
|---|---|
| Router(config-rtr)#**poison-reverse** | Performs poison-reverse processing of updates. Poison reverse causes the advertisement of an unreachable metric when RIPng advertises network IPv6 prefixes on interfaces from which it learned them. If both split horizon and poison reverse are enabled, only split-horizon processing occurs. Poison-reverse is turned off by default. |
| Router(config-rtr)#**split-horizon** | Performs split-horizon processing of updates. Split horizon suppresses the advertisement of network IPv6 prefixes on interfaces from which RIPng learned them. |
| Router(config-rtr)#**port** *udp-port* **multicast-group** *multicast-address* | Defines a different UDP port number and multicast address than the default values. By default, the standardized UDP port 521 and RIP's multicast address FF02::9 are used by the RIPng processes. |
| Router(config-rtr)#**timers** *update expire holddown garbage-collect* | Configures the RIPng routing timers. The *update* parameter defines the periodic updates interval. The default *update* value is 30 seconds. *expire* is a timeout parameter that marks as unreachable network prefixes not heard after *expire* seconds. The default *expire* value is 180 seconds. Information about unreachable network prefixes is ignored for a further *holddown* seconds. The 0 value, the default, is used to not use holddown. The *garbage-collect* parameter deletes an expired entry in the RIPng routing table. The removal is done *garbage-collect* seconds after either the expiration or holddown termination. The default *garbage-collect* value is 120. |
| Router(config-rtr)#**redistribute {bgp I connected I isis I ospf I rip I static}** [**metric** *metric-value* ] [**level-1Ilevel-1-2 I level-2**] [*route-map map-tag*] | Advertises routes learned from other protocols, such as bgp, connected, isis, ospf, rip, and static. Refer to the following section to get detailed information about the **redistribute** command. |
| Router(config-rtr)#**exit** | Exits the RIPng configuration mode. |

## Redistributing IPv6 Routes into RIPng

The redistribution of IPv6 routes into RIPng is similar to the equivalent process in IPv4. BGP4+, IS-IS for IPv6, OSPFv3, and static routes may be redistributed into RIPng. The following section presents commands and examples of redistributing IPv6 routes into RIPng. The redistribution of IPv6 routes with RIPng is performed using the **redistribute** command in the ipv6 router rip subcommand mode. This command is used in the same manner as the IPv4 **redistribute** command with RIPv2. The syntax for the **redistribute** command is as follows:

```
Router(config-rtr)#redistribute {bgp I connected I isis I ospf I rip I static}
```

## Redistributing Static IPv6 Routes into RIPng

You may supply optional parameters such as **metric** and **route-map** with the **redistribute static** command. A new **metric** value may be forced for the static IPv6 routes redistributed instead of the default metric value of 1 for routes redistributed into RIPng. Then, a **route-map** may be used to filter routes against a routing policy. The syntax for the **redistribute static** command in RIPng is as follows:

```
Router(config-rtr)#redistribute static [metric metric-value] [route-map map-tag]
```

The RIPng configuration in Example 4-11 shows the **redistribute** static command used to inject static IPv6 routes into RIPng.

**Example 4-11** *Redistributing Static IPv6 Routes into RIPng*

```
RouterR1#configure terminal
RouterR1(config)#ipv6 router rip RIPNGR1
RouterR1(config-rtr)#redistribute static
```

## Redistributing BGP4+ into RIPng

The **redistribute bgp** command defines the redistribution of BGP4+ routes into RIPng. The *process* argument is the AS number. The optional **metric** parameter identifies a new metric value associated with BGP4+ routes advertised into RIPng. A **route-map** may be used optionally to filter incoming IPv6 routes from the source protocol BGP4+ to RIPng. The syntax for the **redistribute bgp** command in RIPng is as follows:

```
Router(config-rtr)#redistribute bgp process [metric metric-value] [route-map
   map-tag]
```

The RIPng configuration in Example 4-12 shows the **redistribute bgp** command used to inject BGP4+ routes into RIPng. The BGP4+ route 2001:420:ffff::/48 is injected into RIPng. Refer to the section "BGP4+ for IPv6" for detailed information about the configuration presented here.

**Example 4-12** *Redistributing BGP4+ Routes into RIPng*

```
RouterR1#configure terminal
RouterR1(config)#router bgp 65001
RouterR1(config-router)#no bgp default ipv4-unicast
RouterR1(config-router)#bgp router-id 1.1.1.1
RouterR1(config-router)#neighbor 3ffe:b00:ffff:2::2 remote-as 65002
RouterR1(config-router)#address-family ipv6
RouterR1(config-router-af)#neighbor 3ffe:b00:ffff:2::2 activate
RouterR1(config-router-af)#network 2001:420:ffff::/48
RouterR1(config-router-af)#exit-address-family
RouterR1(config-router)#exit
RouterR1(config)#ipv6 router rip RIPNGR1
RouterR1(config-rtr)#redistribute bgp 65001
```

### Redistributing IS-IS for IPv6 into RIPng

The **redistribute isis** command defines the redistribution of IS-IS for IPv6 routes into RIPng. The *process* argument is the IS-IS process on the router. The optional **metric** parameter identifies a new metric value associated with IS-IS for IPv6 routes advertised into RIPng. The **level-1**, **level-2**, and **level-1-2** keywords specify the level of IS-IS routes that is injected into RIPng from IS-IS. A **route-map** may be used optionally to filter incoming IPv6 routes from the source protocol IS-IS to RIPng. The syntax for the **redistribute isis** command is as follows:

```
Router(config-rtr)#redistribute isis process [metric metric-value] {level-1 |
   level-2 | level-1-2} [route-map map-tag]
```

## Managing RIPng

As shown in Table 4-8, you can display the status, the RIPng database, and the next-hop addresses of the RIPng process using the **show ipv6 rip** command. The **show ipv6 rip** command is equivalent to the **show rip** command in IPv4.

**Table 4-8**  show ipv6 rip *Command*

| Command | Description |
|---|---|
| **show ipv6 rip** | Displays the status of the various RIPng processes. |
| **show ipv6 rip database** | Displays the RIPng database. |
| **show ipv6 rip next-hops** | Displays the RIPng next hops. |

You can remove all entries from the RIPng database using the **clear ipv6 rip** command, the syntax for which is as follows:

```
Router#clear ipv6 rip [name]
```

The command **debug ipv6 rip** displays debug information related to the RIPng routing protocol. This command displays RIPng packets sent and received on all interfaces where RIPng is enabled. The **debug ipv6 rip** command is equivalent to the **debug ip rip** command in IPv4. The syntax is as follows:

```
Router#debug ipv6 rip
```

To display RIPng packets sent and received on a specific interface, use the *interface* parameter:

```
Router#debug ipv6 rip interface
```

**NOTE**    When the **debug ipv6 rip** command is used on a busy network, it can seriously affect the router's performance.

# IS-IS for IPv6

ISO/EIC 10589, *Intermediate System to Intermediate System,* is the basic specification that defines the IS-IS intradomain routing exchange protocol for Connectionless Network Service (CLNS) traffic. RFC 1195, *Use of OSI IS-IS for Routing in TCP/IP and Dual Environments,* is the most specific standard of IS-IS for IPv4. IS-IS for IPv4 is also known in Cisco environments as integrated IS-IS. The IS-IS protocol runs on top of the data link layer and requires Connectionless Network Protocol (CLNP) as defined in the ISO 8473 specification. CLNP uses NSAP addresses.

---

**NOTE**     The Cisco IOS Software supports IS-IS for IPv4. However, configuring IS-IS for IPv4 on Cisco is beyond the scope of this book.

---

IPv6 is now supported by the IS-IS protocol. The IETF draft-ietf-isis-ipv6-05.txt "Routing IPv6 with IS-IS" defines the IPv6 support in the IS-IS protocol. Because the IPv6 protocol represents a new address family to support, this section presents the updates added in the IS-IS protocol to support IPv6. The updates added to the protocol specified in the IETF draft-ietf-isis-ipv6-05.txt refer to IS-IS's mechanisms, as described in RFC 1195.

The updates are focused on the two new Type-Length Values (TLVs), which were added to carry information related to the IPv6 routing. The TLV is router information encoded in variable-length fields within the Link State Packets (LSPs). The new TLVs added are as follows:

- **IPv6 Reachability**—This new TLV describes the network reachability such as the IPv6 routing prefix, metric information, and some option bits. The option bits indicate the advertisement of the IPv6 prefix from a higher level, distribution of the prefix from other routing protocols (redistribution), and the existence of sub-TLVs. The decimal value assigned to the IPv6 Reachability TLV is 236 (hex 0xEC). This IPv6 Reachability TLV is equivalent to the IP Internal Reachability and IP External Reachability Information described in RFC 1195.

- **IPv6 Interface Address**—This TLV contains an IPv6 interface address (128-bit) instead of an IPv4 interface address (32-bit). This IPv6 Interface Address is equivalent to the IP Interface Address described in RFC 1195. The decimal value assigned to the IPv6 Reachability TLV is 232 (hex 0xE8). For IS HELLO PDUs, this TLV must contain the link-local address (FE80::/10). However, for the LSP, the TLV must contain the non-link-local address.

A new Network Layer Protocol Identifier (NLPID) has also been defined, allowing IS-IS routers with IPv6 support to advertise packets using the decimal value 142 (hex 0x8E) for IPv6 packets. The NLPID is an 8-bit field identifying the network layer. Different NLPID values are used for IPv4 and OSI.

## IS-IS Network Design with IPv6

The domain in the IS-IS context is equivalent to the AS in BGP. The IS-IS domain is based on a two-level structure: level 1 and level 2. As in IPv4, any IS-IS router with IPv6 support can act as the following:

- **Level-1 (L1) router**—Responsible for intra-area IPv6 routing

- **Level-2 (L2) router**—Responsible for interarea IPv6 routing

- **Level-1-2 (L1/L2) router**—Responsible for both IPv6 intra-area and interarea routing

Before describing the IS-IS command sets for IPv6, the following section presents the considerations to keep in mind during the design of your IS-IS network with the IPv6 protocol.

### Single SPF Restrictions

This section presents the restrictions of IS-IS network design when the IPv6 protocol is enabled concurrently with IPv4. Within an IS-IS area, a single SPF runs on each level for OSI, IPv4, and IPv6. This means that all IS-IS routers in a single IS-IS area must run the same set of protocols.

More specifically, the following sections describe these topics:

- **IS-IS adjacency router considerations for IPv6**—You can design three possible architectures of IS-IS adjacency routers in a single IS-IS area—IPv4-only IS-IS, IPv6-only IS-IS, and IPv4-IPv6 IS-IS (in which both protocols are enabled on all IS-IS routers). However, the section describes specific considerations about IS-IS adjacency that must be taken when both IPv4 and IPv6 are enabled gradually on IPv4-only IS-IS routers.

- **Level-2 router configuration for IPv6**—Level-2 IS-IS routers are responsible for intrarouting. Level-2 IS-IS routers must be contiguous with the same protocol sets. Otherwise, routing black holes result. The section presents the contiguous architectures for Level-2 routers when IPv6 is enabled.

- **Multitopology for IPv6**—An alternative to the restrictions of the IS-IS network design when both IPv4 and IPv6 are enabled is to implement a separate SPF algorithm for each address family. In this case, each protocol may have a separate topology.

### IS-IS Adjacency Router Considerations

Because the IS-IS protocol is a link-state protocol, adjacency routers exchange network information on the same links. Within an IPv4-only network, the IS-IS protocol can be enabled on all adjacency routers without any problem. This rule is also true when IS-IS is enabled on an IPv6-only network.

However, special care must be taken when both protocols are enabled on all adjacency IS-IS routers. In this specific case, the IS-IS protocol must be enabled with both protocols on all adjacency routers at the same time. Otherwise, IS-IS routers drop adjacencies with all their

IS-IS IPv4 neighbors. In fact, when the adjacency-check feature is enabled on Level-1 or Level-1-2 IS-IS routers, the IS-IS protocol checks the hello messages from its IS-IS neighbors and refuses to form an adjacency with a neighbor that is using a different protocol set.

The transition of your IPv4-only IS-IS routers toward IPv6-IPv4 IS-IS routers is very critical. If the adjacency check is not disabled during the transition, the IPv4-only IS-IS routers refuse to form an adjacency with IPv6-IPv4 IS-IS routers. Thus, the adjacencies are dropped. This is a very important consideration to keep in mind.

---

**NOTE**    In IS-IS's address-family ipv6 subcommand mode, the **no adjacency-check** command is specially designed to maintain the adjacencies when you enable IPv4-IPv6 IS-IS on each router in turn during the transition from IPv4-only IS-IS routers. When the **no adjacency-check** is enabled, this prevents IS-IS routers using different protocol sets from performing the hello check and dropping the adjacencies. After the successful transition, when all IS-IS routers support both protocols simultaneously, the **no adjacency-check** command can be removed. The **no adjacency-check** command is described in detail later in this chapter.

---

Here are the possible architectures of IS-IS adjacency routers in a single area:

- **IPv4-only**—The IS-IS protocol in the IS-IS area is enabled only with IPv4 on *all adjacency IS-IS routers*.

- **IPv6-only**—The IS-IS protocol in the IS-IS area is enabled only with IPv6 on *all adjacency IS-IS routers*.

- **IPv4-IPv6**—The IS-IS protocol in the IS-IS area is enabled with IPv6 *and* IPv4 on *all adjacency IS-IS routers*. However, during the transition from IPv4-only IS-IS routers to IPv4-IPv6 IS-IS routers, the **no adjacency-check** command must be enabled. Otherwise, adjacencies between the IS-IS using different protocol sets will be dropped.

Figure 4-7 shows examples of IS-IS network topologies with IPv4 and IPv6. Scenario A represents a correct topology, in which three IS-IS routers are enabled with IPv4 only within an IS-IS area. Scenario B illustrates a correct architecture in which three IS-IS routers are enabled with IPv6 only. Scenario C is an incorrect topology in which one IS-IS router is IPv6-only, and the others are IPv4-only. In this example, the IS-IS router enabled on IPv4 only drops adjacency information. Finally, scenario D shows another correct architecture in which all IS-IS routers are enabled with both IPv4 and IPv6 within the IS-IS area.

## Level-2 Router Considerations

In any IS-IS network design, all level-2 routers that are responsible for interarea routing must be contiguous. Therefore, IS-IS level-2 routers must be contiguous for IPv6-only, IPv4-only, or both IPv6 and IPv4. Otherwise, a routing black hole results. This is another consideration to keep in mind when you design IS-IS networks based on both IPv4 and IPv6.

**Figure 4-7** *Examples of IS-IS Network Topologies in Domains*

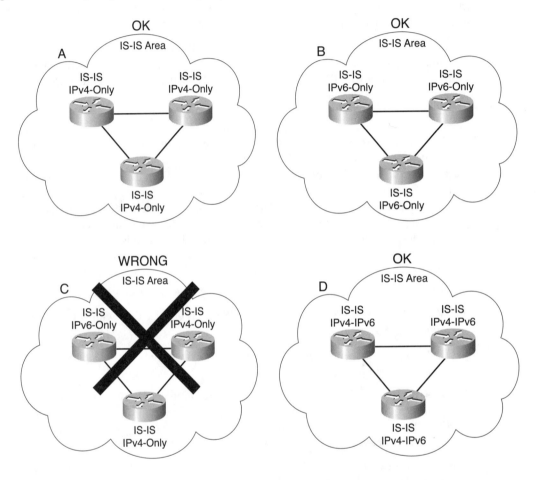

**NOTE** A black hole is caused when you have an IPv4-only IS-IS router on the shortest path for an IPv6 route. Routers at the edge send packets toward the IPv4-only IS-IS router, but the routers that are adjacent to the IPv4-only IS-IS router do not install the route because the next hop does not have an IPv6 address.

Figure 4-8 illustrates this concept. Scenario A shows three IS-IS areas connected with IS-IS level-2 routers. This scenario is wrong because the level-2 IS-IS router in IS-IS Area B is not enabled with IPv6. Therefore, this situation breaks the contiguity for the IPv6 protocol.

However, scenario B presents a correct IS-IS architecture in which all level-2 IS-IS routers are contiguous for both IPv4 and IPv6.

**Figure 4-8**   *Examples of Contiguous and Noncontiguous Level-2 IS-IS Routers for IPv6*

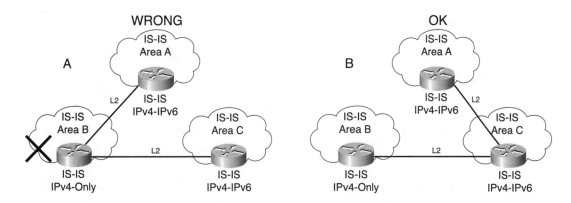

## Multitopology IS-IS for IPv6

To allow more flexibility for the design of IPv6 networks with IS-IS, Cisco added a multitopology feature in its IPv6 implementation of IS-IS. This new feature removes the limitation of having all IS-IS routers of a single area run the exact same set of protocols.

---

**NOTE**    The multitopology IS-IS feature for IPv6 will be available in a future Cisco IOS Software release.

---

## Enabling IS-IS on Cisco

The IPv6-supported IS-IS protocol is available in Cisco IOS Software versions 12.2(8)T, 12.0(21)ST on the Cisco 12000 series, and 12.2(9)S. The same **router isis** command in IPv4 defines the IS-IS process on the router. It defines the IS-IS process on the router. The **router isis** command's syntax is as follows:

```
Router(config)#router isis [tag]
```

The *tag* parameter specifies the name of a process.

The **router isis** command is used on a global basis.

## Configuring IS-IS for IPv6

After the IS-IS routing process is defined on the router, IS-IS can be configured to use the specific attributes of the IPv6 protocol. As with BGP for IPv6, the IPv6 attributes to be configured in the IS-IS configuration are applied under the address-family ipv6 subcommand mode of the IS-IS router (in the Router(config-router-af)# path). Table 4-9 presents the commands available in this subcommand mode to configure IS-IS for IPv6.

**Table 4-9**    *address-family ipv6 Subcommand Mode of IS-IS*

| Command | Description |
|---|---|
| **#address-family ipv6 [unicast]** | Places the router in the address-family ipv6 configuration mode. As with BGP4+, the **unicast** keyword is optional. |
| **#distance** *1-254* | The default administrative distance for IS-IS is 115. This command sets a new administrative distance for IS-IS. |
| **#default-information originate** [**route-map** *name* ] | Generates a default IPv6 route (::/0) into IS-IS. This command is the same as the existing **default-information** command in IPv4. |
| **#maximum-paths** *1-4* | Defines the maximum number of paths allowed for an IPv6 route learned through IS-IS. |
| **#redistribute** {**BGP** ∣ **OSPF** ∣ **RIP** ∣ **static**} [**metric** *metric-value* ] [**metric-type** {**internal** ∣ **external**}] [**level-1** ∣ **level-1-2** ∣ **level-2**] [*route-map-name* ] | Redistributes IPv6 routes learned from other IPv6 routing protocols such as BGP, OSPF, RIP, and static, into IS-IS. A route map may be applied to this command to filter attributes of the incoming routes. This command is the same as the **redistribute** command in IPv4. |
| **#redistribute isis** {**level-1** ∣ **level-2**} into {**level-1** ∣ **level-2**} **distribute-list** *prefix-list-name* | Redistributes the IPv6 routes of the IS-IS routing table between the IS-IS areas. A prefix list can be applied to filter the IPv6 routes to be redistributed between the areas. This command is the same as the **redistribute isis** command in IPv4. |
| **#no adjacency-check** | During the transition from IPv4-only IS-IS routers to IPv4-IPv6 IS-IS routers in a network, the **no adjacency-check** command maintains the adjacencies between IS-IS routers using different protocol sets. The **no adjacency-check** command prevents IS-IS routers using different protocol sets from performing the hello check and dropping the adjacencies. This command must be used only during the transition. After the transition, when all IS-IS routers are supporting both IPv4 and IPv6, the **no adjacency-check** can be removed. |
| **#summary-prefix** *ipv6-prefix/ prefix-length*  [**level-1** ∣ **level-2** ∣ **level-1-2**] | Configures IPv6 summary prefixes. The summary IPv6 prefix, the prefix length, and the IS-IS level must be specified as parameters. |
| **#exit-address-family** | Leaves the address-family ipv6 configuration mode and returns to the IS-IS router configuration mode. |

## Configuring the Network Entity Title IS-IS

After you have properly configured the specific attributes of IPv6, the next step is to identify the router for IS-IS by assigning to it an IS-IS Network Entity Title (NET) address. The SPF calculations rely on the IS-IS NET address to identify the routers. The IS-IS NET address is applied in the IS-IS router configuration mode. Use the **net** command to assign an IS-IS NET address to the routing process:

```
Router(config-router)#net network-entity-title
```

This is the same command as in IPv4.

## Enabling IS-IS on Interfaces

The last step to complete the IS-IS configuration for IPv6 on the router is to enable IS-IS on the router's interfaces. After the IPv6 address has been assigned to the interface, the **ipv6 router isis** command starts the IS-IS IPv6 process on that interface. Finally, as with IS-IS for IPv4, the interface's adjacency type can be specified on an interface basis. Table 4-10 shows the commands used to perform these tasks.

| NOTE | The type of adjacency can also be configured globally on the router. |
|------|----------------------------------------------------------------------|

**Table 4-10**    *Starting IS-IS for IPv6*

| Command | Description |
|---------|-------------|
| Router(config-if)#**ipv6 address** *ipv6-address/prefix-length* | Assigns a static IPv6 address to the network interface. |
| **Example 1** <br> Router(config-if)#**ipv6 address 3ffe:b00:ffff:1::1/64** | Assigns the static IPv6 address 3ffe:b00:ffff:1::1/64 to the network interface. |
| Router(config-if)#**ipv6 router isis** | Starts the IS-IS for IPv6 routing process on an interface. |
| Router(config-if)#**isis circuit-type** {**level-1** ‖ **level-1-2** ‖ **level-2-only**} | Configures the type of adjacency on an interface. This is the same command as in IPv4. |
| **Example 2** <br> Router(config-if)#**isis circuit-type** *level-2-only* | Configures the interface as a level-2-only IS-IS interface. This is the same command as in IPv4. |

Figure 4-9 shows a network architecture in which the IS-IS areas 49.0001 and 49.0002 are connected through level-2 IS-IS Routers R1 and R3. IS-IS support for IPv6 only is enabled on both routers. The level-2 IS-IS adjacency is configured on interface FastEthernet0/0 of Router R1 and on interface Ethernet0 of Router R3. Static IPv6 addresses within the prefix 2001:410:ffff:1::/64 have been assigned to these interfaces.

**Figure 4-9** *IS-IS Areas Interconnected Through IS-IS IPv6-Only Routers*

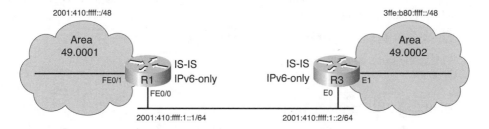

Example 4-13 shows the IS-IS configuration for IPv6 applied on Router R1 in Figure 4-9. As discussed previously, the IS-IS process is defined on the router using the **router isis** command. Then, the **redistribute static** command applied in the address-family ipv6 subcommand mode redistributes the static IPv6 routes known on Router R1 into IS-IS for the IPv6 routing table. The **net 49.0001.1921.6801.0001.00** command assigns the IS-IS NET address to the IS-IS routing process. On the FastEthernet0/0 interface, the **ipv6 address 2001:410:ffff:1::1/64** command represents the assignment of static IPv6. Finally, the IS-IS for IPv6 process is started on the interface FastEthernet0/1 using the command **ipv6 router isis**. The command **isis circuit-type level-2-only** sets that interface as level-2 only.

**Example 4-13** *Enabling IS-IS for IPv6 in Router R1*

```
RouterR1#configure terminal
RouterR1(config)#router isis
RouterR1(config-router)#address-family ipv6
RouterR1(config-router-af)#redistribute static
RouterR1(config-router-af)#exit-address-family
RouterR1(config-router)#net 49.0001.1921.6801.0001.00
RouterR1(config-router)#interface fastethernet0/0
RouterR1(config-if)#ipv6 address 2001:410:ffff:1::1/64
RouterR1(config-if)#ipv6 router isis
RouterR1(config-if)#isis circuit-type level-2-only
RouterR1(config-if)#exit
```

A similar configuration is applied on Router R3, except that the IPv6 address assigned to the Ethernet0 interface is 2001:410:ffff:1::2/64 and the IS-IS area is different. This is a simple example. Additional commands might be required to fine-tune the IS-IS configuration.

## Configuring IS-IS for IPv6 Over a GRE Tunnel

Because the IS-IS protocol runs on top of the data link layer (link-state protocol) and requires CLNP, IS-IS for IPv6 cannot be used by distant IPv6 networks connected through a configured tunnel.

**NOTE**     The configured tunnel is a point-to-point tunnel assigned statically between two nodes over IPv4 that have a dual stack (IPv4 and IPv6 stacks simultaneously). The configured tunnel encapsulates IPv6 packets over IPv4 packets. Then the encapsulated packets are forwarded between the dual-stack nodes using the IPv4 routing domains at the transport layer. At each side of the configured tunnel, IPv4 and IPv6 addresses must be assigned to the tunnel interfaces. Cisco IOS Software supports the configured tunnel. The configured tunnel is discussed in detail in Chapter 5.

IS-IS for IPv6 cannot be used over a configured tunnel (an IPv6-over-IPv4 tunnel) because IS-IS uses CLNP. However, IS-IS for IPv6 can be used by IPv6 networks separated by IPv4 routing domains if the IS-IS for IPv6 routers are configured with a GRE tunnel to carry the IPv6 packets inside a GRE IPv4 tunnel.

**NOTE**     Like the configured tunnel, the GRE tunnel must be configured statically between routers to allow the transport of IPv6 packets over IPv4 routing domains.

Example 4-14 shows the configuration of a GRE tunnel and IS-IS for IPv6 on a router. This configuration shows that Router R9 has the IPv6 address 201:410:ffff:1::1 configured on interface tunnel0 and has IS-IS for IPv6 enabled on this interface using the **ipv6 router isis** command.

**Example 4-14** *Configuring a GRE Tunnel for IS-IS IPv6*

```
RouterR9#configure terminal
RouterR9(config)#router isis
RouterR9(config-router)#net 49.0001.1921.6801.0001.00
RouterR9(config-router)#interface tunnel0
RouterR9(config-if)#ipv6 address 2001:410:ffff:1::1/64
RouterR9(config-if)#tunnel source ethernet0
RouterR9(config-if)#tunnel destination 132.214.1.3
RouterR9(config-if)#tunnel mode gre ipv6
RouterR9(config-if)#ipv6 router isis
RouterR1(config-if)#exit
```

**NOTE**     The configuration of GRE tunnels with IPv6 is described in detail in Chapter 5.

## Redistributing IPv6 Routes into IS-IS

Redistributing IPv6 routes into IS-IS for IPv6 is similar to this task in IPv4. RIPng, BGP4+, OSPF, static routes, and even IPv6 routes between level 1 (L1) and level 2 (L2) can be redistributed into IS-IS for IPv6. The following section presents commands for and examples of redistributing IPv6 routes into IS-IS.

As with BGP4+, the redistribution of IPv6 routes with IS-IS for IPv6 is performed in the address-family ipv6 subcommand mode using the **redistribute** command. This command is used in the same manner as the IPv4 **redistribute** command. The syntax for the **redistribute** command in the address-family ipv6 subcommand mode is as follows:

```
Router(config-router-af)#redistribute {bgp | isis | ospf | rip | static}
```

### Redistributing Static IPv6 Routes into IS-IS for IPv6

The **redistribute static** command is used in the address-family ipv6 subcommand mode to define the redistribution of static routes into IS-IS for IPv6. The **level-1**, **level-2**, and **level-1-2** keywords specify at what level the static routes are injected into IS-IS. The **metric-type** argument identifies the IS-IS metric associated with routes advertised into IS-IS: **internal** means an IS-IS metric less than 63 (the default), and **external** is an IS-IS metric less than 128 but greater than 64. The optional **metric** parameter identifies a new metric value associated with static routes advertised into IS-IS. Finally, a **route-map** may be used optionally to filter static IPv6 routes. The syntax for the **redistribute static** command in the address-family ipv6 subcommand mode is as follows:

```
Router(config-router-af)#redistribute static {level-1 | level-2 | level-1-2}
  [metric-type {external | internal}] [metric metric-value] [route-map map-tag]
```

The IS-IS configuration in Example 4-15 shows the **redistribute static** command in the address-family ipv6 subcommand mode, which injects static IPv6 routes into IS-IS.

**Example 4-15** *Redistributing Static IPv6 Routes into IS-IS for IPv6*

```
RouterR1#configure terminal
RouterR1(config)#router isis
RouterR1(config-router)#address-family ipv6
RouterR1(config-router-af)#redistribute static
```

### Redistributing BGP4+ into IS-IS for IPv6

The **redistribute bgp** command is used in the address-family ipv6 subcommand mode to define the redistribution of BGP4+ routes into IS-IS for IPv6. The *process* argument is the AS number. The **level-1**, **level-2**, and **level-1-2** keywords specify at what level the routes are injected into IS-IS from BGP4+ (the default is level-2). The **metric-type** argument identifies the IS-IS metric associated with routes advertised into IS-IS: **internal** means an IS-IS metric less than 63 (the default), and **external** is an IS-IS metric less than 128 but greater than 64. The optional **metric** parameter identifies a new metric value associated with BGP4+ routes advertised into IS-IS. A

**route-map** may be used optionally to filter incoming IPv6 routes from the source protocol BGP4+ to IS-IS for IPv6. The syntax for the **redistribute bgp** command in the address-family ipv6 subcommand mode is as follows:

```
Router(config-router-af)#redistribute bgp process {level-1 | level-2 | level-1-2}
  [metric-type {external | internal}] [metric metric-value] [route-map map-tag]
```

The IS-IS configuration in Example 4-16 shows the **redistribute bgp** command used in the address-family ipv6 subcommand mode to inject BGP4+ routes into IS-IS. The BGP4+ route 2001:420:ffff::/48 is injected into IS-IS for IPv6 as level-1 routes. The **metric-type** of these routes is **external**. Refer to the section "BGP4+ for IPv6" for detailed information about the BGP4+ configuration.

**Example 4-16** *Redistributing BGP4+ Routes into IS-IS for IPv6*

```
RouterR1#configure terminal
RouterR1(config)#router bgp 65001
RouterR1(config-router)#no bgp default ipv4-unicast
RouterR1(config-router)#bgp router-id 1.1.1.1
RouterR1(config-router)#neighbor 3ffe:b00:ffff:2::2 remote-as 65002
RouterR1(config-router)#address-family ipv6
RouterR1(config-router-af)#neighbor 3ffe:b00:ffff:2::2 activate
RouterR1(config-router-af)#network 2001:420:ffff::/48
RouterR1(config-router-af)#exit-address-family
RouterR1(config-router)#exit
RouterR1(config)#router isis
RouterR1(config-router)#address-family ipv6
RouterR1(config-router-af)#redistribute bgp 65001 level-1 metric-type external
```

## Redistributing RIPng into IS-IS for IPv6

The **redistribute rip** command is used in the address-family ipv6 subcommand mode to define the redistribution of RIPng routes into IS-IS for IPv6. The *process* argument is the RIPng process. The optional **metric** parameter identifies a new metric value associated with RIPng routes advertised into IS-IS. The **level-1**, **level-2**, and **level-1-2** keywords specify at what level the routes are injected into IS-IS from RIPng. The **metric-type** argument identifies the IS-IS metric associated with routes advertised into IS-IS: **internal** means an IS-IS metric less than 63 (the default), and **external** is an IS-IS metric less than 128 but greater than 64. Finally, a **route-map** may be used optionally to filter incoming IPv6 routes from the source protocol RIPng to IS-IS for IPv6. The syntax for the **redistribute rip** command in the address-family ipv6 subcommand mode is as follows:

```
Router(config-router-af)#redistribute rip process {level-1 | level-2 | level-1-2}
  [metric-type {external | internal}] [metric metric-value] [route-map map-tag]
```

The IS-IS configuration in Example 4-17 shows the **redistribute rip** command used in the address-family ipv6 subcommand mode of IS-IS to inject RIPng routes into IS-IS level 1. The 2001:410:ffff:1::/64 route is advertised into IS-IS level 1. Refer to the section "RIPng for IPv6" for detailed information about this configuration.

**Example 4-17** *Redistributing RIPng Routes into IS-IS for IPv6*

```
RouterR1#configure terminal
RouterR1(config)#ipv6 router rip RIPNGR3
RouterR1(config-rtr)#interface fastethernet0/1
RouterR1(config-if)#ipv6 address 2001:410:ffff:1::1/64
RouterR1(config-if)#ipv6 rip RIPNGR3 enable
RouterR1(config-if)#exit
RouterR1(config)#router isis
RouterR1(config-router)#address-family ipv6
RouterR1(config-router-af)#redistribute rip RIPNGR3 level-1
```

## Redistributing IS-IS into IS-IS

The **redistribute isis** command is used in the address-family ipv6 subcommand mode to define the redistribution between IS-IS level 1 and level 2. The **level-1** and **level-2** keywords specify at what source level the routes are injected into the destination level. By default, the IS-IS level-1 routes are automatically redistributed into IS-IS level 2. The **into** argument is an operator. A **distribute-list** may be used optionally with IS-IS to control the sending of IS-IS messages to a specific interface. The syntax for the **redistribute isis** command in the address-family ipv6 subcommand mode is as follows:

```
Router(config-router-af)#redistribute isis {level-1 | level-2} into {level-1 |
   level-2} [distribute-list prefix-list-name]
```

The IS-IS configuration in Example 4-18 shows the **redistribute isis** command used in the address-family ipv6 subcommand mode to inject IS-IS level-2 routes into IS-IS level 1.

**Example 4-18** *Redistributing IS-IS Level-2 Routes into IS-IS Level 1*

```
RouterR1#configure terminal
RouterR1(config)#router isis
RouterR1(config-router)#address-family ipv6
RouterR1(config-router-af)#redistribute isis level-2 into level-1
```

## Verifying and Managing IS-IS for IPv6

You can display IPv6 information related to IS-IS for IPv6 using the **show isis** command. This command is available for both IPv4 and IPv6. Table 4-11 presents the different command options and parameters you can use with the **show isis** command.

**Table 4-11** **show isis** *Command Parameters*

| Command Parameter | Description |
|---|---|
| **show isis database [detail | level-1 | level-2]** | Displays the contents of the IS-IS link-state database. This is the same command as in IPv4. |
| **show isis topology** | Shows a list of all connected routers in all IS-IS areas. This is the same command as in IPv4. |

**Table 4-11**  show isis *Command Parameters (Continued)*

| Command Parameter | Description |
|---|---|
| **show isis route** | Displays the IS-IS level-1 routing table only. This is the same command as in IPv4. |
| **show ipv6 protocols** [*summary* ] | Shows the parameters and current state of the IPv6 routing protocol. |
| **show ipv6 route is-is** | Shows only the IPv6 IS-IS routes. |

It is possible to reset the IS-IS routing using the **clear isis** command. It is available for both IPv4 and IPv6. The syntax of **clear isis** is as follows:

```
Router#clear isis *
```

Use the **clear isis** command to refresh the link-state database and recalculate all routes. To refresh the link-state database and recalculate all routes related to the IS-IS tag specified, use the following:

```
Router#clear isis [* | tag]
```

The **debug isis** command can be used to display debug information and events related to the adjacency packets related to the IS-IS routing protocol. This command is available for both IPv4 and IPv6. The syntax is as follows:

```
Router#debug isis adj-packets
```

To display events related to IS-IS update packets, use the following:

```
Router#debug isis update-packets
```

# OSPFv3 for IPv6

RFC 2328, *OSPF Version 2,* is the latest revision document describing version 2 of OSPF. Version 2 is the most advanced version of OSPF for IPv4 and is mainly used today in Cisco router implementations.

**NOTE**    The Cisco IOS Software supports OSPFv2. However, the configuration of OSPFv2 for IPv4 on Cisco routers is beyond the scope of this book.

OSPF version 3 is defined in RFC 2740, *OSPF for IPv6.* It is the counterpart of OSPFv2 for the IPv6 protocol. It is named OSPFv3 because the version field in RFC 2740 is set to 3. The OSPFv3 specification is mainly based on OSPFv2, but with some enhancements. Adding IPv6 support in the OSPFv2 protocol required important rewrites of the code to remove the IPv4 dependencies, such as the multicast IPv4 addresses 224.0.0.5 and 224.0.0.6, which are not useful in IPv6. After having been updated to support IPv6, OSPFv3 can distribute IPv6 prefixes and run natively over IPv6. Both OSPFv2 and OSPFv3 can be used concurrently, because each address family has a separate SPF.

OSPFv3 has some similarities to OSPFv2:

- OSPFv3 uses the same basic packet types as OSPFv2 such as hello, DBD (also called DDP, database description packets), LSR (link-state request), LSU (link-state update), and LSA (link-state advertisement).

- Mechanisms for neighbor discovery and adjacency formation are identical.

- Operations of OSPFv3 over the RFC-compliant nonbroadcast multiaccess (NBMA) and point-to-multipoint topology modes are supported. OSPFv3 also supports the other modes from Cisco such as point-to-point and broadcast including the interface.

- LSA flooding and aging are the same for both OSPFv2 and OSPFv3.

The main differences between OSPFv3 and OSPFv2 are as follows:

- **OSPFv3 runs over a link**—The network statement in the router subcommand mode of OSPFv2 is replaced by an OSPFv3 command to apply to the interface configuration. It is possible to have multiple instances per link.

- **Router ID**—This 32-bit number indicates that the router is not IPv6-specific. The router ID number is still based on 32-bit. This router ID identifies the OSPFv3 router. As for BGP4+, when no IPv4 address is configured, a router ID must be set.

- **Link ID**—This 32-bit number indicates that the links are not IPv6-specific. The link ID number is still based on 32-bit.

- **Link-local address**—OSPFv3 uses IPv6's link-local addresses to identify the OSPFv3 adjacency neighbors.

- **New LSA types**—The Link-LSA and Intra-Area-Prefix-LSA types are added in OSPFv3:

    — **Link-LSA (LSA type 0x0008)**—There is one Link-LSA per link. This new type provides the router's link-local address and lists all IPv6 prefixes attached to the link.

    — **Intra-Area-Prefix-LSA (LSA type 0x2009)**—There are multiple LSAs with different link-state IDs. The area flooding scope can be an associated prefix with the transit network referencing a Network-LSA, or it can be an associated prefix with a router or a stub referencing a Router-LSA.

- **Transport**—OSPFv3 messages are sent over IPv6 datagrams, allowing the configuration across IPv6-over-IPv4 tunnels.

- **Multicast address**—Two standard multicast addresses are used with OSPFv3:

  — **FF02::5**—Represents all SPF routers on the link-local scope. This multicast address is equivalent to 224.0.0.5 in OSPFv2.

  — **FF02::6**—Represents all Designated Router (DR) routers on the link-local scope. This multicast address is equivalent to 224.0.0.6 in OSPFv2.

- **Security**—OSPFv3 uses Authentication Headers (IPSec AH) and Encapsulating Security Payload (IPSec ESP) extension headers as an authentication mechanism instead of the variety of authentication schemes and procedures defined in OSPFv2. The OSPFv3 implementation in the Cisco IOS Software supports IPSec.

**NOTE**    Although this section presented an overview of the similarities and differences between OSPFv3 and OSPFv2, it is recommended that you read the complete specification in RFC 2740, *OSPF for IPv6*.

## Configuring OSPFv3 on Cisco

Configuring OSPFv3 on Cisco is very similar to configuring it on OSPFv2, because it is a matter of prefixing the existing interface and commands with "**ipv6**." However, keep in mind two important changes from the OSPFv2 configuration:

- **network area command**—The way to identify IPv6 networks that are part of the OSPFv3 network is different than with the OSPFv2 configuration. The **network area** command in OSPFv2 is replaced by a configuration in which interfaces are directly configured to specify that IPv6 networks are part of the OSPFv3 network. Table 4-12 shows you how to identify networks that are part of OSPFv3.

- **Native IPv6 router mode**—The configuration of OSPFv3 is not a subcommand mode of the **router ospf** command (OSPFv2 configuration). With other routing protocols, such as BGP4+ and IS-IS for IPv6, you can place the router in the address-family ipv6 configuration subcommand mode to enable IPv6-specific parameters.

**NOTE**    OSPFv3 is the latest IPv6 IGP added to the Cisco IOS Software. However, currently OSPFv3 is less proven than RIPng and IS-IS over IPv6. Also, this section is based on OSPFv3's beta implementation. OSPFv3 commands and parameters used in this chapter might differ from a recent Cisco IOS Software release you downloaded.

The **ipv6 router ospf** command presented in Step 1 of Table 4-12 enables an OSPFv3 process on the router. The *process-id* is a numeric value local to the router that uniquely identifies an

OSPFv3 process. Similar to IPv4, you can run multiple OSPFv3 processes on the same router. Table 4-12 describes enabling an OSPFv3 process and configuring this routing protocol with IPv6.

| | |
|---|---|
| **NOTE** | Having multiple OSPFv3 processes on the same router is not recommended because it creates multiple databases, which causes more overhead. |

**Table 4-12**   **ipv6 router ospf** *Command*

| Command | Description |
|---|---|
| **Step 1**<br>Router(config)#**ipv6 router ospf** *process-id* | Enables an OSPFv3 process on the router. The *process-id* parameter identifies a unique OSPFv3 process. This command is used on a global basis. |
| **Example**<br>Router(config)#**ipv6 router ospf 100** | Enables the OSPFv3 process number 100 on the router. |
| **Step 2**<br>Router(config-router)#**router-id** *ipv4-address* | For an IPv6-only OSPF router, a **router-id** parameter must be defined in the OSPFv3 configuration as an IPv4 address using the **router-id** *ipv4-address* command. You can use any IPv4 address as the value. |
| **Example**<br>Router(config-router)#**router-id 10.1.1.3** | Defines the **router-id** value as 10.1.1.3. |
| **Step 3**<br>Router(config-router)#**area** *area-id* **range** *ipv6-prefix/prefix-length* | Summarizes IPv6 routes that match the *ipv6-prefix/prefix-length* parameters. |
| **Example**<br>Router(config-router)#**area 1 range 2001:410:ffff::/48** | Configures an area range that summarizes IPv6 routes matching the 2001:410:ffff::/48 prefix. |
| **Step 4**<br>Router(config-router)#**interface** *interface-id* | Enters the interface configuration mode. |
| **Step 5**<br>Router(config-if)#**ipv6 address** *ipv6-address/prefix-length* | Assigns a static IPv6 address to the network interface. |
| **Example**<br>Router(config-if)#**ipv6 address 2001:410:ffff:1::1/64** | Assigns the static IPv6 address 2001:410:ffff:1::1/64 to the network interface. |

**Table 4-12**    **ipv6 router ospf** *Command (Continued)*

| Command | Description |
|---|---|
| **Step 6**<br><br>Router(config-if)#**ipv6 ospf** *process-id* **area** *area-id* | Identifies the IPv6 prefix assigned to this interface as part of the OSPFv3 network. This command replaces the **network area** command used with OSPFv2. |
| **Example**<br><br>Router(config-if)#**ipv6 ospf 100 area 1** | Identifies the IPv6 prefix 2001:410:ffff:1::/64 as part of area 1 in the OSPFv3 process 100. |

Figure 4-10 illustrates a network topology in which Routers R1 and R3 interconnect multiple OSPFv3 areas. Router R1 from OSPF area 1 is interconnected to backbone area 0 using the FastEthernet 0/0 interface. The IPv6 prefix used on OSPF area 1 is 2001:410:ffff:1::/64, and the prefix in use on the backbone is 3ffe:b00:ffff:1::/64. Figure 4-10 also illustrates the aggregatable global unicast IPv6 addresses assigned to the routers' interfaces.

**Figure 4-10**    *Multiple OSPFv3 Area Configurations*

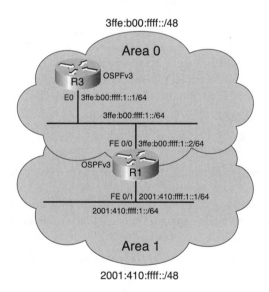

Example 4-19 presents the OSPFv3 configuration applied on Router R1 in Figure 4-10. Th **ipv6 router ospf 100** command configures the OSPFv3 process 100 on the router. The command **area 1 range 2001:410:ffff::/48** configures the range of area 1 within the prefix 2001:410:ffff::/48. The IPv6 addresses 2001:410:ffff:1::/64 and 3ffe:b00:ffff:1::2 are assigned to interfaces FE0/1 and FE0/0, respectively. In the FE0/0 interface configuration mode, the command **ipv6 ospf 100**

**area 1** identifies the prefix 2001:410:ffff:1::/64 as part of area 1 for the OSPFv3 process 100. Because the FE0/0 interface is adjacent to backbone area 0, the command **ipv6 ospf 100 area 0** applied on that interface identifies that the prefix 3ffe:b00:ffff:1::/64 is part of area 0.

**Example 4-19** *Configuring OSPFv3 in Router R1*

```
RouterR1#configure terminal
RouterR1(config)#ipv6 router ospf 100
RouterR1(config-router)#router-id 10.1.1.3
RouterR1(config-router)#area 1 range 2001:410:ffff::/48
RouterR1(config-router)#int FE0/1
RouterR1(config-if)#ipv6 address 2001:410:ffff:1::1/64
RouterR1(config-if)#ipv6 ospf 100 area 1
RouterR1(config-if)#int FE0/0
RouterR1(config-if)#ipv6 address 3ffe:b00:ffff:1::2/64
RouterR1(config-if)#ipv6 ospf 100 area 0
RouterR1(config-if)#exit
```

A similar configuration is also applied on Router R3, except that the area is 0 in this case.

---

**NOTE**    Example 4-19 is a simple example of how to configure OSPFv3 on Cisco. However, because the configuration of OSPFv3 on Cisco is very similar to OSPFv2 (you just add "**ipv6**" to the OSPFv2 commands in most cases), if you have experience with OSPFv2, you should be able to configure advanced IPv6 routing infrastructures using OSPFv3.

---

## Redistributing IPv6 Routes into OSPFv3

Redistributing IPv6 routes into OSPFv3 is similar to this task in IPv4. BGP4+, RIPng, IS-IS for IPv6, and static routes can be redistributed into OSPFv3. The following section is an overview of the command used to redistribute routes into OSPFv3. Redistributing IPv6 with OSPFv3 is performed in the ipv6 router ospf subcommand mode using the **redistribute** command. The syntax for the **redistribute** command with OSPFv3 is as follows:

```
Router(config-router)#redistribute {bgp | isis | rip | static}
```

---

**NOTE**    The **redistribute** command in OSPFv3 is similar to the one in OSPFv2. Refer to the Cisco website for detailed information on IPv6 route redistribution between OSPFv3 and the other protocols.

---

### Verifying and Managing OSPFv3

You can display IPv6 information related to the OSPFv3 protocol using the **show ipv6 ospf** command. Its parameters and options are described in Table 4-13.

**Table 4-13**   **show ipv6 ospf** *Command Parameters*

| Command Parameter | Description |
|---|---|
| **ospf** [*process-id*] | Displays information about an OSPFv3 process configured on the router. |
| **ospf database** | Displays the contents of the topological database maintained by the router. |
| **ospf** [*process-id*] **database link** | Displays the new Link-LSA type added in OSPFv3. |
| **ospf** [*process-id*] **database prefix** | Displays the new Intra-Area-Prefix-LSA type added in OSPFv3. |
| **route ospf** | Displays all IPv6 routes learned by the router through OSPFv3. |

You can reset the IPv6 OSPFv3 routing table using the **clear ipv6 ospf** command, the syntax for which is as follows:

```
Router#clear ipv6 ospf [process-id]
```

## EIGRP for IPv6

IPv6 currently does not support EIGRP. However, the Cisco IOS Software IPv6 road map is considering an IPv6 add-on for EIGRP in a future Cisco IOS Software release.

# Cisco Express Forwarding for IPv6

Cisco Express Forwarding (CEF) is a Layer 3 switching technology designed for routers. It uses a method that optimizes route lookups to achieve very fast forwarding. CEF uses two tables to store the information needed for routing: the Forwarding Information Database (FIB) and the adjacency table.

**NOTE**    CEF is supported on routers 1700, 2600, 3600, 3700, 7100, 7200, 7400, 7500, 7600, and the Catalyst 6500 and 12000 series.

There are two CEF modes:

- **Central CEF**—The route processor handles CEF and adjacency tables. This mode is supported on router series 1700 to 7500.

- **Distributed CEF (dCEF)**—This mode is used on distributed hardware architectures such as the Cisco 7500 VIP and Cisco 12000 line cards. dCEF performs the express forwarding of packets between port adapters and uses interprocess communications (IPC) to synchronize the CEF FIB and adjacency tables between router processors and linecards. The dCEF mode is supported on router series 7500 and 12000(GSR).

CEFv6's behavior is the same as CEF for IPv4. CEFv6 has new configuration commands, and CEFv6 and CEF for IPv4 have some of the same commands. This section presents the new commands used to manage CEF for IPv6 networks.

## Enabling CEFv6 on Cisco

CEFv6 is available on Cisco IOS Software 12.2(13)T and above and 12.2(9)S and above. dCEFv6 is available on Cisco IOS Software 12.0(21)ST1, 12.0(22)S and above for the Cisco 12000 series, and 12.2(13)T for the Cisco 7500 series.

The **ipv6 cef** command enables the central CEFv6 mode. However, before you enable CEFv6, you must enable IPv4 CEF using the **ip cef** command. Similarly, you must enable IPv4 dCEF using the **ip cef distributed** command before you enable dCEFv6 with the **ipv6 cef distributed** command.

## show Commands for CEFv6

You can display IPv6 information related to CEFv6 using the **show ipv6 cef** and the **show cef** commands. Table 4-14 shows the options and parameters of the show ipv6 cef command.

**Table 4-14** show ipv6 cef *Command Parameters*

| Command Parameter | Description |
|---|---|
| **cef** *ipv6-prefix* [*detail*] | Shows IPv6 CEF information for the given IPv6 prefix. |
| **cef** *interface* [*detail*] | Shows all IPv6 prefixes using the interface specified. |
| **cef adjacency** *adjacency* | Shows all IPv6 prefixes resolving through the specified adjacency. |
| **cef non-recursive** [*detail*] | Shows nonrecursive prefixes. |
| **cef summary** | Shows IPv6 CEF table summary information. |
| **cef traffic prefix-length** | Shows per-prefix length accounting statistics. |
| **cef unresolved** | Shows unresolved prefixes. |
| **cef drop** | Shows a counter of IPv6 and IPv4 packets dropped. |
| **cef interface** [*detail*] [*statistics*] *interface* | Shows CEF interface status and configuration. |

**Table 4-14**   **show ipv6 cef** *Command Parameters (Continued)*

| Command Parameter | Description |
|---|---|
| **cef linecard** [*detail*] [*statistics*] *slot* | Shows CEF information related to linecards. |
| **cef not-cef-switched** | Shows counters of IPv6 and IPv4 packets passed on to the next switching layer. |

## debug Commands for CEFv6

You can debug CEFv6 using the **debug ipv6 cef** command. Its options and parameters are shown in Table 4-15.

**Table 4-15**   **debug ipv6 cef** *Command Parameters*

| Command Parameter | Description |
|---|---|
| **drops** | Enables debugging of packets dropped by CEFv6 switching. |
| **events** | Enables debugging of control plane events for CEFv6. |
| **hash** | Enables debugging of load-balancing hash setup events for CEFv6. |
| **receive** | Enables debugging packets passed to IPv6 process-level switching. |
| **table** | Enables debugging of CEFv6 table modification events. |

# Summary

In this chapter, you learned how to configure static and default IPv6 routes. You also learned about the updates applied to the specifications of the interdomain routing protocol such as Border Gateway Protocol (BGP), and intradomain routing protocols such as Routing Information Protocol (RIP), Intermediate System-to-Intermediate System (IS-IS), and Open Shortest Path First (OSPF) to support the IPv6 protocol.

Here is a summary of these updates for each routing protocol:

- **BGP4+**—BGP4+ includes multiprotocol extensions for BGP-4. BGP4+ supports the new address family IPv6. The NEXT_HOP and NLRI attributes are now expressed as IPv6 addresses and prefixes. The NEXT_HOP attribute can handle aggregatable global unicast and link-local addresses.

- **RIPng**—RIPng is based on the design of RIPv2: distance-vector protocol, radius of 15 hops, and so on. RIPng uses IPv6 for transport. The multicast address FF02::9 sends RIPng updates.

- **IS-IS for IPv6**—Two new TLVs are defined for IPv6: IPv6 Reachability and IPv6 Interface Address. A new NLPID value is defined for IPv6. Considerations about the single SPF restrictions must be kept in mind during the design of IS-IS networks based on both the IPv4 and IPv6 protocols.

- **OSPFv3**—To add IPv6 support in OSPFv3, the IPv4 dependencies in this protocol were removed. OSPFv3 uses IPv6 for transport. Link-local addresses are used between adjacency routers. The multicast addresses FF02::5 and FF02::6 are defined for OSPFv3.

Although these routing protocols have been updated to support IPv6, they are similar to their equivalents in IPv4. Moreover, the routing protocols with IPv6 support still use the longest-match prefix as a routing algorithm for route selection, as do their equivalents in IPv4.

The last part of this chapter presented an overview of Cisco Express Forwarding (CEF) for IPv6. CEFv6 is the same as CEF for IPv4. Cisco introduced new commands for the configuration and management of CEFv6. However, common commands are also used for both CEFv6 and CEF for IPv4.

You also learned how to configure BGP4+, RIPng, IS-IS, and OSPFv3 with IPv6 on the Cisco IOS Software technology to be able to minimally deploy them on your networks. For most of these routing protocols, you have seen that the Cisco IOS Software commands to configure them are similar to their equivalents in IPv4. This chapter presented examples, router configurations, and commands to manage these routing protocols on the Cisco IOS Software.

# Case Study: Configuring Static Routes and Routing Protocols with Cisco

Complete the following exercises by configuring static routes and routing protocols with IPv6 to practice the skills you learned in this chapter.

## Objectives

In this exercise, you will complete the following tasks:

- Configuring a static IPv6 route on a router
- Configuring a default IPv6 route
- Verifying an IPv6 route table
- Enabling BGP4+ for IPv6
- Establishing eBGP peerings using an aggregatable global unicast IPv6 address
- Displaying BGP IPv6 neighbors
- Statically configuring an aggregatable global unicast IPv6 address

- Statically configuring a link-local address

- Establishing iBGP peering using a link-local address

- Creating a route map for IPv6

## Commands List

In this configuration exercise, you will use the commands shown in Table 4-16. If necessary, refer to this list during the exercise.

**Table 4-16**   *Commands List*

| Command | Description |
|---|---|
| **address-family ipv6** | Enters the address-family ipv6 subcommand mode of a router configuration. |
| **copy run start** | Saves the current configuration to NVRAM. |
| **ipv6 unicast-routing** | Enables IPv6 traffic forwarding. |
| **ipv6 address 3ffe:b00:ffff:1::2/64** | Configures a static IPv6 address. |
| **ipv6 address 2001:410:ffff:1::2/64** | Configures a static IPv6 address. |
| **ipv6 address 2001:430:ffff:1::1/64** | Configures a static IPv6 address. |
| **ipv6 address fe80::1001 link-local** | Configures a static IPv6 address. This is a link-local address. |
| **ipv6 route 3ffe::/16 fastethernet0/0 fe80::260:3eff:fe47:1533** | Configures a static IPv6 route pointing out a link-local address as the next hop. |
| **ipv6 route::/0 fastethernet0/1 fe80::260:3eff:fe78:3351** | Configures a default IPv6 route pointing out a link-local address as the next hop. |
| **ipv6 nd suppress-ra** | Suppresses router advertisement. |
| **neighbor 2001:410:ffff:1::1 remote-as 65099** | Configures BGP peering using an IPv6 address. |
| **neighbor 2001:410:ffff:1::1 activate** | Activates BGP peering. |
| **network 2001:430:ffff::/48** | Specifies the prefix 2001:430:ffff::/48 to announce via a routing protocol. |
| **no bgp default ipv4-unicast** | Disables the advertisement of BGP-4 routing information for the IPv4 address family. |
| **router bgp 65005** | Enables the BGP4+ router process for the AS65005. |
| **route-map linklocal-iBGP** | Defines a route map. |
| **set ipv6 next-hop 2001:430:ffff:1::1** | Sets the NEXT_HOP attribute. |

*continues*

**Table 4-16** *Commands List (Continued)*

| Command | Description |
|---|---|
| **show ipv6 interface fastEthernet 0/0** | Displays the IPv6 configuration applied to an interface. |
| **show ipv6 interface fastethernet 0/1** | Displays the IPv6 configuration applied to an interface. |
| **show bgp ipv6 neighbors** | Displays information on the state of all IPv6 BGP4+ neighbors. |

# Task 1: Configure Static and Default Routes on a Router

Figure 4-11 shows the network architecture used in Task 1. Your corporate network is getting IPv6 connectivity to the IPv6 Internet through the IPv6 provider using 2001:410::/35 as an aggregatable global unicast network prefix. The IPv6 provider assigned the prefix 2001:410:ffff::/48 to your corporate network. However, your corporate network is also connected to the 6bone network, which is based on the aggregatable global unicast prefix 3ffe::/16. The main goal of this task is to set on Router R4 a static IPv6 route for the prefix 3ffe::/16 that points out the 6bone and then add a default IPv6 route pointing out the IPv6 provider.

**Figure 4-11** *Adding Static IPv6 Routes on a Router*

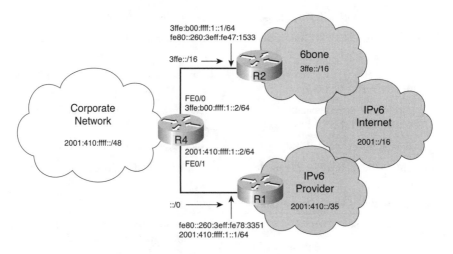

Complete the following steps:

**Step 1** Enter the command to enable IPv6 traffic forwarding on Router R4 to forward unicast IPv6 packets between interfaces. What command should you use?

```
RouterR4#conf t
RouterR4(config)#ipv6 unicast-routing
RouterR4(config)#exit
```

**Step 2**    Based on the following table, assign one static IPv6 address to each interface of
Router R4 specified. Then disable router advertisement on each interface.
What command assigns a static IPv6 to an interface?

| Router R4 Interface | IPv6 Address |
|---|---|
| FastEthernet 0/0 (FE0/0) | 3ffe:b00:ffff:1::2/64 |
| FastEthernet 0/1 (FE0/1) | 2001:410:ffff:1::2/64 |

```
RouterR4#conf t
RouterR4(config)#int fe0/0
RouterR4(config-if)#ipv6 address 3ffe:b00:ffff:1::2/64
RouterR4(config-if)#ipv6 nd suppress-ra
RouterR4(config-if)#int fe0/1
RouterR4(config-if)#ipv6 address 2001:410:ffff:1::2/64
RouterR4(config-if)#ipv6 nd suppress-ra
RouterR4(config-if)#exit
RouterR4(config)#exit
```

**Step 3**    Verify the static IPv6 addresses of each interface. What command displays
IPv6 addresses used on an interface?

```
RouterR4#show ipv6 interface fastEthernet 0/0
RouterR4#show ipv6 interface fastEthernet 0/1
```

**Step 4**    Configure a static IPv6 route on Router R4 to reach the destination network
3ffe::/16, represented in Figure 4-11 as the 6bone. Use the next-hop link-
local address fe80::260:3eff:fe47:1533 through the FastEthernet0/0
interface. What command will you use?

```
RouterR4#conf t
RouterR4(config)#ipv6 route 3ffe::/16 fastethernet0/0 fe80::260:3eff:fe47:1533
RouterR4(config)#exit
```

**Step 5**    Configure a default IPv6 route to reach the IPv6 Internet through the
FastEthernet0/1 interface. Use the next-hop link-local address
fe80::260:3eff:fe78:3351.

```
RouterR4#conf t
RouterR4(config)#ipv6 route ::/0 fastethernet0/1 fe80::260:3eff:fe78:3351
RouterR4(config)#exit
```

**Step 6**    Examine the current IPv6 routing table in Router R4 and verify the static and
default IPv6 routes added. What command is used to display the IPv6 routes?

```
RouterR4#show ipv6 route
```

**Step 7**    Save the current configuration to NVRAM.

```
RouterR4#copy run start
Destination filename [startup-config]?
Building configuration...
[OK]
```

## Task 2: Configure eBGP and iBGP Peerings on Router R2

Figure 4-12 shows the network architecture used for Task 2. Your domain is AS65005, and you have to configure multihop eBGP peering with AS65099 and AS65123 on border Router R2 using the aggregatable global unicast IPv6 addresses of your neighbors. Then, because routers R1 and R2 are adjacent on the same link, you have to configure an iBGP peering with Router R1 but using the link-local address of this iBGP neighbor.

**Figure 4-12** *Configuring eBGP and iBGP Peerings*

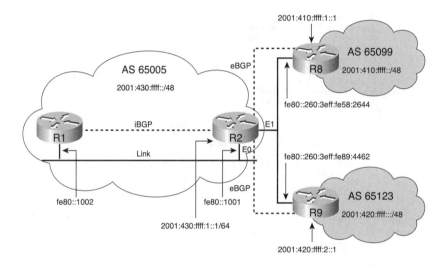

Follow these steps:

**Step 1** Before establishing the eBGP peering with AS65009 and AS65123, add two IPv6 static routes on Router R2 to reach these domains. The destination prefix 2001:410:ffff::/48 can be reached using the next-hop link-local address fe80::260:3eff:fe58:2644. The destination prefix 2001:420:ffff::/48 can be reached through the next-hop link-local address fe80::260:3eff:fe89:4462. What commands will you use to perform these tasks?

```
RouterR2#conf t
RouterR2(config)#ipv6 route 2001:410:ffff::/48 ethernet1 fe80::260:3eff:fe58:2644
RouterR2(config)#ipv6 route 2001:420:ffff::/48 ethernet1 fe80::260:3eff:fe89:4462
RouterR2(config)#exit
```

**Step 2** Enter the command to enable a BGP4+ router process on Router R2 for the AS65005. What command will you use?

```
RouterR2#conf t
RouterR2(config)#router bgp 65005
RouterR2(config-router)#
```

**Step 3**    Disable the advertisement of routing information for the IPv4 address family on the BGP router process. Also define the router ID as 172.16.1.1.

```
RouterR2(config-router)#no bgp default ipv4-unicast
RouterR2(config-router)#bgp router-id 172.16.1.1
RouterR2(config-router)#
```

**Step 4**    Specify the IPv6 prefix of this AS to announce via BGP4+. The IPv6 prefix of this AS is 2001:430:ffff::/48. What command will you use?

```
RouterR2(config-router)#address-family ipv6
RouterR2(config-router-af)#network 2001:430:ffff::/48
RouterR2(config-router-af)#exit
RouterR2(config-router)#exit
```

**Step 5**    Configure the BGP peering with AS65099. Use the aggregatable global unicast IPv6 address 2001:410:ffff:1::1 to establish this BGP peering. Be sure BGP peering is activated. What commands configure BGP peering with a neighbor?

```
RouterR2(config-router)#neighbor 2001:410:ffff:1::1 remote-as 65099
RouterR2(config-router)#address-family ipv6
RouterR2(config-router-af)#neighbor 2001:410:ffff:1::1 activate
RouterR2(config-router-af)#exit
RouterR2(config-router)#
```

**Step 6**    As you did in Step 5, configure BGP4+ peering with AS65123, but use the aggregatable global unicast IPv6 address 2001:420:ffff:2::1.

```
RouterR2(config-router)#neighbor 2001:420:ffff:2::1 remote-as 65123
RouterR2(config-router)#address-family ipv6
RouterR2(config-router-af)#neighbor 2001:420:ffff:2::1 activate
RouterR2(config-router-af)#exit
RouterR2(config-router)#exit
```

**Step 7**    Verify your BGP4+ configuration by displaying information on the state of the IPv6 BGP4+ neighbors. What command configures BGP peering with a neighbor?

```
RouterR2#show bgp ipv6 neighbors
```

**Step 8**    Using the following table, statically assign one aggregatable global unicast and one link-local IPv6 address to Router R2's Ethernet0 interface. The Ethernet0 interface will be used to configure iBGP peering using the link-local address of the adjacent BGP4+ neighbor.

| Type of Address | IPv6 Address |
|---|---|
| Link-local address | fe80::1001 |
| Global IPv6 address | 2001:430:ffff:1::1/64 |

```
RouterR2#conf t
RouterR2(config)#int ethernet0
RouterR2(config-if)#ipv6 address 2001:430:ffff:1::1/64
RouterR2(config-if)#ipv6 address fe80::1001 link-local
RouterR2(config-if)#exit
RouterR2(config)#exit
RouterR2#
```

**Step 9**    Define a **route-map** statement to set the NEXT_HOP attribute on outbound BGP4+ updates to be sent to the iBGP neighbor (Router R1). The NEXT_HOP attribute must be set to the IPv6 address 2001:430:ffff:1::1.

```
RouterR2#conf t
RouterR2(config)#route-map linklocal-iBGP
RouterR2(config-route-map)#set ipv6 next-hop 2001:430:ffff:1::1
RouterR2(config-route-map)#exit
RouterR2(config)#
```

**Step 10**    Configure iBGP peering on Router R2 with Router R1. Use Router R1's link-local address fe80::1002 in the BGP4+ configuration.

```
RouterR2(config)#router bgp 65005
RouterR2(config-router)#neighbor fe80::1002 remote-as 65005
RouterR2(config-router)#neighbor fe80::1002 update-source ethernet0
RouterR2(config-router)#address-family ipv6
RouterR2(config-router-af)#neighbor fe80::1002 activate
RouterR2(config-router-af)#neighbor fe80::1002 route-map linklocal-iBGP out
RouterR2(config-router-af)#exit-address-family
RouterR2(config-router)#
```

**Step 11**    Examine again your BGP4+ configuration by displaying information on the state of all IPv6 BGP4+ neighbors. You should see the new iBGP peering using a link-local address.

```
RouterR2#show bgp ipv6 neighbors
```

**Step 12**    Save the current configuration to NVRAM.

```
RouterR2#copy run start
Destination filename [startup-config]?
Building configuration...
[OK]
```

# Review Questions

Answer the following questions, and then refer to Appendix B, "Answers to Review Questions," for the answers.

  **1**    What command displays the whole IPv6 routing table?

  **2**    Using the following table, specify the commands used to add the static IPv6 routes in the router for each destination IPv6 network given.

| Destination IPv6 Network | Next Hop | Corresponding Interface |
|---|---|---|
| 3ffe::/16 | fe80::260:3eff:fe58:2644 | ethernet0 |
| 2002::/16 | — | Tunnel0 |
| 2001:410:ffff::/48 | fe80::260:3eff:fec5:8888 | ethernet1 |
| Default IPv6 route | fe80::260:3eff:fe69:3322 | fastethernet0/0 |

| Destination IPv6 Network | Command Used in the Cisco IOS Software |
|---|---|
| 3ffe::/16 | |
| 2002::/16 | |
| 2001:410:ffff::/48 | |
| Default IPv6 route | |

3   What changes were made to BGP4+ for IPv6 support?

4   What command is used in the BGP router subcommand mode to disable the advertisement of routing information for the IPv4 address family?

5   How should an IPv6 prefix list be applied in a BGP4+ configuration?

6   List the IPv6 commands that are equivalent to the well-known IPv4 commands listed in the following table.

| IPv4 Command | Equivalent Command in IPv6 |
|---|---|
| **show ip route** | |
| **router bgp** | |
| **ip prefix-list** | |
| **route-map** | |
| **show ip bgp** | |
| **clear bgp** | |
| **debug bgp** | |
| **show ip prefix-list** | |

7   What destination address is used by RIPng in IPv6 to send updates?

8   Which command enables RIPng on an interface?

9   What are the new TLVs and the values they add in the IS-IS specification to support IPv6?

10  What NLPID value is defined in IS-IS for IPv6 support?

11  Which command starts IS-IS for IPv6 on an interface?

12  Which RFC describes the OSPFv3 specification?

13  Which command enables an OSPFv3 process on the router?

14  What replaces the **network area** command in OSPFv3?

# References

RFC 904, *Exterior Gateway Protocol Formal Specification,* D.L. Mills, IETF, www.ietf.org/rfc/rfc904.txt, April 1984

RFC 1058, *Routing Information Protocol,* C. Hedrick, IETF, www.ietf.org/rfc/rfc1058.txt, June 1988

RFC 1195, *Use of OSI IS-IS for Routing in TCP/IP and Dual Environments,* R. Callon, IETF, www.ietf.org/rfc/rfc1195.txt, December 1990

RFC 1723, *RIP Version 2 Carrying Additional Information,* G. Malkin, IETF, www.ietf.org/rfc/rfc1723.txt, November 1994

RFC 1771, *A Border Gateway Protocol 4 (BGP-4),* Y. Rekhter, T. Li, IETF, www.ietf.org/rfc/rfc1771.txt, March 1995

RFC 2080, *RIPng for IPv6,* G. Malkin, R. Minnear, IETF, www.ietf.org/rfc/rfc2080.txt, January 1997

RFC 2328, *OSPF Version 2,* J. Moy, IETF, www.ietf.org/rfc/rfc2328.txt, April 1998

RFC 2545, *Use of BGP-4 Multiprotocol Extensions for IPv6 Inter-Domain Routing,* P. Marques, F. Dupont, IETF, www.ietf.org/rfc/rfc2545.txt, March 1999

RFC 2740, *OSPF for IPv6,* R. Coltun, D. Ferguson, J. Moy, IETF, www.ietf.org/rfc/rfc2740.txt, December 1999

RFC 2858, *Multiprotocol Extensions for BGP-4,* T. Bates et al., IETF, www.ietf.org/rfc/rfc2858.txt, June 2000

Draft-ietf-isis-ipv6-05.txt, *Routing IPv6 with IS-IS,* Christian E. Hopps, IETF, www.ietf.org/internet-drafts/draft-ietf-isis-ipv6-03.txt, October 2002

ISO 8479, *Connectionless Network Protocol (CLNP)*

ISO/EIC 10589, *Intermediate System to Intermediate System*

# IPv4 and IPv6: Coexistence and Integration

The transition from the IPv4 protocol, on which the current Internet core is based, toward IPv6 is crucial for a strong adoption and large-scale deployment of IPv6. The IPv6 protocol has been designed from the beginning with transition in mind to maintain complete backward compatibility with IPv4. Part III describes the coexistence, integration mechanisms, strategies, and approaches in IPv6 designed to provide a smooth transition of IPv4 networks to IPv6. These include dual-stack, the tunneling of IPv6 packets in IPv4, and protocol translation.

On the practical side, Part III presents in detail the new commands added in the Cisco IOS Software for the integration and coexistence mechanisms. Finally, this part explains how to enable IPv6 and configure transition mechanisms on several host operating systems such as Microsoft, Solaris, FreeBSD, Linux, and Tru64 to interact with Cisco routers.

The following chapters comprise this part of the book:

"There is no reason anyone would want a computer in their home."

Ken Olsen, President, Chairman, and Founder of Digital Equipment, 1977

# CHAPTER 5

# IPv6 Integration and Coexistence Strategies

The IPv6 protocol has been designed from the beginning with transition in mind to maintain complete backward compatibility with IPv4. Unlike the Y2K bug, there is no D-day for the switch from IPv4 to IPv6 networks on the Internet. The complete conversion of the Internet to IPv6 will be a long transition period during which IPv6 networks will have to communicate and coexist with IPv4 networks. The transition is expected to take several years.

After reading this chapter, you should understand the main integration and coexistence strategies (defined by IETF) provided in IPv6 to enable a smooth transition of IPv4 networks to IPv6. This chapter also includes examples and configurations of the integration and coexistence mechanisms supported by the Cisco IOS Software.

The NGtrans IETF working group was created to design tools, protocols, and mechanisms that might be used to allow the transition of IPv4 networks toward IPv6. The IETF has defined several mechanisms and protocols for the transition since 1996. This chapter covers the most-used integration and coexistence strategies, especially those supported in the Cisco IOS Software.

Integration and coexistence strategies presented in this chapter are divided into three classes:

- **Dual stack**—The host, server, and router on a network might handle an IPv4 stack and an IPv6 stack simultaneously. When the two stacks are used on nodes connected to networks in which both protocols are enabled concurrently, the dual-stack mode provides the flexibility for nodes to establish end-to-end sessions over either IPv6 or IPv4.

- **Tunneling**—Tunneling allows the isolated IPv6 host, server, router, and domain to communicate with other IPv6 networks over the existing IPv4 infrastructure. Even isolated IPv6 hosts might have to establish end-to-end IPv6 sessions using IPv4 as the transport layer. Tunneling consists of encapsulating IPv6 packets into IPv4 packets and then sending these encapsulated packets to an IPv4 destination node over an IPv4 network. The destination node performs the decapsulation to extract IPv6 packets. Several techniques to deploy and establish tunnels over IPv4 are defined for the tunneling strategy.

| NOTE | Dual-stack support is required on nodes to tunnel IPv6 packets in IPv4. |
|------|--------------------------------------------------------------------------|

- **Protocol translation**—It is possible for IPv6-only nodes on the IPv6 network to communicate with IPv4-only nodes on the IPv4 network. However, these mechanisms require protocol translation between IPv4 and IPv6 at the edge of the two types of networks.

# Dual Stack

This section presents the dual-stack approach used to transition from IPv4 networks to IPv6. The dual stack is a method used by the network's host, server, and router to handle and use the IPv4 and IPv6 protocols simultaneously. This well-known technique was successfully applied in the past for other protocol transitions, especially for the deployment of IPv4 inside Internet Packet Exchange (IPX) networks, Digital Equipment Corporation network protocol (DECnet), and AppleTalk-based networks. Dual-stack support implies that an IPv6 stack is installed on the host, server, and router where both protocols are needed. The management of IPv6 stacks on dual-stack nodes is greatly facilitated by IPv6's stateless autoconfiguration functionality, as discussed in Chapter 2, "IPv6 Addressing."

| NOTE | The assignment of IPv6 addresses on nodes with an IPv6 stack is simplified because a router advertises the IPv6 network prefix on the local links. Therefore, nodes can configure their IPv6 addresses by themselves. |
|------|--------------------------------------------------------------------------|

## Applications Supporting Both IPv4 and IPv6

Before being able to use the dual-stack capability in nodes, IPv4-based applications must be modified to support the IPv6 protocol. Basically, the API of the IPv4-only applications is coded to handle IPv4 addresses only. In fact, the application itself calls an IPv4-only API function that can handle only 32-bit addresses. As shown in Figure 5-1, the IPv4-only application may use either TCP or UDP as the transport layer to deliver data. After arriving at the stack, the data is put into IPv4 packets. Then the IPv4 packets are sent to the node's network interface. The protocol ID value used within Ethernet frames for IPv4 packets is 0x0800. This is a simple example that shows how the data passes from the IPv4-only application to the network interface through the IPv4 stack.

When an IPv4-only application has been modified to handle both IPv4 and IPv6 protocols, the application can continue to run as before over IPv4. The application can now call the right API function that can handle 128-bit addresses. After being updated to support IPv6, the application can select either the IPv4 or IPv6 stack to make the packets.

**Figure 5-1**    *IPv4-Only Application Uses the IPv4 Stack to Send Packets*

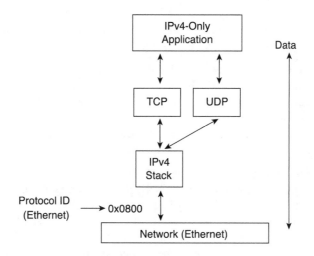

Figure 5-2 illustrates an application supporting both IPv4 and IPv6 protocols. The application uses TCP or UDP as the transport protocol, but it selects the IPv6 stack rather than IPv4. IPv6 packets are made and sent to the network interface. The protocol ID value used within Ethernet frames for IPv6 packets is 0x86DD.

**Figure 5-2**    *Application Supporting Both IPv4 and IPv6 Can Use Both Stacks*

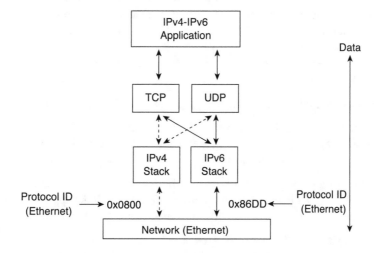

## Stack Selection

Even though an application is coded to handle both IPv4 and IPv6 protocols, the dual-stack node itself cannot randomly decide to use one of the two stacks to communicate. There are two methods to force a dual-stack node to use its IPv6 stack when IPv6 connectivity is available:

- **Manual entry by the user**—If the user knows the IPv6 address of the destination IPv6 host name, he can fill in the IPv6 address to establish the session. However, as mentioned in Chapter 2, the legal format of an IPv6 address must be used. For web applications, do not forget to use the specific format for addresses used in a URL, as defined in RFC 2732. Manually entering an IPv6 address is good enough for debugging purposes, but this is not the best practice for the daily use of applications.

- **Using a naming service**—As you saw in Chapter 3, "IPv6 in Depth," you can configure a fully qualified domain name (FQDN) in the naming service (DNS) with both IPv4 and IPv6 addresses. An FQDN may be available through one IPv4 address represented by an A record or through one IPv6 address represented by an AAAA record in the DNS server. Eventually, the same FQDN might be available with both IPv4 and IPv6 addresses. This means that the DNS servers can be queried to provide information about a server's availability and host service either over IPv4 or IPv6.

As defined in RFC 2553, *Basic Socket Interface Extensions for IPv6,* a new API is defined to handle both IPv4 and IPv6 in DNS queries. The functions **gethostbyname** and **gethostbyaddr** in applications must be modified to get the benefits of the IPv6 protocol in legacy IPv4-based applications.

---

**NOTE**    The **gethostbyname** function translates a host name into its corresponding IPv4 address. **gethostbyaddr** translates an IPv4 address into its corresponding name. Both functions were originally designed to work with IPv4 values only.

---

The following is a list of possible querying scenarios:

- **Querying for an IPv4 address**—An IPv4-only application requests naming services to resolve FQDN into an A record (IPv4 address). If the application receives an A record, it communicates with the host name using the IPv4 address received.

- **Querying for an IPv6 address**—An IPv6-only application requests naming services to resolve FQDN into an AAAA record (IPv6 address). If the application receives an AAAA record, it communicates with the host name using the IPv6 address received.

- **Querying for all types of addresses**—An application with both IPv4 and IPv6 support requests naming services to resolve FQDN into all types of addresses. The application looks for an AAAA record first. If it does not find an AAAA record, it looks for an A record to communicate with a host name.

The following sections describe these scenarios.

## Querying the Naming Service for an IPv4 Address

When an application is IPv4-aware only (it does not support IPv6), the application asks the DNS server to get only the IPv4 address for the host name to communicate. As shown in Figure 5-3, first an IPv4-only application on the dual-stack node X asks the DNS server Y to resolve the FQDN www.example.org into an A record. Then the DNS server Y replies to the dual-stack node X, specifying the IPv4 address 206.123.31.2 of www.example.org. Finally, the IPv4-only application on the dual-stack node X forces node X to establish a session to the destination IPv4 address 206.123.31.2.

**Figure 5-3**    *IPv4-Only Application Requesting an FQDN's A Record from the DNS Server*

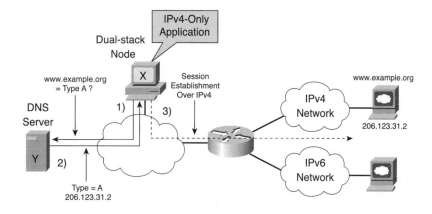

**NOTE**    The naming service presented in this example is a DNS server. However, a simple host file may also be used as a naming service.

## Querying the Naming Service for an IPv6 Address

On the opposite side, the application may also support only IPv6 as the protocol. In this case, the IPv6-only application asks the DNS server to resolve an FQDN to get the host name's IPv6 address to communicate. As shown in Figure 5-4, first an IPv6-only application on the dual-stack node X asks the DNS server Y to resolve the FQDN www.example.org into an AAAA record. Then the DNS server Y replies to the dual-stack node X, specifying the destination IPv6 address 3ffe:b00:ffff:a::1. Finally, the IPv6-only application on the dual-stack node X forces node X to establish a session to the destination IPv6 address 3ffe:b00:ffff:a::1.

**Figure 5-4** *IPv6-Only Application Requesting an FQDN's AAAA Record from the DNS Server*

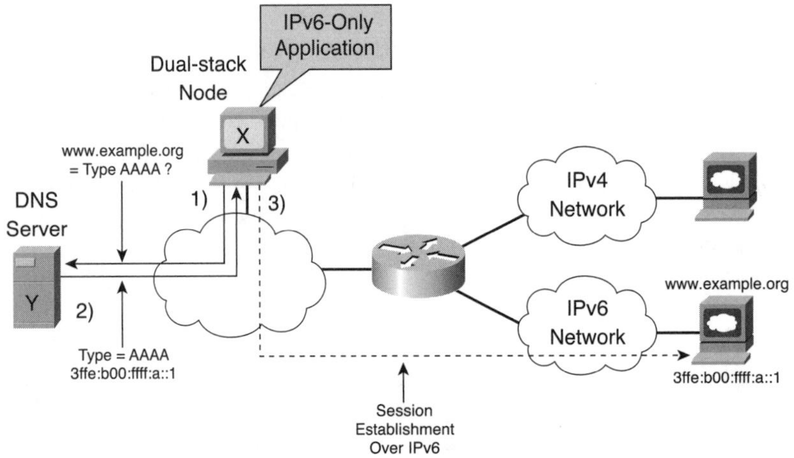

**NOTE**     In Figure 5-4, the DNS query sent to the DNS server Y can be sent over IPv4 or IPv6. The type of address requested in a DNS query is independent of the protocol used to transport the query. However, to send a DNS query over IPv6, the dual-stack node's resolver must handle IPv6, and the DNS server must be reachable using an IPv6 address.

## Querying the Naming Service for All Types of Addresses

The third possibility is an application with both IPv4 and IPv6 support used on a dual-stack node. In this situation, the application asks the DNS server to get all types of addresses. The application first looks for an AAAA record. If it does not find one, it looks for an A record to communicate with a host name. An application supporting both IPv4 and IPv6 is generally coded to give preference to the IPv6 address received from a naming service. As shown in Figure 5-5, an application with both IPv4 and IPv6 support on the dual-stack node X asks the DNS server Y to resolve the FQDN www.example.org into AAAA and A records. Then the DNS server Y replies to the dual-stack node X, specifying 3ffe:b00:ffff:a::1 as the destination IPv6 address and 206.123.31.2 as the destination IPv4 address. Finally, the application on the dual-stack node X prefers the IPv6 address 3ffe:b00:ffff:a::1 to establish the session to the destination node.

**Figure 5-5**    *Application with IPv4 and IPv6 Support Requesting the A and AAAA Records from the DNS Server*

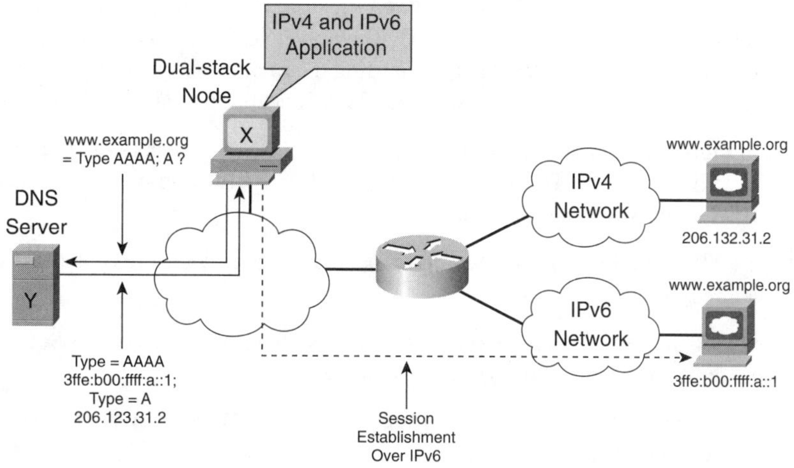

To facilitate the understanding of this concept, Figure 5-5 presents two different hosts (www.example.org) connected on two separate networks: IPv4 and IPv6. Moreover, each server uses a different address family, but they share the same FQDN. In a normal deployment, the same host using a dual stack may use both IPv4 and IPv6 addresses to handle the same service (in Figure 5-5, the web service).

## Enabling Dual-Stack Support on Cisco Routers

On a Cisco router, when both IPv4 and IPv6 addresses are assigned to a network interface, the interface is considered dual-stacked. Therefore, the router can forward both IPv4 and IPv6 packets.

As shown in Example 5-1, the command **ipv6 address 3ffe:b00:ffff:a::1/64** assigns the IPv6 address to the interface. The **ip address 206.123.31.2 255.255.255.0** command enables the IPv4 address on the same network interface, fastethernet0/0.

**Example 5-1**    *Enabling the Dual Stack on the Internet by Configuring Both IPv6 and IPv4 Addresses*

```
Router#configure terminal
Router(config)#int fastethernet 0/0
Router(config-if)#ipv6 address 3ffe:b00:ffff:a::1/64
Router(config-if)#ip address 206.123.31.2 255.255.255.0
Router(config-if)#exit
Router(config)#exit
```

The following is a list of applications that have dual-stack support on the Cisco IOS Software:

- **DNS resolver**—The DNS resolver on the Cisco IOS Software may resolve host names into IPv4 or IPv6 addresses. The DNS resolver on Cisco can be configured to reach naming services over IPv4 and IPv6 using the **ip name-server** *ipv6-address* command, as discussed in Chapter 3. This command may accept up to six different name servers.

- **Telnet**—The Telnet server on the Cisco IOS Software accepts incoming Telnet sessions over IPv4 or IPv6. The Telnet client in the IOS EXEC command accepts both IPv4 and IPv6 addresses as an argument.

- **TFTP**—The TFTP IOS EXEC command accepts either an IPv4 address or an IPv6 address as an argument.

- **HTTP server**—When enabled, the HTTP server on the Cisco IOS Software accepts incoming HTTP sessions over IPv4 and IPv6.

Refer to Chapter 3 for additional information about the DNS resolver, Telnet, TFTP, and the HTTP server with IPv6 on Cisco.

# Tunneling IPv6 Packets Over Existing IPv4 Networks

This section explains the rationale of tunneling data over the network. Then it describes how IPv6 packets are tunneled over IPv4 networks. Finally, it presents protocols and mechanisms standardized by the IETF to establish and deploy IPv6-over-IPv4 tunnels between dual-stack nodes.

## Why Tunneling?

Tunnels are generally used on the network to carry incompatible protocols or specific data over an existing network. For example, Distance Vector Multicast Routing Protocol (DVMRP) tunnels carry multicast datagrams over unicast networks. IPSec in tunnel mode, Layer 2 Tunneling Protocol (L2TP), and other Virtual Private Network (VPN) mechanisms transfer sensitive data over public IP networks using secure tunneling protocols.

For the deployment of IPv6 in the context of existing IPv4 infrastructure everywhere on the Internet, the tunneling approach provides a basic way for IPv6 hosts or islands made of IPv6 hosts, servers, and routers to reach other IPv6 islands and IPv6 networks using IPv4 routing domains as the transport layer. As illustrated in Figure 5-6, a tunnel is deployed between two islands made up of IPv6 nodes over an IPv4-only network such as the Internet. Edge routers at the border of the IPv6 islands and the Internet can handle the tunneling of IPv6 packets in IPv4.

However, any networks, links, and infrastructure made of native IPv6 connectivity should be preferred before any transition and coexistence strategies such as tunneling mechanisms. In fact, the tunneling of IPv6 packets over IPv4 infrastructure should be considered as an alternative only when it is impossible to get native IPv6 connectivity on networks, links, and infrastructure.

**Figure 5-6**    *Tunnel Established Over IPv4 Only Between Two Islands of IPv6 Nodes*

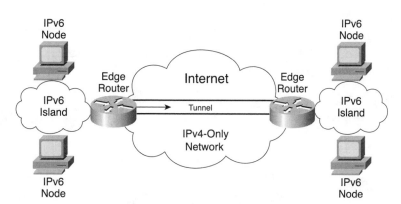

## How Does Tunneling IPv6 Packets in IPv4 Work?

When IPv6 packets are tunneled in IPv4, their original header and payload are not modified. One IPv4 header is inserted before the IPv6 packet. Therefore, the inner header contains the source and destination IPv6 addresses of the end-to-end IPv6 session, and the outer header contains the source and destination IPv4 addresses of the tunnel's endpoints. At each side of the tunnel, encapsulation and decapsulation of IPv6 packets are performed. Devices at each side of the tunnel must support both IPv4 and IPv6 protocols (dual stack) to encapsulate and decapsulate IPv6 packets in IPv4.

As shown in Figure 5-7, IPv6 host A, which knows the destination IPv6 address of IPv6 host B, wants to establish an end-to-end IPv6 session to host B. Both IPv6 networks are isolated, but they are connected using an IPv4 network. A tunnel to carry IPv6 packets in IPv4 is deployed between Routers R1 and R2. To initiate the end-to-end session, host A sends the first IPv6 packet, made up of an IPv6 header and a payload, to host B's IPv6 address as the destination address. Because the destination IPv6 host is on a different IPv6 routing domain, the packet is delivered over IPv6 to the border Router R1, acting as the tunnel's entry point. Therefore, Router R1 encapsulates the IPv6 packet in an IPv4 packet by inserting an IPv4 header. Then it sends the IPv4 packet to Router R2 over the IPv4 network. After receiving the IPv4 packet, Router R2, acting as the tunnel's exit point, performs the decapsulation. Then it forwards the IPv6 packet over IPv6 to the destination, host B. You can see that the IPv6 packet's header and payload are not modified during these steps.

As described in RFC 2893, *IPv6 Transition Mechanisms,* the protocol number assigned to the encapsulation of IPv6 packets in IPv4 is 41. This value is used in the IPv4 header's Protocol Number field to specify the encapsulation of an IPv6 packet in an IPv4 packet.

**Figure 5-7** *IPv6 Packets Delivered Through a Tunnel Over IPv4*

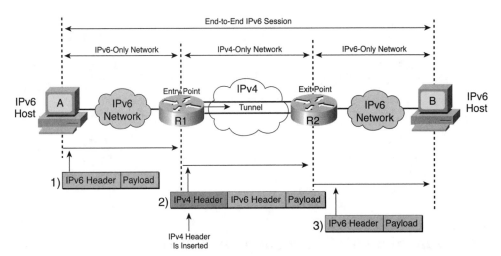

Like any other tunneling technique, such as IPv4-in-IPv4, minimal encapsulation, and generic routing encapsulation (GRE), the encapsulation of IPv6 packets in IPv4 raises some issues:

- **Tunnel Maximum Transmission Unit (MTU) and fragmentation**—Because one IPv4 header of 20 octets is inserted before the IPv6 packet, IPv6's effective MTU is decreased by 20 octets. The minimum MTU for any link layer in IPv6, including any tunnel interface, is 1280 octets. Depending on the MTU values configured on IPv6 and IPv4 link layers, fragmentation at the IPv4 layer might occur. This fragmentation affects performance and requires additional processing in the tunnel's endpoints.

- **Handling IPv4 Internet Control Message Protocol (ICMPv4) Errors**—Many older IPv4 routers return only eight octets of data beyond the packet's IPv4 header in case of error. However, if there is a problem, the IPv6 source node needs to know the address fields of the IPv6 packet in error.

- **Filtering Protocol 41**—If firewalls and routers with access control lists (ACLs) on IPv4 networks are well-configured, these devices should normally block all IPv4 packets from using protocol 41. This issue is more related to network management, but it affects the deployment of IPv6-over-IPv4 tunnels.

- **Network Address Translation (NAT)**—Like other tunneling protocols, it is not possible to establish IPv6 in IPv4 tunnels through NAT when it is enabled in the dynamic port translation and port redirection modes. However, this is possible if the tunnel through NAT is enabled in static mode. The issue of dynamic NAT and tunneling IPv6 packets in IPv4 is currently under discussion at the IETF. See the later section "Teredo Tunneling Mechanism."

**NOTE**        IP-in-IP and minimal encapsulation are well-known tunneling mechanisms that encapsulate IPv4 packets in IPv4 packets. GRE is another tunneling mechanism that can encapsulate IPv4 and other protocols such as IPX and AppleTalk, in IPv4 packets. GRE has been updated on Cisco IOS Software technology to support the encapsulation of IPv6 packets. This is discussed later in this chapter.

Although there are important issues related to the tunneling of IPv6 packets in IPv4, the deployment of the 6bone is proof that tunneling IPv6 packets over the IPv4 infrastructure is acceptable and scalable, provides basic efficiency, and has minimal impacts on network management.

**NOTE**        The 6bone is a worldwide informal collaborative IPv6 test bed that is an outgrowth of the IETF IPng project. The IPng designed and created the IPv6 protocol. The 6bone started in 1996 as a virtual network made of IPv6 in IPv4 tunnels operating over the Internet but slowly migrated to native IPv6 links. For more information on 6bone, refer to Chapter 7, "Connecting to the IPv6 Internet," or go to www.6bone.net.

For the transition of IPv4 networks to IPv6, different scenarios exist in which the tunneling of IPv6 packets in IPv4 can be used:

- **Host to host**—Isolated hosts with a dual stack on an IPv4 network can establish a tunnel to another dual-stack host. This architecture allows only the establishment of end-to-end IPv6 sessions between hosts.

- **Host to router**—Isolated hosts with a dual stack on an IPv4 network can establish a tunnel to the dual-stack router. The router may have native connectivity on another interface. This architecture allows the establishment of end-to-end IPv6 sessions between any destination IPv6 hosts through the router.

- **Router to router**—Routers with a dual stack on an IPv4 network can establish a tunnel to another dual-stack router. Routers can be used to interconnect islands of IPv6 hosts. Therefore, any host can establish end-to-end IPv6 sessions between hosts.

In Figure 5-8, example A shows a tunnel deployed between two dual-stack hosts. Example B illustrates a tunnel established between a dual-stack host and a dual-stack router; in this example, the dual-stack router is connected to a native IPv6 network. Finally, example C presents a tunnel established between two dual-stack routers; each dual-stack router is connected to a native IPv6 network.

**Figure 5-8**    *IPv6 Tunneling Scenarios in IPv4*

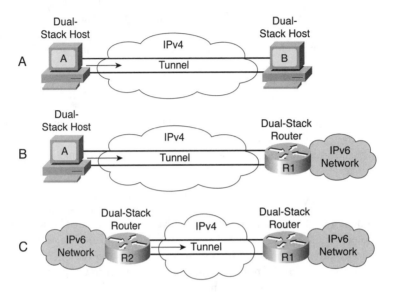

## Deploying Tunnels

The preceding section showed you how tunnels can carry IPv6 packets over an existing IPv4 network when native IPv6 networks or links are unavailable. However, the mechanism used to deploy tunnels between dual-stack nodes is a fundamental functionality that allows a smooth transition from IPv4 networks to IPv6 networks. The IETF defined protocols and techniques for establishing tunnels between dual-stack nodes, especially for the IPv6 protocol. The following is a list of protocols and techniques that are designed for the establishment of tunnels:

- Configured tunnel

- Tunnel broker

- Tunnel server

- 6to4

- GRE tunnel

- ISATAP (Intrasite Automatic Tunnel Addressing Protocol)

- Automatic IPv4-compatible tunnel

This section is organized such that protocols and techniques are presented from the most-prominent to the least-prominent.

| NOTE | Tunneling mechanisms presented in this section have the same mandatory requirement: nodes and routers acting as tunnel endpoints must have dual-stack support. |

## Deploying the Configured Tunnel

Configured tunnels are enabled and configured statically on dual-stack nodes. Because the configured tunnel was one of the first transition mechanisms supported by IPv6, it is mostly supported by all IPv6 implementations available today, including the Cisco IOS Software.

On each side of a configured tunnel, IPv4 and IPv6 addresses must be assigned manually to configure the tunnel interface. The following addresses are assigned to the tunnel interface:

- **Local IPv4 address**—An IPv4 address by which the local dual-stack node can be reached over the IPv4 network. The local IPv4 address is used as the source IPv4 address for outbound traffic.

- **Far-end IPv4 address**—An IPv4 address by which the far-end dual-stack node can be reached over the IPv4 network. The far-end IPv4 address is used as the destination IPv4 for outbound traffic.

- **Local IPv6 address**—The IPv6 address is assigned locally to the tunnel interface.

| NOTE | The configured tunnel is considered a point-to-point link. In the IPv6 world, it is a good practice on a point-to-point link to assign local and far-end IPv6 addresses within the same /64 IPv6 prefix. Therefore, as defined in RFC 3177, *IAB/IESG Recommendations on IPv6 Address Allocations to Sites,* the recommended prefix length for a point-to-point link should be a /64 or even a /128 when you are sure that one and only one device is connecting. |

| NOTE | Assigning a /127 IPv6 prefix to a point-to-point link such as a tunnel interface has been a popular operational practice on IPv6 networks because it was easier to know which address was used at the other end. However, it is not recommended that you use /127 as a prefix length because operational problems occur on point-to-point links established between routers when the subnet-router anycast address is implemented. One of the two available unicast IPv6 addresses of the /127 prefix that is assigned to the tunnel interface causes an address conflict with the subnet-router anycast address. One subnet-router anycast address is automatically configured on the router for each unicast address assigned. When this situation happens, the duplicate address detection (DAD) mechanism fails, and it is impossible to configure the unicast address to the tunnel interface. |

**NOTE**      Refer to the Internet draft www.ietf.org/internet-drafts/draft-savola-ipv6-127-prefixlen-04.txt
to learn about the issues involved with using /127 as a prefix length. Chapter 2 has additional
information on the subnet-router anycast address.

As shown in Figure 5-9, IPv6 network A, represented by the aggregatable global unicast prefix
3ffe:b00:ffff::/48, and IPv6 network B, using the address space 2001:420:ffff::/48, are connected through a configured tunnel. The IPv4 address assigned to the configured tunnel interface on Router R1 is 206.123.31.200, and the IPv6 address assigned to the same interface on
this router is 3ffe:b00:ffff:2::1/64. Router R2 uses 132.214.1.10 as the IPv4 address assigned to
its configured tunnel interface, and 3ffe:b00:ffff:2::2/64 is the IPv6 address applied. The IPv6
addresses assigned to both ends of the configured tunnel are within the same subnet (the same
/64 prefix).

**Figure 5-9**    *Addresses Assigned to a Configured Tunnel Interface*

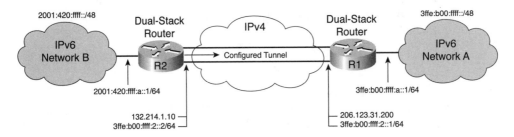

After all the addresses of the configured tunnel interface are assigned, the IPv6 routing must be
configured properly to enable the forwarding of IPv6 packets between the two IPv6 networks.
However, the configured tunnel can be used only after the configuration is fully applied on both
sides. Note that the configured tunnel is of interest to organizations that require strict control
over the establishment of tunnels, for the following reasons:

- Because the source and destination IPv4 addresses of each configured tunnel are well-
  known, security rules in firewalls or ACLs in routers may be enabled. However, for some
  tunneling mechanisms, such as the 6to4 tunnel (discussed later in this chapter), tunnel
  control is restrictive.

- When multiple configured tunnels are deployed, the network staff may disable a configured
  tunnel at any time just by shutting down a tunnel interface. This action affects only the
  traffic on that tunnel interface.

## Enabling Configured Tunnels on Cisco

Table 5-1 presents the steps and parameters required to enable a configured tunnel on a Cisco router.

**Table 5-1**    *Steps and Commands to Enable the Configured Tunnel on Routers*

| Command | Description |
|---------|-------------|
| **Step 1**<br>Router(config)#**interface** *tunnel-interface-number* | Specifies a tunnel interface number to enable a configured tunnel. |
| **Step 2**<br>Router(config-if)#**ipv6 address** *ipv6-address/ prefix-length* | Statically assigns an IPv6 address and a prefix length to the tunnel interface. |
| **Step 3**<br>Router(config-if)#**tunnel source** *ipv4-address* | Defines the local IPv4 address used as the source address for the tunnel interface. |
| **Step 4**<br>Router(config-if)#**tunnel destination** *ipv4-address* | The **tunnel destination** command defines the tunnel endpoint's destination IPv4 address. The destination IPv4 address is the far-end side of the tunnel. |
| **Step 5**<br>Router(config-if)#**tunnel mode ipv6ip** | Defines the type of tunnel interface as a configured tunnel. |
| **Step 6**<br>Router(config-if)#**exit**<br>Router(config)#**ipv6 route** *ipv6-prefix/prefix-length  interface-type interface-number* | After you exit the interface subcommand mode, the **ipv6 route** command may be used to forward matching IPv6 packets to the configured tunnel interface. |

Examples 5-2 and 5-3 are related to Figure 5-9. They show the commands and parameters used on Routers R1 and R2 to establish a configured tunnel.

**Example 5-2**    *Enabling a Configured Tunnel on Router R1*

```
RouterR1#configure terminal
RouterR1(config)#int tunnel0
RouterR1(config-if)#ipv6 address 3ffe:b00:ffff:2::1/64
RouterR1(config-if)#tunnel source 206.123.31.200
RouterR1(config-if)#tunnel destination 132.214.1.10
RouterR1(config-if)#tunnel mode ipv6ip
RouterR2(config-if)#exit
RouterR2(config)#ipv6 route 2001:420:ffff::/48 tunnel0
```

**Example 5-3** *Enabling a Configured Tunnel on Router R2*

```
RouterR2#configure terminal
RouterR2(config)#int tunnel5
RouterR2(config-if)#ipv6 address 3ffe:b00:ffff:2::2/64
RouterR2(config-if)#tunnel source 132.214.1.10
RouterR2(config-if)#tunnel destination 206.123.31.200
RouterR2(config-if)#tunnel mode ipv6ip
RouterR2(config-if)#exit
RouterR2(config)#ipv6 route 3ffe:b00:ffff::/48 tunnel5
```

**NOTE**    Note that the source IPv4 address of tunnel0 on Router R1 is the destination IPv4 address of tunnel5 on Router R2 and vice versa.

## Displaying the Configured Tunnel Interface

You can use the **show ipv6 interface** command to display information about the router's tunnel interface. Example 5-4 shows the command **show ipv6 interface tunnel0** applied on Router R1. The low-order 64-bit of the link-local address is the IPv4 source address of the tunnel interface converted into hexadecimal. In the following example, CE7B:1FC8 is equivalent to the IPv4 source address 206.123.31.200 assigned to the tunnel interface. The aggregatable global unicast IPv6 address assigned is 3ffe:b00:ffff:2::1. The interface automatically joins several multicast assigned addresses such as FF02::1, FF02::2, FF02::1:FF00:1, and FF02::1:FFA8:147. Refer to Chapter 2 for detailed information about multicast assigned addresses on interfaces.

**Example 5-4** *Displaying the Configured Tunnel Interface Using the*          **show ipv6 interface tunnel0** *Command*

```
RouterR1#show ipv6 interface tunnel0
Tunnel0 is up, line protocol is up
  IPv6 is enabled, link-local address is FE80::CE7B:1FC8
  Global unicast address(es):
    3FFE:B00:FFFF:2::1, subnet is 3FFE:B00:FFFF:2::/64
  Joined group address(es):
    FF02::1
    FF02::2
    FF02::1:FF00:1
    FF02::1:FFA8:147
  MTU is 1480 bytes
  ICMP error messages limited to one every 100 milliseconds
  ICMP redirects are enabled
  ND DAD is enabled, number of DAD attempts: 1
  ND reachable time is 30000 milliseconds
  Hosts use stateless autoconfig for addresses.
```

## Tunnel Brokers

As you saw in the preceding section, establishing a configured tunnel between two dual-stack nodes requires manual configuration at both endpoints. Therefore, the configured tunnel mechanism is not scalable when managed statically.

To facilitate the deployment of configured tunnels over an IPv4 network, the IETF defined a mechanism called the *tunnel broker*. As defined in RFC 3053, *IPv6 Tunnel Broker,* the tunnel broker is an external system, rather than a router, that acts as a server on the IPv4 network and that receives requests for tunneling from dual-stack nodes. Basically, requests are sent over IPv4 by dual-stack nodes to the tunnel broker using HTTP. End users can fill a webpage to request a configured tunnel for their dual-stack nodes.

Then the tunnel broker sends back information over HTTP to the dual-stack nodes such as the IPv4 addresses, the IPv6 addresses, and the default IPv6 routes to apply for the establishment of a configured tunnel to a dual-stack router. A tunnel broker may optionally provide a script to the dual nodes to facilitate the configured tunnel configuration on the operating system.

Finally, the tunnel broker remotely applies commands on a dual-stack router to enable a configured tunnel. The dual-stack router must be connected to an IPv6 domain. In the tunnel broker specification, the tunnel broker and the dual-stack router use different IPv4 addresses.

As shown in Figure 5-10, a dual-stack host on an IPv4 network first, over IPv4, reaches the tunnel broker using HTTP. The end user fills a web page, and then he gets IPv4 and IPv6 addresses from the tunnel broker through HTTP. The end user applies the configuration obtained to his dual-stack host to enable a configured tunnel. Simultaneously, the tunnel broker automatically applies the far-end configuration of the configured tunnel on a dual-stack router connected to an IPv6 domain. As soon as the configuration is applied on the dual-stack host and on the dual-stack router, the configured tunnel is properly established and can be used to realize end-to-end IPv6 sessions over an IPv4 network.

**Figure 5-10**   *Dual-Stack Host Establishing a Configured Tunnel Using a Tunnel Broker*

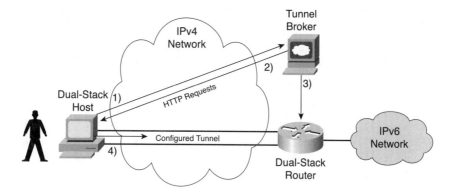

The tunnel broker model assumes that both the dual-stack router and the tunnel broker are controlled by the same authority. To be able to control the router's configuration, the tunnel broker may be physically connected to the router's console port, or it can reach the management console through protocols such as Telnet or Secure Shell (SSH). This also means that the tunnel broker must have the rights and permissions to manage the dual-stack router securely.

| NOTE | Cisco does not support the tunnel broker in the Cisco IOS Software technology. However, several tunnel broker implementations available on the Internet use Cisco routers for their operation. Refer to the 6bone website at www.6bone.net to get information about tunnel brokers available on the Internet. |
| --- | --- |

## Tunnel Servers

The *tunnel server* is a simplified model of the tunnel broker. The tunnel server combines the broker and the dual-stack router in the same system rather than having two separate systems. The way to request a configured tunnel is generally the same as with the tunnel broker: HTTP over IPv4.

As illustrated in Figure 5-11, a dual-stack host on an IPv4 network first, over IPv4, reaches the tunnel server using HTTP. The end user fills a web page and then gets IPv4 and IPv6 addresses from the tunnel server. The end user applies the configuration obtained to his dual-stack host to enable a configured tunnel. Then the tunnel server locally applies the far-end configuration of the configured tunnel. Finally, as with the tunnel broker, as soon as the configuration is fully applied on the dual-stack host and on the tunnel server, the configured tunnel is properly established and can be used to realize end-to-end IPv6 sessions over an IPv4 network.

**Figure 5-11**  *Dual-Stack Host Establishing a Configured Tunnel Using a Tunnel Server*

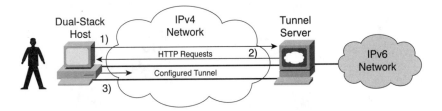

Because the broker and the dual-stack router are within the same device (a single system), the tunnel server is considered an open model that may allow the development of new control and signaling protocols for the establishment of configured tunnels. A signaling protocol with a built-in tunnel server would provide much more flexibility than a tunnel broker for the deployment of IPv6 connectivity on a very large scale over existing IPv4 networks. For example, a signaling protocol may allow the deployment of IPv6 in IPv4 tunnels through IPv4 NAT. Deploying IPv6 in IPv4 tunnels through NAT is difficult with the tunnel broker model.

| | |
|---|---|
| **NOTE** | Cisco does not support the tunnel server in the Cisco IOS Software technology. Tunnel server implementations available on the Internet such as Freenet6 (www.freenet6.net), provide connectivity to the IPv6 Internet and the 6bone through configured tunnels. Moreover, Freenet6 supports the establishment of configured tunnels to Cisco IOS Software technology. |

The tunnel broker and tunnel server are seen as mechanisms to automate the deployment of configured tunnels for dual-stack nodes on IPv4 routing domains without manual operation.

## Deploying 6to4

Establishing, operating, managing, and supporting configured tunnels between IPv6 domains requires synchronization between at least two entities. For some organizations, it is acceptable to statically manage a few tunnels, but for others, this is troublesome and is not a recommended practice. The IETF has defined another mechanism called 6to4 to facilitate the deployment of IPv6 over IPv4 networks through tunnels.

As defined in RFC 3056, *Connection of IPv6 Domains via IPv4 Clouds,* here are the main characteristics of the 6to4 mechanism:

- **Automatic tunneling**—A dynamic method to deploy tunnels between sites made up of IPv6 nodes. You don't need to manually preset source and destination IPv4 addresses to establish tunnels. Tunneling of IPv6 packets between 6to4 sites is done dynamically according to the destination IPv6 addresses of packets originating from IPv6 nodes on 6to4 sites. Like the configured tunnel, 6to4 encapsulates IPv6 packets in IPv4 and uses the IPv4 routing domains as the transport layer.

- **Enabled at the edge of the site**—6to4 should be enabled in border routers at the edge of sites. 6to4 routers must be able to reach other 6to4 sites and 6to4 routers using the IPv4 routing infrastructure.

- **Automatic prefix assignment**—Provides one aggregatable global unicast IPv6 prefix to each 6to4 site:

  - 6to4 prefixes are all based on the 2002::/16 address space assigned by the IANA.

  - Each 6to4 site uses at least one globally unicast IPv4 address assigned on a 6to4 router. This IPv4 32-bit address is converted into hexadecimal format and is appended to the 2002::/16 prefix. The final representation is 2002:*ipv4-address*::/48.

- — Each 6to4 site gets one /48 prefix based on its globally unicast IPv4 addressing. The next 16-bit of the /48 prefix is available for the subnet assignments within the IPv6 domain behind the 6to4 router. Remember that one /48 prefix contains 65,536 /64 prefixes.

- **No IPv6 route propagation**—Because the 6to4 prefixes are based on globally unique IPv4 addresses (IPv4 routing domains), there is no need to propagate /48 IPv6 routes between all other 6to4 sites.

Figure 5-12 shows Routers A and B enabled as 6to4 routers. Router A uses 132.214.1.10 as the globally unique IPv4 unicast address for the 6to4 mapping, and Router B uses 206.123.31.200. Therefore, the IPv6 prefix of IPv4/IPv6 site A is 2002:84d6:010a::/48, where 84d6:010a is the hexadecimal representation of 132.214.1.10. IPv4/IPv6 site B uses the prefix 2002:ce7b:1fc8::/48, which is based on the IPv4 address 206.123.31.200. The 6to4 tunnel between Router A and Router B is established only when hosts within site A send IPv6 packets to the destination network 2002:ce7b:1fc8::/48 or hosts within site B send packets to the destination network 2002:84d6:010a::/48.

**Figure 5-12** *IPv6 Prefixes of the 6to4 Sites Are Based on IPv4 Addresses of the 6to4 Routers*

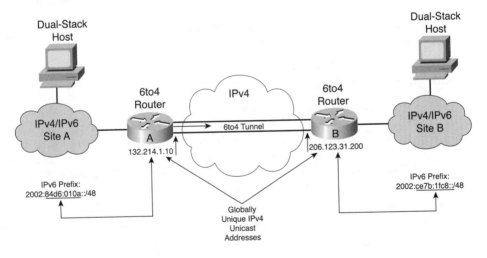

NOTE     Hosts behind 6to4 routers may have either a native IPv6 stack or dual-stack support.

Figure 5-13 illustrates an end-to-end IPv6 session established between host A using the IPv6 address 2002:84d6:010a:1::1 within site A and host B using 2002:ce7b:1fc8:2::2 within site B. Addresses assigned to hosts A and B are based on each site's 6to4 prefixes. Host A initiates the session to host B by sending an IPv6 packet using 2002:84d6:010a:1::1 as the source IPv6 address and 2002:ce7b:1fc8:2::2 as the destination IPv6 address. The IPv6 packet is delivered natively over IPv6 toward the default Router R1 on site A, which acts as the 6to4 router. Then the 6to4 Router R1 looks at the packet's destination IPv6 address and extracts the IPv4 address embedded in the destination address. Following the extraction, the 6to4 Router R1 encapsulates the IPv6 packet in an IPv4 packet using the IPv4 address extracted as the destination IPv4 address for the endpoint tunnel. This destination IPv4 address represents site B's 6to4 edge Router R2. Therefore, the IPv6 packet is encapsulated in IPv4: The packet's source IPv4 address is 132.214.1.10, and the destination IPv4 address is 206.123.31.200. During the encapsulation, the IPv6 packet remains unchanged. The 6to4 Router R2 receives the IPv4 packet and decapsulates the IPv6 packet. Then Router R2 forwards natively over IPv6 the IPv6 packet toward host B.

**Figure 5-13**  *End-to-End IPv6 Session Between IPv6 Hosts Through 6to4 Routers*

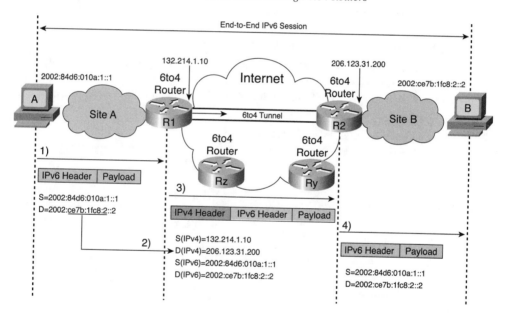

As discussed in this section, the 6to4 operation is based on the IPv4 Internet addressing and routing infrastructure. Therefore, you should take the following into consideration before deploying sites using the 6to4 mechanism:

- **The edge router's IPv4 address might change over time**—Because a 6to4 site's IPv6 prefix is based on the edge router's globally unique IPv4 unicast address, any change of this IPv4 address forces the renumbering of the whole 6to4 site.

- **Private addressing**—The use of private address space such as 10.0.0.0/8, 172.16.0.0/12, and 192.168.0.0/16, is forbidden for the deployment of a 6to4 router on the Internet.

- **Controlling tunnel establishment**—As soon as a 6to4 router is enabled on an edge router, the 6to4 router must accept encapsulated packets from any other 6to4 router on the Internet. Blocking or filtering inbound 6to4 traffic based on source IPv4 addresses breaks the 6to4 model. However, the absence of control for 6to4 tunneling represents a security issue, because malicious users might enable 6to4 sites for short periods of time.

**NOTE** Unlike configured tunnel support, which is available in every IPv6 implementation, 6to4 support requires special code in the implementation. The 6to4 mechanism is supported in the Cisco IOS Software technology. 6to4 support is also available in Microsoft, FreeBSD, OpenBSD, NetBSD, and Linux implementations. Chapter 6, "IPv6 Hosts Internetworking with Cisco," presents examples of interoperability with these operating systems and the Cisco IOS Software.

## Enabling 6to4 Router Configuration on Cisco

Table 5-2 describes the steps required to enable a 6to4 router. Steps 1 and 2 define the IPv4 address and the 6to4 prefix for the 6to4 site. Steps 3 through 7 set the commands and parameters for the configuration of a 6to4 tunnel. Step 8 enables a route for the forwarding of IPv6 packets using the 6to4 prefix as the destination.

**Table 5-2**   *Steps and Commands to Enable a 6to4 Router*

| Command | Description |
|---|---|
| **Step 1**<br><br>Router(config)#**interface** *loopback-interface-number*<br><br>Router(config-if)#**ip address** *ipv4-address netmask* | Assigns an IPv4 address to a loopback interface. This address is used as a source IPv4 address for the IPv6 packets to be tunneled over IPv4. This IPv4 address also determines the 6to4 prefix of the 6to4 site. |
| **Step 2**<br><br>Router(config)#**interface** *interface-type interface-number*<br><br>Router(config-if)#**ipv6 address** *ipv6-prefix/prefix-length* | Assigns an IPv6 address to a network interface inside the 6to4 site. The IPv6 address assigned is based on the concatenation of the IPv6 prefix 2002::/16 and the IPv4 address of the 6to4 router defined in Step 1. The IPv4 address must be represented in hexadecimal. |
| **Step 3**<br><br>Router(config)#**interface** *tunnel-interface-number* | Specifies a tunnel interface number to enable the 6to4 router. |
| **Step 4**<br><br>Router(config-if)#**no ip address** | In the 6to4 operation, there is no IPv4 or IPv6 address to assign to the tunnel interface. The tunnel interface uses the address of another interface instead. Therefore, the **no ip address** command must be used. |

**Table 5-2**   *Steps and Commands to Enable a 6to4 Router (Continued)*

| Command | Description |
|---|---|
| **Step 5**<br><br>Router(config-if)#**ipv6 unnumbered** *interface-type interface-number* | Specifies the interface type and number used by the tunnel interface for the 6to4 operation. This command must point out the interface identified in Step 2. |
| **Step 6**<br><br>Router(config-if)#**tunnel source** *interface-type interface-number* | The tunnel source specifies an interface with an IPv4 address assigned. This interface's IPv4 address is used to determine the 6to4 prefix (/48). This command must point to the interface identified in Step 1. |
| **Step 7**<br><br>Router(config-if)#**tunnel mode ipv6ip 6to4** | Defines the type of tunnel interface used for the 6to4 operation. |
| **Step 8**<br><br>Router(config)#**ipv6 route 2002::/16** *interface-type interface-number* | Forwards all IPv6 packets that match the 2002::/16 prefix through the 6to4 tunnel interface. |

Figure 5-14 shows a typical network topology in which Router R1 acts as the 6to4 router on the Internet. Router R1 can be reached through IPv4 using the address 132.214.1.10. It uses Tunnel1 as an interface for the 6to4 tunneling.

**Figure 5-14**   *R1 Acting as a 6to4 Router*

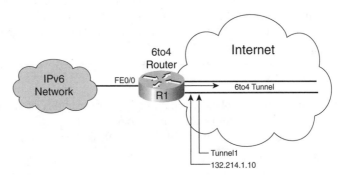

Example 5-5, which is based on Figure 5-14, presents the configuration applied on Router R1 to turn it into a 6to4 router.

**Example 5-5** *Enabling a 6to4 Router on Router R1*

```
RouterR1#configure terminal
RouterR1(config)#int Loopback0
RouterR1(config-if)#ip address 132.214.1.10 255.255.255.0
RouterR1(config-if)#int fastethernet0/0
RouterR1(config-if)#ipv6 address 2002:84d6:010a:0001::1/64
RouterR1(config-if)#int tunnel1
RouterR1(config-if)#no ip address
RouterR1(config-if)#ipv6 unnumbered fastethernet0/0
RouterR1(config-if)#tunnel source Loopack0
RouterR1(config-if)#tunnel mode ipv6ip 6to4
RouterR1(config-if)#exit
RouterR1(config)#ipv6 route 2002::/16 Tunnel1
```

**NOTE**    The IPv6 address assigned to the fastethernet0/0 interface is based on the 2002:84d6:010a::/48 prefix. The value 84d6:010a is the hexadecimal representation of the IPv4 address 132.214.1.10. The subnet ID used is 0001. The IPv6 address is assigned statically to the interface fastethernet0/0. Refer to Chapter 2 for more details about assigning a static IPv6 address to a network interface.

**NOTE**    When you enable a 6to4 site on your router, be sure you do not have an IPv4 ACL denying protocol 41. Otherwise, 6to4 tunnel establishment will fail. With the 6to4 mechanism, you must allow inbound IPv4 packets with protocol 41 from any source address on the IPv4 Internet. Filtering rules (IPv4 ACLs) such as **permit 41 any host 132.214.1.10** (incoming 6to4 traffic) and **permit 41 host 132.214.1.10 any** (outgoing 6to4 traffic) are recommended for such a configuration, as shown in Example 5-5.

As soon as 6to4 is applied, you can verify the reachability of another 6to4 destination on the IPv4 Internet. For example, you can try to ping the 6to4 site operated by Microsoft Research at the IPv6 address 2002:836b:4179::836b:4179, as shown in Example 5-6.

**Example 5-6** *Verifying the Reachability of Another 6to4 Site on the IPv4 Internet*

```
RouterR1#ping ipv6 2002:836b:4179::836b:4179
Type escape sequence to abort.
Sending 5, 100-byte ICMP Echos to 2002:836B:4179::836B:4179, timeout is 2 seconds:
!!!!!
Success rate is 100 percent (5/5), round-trip min/avg/max = 124/160/192 ms
```

| NOTE | Refer to Chapter 3 for more details on the **ping ipv6** command. |
|------|---|

### Using 6to4 Relay

The 6to4 mechanism enabled on an edge router allows the forwarding of IPv6 packets to any destination within the 2002::/16 prefix over the existing IPv4 infrastructure. However, as seen in Chapter 2, other aggregatable global unicast prefixes are used on the IPv6 Internet such as 2001::/16 (Production IPv6 Internet) and 3ffe::/16 (the 6bone). Therefore, all these prefixes other than 2002::/16 are unreachable unless one of the 6to4 routers on the IPv4 Internet offers to act as a gateway to forward the 6to4 traffic to the IPv6 Internet. A 6to4 router providing traffic forwarding to the IPv6 Internet is called a *6to4 relay*. A 6to4 relay is generally at the border of the IPv4 Internet and the IPv6 Internet. On its interface connected to the IPv6 Internet, the 6to4 router advertises the route 2002::/16 as a participant of the IPv6 unicast routing network.

Figure 5-15 shows Router B acting as a 6to4 relay. The Router B configuration is similar to a 6to4 router, except for the routing configuration. Router B gets routes from the IPv6 Internet, and it can forward IPv6 packets received from 6to4 sites (2002::/16 prefix) to the IPv6 Internet. To use a 6to4 relay, a 6to4 router must add a default route in its configuration pointing to the 6to4 relay. Therefore, all non-6to4 traffic is sent to the IPv6 Internet through the 6to4 relay.

**Figure 5-15**  *Router Acting as a 6to4 Relay*

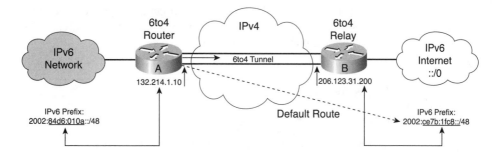

| NOTE | A router enabled into a 6to4 relay may also act as a 6to4 router. |
|------|---|

### Using a 6to4 Relay in a Cisco Configuration

An additional step is necessary to force the forwarding of all non-6to4 traffic to the IPv6 Internet through a 6to4 relay. The **ipv6 route ::/0** command forwards all non-6to4 packets to the IPv6 Internet through a 6to4 relay. The IPv6 address of the 6to4 relay must be specified there. The syntax of the **ipv6 route ::/0** command is as follows:

```
Router(config)#ipv6 route ::/0 ipv6-address-6to4-relay
```

Figure 5-16 shows Router R2 acting as a 6to4 relay on the IPv4 Internet. Router R2 can be reached on IPv4 using the destination IPv4 address 206.123.31.200, and it has the IPv6 address 2002:ce7b:1fc8:1::1 for the 6to4 relay operation. The 6to4 Router R1 can add a default IPv6 route that points to the 6to4 relay (Router R2) to forward non-6to4 traffic to the IPv6 Internet.

**Figure 5-16** *Router Acting as a 6to4 Relay*

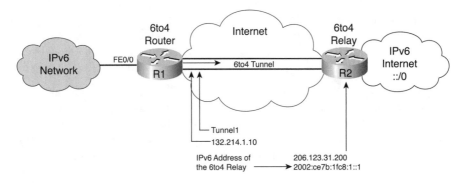

Example 5-7 is based on Figure 5-16. It presents the configuration applied on Router R1 to turn this router into a 6to4 router with a default IPv6 route that points to a 6to4 relay. The shaded line is the default IPv6 route that points to the 6to4 relay.

**Example 5-7** *Enabling a 6to4 Router on Router R1 with a Default Route to a 6to4 Relay*

```
RouterR1#configure terminal
RouterR1(config)#int Loopback0
RouterR1(config-if)#ip address 132.214.1.10 255.255.255.0
RouterR1(config-if)#int fastethernet0/0
RouterR1(config-if)#ipv6 address 2002:84d6:010a:0001::/64 eui-64
RouterR1(config-if)#int tunnel1
RouterR1(config-if)#no ip address
RouterR1(config-if)#ipv6 unnumbered fastethernet0/0
RouterR1(config-if)#tunnel source Loopack0
RouterR1(config-if)#tunnel mode ipv6ip 6to4
RouterR1(config-if)#exit
RouterR1(config)#ipv6 route 2002::/16 Tunnel1
RouterR1(config)#ipv6 route ::/0 2002:ce7b:1fc8:1::1
```

**NOTE**    6to4 routers on the Internet based on private IPv4 addressing cannot use a 6to4 relay, because private addressing is unreachable through the Internet by 6to4 relays.

### Finding a 6to4 Relay on the Internet

The first step before enabling a default route to the IPv6 Internet through a 6to4 relay is to find the IPv4 address of a public 6to4 relay. There are people on the Internet who maintain static lists of public 6to4 relays. Table 5-3 is a sample of some available public 6to4 relays.

**Table 5-3**    *Public 6to4 Relays*

| 6to4 Relay | Country |
| --- | --- |
| 6to4.ipv6.microsoft.com | U.S. |
| 6to4.kfu.com | U.S. |
| kddilab.6to4.jp | Japan |
| 6to4.ipv6.bt.com | England |
| skbys-00-00.6to4.xs26.net | Slovakia |
| 6to4.ipng.nl | Netherlands |

Source: 6bone website (www.6bone.net)

**NOTE**    Before you use a public 6to4 relay on the Internet for testing or even production purposes, be sure it is officially available.

As shown in Table 5-3, a publicly available 6to4 relay is a long distance from your site, resulting in poor network performance for the IPv6 traffic between your site and the IPv6 Internet.

To help 6to4 sites find an available 6to4 relay on the Internet and to add more scalability to the 6to4 mechanism, RFC 3068, *An Anycast Prefix for 6to4 Relay Routers,* introduces a 6to4 relay anycast prefix from which 6to4 packets are automatically routed to the nearest 6to4 relay on the IPv4 Internet.

IANA assigned the 6to4 relay anycast prefix 192.88.99.0/24 for the specific purpose of automatically routing 6to4 packets to the nearest 6to4 relay. The IPv4 address defined in this anycast prefix to reach the nearest 6to4 relay is 192.88.99.1. Therefore, the representation of this address in IPv6 is 2002:c058:6301::. In your 6to4 configuration, you can use the **ipv6 route ::/0 2002:C058:6301::** command to configure the default IPv6 route. After this command is applied in your 6to4 configuration, you can try to ping any IPv6 destination within the aggregatable global unicast IPv6 space (2000::/3).

**NOTE** The details of how an anycast prefix is advertised on the Internet are beyond the scope of this chapter. Refer to Chapter 2 for an overview of the anycast operation.

### Configuring a Cisco Router to Act as a 6to4 Relay with the Anycast IPv4 Prefix

The anycast IPv4 prefix is now supported in the Cisco IOS Software technology. Thus, a Cisco router can act as a 6to4 relay with the anycast IPv4 prefix. Example 5-8 presents the configuration applied on Router R3 to make this router into a 6to4 relay. The **ipv6 address 2002:c058: 6301::/128 anycast** command is the new feature added for the anycast IPv4 prefix. The **ip address 132.214.1.10 255.255.255.0** command defines a global unicast IPv4 address on the router for management purpose. The **ipv6 address 192.88.99.1 255.255.255.0 secondary** command assigns the anycast IPv4 address on the network interface.

**Example 5-8** *Configuring a 6to4 Relay with the Anycast IPv4 Prefix on Router R3*

```
RouterR3#configure terminal
RouterR3(config-if)#int tunnel1
RouterR3(config-if)#no ip address
RouterR3(config-if)#ipv6 unnumbered fastethernet0/0
RouterR3(config-if)#tunnel source fastethernet0/0
RouterR3(config-if)#ipv6 address 2002:c058:6301::/128 anycast
RouterR3(config-if)#tunnel mode ipv6ip 6to4
RouterR3(config-if)#int fastethernet0/0
RouterR3(config-if)#ip address 132.214.1.10 255.255.255.0
RouterR3(config-if)#ip address 192.88.99.1 255.255.255.0 secondary
RouterR3(config-if)#ipv6 address 2002:84d6:010a:0001::/64 eui-64
RouterR3(config-if)#exit
RouterR3(config)#ipv6 route 2002::/16 Tunnel1
```

**NOTE** The IPv4 prefix 192.88.99.0/24 should be injected into a routing protocol on IPv4 Internet. Otherwise, this 6to4 relay will not be reachable on the IPv4 Internet using the anycast prefix.

## Deploying IPv6 Over a GRE Tunnel

The Cisco IOS Software supports the encapsulation of IPv6 packets over GRE tunnels. A GRE tunnel is a well-known standardized tunnel technique that can ensure stable and secure point-to-point links. Like the configured tunnel, a GRE tunnel must be configured statically between routers to allow the transport of IPv6 packets over an existing IPv4 infrastructure.

However, the GRE tunnel provides an additional benefit for organizations using IS-IS for IPv6 as the routing protocol in their domain. Because the IS-IS protocol needs to send link layer messages between adjacent routers on the network, GRE tunneling is the only tunneling protocol that can carry this kind of traffic over an IP infrastructure. Therefore, the same GRE tunnel can be used simultaneously within a wide network to carry both IPv6 packets and IS-IS link layer messages between IS-IS routers.

**NOTE**    Configuring IS-IS for IPv6 with GRE is beyond the scope of this chapter. Refer to Chapter 4, "Routing on IPv6," for more information about IS-IS for IPv6 and GRE.

## Enabling a GRE Tunnel for IPv6 on a Cisco Router

Table 5-4 presents the steps required to enable a GRE tunnel on a Cisco router to carry IPv6 packets over IPv4. Steps 1 through 5 describe the commands and parameters used to configure a GRE tunnel for IPv6.

**Table 5-4**    *Commands to Enable a GRE Tunnel*

| Command | Description |
| --- | --- |
| **Step 1**<br><br>Router(config)#**interface** *tunnel-interface-number* | Specifies the tunnel interface number to enable a GRE tunnel. |
| **Step 2**<br><br>Router(config-if)#**ipv6 address** *ipv6-address/prefix-length* | Statically assigns an IPv6 address and a prefix length to the tunnel interface. |
| **Step 3**<br><br>Router(config-if)#**tunnel source** *ipv4-address* | Defines the IPv4 address used as the source address for the tunnel interface. |
| **Step 4**<br><br>Router(config-if)#**tunnel destination** *ipv4-address* | Identifies the destination IPv4 address of the tunnel endpoint. The destination IPv4 address is the far-end side of the tunnel. |
| **Step 5**<br><br>Router(config-if)#**tunnel mode gre ipv6** | Defines the tunnel interface as the GRE tunnel for IPv6. |

Example 5-9 shows the commands and parameters to be applied on a router to configure a GRE tunnel supporting the encapsulation of IPv6 packets.

**Example 5-9**  *Configuring a GRE Tunnel on Router R1*

```
RouterR1#configure terminal
RouterR1(config)#int tunnel0
RouterR1(config-if)#ipv6 address 3ffe:b00:ffff:2::1/64
RouterR1(config-if)#tunnel source 206.123.31.200
RouterR1(config-if)#tunnel destination 132.214.1.10
RouterR1(config-if)#tunnel mode gre ipv6
RouterR2(config-if)#exit
```

## Deploying ISATAP Tunnels

Intrasite Automatic Tunnel Addressing Protocol (ISATAP), defined in draft-ietf-ngtrans-isatap-12.txt, is a mechanism that tunnels IPv6 packets in IPv4 within an administrative domain (such as a site) to create a virtual IPv6 network over an IPv4 network.

The main functionalities and components of ISATAP are as follows:

- **Automatic tunneling**—The tunneling of IPv6 packets in IPv4 is performed between ISATAP hosts or between an ISATAP host and an ISATAP router. The tunneling is automatic, meaning that there is no need to apply manual configurations on hosts when ISATAP support is enabled. However, for ISATAP host-to-ISATAP router tunneling, the ISATAP host must initially find the IPv4 address of an ISATAP router from the Potential Router List.

**NOTE**  On an ISATAP link, a Potential Router List contains IPv4 addresses representing all ISATAP routers within a site. The ISATAP draft proposes to get the Potential Router List from the naming service as a bootstrap for ISATAP host-to-ISATAP router tunneling.

- **ISATAP address format**—ISATAP addresses assigned to ISATAP hosts and ISATAP routers are made using the concatenation of an aggregatable global unicast IPv6 prefix dedicated to the ISATAP operation and the special format of the interface ID.

- **Prefix**—Represents the high-order 64-bit of the IPv6 address. One ISATAP address is enabled on the ISATAP host using the link-local prefix (FE80::/10). One aggregatable global or site-local /64 prefix must be assigned for the ISATAP operation within the site. This /64 prefix is received by the ISATAP hosts from router advertisement messages sent by ISATAP routers through ISATAP tunnels established over IPv4.

- **Interface ID**—Represents the low-order 64-bit of the IPv6 address assigned to the ISATAP host. Like the 6to4 mechanism, ISATAP embeds IPv4 addresses in ISATAP IPv6 addresses. The interface ID is made by appending the 32-bit of the IPv4 address to the high-order 32-bit value 0000:5EFE, which has been reserved by IANA for ISATAP operation. Because ISATAP operation is scoped to a site, IPv4 addresses used by ISATAP hosts and routers may be either public or private addressing.

As illustrated in Figure 5-17, ISATAP host A on the IPv4 network having the IPv4 address 206.123.20.100 uses the link-local address fe80::5efe:ce7b:1464. This link-local address is based on the ISATAP format. ISATAP host A also has the aggregatable global unicast IPv6 address 3ffe:b00:ffff:2::5efe:ce7b:1464 assigned. The low-order 64-bit of this aggregatable global unicast address is the same as the link-local address. ISATAP host A receives the ISATAP prefix 3ffe:b00:ffff:2::/64 from ISATAP Router R1. When ISATAP host A has to send IPv6 packets to ISATAP Router R1 at 3ffe:b00:ffff:2::5efe:ce7b:1fc8, host A's ISATAP interface automatically encapsulates IPv6 packets in IPv4. The IPv4 packets of the IPv6 encapsulated packet use 206.123.20.100 as the source IPv4 address and 206.123.31.200 as the destination IPv4 address.

**Figure 5-17**  *Address Assignments for the ISATAP Host and the ISATAP Router*

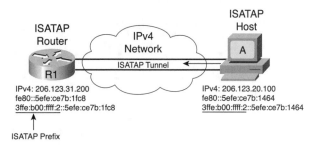

- **ISATAP prefix advertisement**—After the ISATAP host is enabled with its link-local address using ISATAP format in the low-order 64-bit, it sends a router solicitation to an ISATAP router through an ISATAP tunnel. Then the ISATAP router replies with a router advertisement message to the ISATAP host, and it specifies the ISATAP prefix defined within the site. After receiving the ISATAP prefix, the ISATAP host configures its aggregatable global unicast IPv6 address based on this ISATAP format. The ISATAP host uses the ISATAP router's link-local address as the default IPv6 router address.

Figure 5-18 shows all the steps by which an ISATAP prefix is advertised to ISATAP hosts over the IPv4 network using the ISATAP mechanism. First, ISATAP host A, using the link-local address fe80::5efe:ce7b:1464, sends a router solicitation to ISATAP Router R1 at destination fe80::5efe:ce7b:1fc8. This IPv6 packet is encapsulated within an IPv4 packet: The source IPv4 address is 206.123.20.100 and the destination IPv4 address is 206.123.31.200. Then ISATAP Router R1 receives this router solicitation. It replies by sending a router advertisement message to ISATAP host A. This IPv6 packet is also encapsulated in an IPv4 packet: The source IPv4 address is now 206.123.31.200, and the destination IPv4 address is 206.123.20.100. The router advertisement message contains the ISATAP prefix 3ffe:b00:ffff:2::/64, which ISATAP host A uses to configure its IPv6 address.

**Figure 5-18** *Advertisement of the ISATAP Prefix*

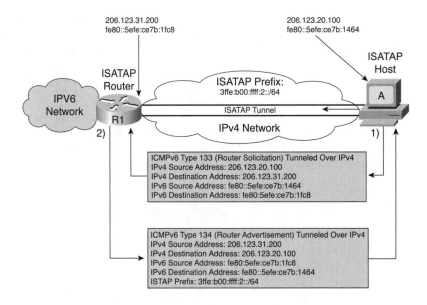

**NOTE**   The ISATAP mechanism is defined in draft-ietf-ngtrans-isatap-12.txt. As with other transition and coexistence mechanisms, dual-stack support is required in hosts and routers for ISATAP operation.

**NOTE**   Cisco IOS Software supports ISATAP. The Cisco router can act as an ISATAP router.

## Enabling an ISATAP Tunnel on a Cisco Router

Table 5-5 presents the steps required to enable an ISATAP tunnel on a Cisco router. Steps 1 through 6 describe the commands and parameters used to configure the router as an ISATAP router.

**Table 5-5**    *Commands to Enable an ISATAP Tunnel*

| Command | Description |
|---|---|
| **Step 1**<br><br>Router(config)#**interface***interface-typeinterface-number*<br><br>Router(config-if)#**ip address** *ipv4-address netmask* | Assigns an IPv4 address to a network interface. This address is used as the source IPv4 address for the IPv6 packets to be tunneled. This IPv4 address also determines the IPv6 ISATAP address of the ISATAP router. |
| **Step 2**<br><br>Router(config)#**interface***tunnel-interface-number* | Specifies a tunnel interface number to enable the ISATAP mechanism on the router. |
| **Step 3**<br><br>Router(config-if)#**tunnel source** *interface-type interface-number* | The tunnel source specifies an interface with an IPv4 address assigned. The IPv4 address on the interface defines the low-order 32-bit of the ISATAP address assigned to the router. |
| **Step 4**<br><br>Router(config-if)#**tunnel mode ipv6ip isatap** | Defines the type of tunnel interface as ISATAP. |
| **Step 5**<br><br>Router(config-if)#**no ipv6 nd suppress-ra** | By default on the Cisco IOS Software, router advertisement is disabled on the tunnel interface. The **no ipv6 nd suppress-ra** command enables router advertisement on the tunnel interface. Router advertisement must be enabled on the tunnel interface for ISATAP. |
| **Step 6**<br><br>Router(config-if)#**ipv6 address** *ipv6-address/ prefix-length*  **eui-64** | The ISATAP IPv6 address has to be configured using EUI-64 format, because the address's low-order 32-bit is based on the IPv4 address. This command also enables prefix advertisement on the tunnel interface. The prefix defined here must be the ISATAP prefix assigned to the site. |

Example 5-10 shows the commands and parameters applied on Router R1 to configure it as an ISATAP router.

**Example 5-10**  *Configuring ISATAP on Router R1*

```
RouterR1#configure terminal
RouterR1(config)#int fastethernet0/0
RouterR1(config-if)#ip address 206.123.31.200 255.255.255.0
RouterR1(config-if)#int tunnel0
RouterR1(config-if)#tunnel source fastethernet0/0
RouterR1(config-if)#tunnel mode ipv6ip isatap
RouterR1(config-if)#no ipv6 nd suppress-ra
RouterR1(config-if)#ipv6 address 3ffe:b00:ffff:2::/64 eui-64
RouterR2(config-if)#exit
```

## Deploying an Automatic IPv4-Compatible Tunnel

This section describes the automatic IPv4-compatible tunnel as another technique used to carry IPv6 packets over IPv4 networks. However, this tunneling technique is supported less in IPv6 implementations, because it is used less and is deployed on the Internet, unlike the configured tunnel and 6to4 mechanisms.

The automatic IPv4-compatible tunnel mechanism was one of the first transition mechanisms defined by the IETF. The automatic IPv4-compatible tunnel mechanism lets automatic tunnels (no manual configuration) over IPv4 networks carry IPv6 packets between dual-stack hosts only. This mechanism allows isolated IPv6 hosts on IPv4 networks to automatically enable tunnels to other isolated IPv6 hosts on IPv4 networks. The low-order 32-bit of the source and destination IPv6 addresses represents the source and destination IPv4 addresses of the tunnel endpoints. The IPv4-compatible IPv6 prefix is ::/96 (made up of 96 0s).

---

**NOTE**     The prefix used for the automatic IPv4-compatible tunnel mechanism is based on the IPv6 prefix ::/96, which is related to the IPv4-compatible IPv6 prefix. Chapter 2 presents in detail the representation of the IPv4-compatible IPv6 prefix.

---

Figure 5-19 shows Router R1 deploying an automatic IPv4-compatible tunnel to Router R2 over the Internet. Router R1's IPv4 address is 206.123.31.200, and its IPv6 address is ::206.123.31.200. Router R2's IPv4 address is 132.214.1.10, and its IPv6 address is ::132.214.1.10. Suppose Router R1 sends a first IPv6 packet to Router R2 using the source IPv6 address ::206.123.31.200 and the destination ::132.214.1.10. Router R1 dynamically deploys an automatic IPv4-compatible tunnel to Router R2 to carry IPv6 packets over the Internet.

**Figure 5-19**  *Automatic IPv4-Compatible Tunnel Deployed Between Two Dual-Stack Routers*

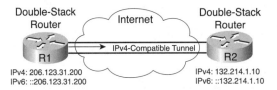

Although the automatic IPv4-compatible tunnel mechanism seems to provide an easy and simple way to deploy tunnels to carry IPv6 packets over IPv4, it has several limitations:

- **Homogeneousness**—Communications are always realized between IPv4-compatible addresses only. Moreover, the mechanism is limited to host-to-host tunneling. A router may also act as a host for some applications, such as the establishment of a Telnet-over-IPv6 session between two routers.

- **Address space limitation**—Because this mechanism and tunnel establishment are only based on the hosts' IPv4 addresses, the automatic IPv4-compatible tunnel mechanism does not offer a solution to the IPv4 space shortage.

- **Scalability**—This mechanism requires one globally unique IPv4 address for each host to allow the deployment of IPv6 at large on the Internet.

| | |
|---|---|
| **NOTE** | Cisco supports the automatic IPv4-compatible tunnel mechanism, but the router acts only as a host. However, the automatic IPv4-compatible tunnel is being deprecated in favor of other transition and coexistence mechanisms, such as 6to4 and ISATAP. |

## Teredo Tunneling Mechanism

*Teredo*, also known as *shipworm,* is a new tunneling mechanism being designed at the IETF for the transition from IPv4 to IPv6. Teredo's main goal is to deliver IPv6 packets to dual-stack nodes that are behind NAT devices on IPv4-only domains, because protocol 41 (used by the configured tunnel and 6to4 mechanisms) does not work through NAT. The delivery of IPv6 connectivity through NAT devices is possible with Teredo by tunneling IPv6 packets over IPv4 UDP datagrams. By using the combination of a single IPv4 address and the UDP mappings of a NAT device, Teredo can deliver IPv6 connectivity over IPv4 UDP datagrams to several nodes that are behind the same NAT.

The following list describes the main components of the Teredo mechanism:

- **Teredo server**—The Teredo server is connected to the IPv4 Internet and can be reached using a single globally unicast IPv4 address. This stateless device manages signalization traffic with the Teredo clients.

- **Teredo relay**—The Teredo relay is the device acting as an IPv6 router. The Teredo relay is connected to the IPv6 Internet and provides IPv6 connectivity over IPv4 UDP packets to Teredo clients that are behind NAT.

- **Teredo client**—The Teredo client is located in an IPv4 domain behind the NAT device. In the Teredo model, the Teredo client (which is behind a NAT) must initiate the request to the Teredo server to get IPv6 connectivity over IPv4 UDP packets from the Teredo relay. However, the Teredo client must be configured with the Teredo server's IPv4 address.

Refer to the Internet-draft www.ietf.org/internet-drafts/draft-ietf-ngtrans-shipworm-08.txt for detailed information about this new tunneling mechanism for IPv6.

## Choosing an Appropriate Tunneling Mechanism

Although several tunneling mechanisms carry IPv6 packets over the exiting IPv4 infrastructure, you should remember that configured tunnel, 6to4, and GRE tunnel probably will be used to interconnect sites. ISATAP may be used to interconnect hosts to exit routers in an IPv4 domain. Tunnel server and tunnel broker may also be used to deploy IPv6 connectivity on a large scale to isolated nodes that are on IPv4-only domains. Teredo delivers IPv6 connectivity to nodes behind NAT devices. The automatic IPv4-compatible tunnel is not used, because it is being deprecated.

# IPv6-Only-to-IPv4-Only Transition Mechanisms

The previous sections presented mechanisms to tunnel IPv6 packets over existing IPv4 networks to interconnect IPv6 domains. This section presents other transition scenarios in which networks made of native IPv6-only and IPv4-only protocols have to interact and coexist.

Early adopters of IPv6 are currently deploying an IPv6-only infrastructure on their production networks. In Asia and Europe, where getting globally unique IPv4 space is a long and costly process (it's almost impossible in some countries), the deployment of IPv6-only networks has already started. This enables more islands and networks made of IPv6-only nodes interconnected to the IPv6 Internet. On the other hand, organizations and providers having IPv4-only networks may wait until there is enough demand for IPv6 before migrating their networks to IPv6. The transition period is expected to take several years.

In the meantime, IPv6-only networks have to interact with IPv4-only networks on the Internet. Full interaction between the two types of networks is mandatory to maintain complete compatibility between both protocols. Here are basic examples of interaction between the two protocols:

- A node in an IPv6-only domain might have to send e-mail messages using Simple Mail Transfer Protocol (SMTP) to a destination node in an IPv4-only domain.

- A node in an IPv4-only domain might have to reply to the source IPv6-only node in the IPv6 domain.

- Nodes in an IPv4-only domain might have to get connected using HTTP to a destination web server running only in an IPv6-only domain.

Because IPv6 has been designed from the beginning with transition in mind to maintain complete backward compatibility with IPv4, typical scenarios and techniques allowing IPv6-only nodes to communicate with IPv4-only domains have been defined. These methods are divided into techniques called application-level gateways (ALGs) and NAT-PT. The following sections provide details about these techniques.

## Using Application-Level Gateways (ALGs)

The *ALG technique* is a network architecture in which gateways with dual-stack support allow nodes in an IPv6-only domain to interact with nodes in an IPv4-only domain.

Figure 5-20 shows a network architecture in which an ALG is deployed between the IPv6-only and IPv4-only domains. The IPv6-only host A establishes an IP session to the IPv4-only server B through ALG C. ALG C maintains one independent session with the IPv6-only host A using IPv6 as the transport protocol and another independent session with the IPv4-only server B over IPv4. ALG C converts the IPv6 session into IPv4, and vice versa. ALG C is located in a subnet where both IPv6 and IPv4 connectivity are enabled. The ALG has dual-stack support.

**Figure 5-20**  *IP Session Established Between an IPv6-Only Host and an IPv4-Only Server Through an ALG*

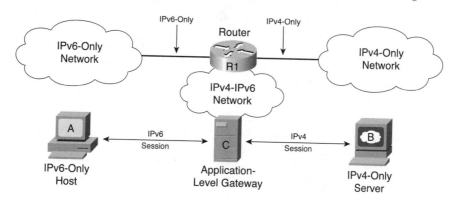

The ALG method can be used for the transition of Internet applications such as mail, the web, and many other protocols:

- **Mail**—IPv6-only hosts on IPv6-only networks can send their e-mail messages using SMTP over IPv6 to their local SMTP server. After receiving messages, the local SMTP server that has dual-stack support and that acts as the ALG for SMTP can send messages to the destination SMTP servers on the Internet. The local SMTP server first tries to reach the destination SMTP servers through IPv6 (using the naming service). Otherwise, it goes back to IPv4 to deliver the messages.

- **Web**—Browsers on IPv6-only hosts can be configured to pass through a proxy web server over IPv6 to reach any destination IPv4 website on the Internet. A local proxy web server with dual-stack support can be enabled within a local network to act as an ALG for HTTP. From one side, the local proxy web server gets HTTP requests over IPv6 from IPv6-only hosts. On the other side, the proxy web server first tries to reach destination web servers through IPv6 (using the naming service). Otherwise, it reaches them using IPv4.

**NOTE**    The ALG technique requires applications already converted to IPv6.

ALG deployed at the border of IPv6-only and IPv4-only networks is an interesting technique. For example, with SMTP, the main advantage of this technique is the transparency for the end users sending and receiving messages. However, applications that are used by nodes must have both IPv4 and IPv6 support in the ALG.

# Using NAT-PT

Another technique that allows IPv6-only nodes to communicate with IPv4-only nodes is Network Address Translation Protocol Translation (NAT-PT). As defined in RFC 2766, *Network Address Translation Protocol Translation,* NAT-PT is a type of NAT that translates IPv6 addresses into IPv4 addresses and vice versa. NAT-PT is based on the Stateless IP/ICMP Translator (SIIT) algorithm defined in RFC 2765. The SIIT algorithm translates between IPv4 and IPv6 packet headers, including ICMP headers.

---

**NOTE**    Although the NAT is undesirable in IPv6, the aim of NAT-PT is to use translation only when there is no other method to allow IPv6-only nodes to communicate with IPv4-only domains. The other alternatives are the deployment of native IPv6 networks, native links, dual-stack operation in nodes, and tunneling techniques such as those described in this chapter.

---

As with ALG, there is no need to add dual-stack support in IPv6-only or IPv4-only nodes to allow them to communicate through NAT-PT. NAT-PT is similar to the well-known NAT mechanism in IPv4 because it is a stateful mechanism. NAT-PT involves network address translation and protocol translation.

For its operation, NAT-PT requires a specific routing configuration within the network in which all IPv6 packets addressed to a predefined /96 prefix must be routed toward the NAT-PT device. The /96 prefix must be reserved within the IPv6 domain for the NAT-PT operation. Then, the NAT-PT device translates destination IPv6 addresses within the /96 prefix into IPv4 addresses according to its mapping rules.

Figure 5-21 illustrates the deployment of a NAT-PT device at the border of the IPv6-only network A and the IPv4 Internet. 3ffe:b00:ffff:0:0:1::/96 is the predefined prefix for the NAT-PT operation in the IPv6-only network A. Packets originating from the IPv6-only network A and using destination addresses in prefix 3ffe:b00:ffff:0:0:1::/96 are routed toward Router R1, acting as the NAT-PT device. Therefore, IPv6 addresses in packets are translated into IPv4 addresses and then are delivered to the IPv4-only nodes on the IPv4 Internet. The IPv6-only network has a native IPv6 link to the IPv6 Internet. A default IPv6 route in the IPv6-only network is configured to point to router R2 to reach the IPv6 Internet.

**Figure 5-21**  *IPv6-Only Node A Communicates with IPv4-Only Node B Through a NAT-PT Device*

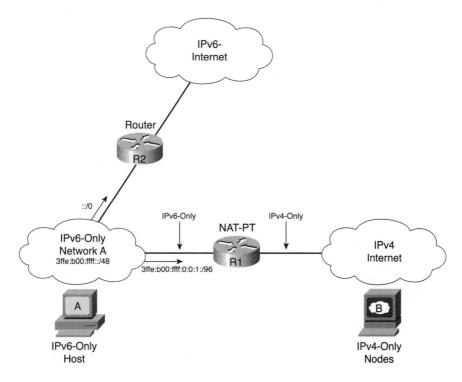

The following list describes the different types of operations defined for the NAT-PT mechanism:

- **Static NAT-PT**—Static mode provides a one-to-one mapping between an IPv6 address and an IPv4 address. Each IPv4 address to be reached on the IPv4-only domain by the nodes within the IPv6-only domain must be configured in the NAT-PT device. The destination of each IPv4 address is mapped in the NAT-PT device to an IPv6 address in the predefined NAT-PT prefix. This mode requires one source IPv4 address for each IPv6-to-IPv4 mapping. Static NAT-PT mode is similar to static NAT in IPv4.

- **Dynamic NAT-PT**—Dynamic mode also provides a one-to-one mapping, but it uses a pool of IPv4 addresses. The number of source IPv4 addresses in the pool determines the maximum number of simultaneous IPv6-to-IPv4 translations. The destination IPv4 address is appended dynamically to the predefined NAT-PT prefix by the IPv6-only nodes in the IPv6 network. This mode requires a pool of IPv4 addresses to perform the dynamic translation. Dynamic NAT-PT mode is similar to dynamic NAT in IPv4.

- **NAPT-PT**—Network Address Port Translation Protocol Translation. NAPT-PT provides a many-to-one dynamic mapping between multiple IPv6 addresses in the NAT-PT prefix and one source IPv4 address. This translation is done simultaneously at Layer 3 (IPv6/IPv4) and at the upper layers (TCP/UDP). The NAPT-PT is similar to NAT port translation in IPv4. NAPT-PT has the same limitations as IPv4: Only TCP, UDP, and ICMP can be translated.

● **NAT-PT DNS ALG**—Dynamic NAT-PT mapping can be combined with the DNS ALG to translate the DNS transactions to automatically build the translated addresses of the destination nodes. NAT-PT can intercept the DNS requests (A-record query) originating from the IPv6 network toward the IPv4 network. A DNS server or even a node in the IPv6 network must first send a DNS query to an IPv4 DNS server through the NAT-PT device. Then NAT-PT automatically translates the content of the DNS response (the A record) to an IPv6 address (AAAA record). A NAT-PT mapping is dynamically configured between the external IPv4 address and an IPv6 address in the NAT-PT prefix. Therefore, the IPv6-only node can get one IPv6 address to reach the IPv4 destination through the NAT-PT device.

## NAT-PT Operation

Figure 5-22 shows the generic operation of NAT-PT at the border of IPv6-only network A and IPv4-only network B. IPv6-only node A, which uses the IPv6 address 3ffe:b00:ffff:1::2, establishes a session to IPv4-only node B at 206.123.31.200 through the NAT-PT device. In this example, the static NAT-PT mapping of 206.123.31.200 to 3ffe:b00:ffff:0:0:1::a is configured in NAT-PT. Therefore, node A sends an IPv6 packet to destination 3ffe:b00:ffff:0:0:1::a using the source address 3ffe:b00:ffff:1::2. NAT-PT translates the packet's IPv6 header into an IPv4 header. Then NAT-PT sends an IPv4 packet to the destination IPv4 address 206.123.31.200 using the source address 206.123.31.1. After receiving the packet, node B sends back the response to NAT-PT using 206.123.31.1 as the destination IPv4 address. NAT-PT translates that packet's IPv4 header into an IPv6 header. Then it sends the IPv6 packet to node A at 3ffe:b00:ffff:1::2 using the source IPv6 address 3ffe:b00:ffff:0:0:1::a.

**Figure 5-22** *NAT-PT Operation Between the IPv6 and IPv4 Networks*

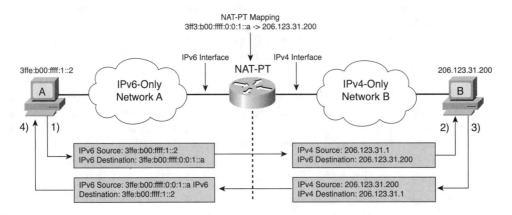

## Limitations of NAT-PT

NAT-PT has several well-known limitations, but it inherits some of them from IPv4 NAT. The following are NAT-PT's main limitations:

- **Single point of failure**—NAT-PT is a stateful device. If NAT-PT goes down, all sessions between IPv6-only domains and IPv4-only domains are lost.

- **Inhibition of end-to-end security**—Because NAT-PT modifies packet headers during the translation, the IP header's integrity check fails. This problem can be partially solved, but the fundamental problem is not easy to fix.

- **Not NAT-friendly**—The NAT-PT does not have full knowledge of applications with dynamic port allocation and rendezvous ports embedded in IP addresses. Therefore, NAT-PT has to be upgraded each time a new non-NAT-friendly application is available.

- **PMTUD (path MTU discovery)**—PMTUD does not work with NAT-PT.

- **IPv4 option**—NAT-PT does not handle IPv4 options.

- **Multicast**—Multicast is not supported.

- **DNS**—DNS Security (DNSSEC), defined in RFC 2535, is not supported. Zone transfer between IPv6 and IPv4 networks is an open issue.

## Enabling NAT-PT on Cisco

Whatever the NAT-PT mode used, the basic steps to enable NAT-PT on a router are the same. Because the translation is done at the border of IPv6 and IPv4 domains, the first step before enabling NAT-PT is to determine the network interfaces on which NAT-PT must be used.

The command **ipv6 nat** is described in Table 5-6. It enables NAT-PT on network interfaces used for the NAT-PT device. Then the **ipv6 nat prefix** command defines the NAT-PT prefix used for the NAT-PT operation within the IPv6 domain. The NAT-PT prefix may be enabled on a global basis or a per-interface basis. Table 5-6 shows the NAT-PT prefix enabled on a global basis.

**Table 5-6**    *Enabling NAT-PT on Cisco*

| Command | Description |
|---|---|
| **Step 1**<br><br>Router(config)#**interface** *interface-type interface-number* | Specifies a network interface to enable the NAT-PT mechanism. |
| **Step 2**<br><br>Router(config-if)#**ipv6 nat** | Enables the NAT-PT mechanism on the interface. This command is enabled on an interface basis. |

*continues*

**Table 5-6**    *Enabling NAT-PT on Cisco (Continued)*

| Command | Description |
|---|---|
| **Step 3**<br><br>Router(config)#**interface** *interface-type interface-number* | Determines another network interface to enable NAT-PT. |
| **Step 4**<br><br>Router(config-if)#**ipv6 nat** | Enables NAT-PT on the interface. |
| **Step 5**<br><br>Router(config)#**ipv6 nat prefix** *ipv6-prefix* **/96** | Defines the IPv6 prefix used as the NAT-PT prefix in the IPv6 domain. The only prefix length supported with NAT-PT is /96. |

Example 5-11 shows the commands and parameters applied on a router to enable the NAT-PT mechanism. The NAT-PT prefix is enabled on a global basis.

**Example 5-11** *Enabling NAT-PT*

```
RouterR1#configure terminal
RouterR1(config)#int fastethernet0/0
RouterR1(config-if)#ip address 206.123.31.200 255.255.255.0
RouterR1(config-if)#ipv6 nat
RouterR1(config-if)#int fastethernet0/1
RouterR1(config-if)#ipv6 address 3ffe:b00:ffff:1::/64 eui-64
RouterR1(config-if)#ipv6 nat
RouterR1(config-if)#exit
RouterR1(config)#ipv6 nat prefix 3ffe:b00:ffff:0:0:1::/96
RouterR2(config)#exit
```

## Applying a Static NAT-PT Configuration

As shown in Table 5-7, the commands **ipv6 nat v6v4 source** and **ipv6 nat v4v6 source** configure static NAT-PT mapping between IPv6 and IPv4 addresses. For a one-to-one static mapping, entries are required for each IPv4 and IPv6 node that needs to communicate with the others.

Figure 5-23 shows a static NAT-PT mapping configuration in which IPv6-only host A using 3ffe:b00:ffff:1::2 can communicate with IPv4-only SSH server B on the IPv4 address 206.123.31.200. The prefix used for the NAT-PT operation on IPv6-only network A is 3ffe:b00:ffff:0:0:1::/96. The IPv4-only SSH server B is 206.123.31.200 statically mapped to the IPv6 address 3ffe:b00:ffff:0:0:1::a in the NAT-PT prefix, and IPv6-only host A is mapped to the IPv4 address 206.123.31.2. By applying a static NAT-PT configuration in Router R1, both IPv6-only and IPv4-only nodes can communicate with each other.

**Table 5-7**    *Enabling Static NAT-PT Mapping*

| Command | Description |
|---|---|
| Router(config)#**ipv6 nat v6v4 source** *ipv6-address ipv4-address* | Forces outbound IPv6 packets using the source IPv6 address (the originating IPv6-only host) identified in the command to be translated into an IPv4 packet. The IPv4 packet uses the IPv4 source address specified in the command to reach the destination IPv4 host. |
| Router(config)#**ipv6 nat v4v6 source** *ipv4-address ipv6-address* | Forces inbound IPv4 packets using the source IPv4 address identified in the command to be translated into an IPv6 packet. The IPv4 address is the destination host on the IPv4-only network. The IPv6 address is the corresponding destination IPv6 address that reaches the destination host on the IPv4-only network. |

**Figure 5-23**  *Static NAT-PT Mapping Configuration*

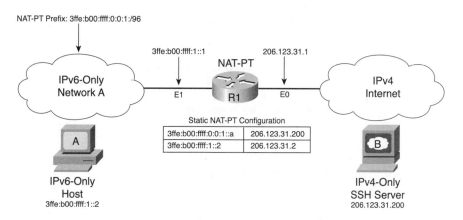

Example 5-12 shows the configuration applied on Router R1 in Figure 5-23 to enable a static NAT-PT mapping configuration.

**Example 5-12**  *Enabling Static NAT-PT Mapping on Router R1*

```
RouterR1#configure terminal
RouterR1(config)#int ethernet0
RouterR1(config-if)#ip address 206.123.31.1 255.255.255.0
RouterR1(config-if)#ipv6 nat
RouterR1(config-if)#int ethernet1
RouterR1(config-if)#ipv6 address 3ffe:b00:ffff:1::1/64
```

*continues*

**Example 5-12** *Enabling Static NAT-PT Mapping on Router R1 (Continued)*

```
RouterR1(config-if)#ipv6 nat
RouterR1(config-if)#exit
RouterR1(config)#ipv6 nat prefix 3ffe:b00:ffff:0:0:1::/96
RouterR1(config)#ipv6 nat v6v4 source 3ffe:b00:ffff:1::2 206.123.31.2
RouterR1(config)#ipv6 nat v4v6 source 206.123.31.200 3ffe:b00:ffff:0:0:1::a

RouterR1(config)#exit
```

## Managing the NAT-PT Translation Table

You can display the content of the NAT-PT translation table using the **show ipv6 nat translations** command. The syntax of this command is as follows:

```
Router#show ipv6 nat translations
```

Example 5-13 presents the NAT-PT translation table after an SSH session has been established by the IPv6-only node 3ffe:b00:ffff:1::1 to the IPv4-only SSH server 206.123.31.200.

**Example 5-13** *Displaying the NAT-PT Translation Table*

```
RouterA#show ipv6 nat translations
Prot  IPv4 source          IPv6 source
      IPv4 destination      IPv6 destination
---   ---                   ---
      206.123.31.200        3FFE:B00:FFFF::1:0:a

tcp   206.123.31.2,1021     3FFE:B00:FFFF:1::2,1021
      206.123.31.200,22     3FFE:B00:FFFF::1:0:a,22
```

Table 5-8 presents the commands that clear, display statistics for, and enable the debugging messages related to the NAT-PT mechanism.

**Table 5-8**    **clear**, **show**, *and* **debug** *Commands for NAT-PT*

| Command | Description |
|---|---|
| Router#**clear ipv6 nat translation** * | Clears the NAT-PT translation table. |
| Router#**show ipv6 nat statistics** | Displays statistics about the translation. |
| Router#**debug ipv6 nat [detailed]** | Enables debugging mode for NAT-PT. The debug output shows all translation events. |

## Applying a Dynamic NAT-PT Configuration

Static NAT-PT mapping is useful in a network in which stable IPv4-only nodes can be reached by IPv6-only nodes. However, static NAT-PT mapping requires one dedicated IPv4 address for each IPv6-only node that needs to communicate with an IPv4-only node.

Dynamic NAT-PT mode instead uses a pool of IPv4 addresses to translate sessions initiated from the IPv6-only network. Each time a new session toward the IPv4 network is initiated, the NAT-PT device dynamically assigns one source IPv4 address from the pool of IPv4 addresses. The number of concurrent IPv6-to-IPv4 sessions is limited by the number of IPv4 addresses in the pool.

Table 5-9 shows the steps required to enable IPv6-to-IPv4 dynamic NAT-PT mapping in a router. Step 1 defines the IPv6 addresses in the IPv6-only network that are allowed to be translated to IPv4 by the NAT-PT mechanism. There are three ways to restrict these addresses: a standard IPv6 ACL, an IPv6 prefix list, and a **route-map** statement. Step 1 shows a configuration using a standard IPv6 ACL. Step 2 defines the pool of IPv4 addresses used for the translation by NAT-PT. Finally, Step 3 represents the dynamic NAT-PT mapping configuration that is applied on the router.

**Table 5-9**    *Enabling IPv6-to-IPv4 Dynamic NAT-PT Mapping*

| Command | Description |
|---|---|
| **Step 1**<br><br>Router(config)#**ipv6 access-list** *name*  **permit** *source-ipv6-prefix/prefix-length destination-ipv6-prefix/prefix-length* | Defines the range of IPv6 addresses in the IPv6-only network that are allowed to be translated. The **ipv6 access-list** command configures a standard IPv6 ACL. Refer to Chapter 3 for detailed instructions on configuring standard IPv6 ACL. |
| **Step 2**<br><br>Router(config)#**ipv6 nat v6v4 pool** *natpt-pool-name start-ipv4 end-ipv4*  **prefix-length** *prefix-length* | Defines a pool of source IPv4 addresses used during the translation. The *natpt-pool-name* argument specifies the name of this pool. The pool's first and last IPv4 addresses, represented by the *start-ipv4* and *end-ipv4* arguments, must be specified as well with the IPv4 pool's prefix length. |
| Step 3<br><br>Router(config)#**ipv6 nat v6v4 source {list | route-map}** *{list-name  | map-name }* **pool** *natpt-pool-name* | Configures dynamic NAT-PT mapping. The **list** keyword used with the *list-name* argument specifies a standard IPv6 ACL to define the range of IPv6 addresses. The **route-map** keyword with the *map-name* argument may be used instead. The **pool** keyword with the *natpt-pool-name* argument defines the pool of source IPv4 addresses. |

Figure 5-24 shows a dynamic NAT-PT mapping configuration in which any IPv6 nodes in IPv6-only network A are dynamically mapped to the IPv4 addresses of the pool 206.123.31.200 to 206.123.31.220 (a maximum of 20 hosts). The prefix used for the NAT-PT operation on IPv6-only network A is 3ffe:b00:ffff:0:0:1::/96. By applying a dynamic NAT-PT configuration in Router R1, IPv6-only nodes can establish sessions toward IPv4 nodes on the IPv4 Internet.

**Figure 5-24** *Dynamic NAT-PT Mapping Configuration*

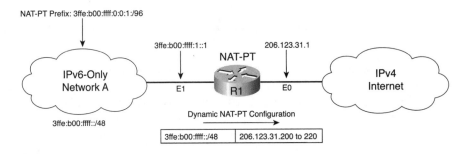

Example 5-14 shows the configuration applied on Router R1 of Figure 5-24 to enable dynamic NAT-PT configuration.

**Example 5-14** *Enabling Dynamic NAT-PT Mapping on Router R1*

```
RouterR1#configure terminal
RouterR1(config)#int ethernet0
RouterR1(config-if)#ip address 206.123.31.1 255.255.255.0
RouterR1(config-if)#ipv6 nat
RouterR1(config-if)#int ethernet1
RouterR1(config-if)#ipv6 address 3ffe:b00:ffff:1::1/64
RouterR1(config-if)#ipv6 nat
RouterR1(config-if)#exit
RouterR1(config)#ipv6 access-list ipv6only-network permit 3ffe:b00:ffff::/48 any
RouterR1(config)#ipv6 nat prefix 3ffe:b00:ffff:0:0:1::/96
RouterR1(config)#ipv6 nat v6v4 pool ipv4-pool 206.123.31.200 206.123.31.220
  prefix-length 24
RouterR1(config)#ipv6 nat v6v4 source list ipv6only-network pool ipv4-pool
RouterR1(config)#exit
```

**NOTE**   The configuration shown in Example 5-14 represents an IPv6-to-IPv4 dynamic NAT-PT mapping configuration only. This is possible, just as it is possible for static NAT-PT mode to configure an IPv4-to-IPv6 dynamic NAT-PT mapping. However, examples of dynamic NAT-PT mapping from IPv4 to IPv6 are not presented in this book. See the Cisco website for examples of dynamic IPv4-to-IPv6 NAT-PT configurations.

## Tuning NAT-PT

By default, there is no limit on the number of translations allowed by NAT-PT. However, you can restrict the number of concurrent translations using the command **ipv6 nat translation max-entries**, as shown in Table 5-10.

The default timeout for dynamic translation entries is 86,400 seconds (1 day). You can modify this global parameter using the **ipv6 nat translation timeout** command, as shown in Table 5-10. The command **ipv6 nat translation** can be used to change the TCP timeout more precisely unless an RST (reset flag) or FIN (finish flag) is seen on the stream. Tuning can also be done for ICMP, UDP, and DNS translations, as shown in Table 5-10.

**Table 5-10**    **ipv6 nat translation** *Command for NAT-PT*

| Command | Description |
|---|---|
| **ipv6 nat translation max-entries** *number* | Limits the number of concurrent translations handled by NAT-PT. By default, there is no limit. |
| **ipv6 nat translation timeout** *seconds* | Defines the global translation timeout for dynamic translations. The default timeout is 86,400 seconds. |
| **ipv6 nat translation tcp-timeout** *seconds* | Defines the translation timeout for TCP. The default timeout is 86,400 seconds. |
| **ipv6 nat translation finrst-timeout** *seconds* | Defines the translation timeout for FIN and RST. The default timeout is 60 seconds. |
| **ipv6 nat translation icmp-timeout** *seconds* | Defines the translation timeout for ICMP. The default timeout is 86,400 seconds. |
| **ipv6 nat translation udp-timeout** *seconds* | Defines the translation timeout for UDP. The default timeout is 300 seconds. |
| **ipv6 nat translation dns-timeout** *seconds* | Defines the translation timeout for DNS sessions. The default timeout is 60 seconds. |

## Other Translation Mechanisms

The IETF defined additional translation mechanisms allowing IPv6-only hosts to exchange packets with IPv4-only nodes. The following list briefly describes each translation mechanism:

- **TCP-UDP relay**—This mechanism is similar to NAT-PT because it must be located between IPv6-only domains and IPv4-only domains. However, the TCP-UDP mechanism performs translation at the transport layer rather than at Layer 3 (IP/ICMP), like NAT-PT. TCP-UDP relay is defined in RFC 3142, *An IPv6-to-IPv4 Transport Relay Translator*.

- **Bump in the Stack (BIS)**—The BIS mechanism is another way to facilitate the transition from IPv4 hosts to IPv6, but it is designed to work on dual-stack hosts only. BIS translates IPv4 packets into IPv6 and vice versa using the SIIT algorithm. One main issue during the transition period is the availability of IPv6-enabled applications on all of a network's hosts. During the early deployment of IPv6, it will be difficult for organizations to get an IPv6 version of all their applications. With BIS, software is added on the dual-stack hosts to intercept and translate packets between the application and the network layers. When the stack receives IPv4 packets from IPv4-only applications, BIS converts IPv4 packets into IPv6 packets and sends them to the IPv6 network using the IPv6 stack. BIS is defined in RFC 2767, *Dual Stack Hosts using the "Bump-In-the-Stack" Technique (BIS)*.

- **Dual-Stack Transition Mechanism (DSTM)** — Within IPv6-only domains, dual-stack hosts might need to reach IPv4-only services on existing IPv4 networks. DSTM defines a method to establish IPv4-over-IPv6 tunnels and the temporary allocation of IPv4 addresses to dual-stack hosts in the IPv6-only domain. The dual-stack hosts with DSTM can reach the IPv4-only services on the IPv4 networks. The IPv4-over-IPv6 tunnels are established between the DSTM server and the DSTM nodes. DSTM is defined in www.ietf.org/internet-drafts/draft-ietf-ngtrans-dstm-08.txt, *Dual Stack Transition Mechanism (DSTM)*.

- **SOCKS-based IPv6/IPv4 gateway** — This translation mechanism is based on the SOCKS protocol (SOCKSv5). The SOCKS mechanism is a well-known proxy protocol defined by the IETF (RFC 1928) for TCP/IP applications. The two components of the SOCKS protocol are the SOCKS server and the SOCKS client. In an IPv6 context, the SOCKS mechanism can allow IPv4-only nodes acting as SOCKS clients to communicate with IPv6-only services and vice versa through a SOCKS server that has dual-stack support. The SOCKS-based IPv6/IPv4 gateway is defined in RFC 3089.

# Summary

During the transition period, integration and coexistence mechanisms maintain complete backward compatibility with the IPv4 protocol and IPv4-only networks. This chapter examined three classes of integration and coexistence strategies — dual stack, tunneling, and protocol translation.

Dual stack allows nodes on the network to handle simultaneously an IPv4 stack and an IPv6 stack. In this context, the naming service (Domain Name System) provides information to dual-stack nodes to force the selection of a stack.

You learned how tunnels carry IPv6 packets over existing IPv4 networks. You explored the main tunneling techniques available for the deployment and establishment of tunnels over IPv4. The following are the key protocols and techniques defined by the IETF for the establishment of tunnels between dual-stack nodes:

- **Configured tunnel** — Tunnels are configured manually between dual-stack nodes to carry IPv6 packets over IPv4.

- **Tunnel broker and tunnel server** — Tunnel broker and tunnel server are mechanisms to automate the deployment of configured tunnels.

- **6to4** — Tunnels are dynamically established between 6to4 sites. The IPv4 address of the 6to4 router is embedded in the 6to4 prefix of the 6to4 sites.

- **GRE tunnel**—Tunneling IPv6 packets in a GRE tunnel is another method to carry IPv6 packets over IPv4 networks. However, the deployment of GRE tunnels is done statically, as for configured tunnels.

- **ISATAP**—Tunnels are dynamically established within a domain to create one virtual IPv6 network over IPv4. Prefixes and addresses assigned to ISATAP hosts and ISATAP routers are based on a specific format.

- **Automatic IPv4-compatible tunnel**—Allows isolated hosts on an IPv4 network to automatically establish tunnels over IPv4 to isolated hosts. This mechanism has several limitations and is being deprecated.

- **Teredo tunnel**—Tunnels to carry IPv6 packets over IPv4 can be established through Network Address Translation (NAT) devices over IPv4 UDP packets. The Teredo tunnel must be initiated by the Teredo clients that are behind a NAT in IPv4 domains.

You also learned how IPv6-only nodes can interact with IPv4-only nodes using Application-Level Gateway (ALG) and NAT-PT. NAT-PT can be used to do protocol translations between the IPv6-only domain and the IPv4-only domain when no other methods are available. The IETF also defined other translation mechanisms that may be used in specific contexts such as TCP-UDP Relay, Bump in the Stack (BIS), Dual-Stack Transition Mechanism (DSTM), and the SOCKS-based IPv6/IPv4 gateway.

Although several mechanisms allow the integration and coexistence of IPv6 and IPv4, infrastructures made of native IPv6 networks and links should be preferred before any of these mechanisms.

Finally, you learned how to configure dual stack, configured tunnel, 6to4, GRE tunnel, ISATAP, and NAT-PT on the Cisco IOS Software to deploy an IPv6 network that interacts with your current IPv4 infrastructure. You also saw examples, router configurations, and Cisco IOS Software commands that manage these mechanisms on the Cisco technology.

# Case Study: Using IPv6 Integration and Coexistence Strategies with Cisco

Practice the skills you learned in this chapter by completing the following exercises. You will configure integration and coexistence mechanisms on networks.

## Objectives

In these exercises, you will complete the following tasks:

- Enabling configured tunnels on a router

- Assigning IPv6 addresses to tunnel interfaces

- Adding a default IPv6 route

- Advertising an IPv6 prefix on a link

- Enabling a 6to4 router

- Adding a default route to a 6to4 relay

- Enabling the NAT-PT mechanism

- Configuring a static NAT-PT mapping

- Verifying NAT-PT mapping

## Commands List

In this configuration exercise, you will use the commands shown in Table 5-11. Refer to this list during the exercise.

**Table 5-11** *Commands List*

| Command | Description |
|---------|-------------|
| **copy run start** | Saves a current configuration to nonvolatile RAM (NVRAM). |
| **ip address 206.123.31.2 255.255.255.0** | Assigns an IPv4 address to an interface. |
| **ipv6 unicast-routing** | Enables IPv6 traffic forwarding. |
| **ipv6 address 2001:420:ffff:0::1/64** | Configures an IPv6 static address. |
| **ipv6 address 2001:420:ffff:1::/64 eui-64** | Configures an IPv6 static address using EUI-64 format. |
| **ipv6 nat** | Enables the NAT-PT mechanism. |
| **ipv6 nat prefix 2001:420:ffff:0:0:1::/96** | Defines a prefix for the NAT-PT operation. |
| **ipv6 nat v4v6 source 10.1.1.100 2001:420:ffff:0:0:1:0:100** | Defines a static mapping between an IPv6 address and 10.1.1.100. |
| **ipv6 nat v4v6 source 10.1.1.150 2001:420:ffff:0:0:1:0:150** | Defines a static mapping between an IPv6 address and 10.1.1.150. |
| **ipv6 nat v6v4 source 2001:420:ffff:2::1 10.1.1.2** | Defines a static mapping between an IPv4 address and 2001:420:ffff:2::1. |
| **ipv6 route ::/0 tunnel0** | Defines a default IPv6 route. |
| **show ipv6 nat translation** | Displays the translation of the NAT-PT mechanism. |

**Table 5-11**  *Commands List (Continued)*

| Command | Description |
|---------|-------------|
| **tunnel destination 132.214.1.199** | Defines the IPv4 destination address of a tunnel interface. |
| **tunnel mode ipv6ip** | Defines the tunnel interface as a configured tunnel. |
| **tunnel mode ipv6ip 6to4** | Defines the tunnel interface as a 6to4 tunnel. |
| **tunnel source 206.123.31.100** | Assigns an IPv4 source address to a tunnel interface. |

# Network Architecture for Task 1

Figure 5-25 shows the network architecture for Task 1. An ISP in your city proposed to provide IPv6 connectivity for your site and to allocate one aggregatable global unicast /48 prefix to it. The ISP received one IPv6 prefix (/32) from ARIN (American Registry for Internet Numbers). The ISP can provide the native IPv6 link and connectivity to your site within the next 12 months. However, your network and the ISP are connected to the IPv4 Internet. In the meantime, you can set up a configured tunnel with the provider to get IPv6 connectivity over the IPv4 Internet.

**Figure 5-25**  *Enabling Configured Tunnels on a Router*

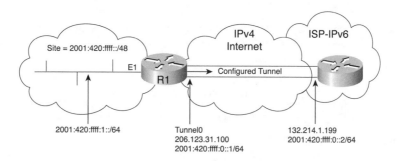

# Task 1: Enable a Configured Tunnel and Default IPv6 Route

Complete the following steps:

**Step 1**  Enter the command to enable IPv6 forwarding on the router to forward unicast IPv6 packets between interfaces. What commands will you use?

```
RouterR1#conf t
RouterR1(config)#ipv6 unicast-routing
RouterR1(config)#exit
```

**Step 2** Based on the following table, enable a configured tunnel on Router R1's tunnel0 interface to get IPv6 connectivity from the ISP. Which commands enable a configured tunnel on Cisco?

| | Address |
|---|---|
| Source IPv4 (your site) | 206.123.31.100 |
| Destination IPv4 | 132.214.1.199 |
| Source IPv6 (your site) | 2001:420:ffff:0::1 |
| Destination IPv6 | 2001:420:ffff:0::2 |
| Point-to-point link prefix length | /64 |

```
RouterR1#conf t
RouterR1(config)#int tunnel0
RouterR1(config-if)#ipv6 address 2001:420:ffff:0::1/64
RouterR1(config-if)#tunnel source 206.123.31.100
RouterR1(config-if)#tunnel destination 132.214.1.199
RouterR1(config-if)#tunnel mode ipv6ip
RouterR1(config-if)#exit
RouterR1(config)#exit
```

**Step 3** The IPv6 Internet can be reached through the ISP-IPv6. Add a default IPv6 route in the router that points to the configured tunnel interface tunnel0. What commands will you use?

```
RouterR1#conf t
RouterR1(config)#ipv6 route ::/0 tunnel0
RouterR1(config)#exit
```

**Step 4** Assign an IPv6 address to the interface ethernet1 using EUI-64 format, and advertise the prefix 2001:420:ffff:1::/64 on the ethernet1 interface. Which commands will you use?

```
RouterR1#conf t
RouterR1(config)#int ethernet1
RouterR1(config-if)#ipv6 address 2001:420:ffff:1::/64 eui-64
RouterR1(config-if)#exit
```

**Step 5** Save the current configuration to NVRAM.

```
RouterR1#copy run start
Destination filename [startup-config]?
Building configuration...
```

# Network Architecture for Task 2

Figure 5-26 shows the network topology for Task 2. Your site can't get IPv6 connectivity from an ISP-IPv6. However, getting IPv6 connectivity using the 6to4 mechanism is an interesting alternative for your site. Your network is already connected to the IPv4 Internet. Therefore, one of your border routers can be configured to act as a 6to4 router, and a 6to4 prefix must be advertised within your internal network on the link behind the 6to4 router.

**Figure 5-26**  *Enabling a 6to4 Site*

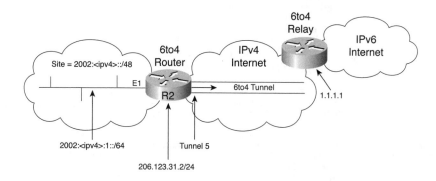

## Task 2: Enable a 6to4 Router

Complete the following steps:

**Step 1**    Assign an IPv4 address to Router R2's loopback0 interface, as shown in the following table. This address will be used for the 6to4 operation. What commands will you use?

| Router Interface | IPv4 Address | Netmask |
|------------------|--------------|---------|
|                  |              |         |
| Loopback0        | 206.123.31.2 | 255.255.255.0 |

```
RouterR2#conf t
RouterR2(config)#int loopback0
RouterR2(config-if)#ip address 206.123.31.2 255.255.255.0
RouterR2(config-if)#exit
```

**Step 2**    The source IPv4 address for the 6to4 router is 206.123.31.2. Calculate the /48 prefix of your 6to4 site. Then append the result to the 2002::/16 prefix to get the /48 prefix for your site.

206.123.31.2 converted to hexadecimal = CE7B:1F02

/48 prefix of the 6to4 site = 2002:CE7B:1F02::/48

**Step 3** Assign an IPv6 address in your /48 prefix to Router R1's ethernet1 interface using EUI-64 format, and advertise the prefix 2002:CE7B:1F02:1::/64 on that interface.

```
RouterR2#conf t
RouterR2(config)#int ethernet1
RouterR2(config-if)#ipv6 address 2002:ce7b:1f02:1::/64 eui-64
RouterR2(config-if)#exit
```

**Step 4** Enable the 6to4 router using the tunnel5 interface. What commands enable a router into a 6to4 site?

```
RouterR2#conf t
RouterR2(config)#int tunnel5
RouterR2(config-if)#no ip address
RouterR2(config-if)#ipv6 unnumbered ethernet1
RouterR2(config-if)#tunnel source loopback0
RouterR2(config-if)#tunnel mode ipv6ip 6to4
RouterR2(config-if)#exit
RouterR2(config)#ipv6 route 2002::/16 tunnel5
RouterR2(config)#exit
```

**Step 5** The IPv6 Internet can be reached through the 6to4 relay, as shown in Figure 2-26. Add a default IPv6 route pointing to this 6to4 relay. What commands will you use?

```
RouterR2#conf t
RouterR2(config)#ipv6 route ::/0 2002:0101:0101::
RouterR2(config)#exit
```

**Step 6** Save the current configuration to NVRAM.

```
RouterR2#copy run start
Destination filename [startup-config]?
Building configuration...
```

# Network Architecture for Task 3

Figure 5-27 shows the network topology for Task 3. Your domain is divided into two subnets. Inside the IPv6-only subnet A, you enable only the IPv6 protocol, and IPv6-only hosts are deployed. Inside the IPv4/IPv6 subnet B, you enable both IPv4 and IPv6, and all nodes deployed in subnet B have dual-stack support. However, some legacy systems, such as the mainframe and the printer on subnet B, support only IPv4 as the protocol. Therefore, configure Router R3 to act as NAT-PT to allow the IPv6-only host A on subnet A to communicate with the mainframe and the printer.

**Figure 5-27**  *Enabling a Router to Act as NAT-PT*

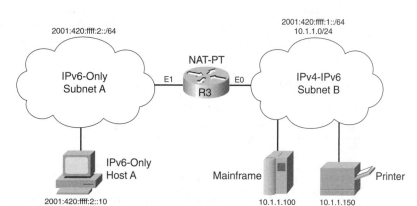

# Task 3: Enable the NAT-PT Mechanism with Static Mapping

Complete the following steps:

**Step 1**  Assign IPv4 and IPv6 addresses to Router R3's interfaces according to the following table. What commands will you use?

| Router Interface | IP Address/Prefix Length |
|---|---|
| Ethernet0 | 10.1.1.1/24 |
| Ethernet1 | 2001:420:ffff:2::1/64 |

```
RouterR3#configure terminal
RouterR3(config)#int ethernet0
RouterR3(config-if)#ip address 10.1.1.1 255.255.255.0
RouterR3(config-if)#int ethernet1
RouterR3(config-if)#ipv6 address 2001:420:ffff:2::1/64
```

**Step 2**  Enable the NAT-PT mechanism on both interfaces of Router R3. What commands enable the NAT-PT mechanism on interfaces?

```
RouterR3#configure terminal
RouterR3(config)#int ethernet0
RouterR3(config-if)#ipv6 nat
RouterR3(config-if)#int ethernet1
RouterR3(config-if)#ipv6 nat
RouterR3(config-if)#exit
```

**Step 3**  The dedicated prefix for NAT-PT is 2001:420:ffff:0:0:1::/96. Define this prefix as global for the NAT-PT operation on Router R3.

```
RouterR3#configure terminal
RouterR3(config)#ipv6 nat prefix 2001:420:ffff:0:0:1::/96
RouterR3(config)#exit
```

**Step 4** Enable static NAT-PT mapping for the mainframe and the printer. The static NAT-PT mapping must allow the IPv6-only host A (2001:420:ffff:2::10) to communicate with the legacy IPv4 systems. Use 10.1.1.2 as the source IPv4 address for the static NAT-PT mapping. Refer to the following table for the configuration of the static mapping.

| System | IPv4 Address | IPv6 Address |
|---|---|---|
| Mainframe | 10.1.1.100 | 2001:420:ffff:0:0:1:0:100 |
| Printer | 10.1.1.150 | 2001:420:ffff:0:0:1:0:150 |

```
RouterR3#configure terminal
RouterR3(config)#ipv6 nat v4v6 source 10.1.1.100 2001:420:ffff:0:0:1:0:100
RouterR3(config)#ipv6 nat v4v6 source 10.1.1.150 2001:420:ffff:0:0:1:0:150
RouterR3(config)#ipv6 nat v6v4 source 2001:420:ffff:2::10 10.1.1.2
RouterR3(config)#exit
```

**Step 5** Display the static NAT-PT configuration to verify your setup. What is the command to display the NAT-PT mapping?

```
RouterR3#show ipv6 nat translation
Prot  IPv4 source          IPv6 source
      IPv4 destination      IPv6 destination
---   ---                  ---
      10.1.1.100            2001:420:FFFF:0:0:1:0:100

---   ---                  ---
      10.1.1.150            2001:420:FFFF:0:0:1:0:150

---   10.1.1.2             2001:420:FFFF:2::10
      ---                  ---
```

**Step 6** Save the current configuration to NVRAM.

```
RouterR3#copy run start
Destination filename [startup-config]?
Building configuration...
```

# Review Questions

Answer the following questions, and then refer to Appendix B, "Answers to Review Questions," for the answers.

**1** List the three classes of integration and coexistence strategies presented in this chapter.

**2** Describe the dual-stack approach.

**3** What type of Ethernet frame is made by IPv6-only applications on nodes?

**4** How do IPv4- and IPv6-enabled applications choose the IP stack when both IPv6 and IPv4 stacks are available?

**5**  Which type of address is preferred by IPv4- and IPv6-enabled applications when the naming service provides both IPv4 (A-record) and IPv6 (AAAA-record) address types?

**6**  When should you consider using integration and coexistence mechanisms?

**7**  What is the protocol number defined for the encapsulation of IPv6 packets in IPv4?

**8**  List the three scenarios presented in this chapter in which the tunneling of IPv6 packets in IPv4 is possible.

**9**  What is the main requirement of tunneling?

**10**  List all the tunneling techniques presented in this chapter.

**11**  What is the main characteristic of a configured tunnel?

**12**  What is the purpose of the tunnel broker and the tunnel server?

**13**  Describe how the prefix to a 6to4 site is assigned.

**14**  What is the purpose of the 6to4 relay?

**15**  Define the ISATAP address format.

**16**  Describe how the ISATAP unicast prefix is advertised to the ISATAP host by an ISATAP router.

**17**  Does the IPv4-compatible tunnel mechanism provide a solution to the IPv4 address space exhaustion?

**18**  List the two methods that allow IPv6-only nodes in an IPv6-only network to communicate with IPv4-only nodes in an IPv4-only network.

**19**  List the different types of operations defined for the NAT-PT mechanism.

**20**  What is the purpose of the 96-bit prefix for the NAT-PT mechanism?

# References

RFC 2473, *Generic Packet Tunneling in IPv6 Specification,* A. Conta, S. Deering, IETF, www.ietf.org/rfc/rfc2473.txt, December 1998

RFC 2553, *Basic Socket Interface Extensions for IPv6,* R. Gilligan et al., IETF, www.ietf.org/rfc/rfc2553.txt, March 1999

RFC 2732, *Format for Literal IPv6 Addresses in URL's,* R. Hinden, B. Carpenter, L. Masinter, IETF, www.ietf.org/rfc/rfc2732.txt, December 1999

RFC 2765, *Stateless IP/ICMP Translation Algorithm (SIIT),* E. Nordmark, IETF, www.ietf.org/rfc/rfc2765.txt, February 2000

RFC 2766, *Network Address Translation Protocol Translation,* G. Tsirtsis, P. Srisuresh, IETF, www.ietf.org/rfc/rfc2766.txt, February 2000

RFC 2767, *Dual Stack Hosts using the "Bump-In-the-Stack" Technique (BIS),* K. Tsuchiya, H. Higuchi, Y. Atarashi, www.ietf.org/rfc/rfc2767.txt, February 2000

RFC 2893, *Transition Mechanisms for IPv6 Hosts and Routers,* R. Gilligan, E. Nordmark, IETF, www.ietf.org/rfc/rfc2893.txt, August 2000

RFC 3053, *IPv6 Tunnel Broker,* A. Durand et al., IETF, www.ietf.org/rfc/rfc3053.txt, January 2001

RFC 3056, *Connection of IPv6 Domains via IPv4 Clouds,* B. Carpenter, K. Moore, IETF, www.ietf.org/rfc/rfc3056.txt, February 2001

RFC 3068, *An Anycast Prefix for 6to4 Relay Routers,* C. Huitema, IETF, www.ietf.org/rfc/rfc3068.txt, June 2001

RFC 3089, *A SOCKS-based IPv6/IPv4 Gateway Mechanism,* H. Kitamura, IETF, www.ietf.org/rfc/rfc3089.txt, April 2001

RFC 3142, *An IPv6-to-IPv4 Transport Relay Translator,* J. Hagino, K. Yamamoto, IETF, www.ietf.org/rfc/rfc3142.txt, June 2001

RFC 3177, *IAB/IESG Recommendations on IPv6 Address Allocations to Sites,* IAB, IETF, www.ietf.org/rfc/rfc3177.txt, September 2001

*Dual Stack Transition Mechanism (DSTM),* Jim Bound et al., IETF, www.ietf.org/internet-drafts/draft-ietf-ngtrans-dstm-08.txt

*Intra-Site Automatic Tunnel Addressing Protocol (ISATAP),* F. Templin et al., IETF, www.ietf.org/internet-drafts/draft-ietf-ngtrans-isatap-12.txt

*Teredo: Tunneling IPv6 over UDP through NATs,* C. Huitema, IETF, www.ietf.org/internet-drafts/draft-ietf-ngtrans-shipworm-08.txt

*Use of /127 Prefix Length Between Routers Considered Harmful,* P. Savola, IETF, www.ietf.org/internet-drafts/draft-savola-ipv6-127-prefixlen-12.txt

"640K is enough for anybody."

Bill Gates, 1981

# CHAPTER 6

# IPv6 Hosts Internetworking with Cisco

As you saw in Chapter 2, "IPv6 Addressing," the built-in stateless autoconfiguration mechanism in IPv6 allows nodes on local links to configure their IPv6 addresses by themselves. Chapter 5, "IPv6 Integration and Coexistence Strategies," described the transition and coexistence mechanisms used to move your current IPv4 network infrastructures toward IPv6. Both chapters discussed the interactions between the routers and IPv6 nodes deployed on networks.

The primary objective of this chapter is to show you how to enable and configure IPv6 support on the most common host operating systems, such as Microsoft Windows, Solaris, FreeBSD, Linux, and Tru64 when deploying IPv6 over networks with Cisco routers.

This chapter also explains how to enable stateless autoconfiguration on these host implementations and how they interact with Cisco routers using transition and coexistence mechanisms such as configured tunnel and 6to4.

After completing this chapter, you will be able to configure and manage Microsoft Windows NT, Microsoft Windows 2000, Microsoft Windows XP, Solaris 8, FreeBSD 4.x, Linux, and Tru64 with IPv6 support. This chapter also presents examples of host and router configurations with IPv6.

## IPv6 on Microsoft Windows

Microsoft has been a leading host operating system for years, especially with the growth of the Internet during the 1990s. In 2001, Microsoft made a clear commitment to supporting IPv6 by including IPv6 support in the mainstream code of Windows XP. IPv6 support for the well-known Windows NT and Windows 2000 platforms has been available since 1998 for research, experimental, and learning purposes only.

In 1998, Microsoft Research (MSR), with contributions from USC/ISI East, started developing an IPv6 stack for the Windows NT and Windows 2000 platforms. For many years, MSR has publicly offered the source and binary code of this beta IPv6 implementation to the whole Internet community for research purposes only.

In 2000, Microsoft released the IPv6 Technology Preview For Windows 2000 and distributed it to the Internet community. The other version of the IPv6 stack was derived from the MSR code, but it was specifically coded to run only on Windows 2000. The Technology Preview For Windows 2000 version targeted people who wanted to learn, experiment with, and develop with IPv6 on Windows platforms. In 2001, Microsoft bundled IPv6 support into Windows XP. IPv6 support is available in Windows XP Professional, Windows XP Home Edition, Windows XP Pro, and Windows XP Home Edition Service Pack 1. Before these, Microsoft did not officially support IPv6. Microsoft also includes IPv6 support on .NET Server Windows Server 2003.

---

**NOTE**   If you want more information on IPv6 support on Microsoft Windows, refer to www.microsoft.com/windows.netserver/technologies/ipv6/default.asp or www.microsoft.com/ipv6.

---

The different versions of IPv6 support for Windows are similar and support the main features of the IPv6 protocol, such as stateless autoconfiguration and some of the transition mechanisms. Users of Windows NT and Windows 2000 can download and install the IPv6 code on their computers to add IPv6 support. However, with Windows XP, IPv6 support is built in; the user just enables it using a command. This section presents the steps used to install and enable IPv6 support on Windows NT, Windows 2000, and Windows XP. First, however, you'll see how IPv6 internetworks with Windows.

## Internetworking Microsoft Windows with IPv6

As soon as IPv6 support is installed successfully and enabled on Windows, the IPv6 stack is interpreted as a separate protocol from IPv4. This stack is IPv6-compliant and can interoperate with IPv6 nodes and router implementations on the market, including the Cisco IOS Software. In the context of internetworking Windows IPv6 nodes with Cisco routers, the IPv6 support provided by Microsoft can basically handle stateless autoconfiguration and some transition mechanisms such as configured tunnel and 6to4.

The Microsoft implementation includes applications, utilities, and tools used for networking that have been ported to IPv6 such as client Telnet, client FTP, ping, nslookup, tracert, DNS resolver, and file and print sharing. Moreover, IPv6 support is also included in Internet Explorer, .NET Server, IIS, Microsoft Media Server, and Microsoft RPC, in theory allowing any application based on RPC to run over IPv6.

Open software applications such as NTEmacs, Teraterm Pro with SSH, Cygwin Net (with IPv6 extensions), Apache for Win32 (with IPv6 extensions), NcFTP, Windump, Ethereal, ISC Bind 8 for NT, Emacs, Ruby, PuTTY, psyBNC, and AsyProxy are available with IPv6 support for Windows. Of course, this list is incomplete. An increasing number of IPv4-only open software and commercial applications that run on Windows are scheduled to be ported to IPv6.

After you see how to install and enable IPv6 support on Windows in the following sections, you will learn the steps and commands used to enable stateless autoconfiguration and to configure the transition mechanisms on Windows.

# Enabling IPv6 on Microsoft Windows

This section presents the steps to install and enable IPv6 support on Windows XP, Windows 2000, and Windows NT.

## Enabling IPv6 on Microsoft Windows XP

As mentioned, IPv6 support is already integrated into Windows XP in the Professional and Home Edition versions. However, IPv6 support must be enabled manually.

To enable IPv6 support, you enter the command **ipv6 install** in the DOS shell of Windows XP, as shown in Example 6-1.

**Example 6-1**    *Enabling IPv6 on Windows XP by Running ipv6.exe in the DOS Shell*

```
C:\Documents and Settings\REGIS>ipv6 install
Installing...
Succeeded.
```

Microsoft has introduced the command interface **netsh** for the DOS shell on Windows XP and .NET Server operating systems. You can use it to enable, configure, manage, and reset IPv4/IPv6 stacks. The **netsh interface ipv6 [...]** command is equivalent to the **ipv6** command. It is available only on the Windows XP and .NET Server operating systems. This section describes the **netsh** commands that are equivalent to the **ipv6** commands for the Windows XP environment. To see the different syntaxes of the **netsh** command for the IPv6 stack on Windows XP, enter **netsh interface ipv6 ?** in the DOS shell. You can also see the corresponding **ipv6** and **netsh** commands on the Microsoft Windows website at www.microsoft.com/windows.netserver/technologies/ipv6/ipv62netshtable.mspx.

**NOTE**    The **netsh interface ipv6 install** command on Windows XP is equivalent to the **ipv6 install** command.

**NOTE**    Installing IPv6 support on any Windows version requires administrator privileges.

| | |
|---|---|
| **NOTE** | Enabling IPv6 support on Windows XP does not require rebooting the computer. However, removing IPv6 support does require a reboot. |

| | |
|---|---|
| **TIP** | You can uninstall IPv6 support on Windows XP by entering **ipv6 uninstall** in the DOS shell. The **netsh interface ipv6 uninstall** command in Windows XP is equivalent to this command. |

You can find more information about IPv6 support for Windows XP at www.microsoft.com/windowsxp/pro/techinfo/administration/default.asp. The Frequently Asked Questions section on IPv6 support in Windows XP is available at www.microsoft.com/windowsxp/pro/techinfo/administration/ipv6/default.asp.

## Enabling IPv6 on Microsoft Windows 2000

The first step in enabling IPv6 support on Windows 2000 is to download the Microsoft IPv6 Technology Preview For Windows 2000 from the Microsoft website.

| | |
|---|---|
| **NOTE** | The Microsoft IPv6 Technology Preview For Windows 2000 code is available at msdn.microsoft.com/downloads/sdks/platform/tpipv6.asp. |

After you download the Microsoft IPv6 Technology Preview For Windows 2000 code, it is strongly recommended that you read all the documentation provided by Microsoft before installing the IPv6 support on your Windows 2000 platform. (Installing the IPv6 support on Windows 2000 is beyond the scope of this chapter.)

| | |
|---|---|
| **NOTE** | Installing the Microsoft IPv6 Technology Preview For Windows 2000 on Windows 2000 forces the reboot of the computer. |

The Frequently Asked Questions section for the Microsoft IPv6 Technology Preview For Windows 2000 is available at msdn.microsoft.com/downloads/sdks/platform/tpipv6/faq.asp.

### Enabling IPv6 on Microsoft Windows NT

The first step in enabling IPv6 support on Windows NT is to download the Microsoft Research IPv6 support from the Microsoft Research website. The Microsoft Research IPv6 code is labeled as outdated by Microsoft. However, considering the large number of users still using Windows NT, this section should be useful.

---

**NOTE**    The Microsoft Research IPv6 code is available at research.microsoft.com/msrIPv6/msripv6.htm.

---

After you download the Microsoft Research IPv6 code, it is strongly recommended that you read all the documentation provided by Microsoft before installing the IPv6 support on your Windows NT platform. (Installing the IPv6 support for Windows NT is beyond the scope of this chapter.)

---

**NOTE**    Installing the Microsoft Research IPv6 support on Windows NT forces the reboot of the computer.

---

## Verifying IPv6 on Microsoft Windows

After you've installed the IPv6 support on your computer, you can verify the installation using the **ipv6 if** command in the DOS shell. When you enter this command, the system displays a list of all the IPv6 pseudo-interfaces defined on Windows.

Example 6-2 shows the output of the **ipv6 if** command applied on Windows XP. Keep in mind that the computer used to produce this output has only one Ethernet interface. This output might differ slightly if you are using Windows 2000 or Windows NT or if the computer used has multiple interfaces. Example 6-2 shows IPv6 pseudo-interfaces 1 through 4. Pseudo-interface 4 represents this computer's physical Ethernet interface, and pseudo-interfaces 1 through 3 are virtual interfaces assigned for IPv6 support.

**Example 6-2**    *Showing IPv6 Pseudo-Interfaces on Windows XP*

```
C:\Documents and Settings\REGIS>ipv6 if
Interface 4: Ethernet: Local Area Connection
  uses Neighbor Discovery
  uses Router Discovery
  link-layer address: 00-08-02-2d-6f-4f
    preferred link-local fe80::208:2ff:fe2d:6f4f, life infinite
    multicast interface-local ff01::1, 1 refs, not reportable
    multicast link-local ff02::1, 1 refs, not reportable
```

*continues*

**Example 6-2** *Showing IPv6 Pseudo-Interfaces on Windows XP (Continued)*

```
link MTU 1500 (true link MTU 1500)
  current hop limit 64
  reachable time 18000ms (base 30000ms)
  retransmission interval 1000ms
  DAD transmits 1
Interface 3: 6to4 Tunneling Pseudo-Interface
  does not use Neighbor Discovery
  does not use Router Discovery
  link MTU 1280 (true link MTU 65515)
  current hop limit 128
  reachable time 22500ms (base 30000ms)
  retransmission interval 1000ms
  DAD transmits 0
Interface 2: Automatic Tunneling Pseudo-Interface
  does not use Neighbor Discovery
  does not use Router Discovery
  router link-layer address: 0.0.0.0
  EUI-64 embedded IPv4 address: 0.0.0.0
    preferred link-local fe80::5efe:192.168.1.51, life infinite
  link MTU 1280 (true link MTU 65515)
  current hop limit 128
  reachable time 43000ms (base 30000ms)
  retransmission interval 1000ms
  DAD transmits 0
Interface 1: Loopback Pseudo-Interface
  does not use Neighbor Discovery
  does not use Router Discovery
  link-layer address:
    preferred link-local ::1, life infinite
    preferred link-local fe80::1, life infinite
  link MTU 1500 (true link MTU 4294967295)
  current hop limit 128
  reachable time 21500ms (base 30000ms)
  retransmission interval 1000ms
  DAD transmits 0
```

NOTE    The **netsh interface ipv6 show address** and **netsh interface ipv6 show interface** commands on Windows XP can provide output similar to that for the **ipv6 if** command.

Here are descriptions of these IPv6 pseudo-interfaces:

- **Interface 4**—The pseudo-interface representing this computer's physical Ethernet interface. When more than one physical interface is present, they are numbered sequentially. Example 6-2 shows information such as the interface's Ethernet MAC address, the link-local address (FE80::/10), and the multicast addresses (FF00::/8).

- **Interface 3**—The pseudo-interface used to enable the 6to4 mechanism on Windows XP. See Chapter 5 for more information about the 6to4 mechanism.

- **Interface 2**—The pseudo-interface used to deploy automatic IPv4-compatible tunnels on Windows XP. See Chapter 5 for more information about automatic IPv4-compatible tunnels. *This mechanism is being deprecated.*

- **Interface 1**—The pseudo-interface representing this computer's IPv6 loopback address. The loopback address is represented as ::1. Refer to Chapter 2 for more information about the loopback address for IPv6.

---

**NOTE**    You can display information about a specific pseudo-interface in Windows by entering the pseudo-interface number as an argument with the command **ipv6 if** *number*. The **netsh interface ipv6 show interface** *number* command is equivalent in Windows XP.

---

## Stateless Autoconfiguration on Microsoft Windows

As soon as IPv6 support is enabled in Windows, stateless autoconfiguration is enabled by default. Therefore, no specific command or configuration needs to be applied in Windows to enable stateless autoconfiguration on the network interfaces.

At the boot of any IPv6 host, including the Windows implementation, the node starts by completing duplicate address detection (DAD) (discussed in Chapter 3, "IPv6 in Depth") to ensure that the interface's link-local address is unique on the local link. At this step, the link-local address of the interface on Windows is enabled.

After assigning the interface's link-local address, the Windows node performs stateless auto-configuration (discussed in Chapter 3) by sending a router solicitation request (ICMPv6 type 133) to the multicast address FF02::2 (all routers on the link-local scope). When a router is present and is properly configured with IPv6 on the local link, the router responds with a router advertisement message (ICMPv6 type 134) to the multicast address FF01::2 (all nodes on the link-local scope) with the necessary information to enable the node's IPv6 configuration. Therefore, the Windows node can configure its IPv6 address using stateless autoconfiguration.

Figure 6-1 illustrates a Windows XP node and an IPv6 router on the same local link. The Windows XP node starts by sending a router solicitation request on the local link via pseudo-interface 4 (the Ethernet interface). Then the IPv6 router responds by sending a router advertisement containing the aggregatable global unicast prefix 3ffe:b00:ffff:1::/64 on the ethernet0 interface. Therefore, the Windows XP node can configure its IPv6 address with the prefix given using stateless autoconfiguration.

**Figure 6-1** *Windows XP Node Receiving a Router Advertisement to Perform Stateless Autoconfiguration*

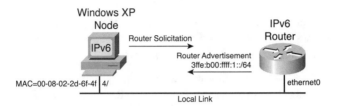

Example 6-3 shows a sample of the configuration applied on the IPv6 router in Figure 6-1 to enable stateless autoconfiguration. By using the **ipv6 address 3ffe:b00:ffff:1::1/64** command on the ethernet0 interface, IPv6 is enabled on the interface, a static IPv6 address is assigned, and stateless autoconfiguration is enabled.

**Example 6-3** *Enabling IPv6 and Stateless Autoconfiguration on Cisco*

```
Router(config)#int ethernet0
Router(config-if)#ipv6 address 3ffe:b00:ffff:1::1/64
Router(config-if)#exit
```

Following the router configuration, Example 6-4 displays the pseudo-interface 4 configuration on Windows XP after the node has successfully completed stateless autoconfiguration.

**Example 6-4** *Pseudo-Interface 4 on Windows XP After Stateless Autoconfiguration Is Performed*

```
C:\Documents and Settings\REGIS>ipv6 if 4
Interface 4: Ethernet: Local Area Connection
  uses Neighbor Discovery
  uses Router Discovery
  link-layer address: 00-08-02-2d-6f-4f
    preferred global 3ffe:b00:ffff:1:853c:f894:6648:3cdc, life
6d23h56m36s/23h54m15s (anonyme)
    preferred global 3ffe:b00:ffff:1:208:2ff:fe2d:6f4f, life
29d23h59m53s/6d23h59m53s (public)
    preferred link-local fe80::208:2ff:fe2d:6f4f, life infinite
    multicast interface-local ff01::1, 1 refs, not reportable
    multicast link-local ff02::1, 1 refs, not reportable
    multicast link-local ff02::1:ff2d:6f4f, 1 refs, last reporter
    multicast link-local ff02::1:ff48:3cdc, 1 refs, last reporter
link MTU 1500 (true link MTU 1500)
  current hop limit 64
  reachable time 18000ms (base 30000ms)
  retransmission interval 1000ms
  DAD transmits 1
```

**NOTE**    The **netsh interface ipv6 show interface 4** command on Windows XP can provide  details similar to the **ipv6 if 4** command.

Compared to Example 6-2, Example 6-4 has four new lines. The second highlighted line shows that aggregatable global unicast address 3ffe:b00:ffff:1:208:2ff:fe2d:6f4f is assigned to pseudo-interface 4 through stateless autoconfiguration. The first highlighted line is an additional unicast IPv6 address assigned to pseudo-interface 4. This address is generated using the privacy extension for stateless autoconfiguration, as defined in RFC 3041, *Privacy Extensions for Stateless Address Autoconfiguration in IPv6.*

**NOTE**    The privacy extension when supported and enabled allows a node to randomly generate the low-order 64-bit of the address rather than using the link-layer address in EUI-64 format. These addresses are considered temporary IPv6 addresses. The privacy extension is supported on Windows XP but not on Windows NT and Windows 2000.

The lifetime values for the address generated using the privacy extension are managed by the Windows XP node instead of being provided by the lifetime values in the router advertisement messages. You can display the various parameters and default lifetimes for the privacy extension on Windows XP by using the **netsh interface ipv6 show privacy** command. The command **netsh interface ipv6 set privacy maxpreferredlifetime=lifetime_in_seconds** can be used to set the lifetime values of the privacy extension.

**NOTE**    The privacy extension can be disabled on Windows XP using the **netsh interface ipv6 set privacy state=disabled** command.

The low-order 64-bit in the second highlighted line and the link-local addresses are generated using the Ethernet MAC address 00-08-02-2d-6f-4f of pseudo-interface 4 converted into EUI-64 format. Finally, the ff02::1:ff2d:6f4f and ff02::1:ff48:3cdc addresses are the solicited-node multicast addresses corresponding to the two aggregatable global unicast IPv6 addresses assigned to the interface.

NOTE     It is possible for Windows XP, Windows 2000, and Windows NT to act as IPv6 routers
         and to send router advertisements on the local link. However, configuring Windows to
         act as an IPv6 router is beyond the scope of this book. Refer to the Microsoft website at
         www.microsoft.com/ipv6 for detailed information on enabling a Microsoft node as an IPv6
         router.

## Assigning a Static IPv6 Address and a Default Route on Microsoft Windows

When no IPv6 router on the local link provides stateless autoconfiguration, you can manually
assign static IPv6 addresses to interfaces in Windows. The command **ipv6 adu** is used in the
DOS shell to perform this task. The syntax for the **ipv6 adu** command is as follows:

```
C:\ipv6 adu ifindex/ipv6-address [life validlifetime[/preflifetime]]
   [anycast] [unicast]
```

The **ipv6 adu** command assigns a static IPv6 address to the given pseudo-interface *ifindex*. The
*ipv6-address* is the static address to assign to the pseudo-interface. The prefix length is locked
at 64 bits on Microsoft. The *validlifetime* and *preflifetime* can be assigned following the **life**
keyword. By default, the lifetime is infinite. Specifying a lifetime of 0 causes the static IPv6
address to be removed. By default, the static IPv6 addresses assigned are **unicast**.

Here is an example of the **ipv6 adu** command:

```
C:\ipv6 adu 4/3ffe:b00:ffff:2000::1
```

This command assigns the static IPv6 address 3ffe:b00:ffff:2000::1/64 to pseudo-interface 4
(the Ethernet interface).

NOTE     The **netsh interface ipv6 add address 4 3ffe:b00:ffff:2000::1** command in Windows XP is
         equivalent to the **ipv6 adu 4/3ffe:b00:ffff:2000::1** command.

On the Windows node that has IPv6 support, you can add a default IPv6 route using the **ipv6
rtu** command, as shown here:

```
C:\ipv6 rtu ::/0 ifindex/gateway
```

This adds a default router that points to the *gateway* address given as an argument. For
example, the following adds a default IPv6 route that points to the link-local address
fe80::290:27ff:fe3a:9e9a via pseudo-interface 4:

```
C:\ipv6 rtu ::/0 4/fe80::290:27ff:fe3a:9e9a
```

| | |
|---|---|
| **NOTE** | The **netsh interface ipv6 add route ::/0 4 nexthop= fe80::290:27ff:fe3a:9e9a** command in Windows XP is equivalent to the **ipv6 rtu ::/0 4/fe80::290:27ff:fe3a:9e9a** command. |

## Managing IPv6 on Microsoft Windows

**ipv6** is the main command used in Windows XP, Windows 2000, and Windows NT to manage IPv6 support. Table 6-1 describes the **ipv6** and **tracert6** commands used to manage IPv6 addresses and routes in Windows.

**Table 6-1**    **ipv6** *and* **tracert6** *Commands on Windows*

| Command | Description |
|---|---|
| **C:\ipv6 if** | Displays the pseudo-interfaces list. The **netsh interface ipv6 show interface** command can perform the same task in Windows XP. |
| **C:\ipv6 adu** | Adds a static IPv6 address to a pseudo-interface. The **netsh interface ipv6 add address** command can perform the same task in Windows XP. |
| **C:\ipv6 rt** | Displays the local IPv6 routing table. The **netsh interface ipv6 show route** command can perform the same task in Windows XP. |
| **C:\ipv6 rtu** | Adds a static IPv6 route to the local IPv6 routing table. The **netsh interface ipv6 add route** command can perform the same task in Windows XP. |
| **C:\tracert6** *ipv6-address* | Traces the route to the destination *ipv6-address* using IPv6. |

You can list all the parameters of these commands by running them without an argument.

### ping6 on Microsoft Windows

The new **ping6** command on Microsoft sends ICMPv6 echo request messages to the specified destination to display the reachability of a destination IPv6 node. The syntax for the **ping6** command is as follows:

```
C:\ping6 ipv6-address[%zoneid]
```

The **ping6** command sends echo request messages to the given destination *ipv6-address* node. The optional *%zoneid* argument specifies the scope of the destination *ipv6-address*. The *%zoneid* argument is used when the destination *ipv6-address* is a link-local address (fe80::/10) or a site-local address (fec0::/10):

- **Link-local address**—In this case, the syntax of the *%zoneid* argument is represented by the % character followed by a number corresponding to the node's pseudo-interface on which the ICMPv6 packets must be sent to the destination link-local address. For example, because the pseudo-interface number corresponding to the Ethernet interface in Example 6-2 is 4, you must use the following command to ping the link-local address fe80::290:27ff:fe3a:9e9a from this node:

```
ping6 fe80::290:27ff:fe3a:9e9a%4
```

- **Site-local address**—When the destination *ipv6-address* is a site-local address, the syntax of the %*zoneid* argument is represented by the % character followed by the site number. Use the following command to find out the site number on your Microsoft node:

  ```
  netsh interface ipv6 show interface level=verbose
  ```

  If multiple sites are not being used, the %*zoneid* argument for site-local addresses is not required.

The %*zoneid* argument is not required when the destination IPv6 address is an aggregatable global unicast address.

## Defining Configured Tunnels on Microsoft Windows

Microsoft supports the configured tunnel as a transition and coexistence mechanism to deliver IPv6 packets over existing IPv4 networks. This section covers establishing a configured tunnel between a Windows node and a Cisco router. As discussed in Chapter 5, the configured tunnel is a transition mechanism providing a basic way for an IPv6 node to reach an IPv6 network using IPv4 as the transport layer. The configured tunnel allows IPv6 packets to be tunneled over IPv4 packets.

However, establishing a configured tunnel between two nodes such as Windows and a Cisco router requires dual-stack support and a static configuration on both devices. On the Windows node and on the Cisco router you must specify the other's source and destination IPv4 addresses to enable a configured tunnel. The static configuration of IPv6 addresses at both ends of the tunnel is also necessary.

Figure 6-2 illustrates a basic topology in which the Windows dual-stack node A has established a configured tunnel to the Cisco dual-stack Router R1. The IPv4 address assigned to the configured tunnel interface tunnel0 on Router R1 is 206.123.31.200, and the IPv6 address is 3ffe:b00:ffff:8::1/64. On Windows node A, the IPv4 address 132.214.1.10 and the IPv6 address 3ffe:b00:ffff:8::2/64 have been assigned to the configured tunnel pseudo-interface.

**Figure 6-2**   *Establishing a Configured Tunnel Between Windows and a Cisco Router*

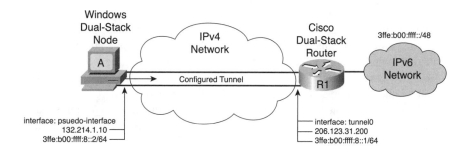

Example 6-5 shows the configuration applied on Cisco Router R1 in Figure 6-2 to set the configured tunnel to Windows node A. The IPv6 source address of the tunnel0 interface is assigned using the **ipv6 address 3ffe:b00:ffff:8::1/64** command. Then the **tunnel source 206.123.31.200** and **tunnel destination 132.214.1.10** commands define the source and destination IPv4 addresses for this configured tunnel. Finally, the **tunnel mode ipv6ip** command defines the type of tunneling as a configured tunnel. For more information on this configuration, refer to Chapter 5, which has the complete description of the commands used to set a configured tunnel on a Cisco router.

**Example 6-5**   *Setting a Configured Tunnel on Cisco Router R1*

```
RouterR1(config)#int tunnel0
RouterR1(config-if)#ipv6 address 3ffe:b00:ffff:8::1/64
RouterR1(config-if)#tunnel source 206.123.31.200
RouterR1(config-if)#tunnel destination 132.214.1.10
RouterR1(config-if)#tunnel mode ipv6ip
RouterR1(config-if)#exit
RouterR1(config)#
```

The pseudo-interface number for the configured tunnel on Windows XP differs from the pseudo-interface number on Windows NT and Windows 2000. The following sections describe how to set a configured tunnel on Windows 2000 and Windows NT compared to Windows XP.

## Defining a Configured Tunnel on Microsoft Windows 2000/NT

With the MSR IPv6 support and the Microsoft IPv6 Technology Preview For Windows 2000, the default pseudo-interface assigned as a configured tunnel interface in the operating system is pseudo-interface 2. The same pseudo-interface number 2 is used on both Windows 2000 and Windows NT to define a configured tunnel.

Example 6-6 is based on Figure 6-2. It shows the configuration applied on a Windows 2000 or Windows NT node A to set the configured tunnel to Cisco Router R1. First, the IPv6 source address of the configured tunnel 3ffe:b00:ffff:8::2 on Windows is assigned with the **ipv6 adu 2/3ffe:b00:ffff:8::2** command. The 2/ represents pseudo-interface 2. The default prefix length on Microsoft for any interface is locked at 64 bits. Then the **ipv6 rtu ::/0 2/::206.123.31.200 pub** command adds a default IPv6 route entry to the IPv6 routing table of Windows node A. It configures the default IPv6 route ::/0 to be routed through pseudo-interface 2 with the tunnel going to the next-hop address ::206.123.31.200. The next-hop IPv6 address for this command on Windows 2000 and Windows NT uses the IPv4-compatible IPv6 address format described in Chapter 2. The IPv4 address 206.123.31.200 represents the destination IPv6 address of Cisco Router R1 for the establishment of the configured tunnel.

**Example 6-6**   *Setting the Configured Tunnel in Figure 6-2 on Windows 2000 and Windows NT*

```
C:\Windows\system32>ipv6 adu 2/3ffe:b00:ffff:8::2
C:\Windows\system32>ipv6 rtu ::/0 2/::206.123.31.200 pub
```

As soon as this configuration is successfully applied, it can be displayed on Windows 2000 and Windows NT using the **ipv6 if 2** command. With **ipv6 if 2**, you should display the tunnel's IPv6 source address 3ffe:b00:ffff:8::2, as well as the IPv4-compatible IPv6 address of Cisco Router R1, ::206.123.31.200. To validate this setup with the Cisco router, you can **ping6** the router's IPv6 address 3ffe:b00:ffff:8::1 from this node.

## Defining a Configured Tunnel on Microsoft Windows XP

The design of the configured tunnel's pseudo-interface is different on Windows XP compared to Windows 2000 and Windows NT. In Windows XP, the configured tunnel's pseudo-interface must be enabled using the **ipv6 ifcr v6v4** *ipv4-source-address ipv4-destination-address* command. The *ipv4-source-address* and *ipv4-destination-address* arguments are the source and destination IPv4 addresses of the configured tunnels. After the command is successfully applied, a new pseudo-interface number is added in Windows XP for the configured tunnel. Then you set the configured tunnel the same way you would for Windows 2000 and Windows NT.

Example 6-7 is based on Figure 6-2. It shows the configuration applied on Windows XP node A to define the configured tunnel to Cisco Router R1. First, the **ipv6 ifcr v6v4 132.214.1.10 206.123.31.200** command adds a new pseudo-interface number for a configured tunnel. As soon as this is done, the operating system displays the new pseudo-interface number, 5. Then the configured tunnel's IPv6 source address 3ffe:b00:ffff:8::2 on Windows XP is assigned with the **ipv6 adu 5/3ffe:b00:ffff:8::2** command, which is the same step in Windows 2000 and Windows NT. Finally, you add the default IPv6 route entry in the node's IPv6 routing table by specifying the command **ipv6 rtu ::/0 5/3ffe:b00:ffff:8::1**. The next-hop IPv6 address for this command in Windows XP does not support the IPv4-compatible IPv6 address format, so you must provide the IPv6 address.

**Example 6-7**  *Setting the Configured Tunnel on Windows XP*

```
C:\Documents and Settings\REGIS>ipv6 ifcr v6v4 132.214.1.10 206.123.31.200
Interface 5 added.
C:\Documents and Settings\REGIS>ipv6 adu 5/3ffe:b00:ffff:8::2
C:\Documents and Settings\REGIS>ipv6 rtu ::/0 5/3ffe:b00:ffff:8::1
```

**NOTE**    The **netsh interface ipv6 add v6v4tunnel interface=TUNNEL-CISCO localaddress= 132.214.1.10 remoteaddress=206.123.31.200** command on Windows XP is equivalent to the **ipv6 ifcr v6v4 132.214.1.10 206.123.31.200** command.

**NOTE**    The **netsh interface ipv6 add address 5 3ffe:b00:ffff:8::2** command on Windows XP is equivalent to the **ipv6 adu 5/3ffe:b00:ffff:8::2** command.

**NOTE**    The **netsh interface ipv6 add route ::/0 5 3ffe:b00:ffff:8::1** command in Windows XP is equivalent to the **ipv6 rtu ::/0 5/3ffe:b00:ffff:8::1** command.

The **ipv6 if 5** command can be used to verify the configuration of the configured tunnel and to display the status of pseudo-interface 5. You should see the tunnel's IPv6 source address 3ffe:b00:ffff:8::2, as well as the IPv4 destination address of Cisco Router R1, 206.123.31.200. To validate this setup with the Cisco router, you can **ping6** the router's IPv6 address 3ffe:b00:ffff:8::1 from this node.

## Using a 6to4 Tunnel on Microsoft Windows

The 6to4 tunnel is another transition mechanism supported in Windows. This section describes the configuration of a 6to4 tunnel that can interact with a Windows node and a Cisco router. As discussed in Chapter 5, 6to4 is a transition mechanism that provides IPv6 connectivity over existing IPv4 infrastructures. Like configured tunnel, IPv6 packets are tunneled over IPv4 packets with 6to4.

Rather than manually defining the tunnel as you would for a configured tunnel, the 6to4 mechanism provides automatic tunneling. The tunneling of IPv6 packets between 6to4 sites is done dynamically according to the destination IPv6 addresses of packets originating from IPv6 nodes on 6to4 sites. Therefore, tunnels are deployed only when needed.

Figure 6-3 illustrates a basic 6to4 topology in which Windows dual-stack node B enables the 6to4 mechanism that can interact with Cisco Router R2. Cisco Router R2 is also enabled with 6to4 support. Because the IPv4 address assigned to Router R2 is 206.123.31.200, the IPv6 prefix of this 6to4 site is 2002:ce7b:1fc8::/48 (206.123.31.200 converted into hexadecimal equals ce7b:1fc8). The IPv6 address 2002:ce7b:1fc8:1::1 is assigned to R2's ethernet0 interface. On Windows node B, the IPv4 address 132.214.1.10 is assigned to the pseudo-interface assigned for the 6to4 operation. Therefore, the IPv6 prefix of this 6to4 site is 2002:84d6:010a::/48.

In Figure 6-3, the IPv6 address 2002:84d6:010a:1::1 is assigned to the 6to4 Windows interface.

**Figure 6-3**   *Enabling 6to4 Between a Windows Host and a Cisco Router*

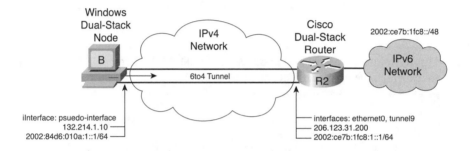

Example 6-8 is based on Figure 6-3. It shows the configuration applied on Cisco Router R2 to enable the 6to4 mechanism. Both the IPv4 and IPv6 addresses are assigned to the ethernet0 interface using the commands **ip address 206.123.31.200 255.255.255.0** and **ipv6 address 2002:ce7b:1fc8:1::1/64**. Then 6to4 is enabled on the tunnel9 interface using the **ipv6 unnumbered ethernet0**, **tunnel source ethernet0**, and **tunnel mode ipv6ip 6to4** commands. Finally, an IPv6 route for the destination network 2002::/16 is added to point to the tunnel9 interface.

**Example 6-8**   *Enabling 6to4 on Cisco Router R2*

```
RouterR2#configure terminal
RouterR2(config)#int ethernet0
RouterR2(config-if)#ip address 206.123.31.200 255.255.255.0
RouterR2(config-if)#ipv6 address 2002:ce7b:1fc8:1::1/64
RouterR2(config-if)#int tunnel9
RouterR2(config-if)#no ip address
RouterR2(config-if)#ipv6 unnumbered ethernet0
RouterR2(config-if)#tunnel source ethernet0
RouterR2(config-if)#tunnel mode ipv6ip 6to4
RouterR2(config-if)#exit
RouterR2(config)#ipv6 route 2002::/16 Tunnel9
```

For more information on this 6to4 configuration, refer to Chapter 5 for the complete description of commands used to enable 6to4 support on Cisco.

The pseudo-interface for enabling the 6to4 mechanism differs on Windows 2000 and Windows NT compared to Windows XP. The following sections discuss these configurations separately.

## Enabling 6to4 on Microsoft Windows 2000/Windows NT

With MSR IPv6 support and Microsoft IPv6 Technology Preview For Windows 2000, the default interface assigned to the 6to4 mechanism is pseudo-interface 2. This is the same pseudo-interface number for both Windows 2000 and Windows NT.

**NOTE**    Recall that pseudo-interface 2 was used on Windows 2000 and Windows NT to set a configured tunnel. You cannot simultaneously enable a configured tunnel and the 6to4 mechanism on Windows 2000 and Windows NT. However, the pseudo-interface architecture is different in Windows XP, making it possible to use both transition mechanisms at the same time.

Example 6-9 is based on Figure 6-3. It shows the configuration applied on Windows 2000 and Windows NT to enable the 6to4 mechanism. First, the **ipv6 rtu 2002::/16 2** command adds a route entry in the IPv6 routing table for the destination network 2002::/16, which points to the pseudo-interface 2. When an IPv6 packet with a destination IPv6 address matches the 2002::/16 prefix, then the router forwards the packet through the 6to4 tunnel interface (pseudo-interface 2) by encapsulating the IPv6 packet in IPv4. Then the IPv6 source address of the Windows pseudo-interface 2 is assigned using the command **ipv6 adu 2/2002:84d6:010a:1::1**. The 2/ represents pseudo-interface 2.

**Example 6-9**    *Enabling 6to4 on Windows 2000 and Windows NT*

```
C:\Windows\system32>ipv6 rtu 2002::/16 2
C:\Windows\system32>ipv6 adu 2/2002:84d6:010a:1::1
```

As soon as the configuration is applied, it can be displayed on Windows 2000 and Windows NT using the **ipv6 if 2** command. You should see the IPv6 source address 2002:84d6:010a:1::1 of this pseudo-interface. To validate this setup with the Cisco router enabled into a 6to4 router, you can **ping6** the router's IPv6 address 2002:ce7b:1fc8:1::1 from this node.

## Enabling 6to4 on Microsoft Windows XP

In Windows XP, the interface assigned for the 6to4 mechanism is pseudo-interface 3 instead of pseudo-interface 2 for Windows 2000 and Windows NT. The commands to enable the 6to4 mechanism on pseudo-interface 3 are the same as those used for Windows 2000 and Windows NT. Example 6-10 presents the 6to4 configuration applied on Windows XP.

**Example 6-10** *Enabling 6to4 on Windows XP*

```
C:\Documents and Settings\REGIS>ipv6 rtu 2002::/16 3
C:\Documents and Settings\REGIS>ipv6 adu 3/2002:84d6:010a:1::1
```

NOTE    The **netsh interface ipv6 add route 2002::/16 3** command in Windows XP is equivalent to the **ipv6 rtu 2002::/16 3** command.

NOTE    The **netsh interface ipv6 add address 3 2002:84d6:010a:1::1** command in Windows XP is equivalent to the **ipv6 adu 3/2002:84d6:010a:1::1** command.

As soon as the configuration is applied, it can be displayed in Windows XP using the **ipv6 if 3** command. You should see the IPv6 source address 2002:84d6:010a:1::1 of this pseudo-interface. To validate this setup with the Cisco router enabled as a 6to4 router, you can **ping6** the router's IPv6 address 2002:ce7b:1fc8:1::1 from this node.

NOTE    Windows XP refuses to assign IPv6 addresses to pseudo-interface 3 when the 6to4 prefix is based on private address ranges such as 10.0.0.0/8, 172.16.0.0/12, and 192.168.0.0/16.

TIP    When needed, you can disable the 6to4 interface on Windows XP using the **netsh interface ipv6 6to4 set state disabled** command.

## Using 6to4 Relay on Microsoft Windows

As seen in Chapter 5, a 6to4 relay is a 6to4 router acting as a gateway between the IPv6 Internet and the 6to4 sites on the Internet. The 6to4 relay is a router at the border of the IPv4 Internet and the IPv6 Internet. The 6to4 relay forwards all non-6to4 traffic such as 2001::/16 and 3ffe::/16 prefixes, to the IPv6 Internet.

To use a 6to4 relay, a 6to4 node such as Windows must add a default IPv6 route in its configuration pointing to the 6to4 relay. Therefore, all non-6to4 traffic is sent to the IPv6 Internet through the 6to4 relay.

Cisco Router R2 in Figure 6-3 acts as a 6to4 relay. Examples 6-11 and 6-12 show the configuration for using a 6to4 relay applied on Windows 2000, Windows NT, and Windows XP.

**Example 6-11** *Using 6to4 Relay on Windows 2000 and Windows NT*

```
C:\Windows\system32>ipv6 rtu 2002::/16 2
C:\Windows\system32>ipv6 adu 2/2002:84d6:010a:1::1
C:\Windows\system32>ipv6 rtu ::/0 2/::206.123.31.200
```

**Example 6-12** *Using 6to4 Relay on Windows XP*

```
C:\Documents and Settings\REGIS>ipv6 rtu 2002::/16 3
C:\Documents and Settings\REGIS>ipv6 adu 3/2002:84d6:010a:1::1
C:\Documents and Settings\REGIS>ipv6 rtu ::/0 3/2002:ce7b:1fc8:1::1
```

**NOTE**    Trumpet provides an IPv6 Winsock implementation for Windows 95 and Windows 98. However, the configuration of IPv6 on Windows 95 and Windows 98 is beyond the scope of this book. Information about the IPv6 Winsock implementation can be found on the Trumpet website at www.trumpet.com.au/ipv6.htm.

# IPv6 on Solaris

Solaris 8 was the first Solaris release containing the IPv6 protocol as a supported feature on all hardware platforms. IPv6 support was available on previous releases of Solaris, but for testing purposes only. Sun Microsystems was one of the leading manufacturers to provide an IPv6 implementation in the early stages of the IPv6 design.

## Internetworking Solaris with IPv6

The Solaris implementation includes IPv6 applications, utilities, and tools such as Telnet, TFTP, ping, traceroute, netstat, route, nslookup, NIS, NIS+, ifconfig, snoop, getent, ndd, inetd, printing, rcp, rsh, rlogin, rdist, and rdate. These IPv6-enabled applications are integrated in Solaris 8's standard directories, allowing nodes based on this operating system to interact with other nodes on the IPv6 Internet.

Open software applications such as apache, mozilla, lynx, mosaic, sendmail, bind, wuftpd, tin, qpopper, ircii, tcpdump, and ipfilter are available with IPv6 support for Solaris 8. Of course, this list is incomplete. If you want more information about IPv6-enabled applications for Solaris, visit wwws.sun.com/software/solaris/ds/ds-ipv6networking/ds-ipv6n.pdf and www.dhis.org/ipv6/solaris/.

## Enabling IPv6 on Solaris

IPv6 support is easy to install on Solaris 8 and above, especially for any new installation of this operating system on a Sun hardware platform or even on any Intel-compatible architecture. During the installation of Solaris 8, you can enable IPv6 support simply by responding "YES" to the question proposing the activation of IPv6.

| NOTE | The complete procedure to install IPv6 support on Solaris 8 that was not enabled with IPv6 at the original installation is beyond the scope of this book. |
| --- | --- |

## Stateless Autoconfiguration on Solaris

To enable IPv6 and stateless autoconfiguration on network interfaces on Solaris 8 after a successful installation of the operating system, you must create an empty file such as /etc/hostname6.*interface* using the **touch** command, as shown in Example 6-13. The *interface* argument must be replaced by the network interface name. The network interface in this example is hme0.

**Example 6-13** *Creating the Empty hostname6 File in Solaris*

```
solaris#touch /etc/hostname6.hme0
```

As soon as the hostname6 file is created, you must restart the computer. Following the reboot, you should be able to verify that IPv6 support has been enabled on Solaris using the **ifconfig hme0 inet6** command, as shown in Example 6-14. In this example, you can see the link-local address fe80::290:27ff:fe3a:9e9a/10 of the hme0 interface confirming that IPv6 is enabled on Solaris.

**Example 6-14** *Verifying IPv6 Support in Solaris*

```
solaris#ifconfig hme0 inet6
hme0: flags=2000841<UP,RUNNING,MULTICAST,IPv6> mtu 1500 index 2
inet6 fe80::290:27ff:fe3a:9e9a/10
```

When an /etc/hostname6.*interface* file is present on Solaris for a given interface, the computer at the boot starts the stateless autoconfiguration mechanism by sending a router solicitation request on the local link. If an IPv6 router is properly configured and present on the link, the router responds with a router advertisement message including the necessary information to process the stateless autoconfiguration mechanism on the IPv6-enabled interfaces of the Solaris node.

Figure 6-4 illustrates a Solaris node and an IPv6 router on the same local link. The Solaris node starts by sending a router solicitation request on the local link through the hme0 interface. Then the IPv6 router responds with a router advertisement message containing the prefix 3ffe:b00:ffff:2::/64 on the ethernet0 interface. The Solaris node can configure its IPv6 address on the hme0 interface with the prefix given using stateless autoconfiguration.

**Figure 6-4**   *Solaris Node Receiving a Router Advertisement to Perform Stateless Autoconfiguration*

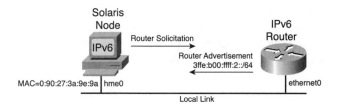

Example 6-15 shows a sample of the configuration applied on the IPv6 router in Figure 6-4 to enable stateless autoconfiguration. By using the **ipv6 address 3ffe:b00:ffff:2::1/64** command on the ethernet0 interface, IPv6 is enabled on the interface, a static IPv6 address is assigned, and stateless autoconfiguration is enabled.

**Example 6-15** *Enabling IPv6 and Stateless Autoconfiguration on Cisco*

```
Router(config)#int ethernet0
Router(config-if)#ipv6 address 3ffe:b00:ffff:2::1/64
Router(config-if)#exit
```

Following the router configuration, Example 6-16 displays the hme0 interface configuration on Solaris after the node has successfully performed stateless autoconfiguration. The highlighted line shows that the IPv6 address 3ffe:b00:ffff:2:290:27ff:fe3a:9e9a/64 is assigned to the logical interface hme0:1. The low-order 64-bit of the link-local and 3ffe:b00:ffff:2:290:27ff:fe3a:9e9a/64 addresses is generated using the Ethernet MAC address of the hme0 interface in EUI-64 format.

**Example 6-16** *Interface Configuration on Solaris After the Node Performs Stateless Autoconfiguration*

```
solaris#ifconfig hme0 inet6
hme0: flags=2000841<UP,RUNNING,MULTICAST,IPv6> mtu 1500 index 2
      inet6 fe80::290:27ff:fe3a:9e9a/10
hme0:1: flags=2000841<UP,RUNNING,MULTICAST,ADDRCONF,IPv6> mtu 1500 index 2
      inet6 3ffe:b00:ffff:2:290:27ff:fe3a:9e9a/64
```

| NOTE | For each IPv6 address assigned to an interface on Solaris, a logical subinterface is created using the following syntax: |
|------|------|
| | *physical_interface*:*logical_number* |
| | In Example 6-16, hme0:1 is logical subinterface 1 of the physical interface hme0. |

| NOTE | As with the Windows and FreeBSD examples presented later in this chapter, Solaris 8 can act as an IPv6 router and send router advertisements on the local link. Configuring Solaris to act as an IPv6 router is beyond the scope of this book. |
|------|------|

## Assigning a Static IPv6 Address and Default Route on Solaris

When no IPv6 router is available on the local link providing stateless autoconfiguration, you can manually assign static IPv6 addresses to interfaces on Solaris. Here is the **ifconfig** command syntax:

```
solaris#ifconfig interface inet6 addif ipv6-address/length up
```

The **ifconfig** command assigns a static IPv6 address to the given *interface*. The **inet6** argument identifies the address family IPv6. The **addif** parameter creates the next available logical subinterface. *ipv6-address* is the static address to assign to the interface. *length* defines the prefix's length. The **up** parameter enables the interface.

Here's an example:

```
solaris#ifconfig hme0 inet6 addif fec0:0:0:1::1/64 up
```

This command assigns the static IPv6 address fec0:0:0:1::1 to the interface hme0 with a prefix length of 64 bits.

| TIP | By adding the line **addif fec0:0:0:1::1/64 up** to the /etc/hostname6.hme0 file, you can save this network configuration. Solaris uses this parameter at the computer's next boot to assign the static IPv6 address to the hme0 interface. |
|------|------|

On the Solaris node with IPv6 support, you can add a default IPv6 route using the **route add -inet6 default** command:

```
solaris#route add -inet6 default gateway [-ifp interface]
```

The **route** command adds a default IPv6 route pointing to the *gateway* address given as an argument. The **-ifp** keyword is an optional parameter that must be used to determine the interface when the IPv6 address of the *gateway* is a link-local address.

The following example adds a default IPv6 route that points to the next-hop link-local address fe80::290:27ff:fe3a:9e9a:

```
solaris#route add -inet6 default fe80::290:27ff:fe3a:9e9a -ifp hme0
```

This other example adds a default IPv6 route that points out the aggregatable global unicast address 3ffe:b00:ffff:10::1:

```
solaris#route add -inet6 default 3ffe:b00:ffff:10::1
```

| | |
|---|---|
| **TIP** | On Solaris 8, you cannot put an IPv6 address in the /etc/defaultrouter file to point to a default IPv6 router. The /etc/defaultrouter configuration file is reserved for IPv4 configuration. Instead, you must create a shell script such as /etc/rc2.d/S99ipv6_routes and add the command **/usr/bin/route add -inet6 default fe80::290:27ff:fe3a:9e9a -ifp hme0**. Solaris uses this script at the computer's next boot to add the default IPv6 route to the routing table. |

## Managing IPv6 on Solaris

The **ifconfig**, **netstat**, **route**, **ping**, and **traceroute** commands are used on UNIX platforms to manage IPv4 addresses and routes. Table 6-2 shows how these commands can be used to manage IPv6 addresses and routes on Solaris.

**Table 6-2**    **ifconfig**, **netstat**, **route**, **ping**, *and* **traceroute** *Commands on Solaris*

| Command | Description |
|---|---|
| **Removing IPv6 Addresses** | |
| solaris#**ifconfig** *interface*  **inet6 removeif** *ipv6-address* | Deletes a logical *interface*  with a given *ipv6-address* . |
| **Example**<br>solaris#**ifconfig hme0 inet6 removeif fec0:0:0:1::1** | Deletes the static IPv6 address fec0:0:0:1::1 on the hme0 interface. |
| **Displaying IPv6 Routes** | |
| solaris#**netstat -rn** | Displays both the IPv4 and IPv6 routing tables. |

*continues*

**Table 6-2**    **ifconfig**, **netstat**, **route**, **ping**, *and* **traceroute** *Commands on Solaris (Continued)*

| Command | Description |
|---|---|
| **Adding IPv6 Routes** | |
| solaris#**route add -inet6** *ipv6-prefix/length gateway* [**-ifp** *interface* ] | Adds a static IPv6 route for the destination network specified by the arguments *ipv6-prefix* and *length* . A *gateway* address must be specified. If the next-hop IPv6 address is a link-local address, the **-ifp** optional keyword must be used. |
| **Example** <br> solaris#**route add -inet6 3ffe:b00:ffff::/48 fe80::290:27ff:fe3a:9e9a -ipf hme0** | The static IPv6 route 3ffe:b00:ffff::/48 is added to the IPv6 routing table. This destination can be reached through the link-local address fe80::290:27ff:fe3a:9e9a. |
| **Removing IPv6 Routes** | |
| solaris#**route delete -inet6** *ipv6-prefix/length* | Deletes a static IPv6 route for the destination network specified by the arguments *ipv6-prefix* and *length* . |
| **Example** <br> solaris#**route delete -inet6 3ffe:b00:ffff::/48** | The static IPv6 route 3ffe:b00:ffff::/48 is removed from the IPv6 routing table. |
| **ping and traceroute** | |
| solaris#**ping -A inet6 -s www.6bone.net** | Pings the destination www.6bone.net using the address family IPv6. |
| solaris#**traceroute -A inet6 www.6bone.net** | Traces the route to the destination www.6bone.net using the address family IPv6. |

## Defining a Configured Tunnel on Solaris

Solaris supports the configured tunnel as a transition and coexistence mechanism to deliver IPv6 packets over existing IPv4 networks.

This section discusses establishing a configured tunnel between a Solaris node and a Cisco router. Figure 6-5 illustrates a basic topology in which the Solaris dual-stack node C has established a configured tunnel to the Cisco dual-stack Router R3. The IPv4 address assigned to the configured tunnel interface tunnel0 on Router R3 is 206.123.31.150, and the IPv6 address is 3ffe:b00:ffff:1::1/64. On Solaris node C, the IPv4 address 132.214.20.1 and the IPv6 address 3ffe:b00:ffff:1::2/128 are assigned to the configured tunnel interface ip.tun0.

---

**NOTE**    The recommended prefix length for a point-to-point link should be a /64 or even a /128 when you know for sure that one and only one device is connecting. Because there is only one device in Figure 6-5, a /128 prefix length is used for the Solaris node. Refer to Chapter 5 to understand the rationale of the /128 prefix length.

---

**Figure 6-5**    *Establishing a Configured Tunnel Between Solaris and a Cisco Router*

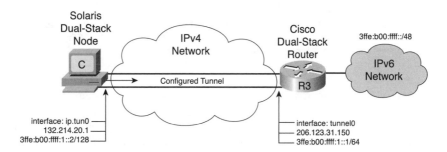

Example 6-17 is based on Figure 6-5. It shows the configuration applied on Cisco Router R3 to set the configured tunnel to Solaris node C. The IPv6 source address of the tunnel0 interface is assigned using the **ipv6 address 3ffe:b00:ffff:1::1/64** command. Then the **tunnel source 206.123.31.150** and **tunnel destination 132.214.20.1** commands define the configured tunnel's source and destination IPv4 addresses. Finally, **tunnel mode ipv6ip** defines the type of tunneling as the configured tunnel.

**Example 6-17** *Establishing the Configured Tunnel on Cisco Router R3*

```
RouterR3(config)#int tunnel0
RouterR3(config-if)#ipv6 address 3ffe:b00:ffff:1::1/64
RouterR3(config-if)#tunnel source 206.123.31.150
RouterR3(config-if)#tunnel destination 132.214.20.1
RouterR3(config-if)#tunnel mode ipv6ip
RouterR3(config-if)#exit
```

The pseudo-interface assigned as the configured tunnel interface on Solaris is the logical interface ip.tun0. Therefore, the logical interface ip.tun0 establishes a configured tunnel carrying IPv6 packets over IPv4. The configured tunnel on Solaris is established using the **ifconfig** command.

Example 6-18 is based on Figure 6-5. It shows the configuration applied on Solaris node C to set a configured tunnel to Cisco Router R3. First, the **ifconfig ip.tun0 inet6 plumb** command enables the logical interface ip.tun0 on Solaris. Then the **ifconfig ip.tun0 inet6 tsrc 132.214.20.1 tdst 206.123.31.150 up** command defines this tunnel's source and destination IPv4 addresses. **ifconfig ip.tun0 inet6 addif 3ffe:b00:ffff:1::2/128 3ffe:b00:ffff:1::1 up** assigns the static IPv6 addresses to the configured tunnel ip.tun0 interface. Finally, the **route add -inet6 default 3ffe:b00:ffff:1::1** command adds a default IPv6 route pointing to the IPv6 address of the tunnel endpoint.

**Example 6-18** *Establishing a Configured Tunnel on Solaris's ip.tun0 Interface*

```
solaris# ifconfig ip.tun0 inet6 plumb
solaris# ifconfig ip.tun0 inet6 tsrc 132.214.20.1 tdst 206.123.31.150 up
solaris# ifconfig ip.tun0 inet6 addif 3ffe:b00:ffff:1::2/128 3ffe:b00:ffff:1::1 up
solaris# route add -inet6 default 3ffe:b00:ffff:1::1
```

As soon as this configuration is successfully applied, you can display it in Solaris using the **ifconfig ip.tun0 inet6** command. With **ifconfig**, you should see the source, destination IPv4 addresses, and link-local address assigned to the logical interface ip.tun0. The command should also display the IPv6 addresses assigned on the subinterface ip.tun0:1. To validate this setup with the Cisco router, you can **ping6** the router's IPv6 address 3ffe:b00:ffff:1::1 from this node.

---

**TIP**     You can save the configured tunnel setup by creating the file /etc/hostname6.ip.tun0. If you add the lines **tsrc 132.214.20.1 tdst 206.123.31.150 up** and **addif 3ffe:b00:ffff:1::2/128 3ffe:b00:ffff:1::1 up** to the file /etc/hostname6.ip.tun0, Solaris automatically enables this tunnel at the computer's next boot. To save the default IPv6 route, create the file /etc/rc2.d/S99ipv6_routes and add the command **/usr/bin/route add -inet6 default 3ffe:b00:ffff:1::1** to this file.

---

# IPv6 on FreeBSD

FreeBSD has long been considered a leading IPv6 host implementation. Beta code for the IPv6 support was available as soon as 1996, and new code releases from different groups of contributors have steadily come out in Japan, France, and the U.S. Moreover, FreeBSD is considered the IPv6-enabled operating system that has the biggest collection of IPv6-enabled applications available for production purposes. In 2000, FreeBSD version 4.0 was the first release that included IPv6 as a supported feature: IPv6 support is bundled in FreeBSD's mainstream code. Previously, the KAME Project, INRIA, and NRL were separate implementations of the IPv6 stack for the FreeBSD platform. Each of these is described in the following list:

- **KAME**—The KAME Project is a joint effort of six companies in Japan to provide a free IPv6 and IPSec stack for BSD variants to the world, including FreeBSD. Officially, KAME is an abbreviation for Karigome, where the KAME project office is located. KAME also means turtle in Japanese. More information about the KAME project can be found at www.kame.net.

- **INRIA**—The French National Institute for Research in Computer Science and Control developed a free IPv6 implementation for platforms such NetBSD and FreeBSD. More information about INRIA and IPv6 can be found at www.inria.fr.

- **NRL**—The Naval Research Laboratory in the U.S. developed a free IPv6 implementation for FreeBSD.

All these IPv6 implementations merged in 2000 using the KAME Project code as the base IPv6 stack. Since FreeBSD version 4.0 and beyond, the KAME code is merged in the mainstream code of FreeBSD.

## Internetworking FreeBSD with IPv6

The FreeBSD implementation includes networking applications, utilities, and tools that were ported to IPv6 years ago such as Telnet, FTP, TFTP, traceroute6, ping6, ifconfig, netstat, route, nslookup, name resolver, lpr, syslog, whois, tcpwrappers, ipfilter, ip6fw, and IPSec. These IPv6-enabled applications are integrated into the standard directories of FreeBSD version 4 and beyond, allowing nodes based on this operating system to interact with other nodes on the IPv6 Internet.

The FreeBSD platform is one of the richest operating systems in the number of software applications already supporting IPv6. The FreeBSD ports collection and the KAME website together contain an impressive collection of IPv6-ready applications such as apache, mozilla, lynx, bind, sendmail, sylpheed, fetchmail, cvs, ssh, openssh, irc, emacs, ethereal, rat, ruby, and many others. This list is incomplete. Other IPv4-only applications are scheduled to be ported to IPv6 for FreeBSD.

For more information on IPv6-enabled applications for FreeBSD in the ports collection and on the KAME Project website, refer to www.freebsd.org/ports/ipv6.html and www.kame.net/.

The availability of IPv6-enabled applications for FreeBSD is allowing an increasing number of network professionals around the world to run all their day-to-day Internet applications over IPv6 only. This is a trend in Asia and Europe, where IPv4 spaces are difficult to obtain.

## Verifying IPv6 Support on FreeBSD

IPv6 support is bundled in FreeBSD version 4.0 and beyond. By using the **ifconfig -a** command on FreeBSD, as shown in Example 6-19, you can see whether the FreeBSD version supports IPv6. In Example 6-19, the link-local address fe80::260:8ff:fe37:f2f has been automatically enabled on the ep0 interface at this computer's boot. The low-order 64-bit of the link-local address has been created using the given Ethernet MAC address 00:60:08:37:0f:2f of the ep0 interface converted into EUI-64 format.

**Example 6-19** *Verifying IPv6 Support on FreeBSD*

```
freebsd# ifconfig -a
ep0: flags=8843<UP,BROADCAST,RUNNING,SIMPLEX,MULTICAST> mtu 1500
        inet6 fe80::260:8ff:fe37:f2f%ep0 prefixlen 64 scopeid 0x1
        ether 00:60:08:37:0f:2f
        media: Ethernet 10baseT/UTP
```

## Stateless Autoconfiguration on FreeBSD

Although IPv6 support is bundled in FreeBSD, you must enable stateless autoconfiguration on all FreeBSD interfaces by adding the line **ipv6_enable="YES"** to the /etc/rc.conf file. The /etc/rc.network6 script uses this parameter at the boot of the FreeBSD node to enable IPv6 and stateless autoconfiguration on all interfaces.

When this parameter is present, the computer at bootup starts the stateless autoconfiguration mechanism by sending a router solicitation request on the local link. If an IPv6 router is properly configured and present on the link, the router responds with a router advertisement message including the necessary information to process the stateless autoconfiguration mechanism on the FreeBSD node's interfaces.

Figure 6-6 illustrates a FreeBSD node and an IPv6 router on the same local link. The FreeBSD node starts by sending a router solicitation request on the local link through the ep0 interface. Then the IPv6 router responds with a router advertisement message containing the prefix 2001:410:ffff:3::/64 on the ethernet0 interface. Therefore, the FreeBSD node can configure its IPv6 address on the ep0 interface with the prefix given using stateless autoconfiguration.

**Figure 6-6**  *FreeBSD Node Receiving a Router Advertisement to Perform Stateless Autoconfiguration*

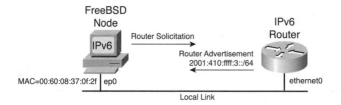

Example 6-20 shows a sample of the configuration applied to the IPv6 router in Figure 6-6 to enable stateless autoconfiguration. By using the **ipv6 address 2001:410:ffff:3::1/64** command on the ethernet0 interface, IPv6 is enabled on the interface, a static IPv6 address is assigned, and stateless autoconfiguration is enabled.

**Example 6-20**  *Enabling IPv6 and Stateless Autoconfiguration on Cisco*

```
Router(config)#int ethernet0
Router(config-if)#ipv6 address 2001:410:ffff:3::1/64
Router(config-if)#exit
```

Following the router configuration, Example 6-21 displays the ep0 interface configuration on FreeBSD after the node has successfully completed stateless autoconfiguration. The highlighted line shows that the aggregatable global unicast IPv6 address 2001:410:ffff:3:260:8ff:fe37:f2f is assigned to the ep0 interface. The low-order 64-bit of the link-local fe80::260:8ff:fe37:f2f and 2001:410:ffff:3:260:8ff:fe37:f2f addresses has been generated using the Ethernet MAC address 00:60:08:37:0f:2f of the ep0 interface converted into EUI-64 format.

**Example 6-21** *Interface Configuration on FreeBSD After Stateless Autoconfiguration Is Performed*

```
Freebsd# ifconfig -a
ep0: flags=8843<UP,BROADCAST,RUNNING,SIMPLEX,MULTICAST> mtu 1500
        inet6 fe80::260:8ff:fe37:f2f%ep0 prefixlen 64 scopeid 0x1
        inet6 2001:410:ffff:3:260:8ff:fe37:f2f prefixlen 64 autoconf
        ether 00:60:08:37:0f:2f
        media: Ethernet 10baseT/UTP
```

**NOTE**    The **ifconfig** *interface* or **ifconfig** *interface* **inet6** commands can also be used on FreeBSD to display the IPv6 configuration of a given interface.

**NOTE**    It is possible for FreeBSD to act as an IPv6 router and to send a router advertisement on the local link. Configuring FreeBSD to act as an IPv6 router is beyond the scope of this book.

## Assigning a Static IPv6 Address and Default Route on FreeBSD

When no IPv6 router is available on the local link providing stateless autoconfiguration, you can manually assign static IPv6 addresses to interfaces on FreeBSD. The **ifconfig** command performs this task:

```
freebsd#ifconfig interface inet6 ipv6-address prefixlen length
```

This command assigns a static IPv6 address to the given *interface*. The **inet6** argument identifies the address family IPv6. The *ipv6-address* is the static address to assign to the interface. The **prefixlen** argument defines the *length* of the prefix.

The following example assigns the static IPv6 address fec0:0:0:1::1 to the interface ep0 with a prefix length of 64 bits:

```
freebsd#ifconfig ep0 inet6 fec0:0:0:1::1 prefixlen 64
```

**TIP**    By adding the line **ipv6_ifconfig_ep0="fec0:0:0:1::1 prefixlen 64"** to the /etc/rc.conf file, you can save this network configuration. This parameter is used by the /etc/rc.network6 script at the computer's next boot to assign the static IPv6 address to the ep0 interface.

On FreeBSD, you can add a default IPv6 route using the **route add -inet6 default** command:

```
freebsd#route add -inet6 default gateway[%interface]
```

The **route** command adds a default IPv6 route pointing to the *gateway* address given as an argument. The *%interface* argument must be used to determine the interface when the IPv6 address of the *gateway* is a link-local address.

The following example adds a default IPv6 route that points to the next-hop link-local address fe80::260:3eff:fe47:1533 via the ep0 interface:

```
freebsd#route add -inet6 default fe80::260:3eff:fe47:1533%ep0
```

This other example adds a default IPv6 route that points to the aggregatable global unicast address 3ffe:b00:ffff:10::1. In this case, the *%interface* argument is not needed.

```
freebsd#route add -inet6 default 3ffe:b00:ffff:10::1
```

TIP     By adding the line **ipv6_defaultrouter="fe80::260:3eff:fe47:1533%ep0"** to the /etc/rc.conf file, you can save this network configuration. This parameter is used by the /etc/rc.network6 script at the computer's next boot to add the default IPv6 route to the routing table.

## Managing IPv6 on FreeBSD

The **ifconfig**, **netstat**, **route**, **ping6**, and **traceroute6** commands are used on UNIX platforms to manage IPv4 addresses and routes. Table 6-3 shows how these commands can be used to manage IPv6 addresses and routes on FreeBSD.

**Table 6-3**     **ifconfig**, **netstat**, **route**, **ping6**, *and* **traceroute6** *Commands on FreeBSD*

| Command | Description |
|---------|-------------|
| **Removing IPv6 Addresses** | |
| freebsd#**ifconfig** *interface* **inet6** *ipv6-address* **delete** | Deletes an *ipv6-address* on a given interface. |
| **Example** <br> freebsd#**ifconfig ep0 inet6 fec0:0:0:1::1 delete** | Deletes the ipv6 address fec0:0:0:1::1 on the ep0 interface. |
| **Displaying IPv6 Routes** | |
| freebsd#**netstat -f inet6 -rn** | Displays the local IPv6 routing table. The **inet6** argument is the address family IPv6. |
| **Adding IPv6 Routes** | |
| freebsd#**route add -inet6** *ipv6-prefix* **-prefixlen** *length gateway* [ *%interface* ] | Adds a static IPv6 route for the destination network specified by the arguments *ipv6-prefix* and *length* . A *gateway* address must be specified. If the gateway is a link-local address, the optional parameter *%interface*  must be used. |

**Table 6-3**    **ifconfig**, **netstat**, **route**, **ping6**, *and*  **traceroute6** *Commands on FreeBSD (Continued)*

| Command | Description |
|---|---|
| **Example**<br><br>freebsd#**route add -inet6 3ffe:b00:ffff::**<br>**-prefixlen 48 fe80::260:3eff:fe47:1533%ep0** | The static IPv6 route 3ffe:b00:ffff::/48 is added to the IPv6 routing table. This destination can be reached through the link-local address fe80::260:3eff:fe47:1533 via the ep0 interface. |
| **Removing IPv6 Routes** | |
| freebsd#**route delete -inet6** *ipv6-prefix*<br>**-prefixlen** *length* | Deletes a static IPv6 route for the destination network specified by the arguments *ipv6-prefix* and *length* . |
| **Example**<br><br>freebsd#**route delete -inet6 3ffe:b00:ffff::**<br>**-prefixlen 48** | The static IPv6 route 3ffe:b00:ffff::/48 is removed from the IPv6 routing table. |
| **ping6 and traceroute6** | |
| freebsd#**ping6 www.6bone.net** | Pings the destination www.6bone.net using IPv6. |
| freebsd#**traceroute6 www.6bone.net** | Traces the route to the destination www.6bone.net using IPv6. |

**NOTE**    Additional information about the **ifconfig**, **netstat**, **route**, **ping6**, and **traceroute6** commands, including IPv6 support, is available in FreeBSD's man pages.

# Defining a Configured Tunnel on FreeBSD

FreeBSD supports the configured tunnel as a transition and coexistence mechanism to deliver IPv6 packets over existing IPv4 networks. This section covers the establishment of a configured tunnel between a FreeBSD node and a Cisco router. Figure 6-7 illustrates a basic topology in which FreeBSD dual-stack node E has established a configured tunnel to Cisco dual-stack Router R5. The IPv4 address assigned to the configured tunnel interface tunnel0 on Router R5 is 206.123.31.100, and the IPv6 address is 3ffe:b00:ffff:2::1/64. On FreeBSD node E, the IPv4 address 132.214.10.1 and the IPv6 address 3ffe:b00:ffff:2::2/128 have been assigned to the configured tunnel interface gif0.

**NOTE**    The recommended prefix length for a point-to-point link should be a /64 or even a /128 when you know for sure that one and only one device is connecting. Because there is only one device in Figure 6-7, a /128 prefix length is used for the FreeBSD node. Refer to Chapter 5 to understand the rationale of the /128 prefix length.

**Figure 6-7**    *Establishing a Configured Tunnel Between FreeBSD and a Cisco Router*

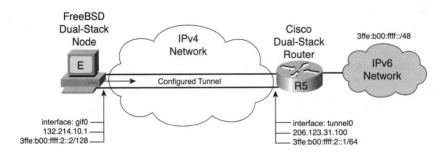

Example 6-22 is based on Figure 6-7. It shows the configuration applied on Cisco Router R5 to set the configured tunnel to FreeBSD node E. The IPv6 source address of the tunnel0 interface is assigned using the **ipv6 address 3ffe:b00:ffff:2::1/64** command. Then the **tunnel source 206.123.31.100** and **tunnel destination 132.214.10.1** commands define the source and destination IPv4 addresses of the configured tunnel. Finally, **tunnel mode ipv6ip** defines the type of tunneling as the configured tunnel.

**Example 6-22**  *Establishing the Configured Tunnel on Cisco Router R5*

```
RouterR5(config)#int tunnel0
RouterR5(config-if)#ipv6 address 3ffe:b00:ffff:2::1/64
RouterR5(config-if)#tunnel source 206.123.31.100
RouterR5(config-if)#tunnel destination 132.214.10.1
RouterR5(config-if)#tunnel mode ipv6ip
RouterR5(config-if)#exit
```

**NOTE**    The commands used to define a configured tunnel on the FreeBSD versions before 4.4 differ from commands applied on FreeBSD version 4.4 and beyond. This book presents only commands for FreeBSD version 4.4 and higher.

The following covers the configured tunnel setup applied on FreeBSD version 4.4 and beyond.

The pseudo-interface assigned as the configured tunnel interface on FreeBSD is called the *gif interface*. FreeBSD with IPv6 support has been designed to handle multiple gif interfaces simultaneously. The gif interface used to establish a configured tunnel carrying IPv6 packets over IPv4 must be enabled and established using a combination of **gifconfig** and **ifconfig** commands.

Example 6-23 is based on Figure 6-7. It shows the configuration applied on FreeBSD node E to set a configured tunnel to Cisco Router R5. First, the **ifconfig gif0 create** command enables the configured interface gif0 on FreeBSD. Then the **gifconfig** command defines the source and destination IPv4 address for the configured tunnel. **ifconfig gif0 inet6 3ffe:b00:ffff:2::2 3ffe:b00:ffff:2::1 prefixlen 128 alias** assigns the static IPv6 addresses to the configured tunnel gif0 interface. Finally, the route **add -inet6 default 3ffe:b00:ffff:2::1** command adds a default IPv6 route pointing to the IPv6 address of the tunnel endpoint.

**Example 6-23** *Establishing a Configured Tunnel on the gif0 Interface on FreeBSD*

```
freebsd#ifconfig gif0 create
freebsd#gifconfig gif0 132.214.10.1 206.123.31.100
freebsd#ifconfig gif0 inet6 3ffe:b00:ffff:2::2 3ffe:b00:ffff:2::1 prefixlen 128
  alias
freebsd#route add -inet6 default 3ffe:b00:ffff:2::1
```

As soon as this configuration is successfully applied, it can be displayed on FreeBSD using the **ifconfig gif0** and **gifconfig gif0** commands. With **ifconfig**, you should see both IPv4 and IPv6 addresses assigned to the configured tunnel gif0 interface. To validate this setup with the Cisco router, you can **ping6** the router's IPv6 address 3ffe:b00:ffff:2::1 from this node.

**TIP**     By adding the lines **gif_interfaces="gif0"**, **gifconfig_gif0="132.214.10.1 206.123.31.100"** and **ipv6_ifconfig_gif0="3ffe:b00:ffff:2::2 3ffe:b00:ffff:2::1 prefixlen 128 alias"** to the /etc/rc.conf file, you can save this network configuration. This parameter is used by the /etc/rc.network6 script at the computer's next boot to enable and set the configured tunnel interface gif0.

## Using 6to4 on FreeBSD

The 6to4 tunnel is another transition mechanism supported on FreeBSD. This section presents the configuration of a 6to4 tunnel between a FreeBSD node and the Cisco router.

Figure 6-8 illustrates a basic topology in which FreeBSD dual-stack node F has enabled the 6to4 mechanism to establish automatic tunneling to Cisco Router R6. Cisco Router R6 also uses the 6to4 support. Because the IPv4 address assigned to Cisco Router R6 is 206.123.31.100, the IPv6 prefix of this 6to4 site is 2002:ce7b:1f64::/48. The IPv6 address 2002:ce7b:1f64:1::1 is assigned to Cisco Router R6's ethernet0 interface. On FreeBSD node F, the IPv4 address 132.214.10.1 is assigned to the ep0 interface. Therefore, the IPv6 prefix of the 6to4 site is 2002:84d6:0a01::/48. The IPv6 address 2002:84d6:0a01:1::1 is assigned to the FreeBSD 6to4 interface stf0.

**Figure 6-8** *Enabling 6to4 Between FreeBSD and Cisco*

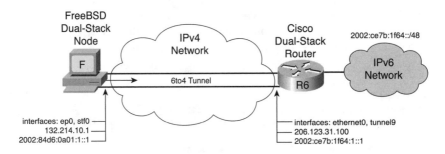

Example 6-24 is based on Figure 6-8. It shows the configuration applied on Cisco Router R6 that enables the 6to4 mechanism. Both the IPv4 and IPv6 addresses are assigned to the ethernet0 interface using the commands **ip address 206.123.31.100 255.255.255.0** and **ipv6 address 2002:ce7b:1f64:1::1/64**. Then 6to4 is enabled on the tunnel9 interface using the **ipv6 unnumbered ethernet0**, **tunnel source ethernet0** and **tunnel mode ipv6ip 6to4** commands. Finally, an IPv6 route to the destination network 2002::/16 points out that the tunnel9 interface is added.

**Example 6-24** *Enabling 6to4 on Cisco Router R6*

```
RouterR6#configure terminal
RouterR6(config)#int ethernet0
RouterR6(config-if)#ip address 206.123.31.100 255.255.255.0
RouterR6(config-if)#ipv6 address 2002:ce7b:1f64:1::1/64
RouterR6(config-if)#int tunnel9
RouterR6(config-if)#no ip address
RouterR6(config-if)#ipv6 unnumbered ethernet0
RouterR6(config-if)#tunnel source ethernet0
RouterR6(config-if)#tunnel mode ipv6ip 6to4
RouterR6(config-if)#exit
RouterR6(config)#ipv6 route 2002::/16 Tunnel9
```

The pseudo-interface assigned as the 6to4 mechanism on FreeBSD is the stf0 interface. Only one stf interface at a time is allowed on a FreeBSD node. However, in the default FreeBSD installation, the stf0 interface is not supported by the running kernel. 6to4 support on FreeBSD requires a properly compiled kernel that enables the pseudo-device stf option. After a new release of the kernel with 6to4 support has been compiled, reboot the computer. You should be able to display the stf0 interface using the **ifconfig -a** command.

Example 6-25 is based on Figure 6-8. It shows the configuration applied on FreeBSD that enables the 6to4 mechanism. First, the **ifconfig ep0 inet 132.214.10.1 netmask 255.255.255.0** command assigns the IPv4 address to the ep0 interface on FreeBSD. Then the **ifconfig stf0**

**inet6 2002:84d6:0a01:1::1 prefixlen 16 alias** command defines the 6to4 prefix and the IPv6 address for this 6to4 site. The 6to4 prefix is created using the IPv4 address assigned to the ep0 interface.

**Example 6-25**  *Enabling 6to4 on FreeBSD*

```
freebsd#ifconfig ep0 inet 132.214.10.1 netmask 255.255.255.0
freebsd#ifconfig stf0 inet6 2002:84d6:0a01:1::1 prefixlen 16 alias
```

The 2002::/16 route is automatically added to the routing table after the completion of the last command. As soon as this configuration is applied, it can be displayed on FreeBSD using the **ifconfig stf0** command. To validate this setup with the Cisco router enabled as a 6to4 router, you can **ping6** the router's IPv6 address 2002:ce7b:1f64:1::1 from this node.

---

**TIP**  By adding the lines **stf_interface_ipv4addr="132.214.10.1"**, **stf_interface_ipv4plen="16"**, **stf_interface_ipv6_ifid="0:0:0:1"**, and **stf_interface_ipv6_slaid="0001"** to the /etc/rc.conf file, you can save this network configuration. stf_interface_ipv4addr is the local IPv4 address used for the 6to4 operation. stf_interface_ipv4plen is the prefix length of the 6to4 prefix. stf_interface_ipv6_ifid is the interface ID (low-order 64-bit). stf_interface_ipv6_slaid represents bits 48 to 64 of the IPv6 address (site-level aggregator). These parameters are used by the /etc/rc.network6 script at the computer's next boot to enable and configure the 6to4 mechanism on FreeBSD.

---

## Using 6to4 Relay on FreeBSD

As with Microsoft, it is possible on FreeBSD to point out a 6to4 relay on the Internet to deliver all non-6to4 traffic. Example 6-26 presents the configuration applied on a FreeBSD node to point out a 6to4 relay. Example 6-26 considers that Cisco Router R6 shown in Figure 6-8 is a 6to4 relay router. The default IPv6 route that points out a 6to4 relay is added using the **route add -inet6 default 2002:ce7b:1f64:1::1** command.

**Example 6-26**  *Using a 6to4 Relay on FreeBSD*

```
freebsd#ifconfig ep0 inet 132.214.10.1 netmask 255.255.255.0
freebsd#ifconfig stf0 inet6 2002:84d6:0a01:1::1 prefixlen 16 alias
freebsd#route add -inet6 default 2002:ce7b:1f64:1::1
```

FreeBSD version 4 and beyond are compliant with RFC 3068, *An Anycast Prefix for 6to4 Relay Routers*. Therefore, the 6to4 prefix 2002:c058:6301::, which is based on the defined IPv4 anycast prefix, can be used to reach a public 6to4 relay on the Internet. The **route add -inet6 default 2002:c058:6301::** command might be used for route configuration in this situation. See Chapter 5 for more information about the 6to4 relay.

## OpenBSD and NetBSD

Because the KAME Project code has also been merged into OpenBSD version 2.7 and NetBSD 1.5 and beyond, the supported features and the commands used on these BSD platforms are very similar to FreeBSD.

More information about IPv6 support on OpenBSD and NetBSD can be found at the KAME Project website at www.kame.net.

# IPv6 on Linux

According to the Linux IPv6 website managed by Peter Bieringer, the first Linux code with IPv6 support appeared in 1996 for the kernel version 2.1.8. Today, IPv6 support for Linux version 2.4.x and higher is available in two different ways:

- **Native IPv6 support**—The several Linux distributions such as Red Hat, Debian, SuSe, Slackware, and Turbo, support IPv6. However, to enable IPv6 on your Linux system, you need to build a kernel with IPv6 support. More information about native IPv6 support on Linux can be found on the website www.tldp.org/HOWTO/Linux+IPv6-HOWTO/. This is the official Linux IPv6 HOWTO website managed by Peter Bieringer.

- **USAGI (universal playground for IPv6)**—The USAGI development project works to deliver a production-quality IPv6 stack for the Linux system, tightly collaborating with the WIDE Project, KAME Project, and TAHI Project. The USAGI project is supported by several Japanese institutions such as Hitachi, NTT, Toshiba, Yogogawa Electric Corporation, the University of Tokyo, and Keio University. Like the IPv6 stack developed by the KAME Project for BSD implementations, USAGI aims to unify the development of IPv6 for Linux to provide one unique IPv6 implementation for all Linux distributions. To enable IPv6 using the USAGI implementation on your Linux system, you need to download the USAGI code and build a kernel. Snapshot kits are released every two weeks, and stable kits are released three or four times a year. You can find more information about the USAGI project and Linux code with IPv6 support at www.linux-ipv6.org.

## Internetworking Linux with IPv6

When the net-tools (version 1.60) and iputils (version 20000121 or newer) packages are installed on Linux, applications, utilities, and tools with IPv6 support are available for networking configuration and operation. The programs in these packages include Telnet, FTP, TFTP, traceroute6, ping6, tracepath6, ifconfig, ip, netstat, route, name resolver, whois, tcpwrappers, netfilter6, and tcpdump.

The Linux platform is another rich operating system in terms of how many software applications are already IPv6-enabled. Applications with IPv6 support that are available for Linux include apache, mozilla, lynx, Mosaic, Netscape 6, opera, squid, bind, sendmail, qmail, zmailer, fetchmail, elm, pine, qpopper, nfs, samba, NNTP clients and servers, several IRC clients, ssh, openssh, vic, rat, cvs, and XFree86. This list is incomplete. Other IPv4-only applications are scheduled to be ported to IPv6 for Linux. If you want more information about IPv6-enabled applications for Linux, go to www.bieringer.de/linux/IPv6/status/IPv6+Linux-status-apps.html.

## Verifying IPv6 Support on Linux

As mentioned, IPv6 support on Linux is available either natively from the distribution or from the USAGI code. There are different ways to verify whether IPv6 support is enabled on a running kernel:

- **Checking the /proc/net directory**—After having compiled a vanilla kernel that has IPv6 support, you may verify the presence of the if_inet6 file in the /proc/net directory. If this file is not present, the IPv6 module is not loaded in the running kernel. In this situation, you should try to load the IPv6 module manually by using the **modprobe ipv6** command.

- **Displaying the existing IPv6 configuration on network interfaces**—By using the **ifconfig** *interface* or **ifconfig -a** or **ip -f inet6 addr show** [**dev** *interface*] commands, you can validate that the running kernel is enabled with IPv6 support. If IPv6 is enabled, you should be able to display the link-local addresses of the network interfaces. As shown in Example 6-27, the link-local address fe80::200:c0ff:fe9a:5fd0 was automatically enabled on the eth0 interface at this computer's boot.

**Example 6-27** *Verifying IPv6 Support on Linux with the* **ifconfig** *and* **ip** *Commands*

```
linux# ifconfig eth0
eth0      Link encap:Ethernet  HWaddr 00:00:C0:9A:5F:D0
          inet6 addr: fe80::200:c0ff:fe9a:5fd0/10 Scope:Link
          UP BROADCAST RUNNING MULTICAST  MTU:1500  Metric:1
<output omitted>
linux# ip -f inet6 addr show dev eth0
2: eth0: <BROADCAST,MULTICAST,UP> mtu 1500 qdisc pfifo_fast qlen 100
    inet6 fe80::200:c0ff:fe9a:5fd0/10 scope link
```

**NOTE**     The command **ip -f inet6 [..]** is equivalent to the **ip -6 [..]** command on other distributions of Linux. This chapter uses the **ip -f inet6** syntax.

- **Displaying existing IPv6 routes**—By using the **route -A inet6** or **ip -f inet6 route show** [**dev** *interface*] command, you can verify IPv6 support. If IPv6 is enabled, you should be able to display an IPv6 route for the link-local prefix fe80::/10 and another route for the multicast prefix ff00::/8, as shown in Example 6-28.

**Example 6-28** *Verifying IPv6 Support on Linux with the* **route** *and* **ip** *Commands*

```
linux#route -A inet6
Kernel IPv6 routing table
Destination                          Next Hop      Flags Metric Ref   Use Iface
::1/128                              ::            U     0      0       0 lo
fe80::200:c0ff:fe9a:5fd0/128         ::            U     0      0       0 lo
fe80::/10                            ::            UA    256    0       0 eth0
ff00::/8                             ::            UA    256    0       0 eth0
::/0                                 ::            UDA   256    0       0 eth0
<output omitted>
linux# ip -f inet6 route show
fe80::/10  proto kernel  metric 256  mtu 1500
ff00::/8  proto kernel  metric 256  mtu 1500
default  proto kernel  metric 256  mtu 1500
```

**NOTE**    Describing the steps to compile Linux with IPv6 support is beyond the scope of this book. Refer to the Linux IPv6 HOWTO website at www.tldp.org/HOWTO/Linux+IPv6-HOWTO/ for instructions on enabling IPv6 on Linux.

IPv6 support in Linux evolved over the time, so different commands and scripts in Linux are available to manage IPv6. The following sections show you how to manage IPv6 addresses and routes on Linux using some of these commands. The examples presented in the next sections are based on Linux 2.4.x, with the native IPv6 support provided in the RedHat implementation. Commands presented in this book are also available on other distributions of Linux. However, it is strongly recommended that you read the documentation provided with your Linux distribution before configuring IPv6 on your systems.

## Stateless Autoconfiguration on Linux

As soon as IPv6 support is enabled on the Linux kernel, stateless autoconfiguration may be enabled at the boot on the network interfaces by adding the line **NETWORKING_IPV6=YES** to the /etc/sysconfig/network file and by inserting the line **IPV6INT=yes** into each network configuration script, such as /etc/sysconfig/network-scripts/ifcfg-eth0 for the eth0 interface. These parameters are used at the boot of the Linux node to enable IPv6 and stateless autoconfiguration on the network interfaces.

**TIP**    You can disable stateless autoconfiguration globally (in the file /etc/sysconfig/network) or on a per-interface basis (in the file /etc/sysconfig/network-scripts/ifcfg-eth0) by adding the line **IPV6_AUTOCONF=no** to the network configuration script.

**TIP**    After the lines are added, you can reboot Linux or run the command **/etc/rc.d/init.d/network restart** to perform the change.

As with the Microsoft, Solaris, and FreeBSD implementations, the Linux kernel at the boot starts the stateless autoconfiguration mechanism by sending a router solicitation request on the local link. If an IPv6 router is present on the link, the router responds with a router advertisement message including all the necessary information to process the stateless autoconfiguration mechanism on the interfaces of the Linux node.

Figure 6-9 illustrates a Linux node and an IPv6 router on the same local link. The Linux node starts by sending a router solicitation request on the local link through its eth0 interface. Then the IPv6 router responds with a router advertisement message containing the prefix 2001:410:ffff:4::/64 on its ethernet0 interface. Therefore, the Linux node can configure its IPv6 address on the eth0 interface with the prefix given using stateless autoconfiguration.

**Figure 6-9**    *Linux Node Receiving Router Advertisement to Perform Stateless Autoconfiguration*

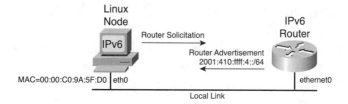

Example 6-29 shows a sample of the configuration applied to the IPv6 router in Figure 6-9 to enable stateless autoconfiguration. By using the **ipv6 address 2001:410:ffff:4::1/64** command on the ethernet0 interface, IPv6 is enabled on the interface, a static IPv6 address is assigned, and stateless autoconfiguration is enabled.

**Example 6-29** *Enabling IPv6 and Stateless Autoconfiguration on Cisco*

```
Router(config)#int ethernet0
Router(config-if)#ipv6 address 2001:410:ffff:4::1/64
Router(config-if)#exit
```

Following the router configuration, Example 6-30 displays the eth0 interface configuration on Linux after the node has successfully completed stateless autoconfiguration. The highlighted line shows that the aggregatable global unicast IPv6 address 2001:410:ffff:4:200:c0ff:fe9a:5fd0 is assigned to the eth0 interface. The low-order 64-bit of the link-local fe80::200:c0ff:fe9a:5fd0 and the 2001:410:ffff:4:200:c0ff:fe9a:5fd0 addresses has been generated using the Ethernet MAC address 00:00:C0:9A:5F:D0 of the eth0 interface converted to EUI-64 format.

**Example 6-30** *Interface Configuration on Linux After Stateless Autoconfiguration Is Performed*

```
linux#ifconfig eth0
eth0      Link encap:Ethernet  HWaddr 00:00:C0:9A:5F:D0
          inet6 addr: 2001:410:ffff:4:200:c0ff:fe9a:5fd0/64 Scope:Global
          inet6 addr: fe80::200:c0ff:fe9a:5fd0/10 Scope:Link
          UP BROADCAST RUNNING MULTICAST  MTU:1500  Metric:1
```

NOTE    The **ip -f inet6 addr show dev eth0** command may also be used as the equivalent command on Linux to display the IPv6 configuration of a given interface.

NOTE    Linux can act as an IPv6 router and can send router advertisements on the local link. However, configuring Linux to act as an IPv6 router is beyond the scope of this book.

## Assigning Static IPv6 Addresses and Default Routes on Linux

When no IPv6 router is available on the local link providing stateless autoconfiguration to Linux hosts, you can manually assign static IPv6 addresses to interfaces. The **ifconfig** and **ip** commands are used to perform this task, as shown in Table 6-4.

**Table 6-4**    **ifconfig** *and* **ip** *Commands for the Assignment of IPv6 Addresses to Interfaces on Linux*

| Command | Description |
|---|---|
| linux#**ifconfig** *interface* **inet6 add** *ipv6-address/prefixlength* | Assigns a static IPv6 address to the given *interface* using the **ifconfig** command. The **inet6 add** argument specifies the adding of an IPv6 address. *ipv6-address* is the static address to assign to the interface. The *prefixlength*  argument defines the length of the prefix. |
| linux#**ip -f inet6 addr add** *ipv6-address/ prefixlength* **dev** *interface* | Assigns a static IPv6 address to the given *interface* using the **ip** command. The **-f inet6 addr add** arguments specify the adding of an IPv6 address. *ipv6-address* is the static address to assign to the interface. The *prefixlength*  argument defines the length of the prefix. The **dev** argument identifies the given *interface* . This command and the preceding one provide the same result. |

**Table 6-4**    **ifconfig** *and* **ip** *Commands for the Assignment of IPv6 Addresses to Interfaces on Linux*

| Command | Description |
|---|---|
| **Example with ifconfig**<br>linux#**ifconfig eth0 inet6 add fec0:0:0:1::1/64**<br>**Example with ip**<br>linux#**ip -f inet6 addr add fec0:0:0:1::1/64**<br>**dev eth0** | Assigns the static IPv6 address fec0:0:0:1::1 to the interface eth0 with a prefix length of 64 bits. |

**TIP**    By adding the line **IPV6ADDR=fec0:0:0:1::1/64** to the /etc/sysconfig/network-scripts/ifcfg-eth0 file, you can save this network configuration. This parameter is used at the computer's next boot to assign this static IPv6 address to the eth0 interface.

On Linux, you can add a default IPv6 route using the **route** or **ip** commands, as shown in Table 6-5.

**Table 6-5**    **route** *and* **ip** *Commands to Add a Default IPv6 Route on Linux*

| Command | Description |
|---|---|
| linux#**route -A inet6 add ::/0 gw** *gateway*<br>[**dev** *interface* ] | Adds a default IPv6 route. Points to the link-local address of the next-hop *gateway*. The **::/0** value means any IPv6 address (the default). When a link-local address is defined as the next hop, the *interface* must be specified following the **dev** argument. |
| linux#**ip -f inet6 route add ::/0 via** *gateway*<br>[**dev** *interface* ] | Adds a default IPv6 route. Points to the link-local address of the next-hop *gateway*. The **::/0** value means any IPv6 address (the default). When a link-local address is defined, the *interface*  must be specified following the **dev** argument. This command and the preceding one provide the same result. |
| **Example with ifconfig**<br>linux#**route -A inet6 add ::/0 gw**<br>**fe80::260:3eff:fe47:1533 dev eth0**<br>**Example with ip**<br>linux#**ip -f inet6 route add ::/0 via**<br>**fe80::260:3eff:fe47:1533 dev eth0** | Adds a default IPv6 route that points to the link-local address fe80::260:3eff:fe47:1533. This default route can be reached through the node's eth0 interface. |

| TIP | By adding the line **eth0 ::/0 fe80::260:3eff:fe47:1533** to the /etc/sysconfig/static-routes-ipv6 file, you can save this network configuration. This parameter is used at the computer's next boot to add the default IPv6 route to the routing table. |
|---|---|

## Managing IPv6 on Linux

The **ifconfig**, **ip**, **netstat**, **route**, **ping6**, **traceroute6**, and **tracepath6** commands are used on UNIX platforms to manage addresses and routes. Table 6-6 shows how these commands can be used to manage IPv6 addresses and routes on Linux.

**Table 6-6**    ifconfig, ip, netstat, route, ping6, traceroute6, *and* tracepath6 *Commands on Linux*

| Command | Description |
|---|---|
| **Removing IPv6 Addresses** | |
| linux#**ifconfig** *interface* **inet6 del** *ipv6-address/prefixlength* | Removes an *ipv6-address* on a given interface. |
| linux#**ip -f inet6 addr del** *ipv6-address/prefixlength* **dev** *interface* | Removes an *ipv6-address* on a given interface. |
| **Example with ifconfig** <br> linux#**ifconfig eth0 inet6 del fec0:0:0:1::1/64** <br> **Example with ip** <br> linux#**ip -f inet6 addr del fec0:0:0:1::1/64 dev eth0** | Removes the IPv6 address fec0:0:0:1::1/64 on the eth0 interface. |
| **Displaying IPv6 Routes** | |
| linux#**route -A inet6** | Displays IPv6 routes of the routing table. |
| linux#**ip -f inet6 route show** | Displays IPv6 routes of the routing table. |
| linux#**netstat -A inet6 -rn** | Displays IPv6 routes of the routing table. |
| **Adding IPv6 Routes** | |
| linux#**route -A inet6 add** *ipv6-prefix/ prefixlength* **gw** *gateway* [**dev** *interface* ] | Adds a static IPv6 route for the destination network specified by the *ipv6-prefix/prefixlength* value. A gateway may be specified as the next-hop IPv6 address using the **gw** argument. When the gateway's IPv6 address is a link-local address, the interface must be specified following the **dev** argument. |
| linux#**ip -f inet6 route add** *ipv6-prefix/ prefixlength* **via** *gateway* [**dev** *interface* ] | Adds a static IPv6 route for the destination network specified by the *ipv6-prefix/prefixlength* value. A gateway may be specified as the next-hop IPv6 address using the **via** argument. When the gateway's IPv6 address is a link-local address, the interface must be specified following the **dev** argument. |

**Table 6-6**    **ifconfig**, **ip**, **netstat**, **route**, **ping6**, **traceroute6**, *and* **tracepath6** *Commands on Linux (Continued)*

| Command | Description |
|---|---|
| **Example with ifconfig**<br><br>linux#**route -A inet6 add 3ffe:b00:ffff::/48 gw fe80::260:3eff:fe47:1533 dev eth0**<br><br>**Example with ip**<br><br>linux#**ip -f inet6 route add 3ffe:b00:ffff::/48 via fe80::260:3eff:fe47:1533 dev eth0** | The static IPv6 route 3ffe:b00:ffff::/48 is added to the IPv6 routing table. This destination can be reached using the link-local address fe80::260:3eff:fe47:1533 through the eth0 interface. |
| **Removing IPv6 Routes** | |
| linux#**route -A inet6 del** *ipv6-prefix/ prefixlength*  **gw** *gateway*  [**dev** *interface* ] | Deletes a static IPv6 route for the destination network specified by the arguments *ipv6-prefix/ prefixlength* . |
| linux#**ip -f inet6 route del** *ipv6-prefix/ prefixlength*  **via** *gateway*  [**dev** *interface* ] | Deletes a static IPv6 route for the destination network specified by the arguments *ipv6-prefix/ prefixlength* . |
| **Example with ifconfig**<br><br>linux#**route -A inet6 del 3ffe:b00:ffff::/48 gw fe80::260:3eff:fe47:1533**<br><br>**Example with ip**<br><br>linux#**ip -f inet6 route del 3ffe:b00:ffff::/48 via fe80::260:3eff:fe47:1533** | The static IPv6 route 3ffe:b00:ffff::/48 is removed from the IPv6 routing table. |
| **ping6, traceroute6, and tracepath6** | |
| linux#**ping6 www.6bone.net** | Pings the destination www.6bone.net using IPv6. |
| linux#**ping6 -I eth0 fe80::260:3eff:fe47:1533** | Pings the link-local address fe80::260:3eff:fe47:1533 using the network interface eth0. The **I** keyword must be used to specify an interface when this is a link-local address. |
| linux#**traceroute6 www.6bone.net** | Traces the route to the destination www.6bone.net using IPv6. |
| linux#**tracepath6 www.6bone.net** | Traces the path and discovers the MTU values to the destination www.6bone.net. |

**NOTE**    Additional information about the **ifconfig**, **ip**, **netstat**, **route**, **ping6**, **traceroute6**, and **tracepath6** commands with IPv6 support is available in the Linux man pages.

## Defining Configured Tunnels on Linux

Linux supports the configured tunnel as a transition and coexistence mechanism to deliver IPv6 packets over existing IPv4 networks. This section discusses how you can establish a configured tunnel between a Linux node and a Cisco router. Figure 6-10 illustrates a basic topology in which Linux dual-stack node G has established a configured tunnel to Cisco dual-stack Router R7. The IPv4 address assigned to the configured tunnel interface tunnel0 on Router R7 is 206.123.31.50, and its IPv6 address is 3ffe:b00:ffff:a::1/64. On Linux node G, the IPv4 address 132.214.30.1 and the IPv6 address 3ffe:b00:ffff:a::2 define the configured tunnel on interface sit1.

**Figure 6-10** *Establishing a Configured Tunnel Between Linux and a Cisco Router*

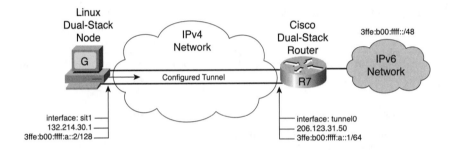

Example 6-31 is based on Figure 6-10. It shows the configuration applied on Cisco Router R7 to define the configured tunnel to Linux node G. The IPv6 source address of the tunnel0 interface is assigned using the **ipv6 address 3ffe:b00:ffff:a::1/64** command on the Cisco router. Then the **tunnel source 206.123.31.50** and **tunnel destination 132.214.30.1** commands define the source and destination IPv4 addresses for this configured tunnel. Finally, **tunnel mode ipv6ip** defines the type of tunneling as the configured tunnel.

**Example 6-31** *Setting a Configured Tunnel on Cisco Router R7*

```
RouterR7(config)#int tunnel0
RouterR7(config-if)#ipv6 address 3ffe:b00:ffff:a::1/64
RouterR7(config-if)#tunnel source 206.123.31.50
RouterR7(config-if)#tunnel destination 132.214.30.1
RouterR7(config-if)#tunnel mode ipv6ip
RouterR7(config-if)#exit
```

The following section presents the counterpart of tunnel configuration applied on the Linux node.

The pseudo-interfaces used as configured tunnel interfaces on Linux are called *sit interfaces*. Linux with IPv6 support has been designed to handle multiple sit interfaces simultaneously. The sit interface used to establish a configured tunnel carrying IPv6 packets over IPv4 can be defined on Linux using different commands such as **ifconfig**, **route**, **iptunnel**, and **ip**.

**NOTE**    Use sit1 for the first configured tunnel you have to define, sit2 for the second configured tunnel, sit3 for the third, and so on. The sit0 interface should be used as the interface for the 6to4 operation on Linux. On old releases of Linux with IPv6 support, the interface sit0 was reserved for 6to4. However, the use of sit0 for 6to4 on Linux is being deprecated in favor of a new tunnel interface designated for the 6to4 operation. See the next section for additional information on 6to4 configuration on Linux.

Example 6-32 is based on Figure 6-10. It shows the configuration applied on Linux node G to enable a configured tunnel to Cisco Router R7. First, the **iptunnel add sit1 remote 206.123.31.50 mode sit ttl 64** command creates the configured interface sit1 on Linux. This command also defines this tunnel's destination IPv4 address: Router R7's IPv4 address. Because the TTL value for a sit interface is set to 0 by default, a TTL value of 64 is defined here. Then the interface sit1 is enabled on Linux using the **ifconfig sit1 up** command. The **ifconfig eth0 inet6 add 3ffe:b00:ffff:a::2/128** command assigns an IPv6 address to the eth0 interface of Linux node G. Finally, the **route add -A inet6 ::/0 dev sit1** command adds a default IPv6 route that points to the tunnel interface sit1.

**Example 6-32** *Defining the Configured Tunnel sit1 Interface on Linux Using the* **ifconfig** *and* **route** *Commands*

```
linux#iptunnel add sit1 remote 206.123.31.50 mode sit ttl 64
linux#ifconfig sit1 up
linux#ifconfig eth0 inet6 add 3ffe:b00:ffff:a::2/128
linux#route add -A inet6 ::/0 dev sit1
```

Example 6-33 presents the same configuration as the previous example, but it uses the **ip** command to define the configured tunnel. In the first command, both source and destination IPv4 addresses of the tunnel are defined when the interface is created using the **ip tunnel add sit1 mode sit ttl 64 remote 206.123.31.50 local 132.214.30.1** command. Then the **ip link set dev sit1 up** command enables the configured tunnel interface sit1. Finally, the **ip -f inet6 addr add 3ffe:b00:ffff:a::2/128 dev eth0** command assigns an IPv6 address to the eth0 interface, and the **ip -f inet6 route add ::/0 dev sit1 metric 1** command adds the default IPv6 route to the routing table.

**Example 6-33** *Defining the Configured Tunnel sit1 Interface on Linux Using the* **ip** *Command*

```
linux#ip tunnel add sit1 mode sit ttl 64 remote 206.123.31.50 local 132.214.30.1
linux#ip link set dev sit1 up
linux#ip -f inet6 addr add 3ffe:b00:ffff:a::2/128 dev eth0
linux#ip -f inet6 route add ::/0 dev sit1 metric 1
```

As soon as this configuration is successfully applied, you can display it on Linux using different commands such as **ifconfig sit1**, **ifconfig eth0**, **ifconfig -a**, **route -A inet6**, and **ip -f inet6 route**

**show**. To validate this setup with the Cisco router, you can **ping6** the router's IPv6 address 3ffe:b00:ffff:a::1 from this node.

| TIP | You can save this network configuration by adding the lines **DEVICE=sit1**, **ONBOOT=yes**, **IPV6INIT=yes**, **IPV6TUNNELIPV4=206.123.31.50**, and **IPV6TUNNELIPV4LOCAL=132.214.30.1** to the /etc/sysconfig/network-scripts/ifcfg-sit1 file; the lines **IPV6INIT=yes** and **IPV6ADDR=3ffe:b00:ffff:a::2/128** to the /etc/sysconfig/network-scripts/ifcfg-eth0 file; and the line sit1 ::/0 to the /etc/sysconfig/static-routes-ipv6 file. These parameters are used at the computer's next boot to enable the configured tunnel interface sit1. |
| --- | --- |

## Using 6to4 on Linux

6to4 is another transition mechanism supported on Linux. The following section presents the 6to4 configuration on a Linux node that can interact with a 6to4 interface on a Cisco router.

Figure 6-11 shows a basic topology in which Linux dual-stack node H has enabled the 6to4 mechanism to automatically establish tunneling to Cisco Router R8. Cisco Router R8 is also enabled with 6to4 support. Because the IPv4 address assigned to Cisco Router R8 is 206.123.31.50, the IPv6 prefix of this 6to4 site is 2002:ce7b:1f32::/48. The IPv6 address 2002:ce7b:1f32:1::1 is assigned to Cisco Router R8's ethernet0 interface. On Linux node H, the IPv4 address 132.214.30.1 is assigned to the eth0 interface. Thus, the IPv6 prefix of the 6to4 site based on Linux is 2002:84d6:1e01::/48. Moreover, the IPv6 address 2002:84d6:1e01::1 is assigned to the Linux 6to4 interface sit0.

**Figure 6-11** *Enabling 6to4 Between Linux and Cisco*

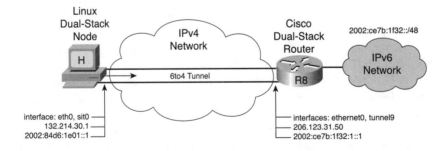

Example 6-34 is based on Figure 6-11. It shows the configuration applied on Cisco Router R8 to enable the 6to4 mechanism. Both the IPv4 and IPv6 addresses are assigned to the ethernet0 interface using the commands **ip address 206.123.31.50 255.255.255.0** and **ipv6 address 2002:ce7b:1f32:1::1/64**. Then 6to4 is enabled on the tunnel9 interface using the **ipv6 unnumbered ethernet0**, **tunnel source ethernet0**, and **tunnel mode ipv6ip 6to4** commands.

Finally, an IPv6 route to the destination network 2002::/16 that points to the tunnel9 interface is added.

**Example 6-34** *Enabling 6to4 on Cisco Router R8*

```
RouterR8#configure terminal
RouterR8(config)#int ethernet0
RouterR8(config-if)#ip address 206.123.31.50 255.255.255.0
RouterR8(config-if)#ipv6 address 2002:ce7b:1f32:1::1/64
RouterR8(config-if)#int tunnel9
RouterR8(config-if)#no ip address
RouterR8(config-if)#ipv6 unnumbered ethernet0
RouterR8(config-if)#tunnel source ethernet0
RouterR8(config-if)#tunnel mode ipv6ip 6to4
RouterR8(config-if)#exit
RouterR8(config)#ipv6 route 2002::/16 Tunnel9
```

In the old release of Linux, the pseudo-interface sit0 was used for the 6to4 operation. Today the sit0 interface is still available for 6to4, but it is being deprecated in favor of the new tunnel interface tun6to4. This section presents the two ways to enable 6to4 on Linux.

Example 6-35 is based on Figure 6-11. It shows the configuration applied on Linux to enable the 6to4 mechanism. First, the **ifconfig eth0 132.214.30.1 netmask 255.255.255.0** command represents the assignment of the IPv4 address to the eth0 interface on Linux. Then the command **ifconfig sit0 up** enables the 6to4 interface, and the command **ifconfig sit0 add 2002:84d6:1e01::1/16** defines the 6to4 prefix and the IPv6 address for this 6to4 site. The 6to4 prefix is generated using the IPv4 address assigned to the eth0 interface. Finally, the **route -A inet6 add 2002::/16 dev sit0** command creates a route entry for the outbound 6to4 traffic through the sit0 interface.

**Example 6-35** *Enabling 6to4 on Linux with the sit0 Interface*

```
linux#ifconfig eth0 132.214.30.1 netmask 255.255.255.0
linux#ifconfig sit0 up
linux#ifconfig sit0 add 2002:84d6:1e01::1/16
linux#route -A inet6 add 2002::/16 dev sit0
```

As soon as this configuration is applied, it can be displayed on Linux using the **ifconfig sit0** and **route -A inet6** commands.

Example 6-36 presents the same configuration as the previous example, but it uses the **ip** command to define the 6to4 interface. The first command creates the tun6to4 interface and defines the local IPv4 address for the 6to4 operation. Then the tun6to4 interface is enabled using **ip link set dev tun6to4 up**. The **ip -f inet6 addr add 2002:84d6:1e01::1/16 dev tun6to4** command defines the 6to4 prefix and the IPv6 address for this 6to4 site. Finally, **ip -f inet6 route add 2002::/16 dev tun6to4 metric 1** creates a route entry for the outbound 6to4 traffic through the tun6to4 interface.

**Example 6-36** *Enabling 6to4 on Linux with the tun6to4 Interface*

```
linux#ip tunnel add tun6to4 mode sit ttl 64 remote any local 132.214.30.1
linux#ip link set dev tun6to4 up
linux#ip -f inet6 addr add 2002:84d6:1e01::1/16 dev tun6to4
linux#ip -f inet6 route add 2002::/16 dev tun6to4 metric 1
```

As soon as this configuration is applied, it can be displayed on Linux using the **ifconfig tun6to4** and **route -A inet6** commands. To validate this setup with the Cisco router enabled as a 6to4 router, you can **ping6** the router's IPv6 address 2002:ce7b:1f32:1::1 from this node.

### Using 6to4 Relay on Linux

As with Microsoft and FreeBSD, on Linux you can point to a 6to4 relay on the Internet to deliver all non-6to4 traffic. The following commands present the configuration applied on Linux to point to a 6to4 relay. These commands consider that Cisco Router R8 shown in Figure 6-11 acts as 6to4 relay. The default IPv6 route on Linux may be added using the **route -A inet6 add ::/0 gw ::206.123.31.50 dev sit0** command or the **ip -f inet6 route add ::/0 via ::206.123.31.50 dev tun6to4 metric 1** command. The default IPv6 route on the Linux node points to the 6to4 address of Cisco Router R8.

Linux is also compliant with RFC 3068, *An Anycast Prefix for 6to4 Relay Routers*, as discussed in Chapter 5. Thus, the 6to4 anycast prefix can be used to automatically reach a public 6to4 relay on the Internet. The **route -A inet6 add ::/0 gw ::192.88.99.1 dev sit0** command or the **ip -f inet6 route add ::/0 via :: 192.88.99.1 dev tun6to4 metric 1** command may be used to perform this task.

# IPv6 on Tru64 UNIX

Tru64 UNIX version 5.1 was the first supported release for IPv6 in 2000. Compaq provided Early Adopters Kits (EAKs) for previous versions of Tru64 UNIX, but on an experimental basis. Compaq was one of the leading manufacturers to offer an IPv6 implementation in the early stages of the IPv6 design.

Currently, not all applications and packages that are available on Tru64 UNIX support IPv6, but most networking services are IPv6-enabled.

## Stateless Autoconfiguration on Tru64

As soon as IPv6 support is enabled on Tru64, you can enable stateless autoconfiguration on a given interface by following this procedure:

**Step 1**    Run the /usr/sbin/ip6_setup script.

**Step 2**    Enter **yes** to enable inet services.

**Step 3**    Enter **no** to configure the system as an IPv6 router.

**Step 4**    Specify an interface, and enter **yes** to start IPv6.

The script places all the correct flags and values in the /etc/rc.config file. This file is used at the boot of Tru64 to enable IPv6 and stateless autoconfiguration on the network interfaces.

As with the Microsoft, Solaris, FreeBSD, and Linux implementations discussed earlier, the Tru64 kernel at the boot starts the stateless autoconfiguration mechanism by sending a router solicitation request on the local link. If an IPv6 router is present on the link, the router responds with a router advertisement message including all the necessary information to process the stateless autoconfiguration mechanism on the interfaces of the Tru64 node.

Figure 6-12 illustrates a Tru64 node and an IPv6 router on the same local link. The Tru64 node starts by sending a router solicitation request on the local link through its ln0 interface. Then the IPv6 router responds with a router advertisement message containing the prefix 2001:410:ffff:5::/64 on its ethernet0 interface. Therefore, the Tru64 node can configure its IPv6 address on the ln0 interface with the prefix given using stateless autoconfiguration.

**Figure 6-12**    *Tru64 Node Receiving a Router Advertisement to Perform Stateless Autoconfiguration*

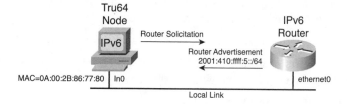

Example 6-37 shows a sample of the configuration applied to the IPv6 router in Figure 6-12 to enable stateless autoconfiguration. By using the **ipv6 address 2001:410:ffff:5::1/64** command on the ethernet0 interface, IPv6 is enabled on the interface, a static IPv6 address is assigned, and stateless autoconfiguration is enabled.

**Example 6-37**    *Enabling IPv6 and Stateless Autoconfiguration on Cisco*

```
Router(config)#int ethernet0
Router(config-if)#ipv6 address 2001:410:ffff:5::1/64
Router(config-if)#exit
```

Following the router configuration, Example 6-38 displays the ln0 interface configuration on Tru64 after the node has successfully completed the stateless autoconfiguration. The highlighted line shows that the aggregatable global unicast IPv6 address 2001:410:ffff:5:a00: 2bff:fe86:7780 is assigned to the ln0 interface. The low-order 64-bit of the link-local fe80::a00:2bff:fe86:7780 and the 2001:410:ffff:5:a00:2bff:fe86:7780 addresses is generated using the Ethernet MAC address 0a:00:2b:fe:86:77:80 of the ln0 interface converted into EUI-64 format.

**Example 6-38** *Interface Configuration on Tru64 After Stateless Autoconfiguration Is Performed*

```
tru64#ifconfig ln0 inet6
ln0 :   flags=c63<UP,BROADCAST,NOTRAILERS,RUNNING,MULTICAST,SIMPLEX>
        inet6 fe80::a00:2bff:fe86:7780
        inet6 2001:410:ffff:5:a00:2bff:fe86:7780
```

NOTE    It is possible for Tru64 to act as an IPv6 router and to send router advertisements on the local link. However, configuring Tru64 to act as an IPv6 router is beyond the scope of this book.

## Assigning Static IPv6 Addresses and Default Routes on Tru64

When no IPv6 router is available on the local link providing stateless autoconfiguration to Tru64 hosts, you can manually assign static IPv6 addresses to interfaces. The **ifconfig** command performs this task. Its syntax is as follows:

```
tru64# ifconfig interface inet6 ipv6-address
```

By default, the prefix length is 64 bits. The following example assigns the static IPv6 address fec0:0:0:1::1 to the interface ln0 with a prefix length of 64 bits:

```
tru64#ifconfig ln0 inet6 fec0:0:0:1::1
```

On Tru64, you can add a default IPv6 route using the **route** command:

```
tru64#route add -inet6 default gateway -I interface
```

This command adds a default IPv6 route that points to a next-hop *gateway*. When a link-local address is defined as the next hop, the *interface* must be specified following the **-I** argument. The following example adds a default IPv6 route that points to the link-local address fe80::260:3eff:fe47:1533. This default route can be reached through the ln0 interface:

```
tru64#route add -inet6 default fe80::260:3eff:fe47:1533 -I ln0
```

## Managing IPv6 on Tru64

The **ifconfig**, **netstat**, **route**, **ping**, and **traceroute** commands are used on UNIX platforms to manage addresses and routes. Table 6-7 shows how these commands can be used to manage IPv6 addresses and routes on Tru64.

**Table 6-7**    **ifconfig**, **netstat**, **route**, **ping**, *and* traceroute *Commands on Tru64*

| Command | Description |
|---|---|
| **Removing IPv6 Addresses** | |
| tru64#**ifconfig** *interface* **inet6 delete** *ipv6-address* | Removes an IPv6 address on a given interface. |
| **Example** tru64#**ifconfig ln0 inet6 delete fec0:0:0:1::1** | Removes the IPv6 address fec0:0:0:1::1 on the ln0 interface. |
| **Displaying IPv6 Routes** | |
| tru64#**netstat -f inet6 -rn** | Displays IPv6 routes of the routing table. |
| **Adding IPv6 Routes** | |
| tru64#**route add -inet6** *ipv6-prefix/ prefixlength* *gateway* **-I** *interface* | Adds a static IPv6 route for the destination network specified by the *ipv6-prefix/prefixlength* value. A gateway must be specified as the next-hop IPv6 address. When the gateway's IPv6 address is a link-local address, the *interface* must be specified following the **-I** keyword. |
| **Example** tru64#**route add -inet6 add 3ffe:b00:ffff::/48 fe80::260:3eff:fe47:1533 -I ln0** | The static IPv6 route 3ffe:b00:ffff::/48 is added to the IPv6 routing table. This destination can be reached using the link-local address fe80::260: 3eff:fe47:1533 through the ln0 interface. |
| **Removing IPv6 Routes** | |
| tru64#**route delete -inet6** *ipv6-prefix/ prefixlength* *gateway* **-I** *interface* | Deletes a static IPv6 route for the destination network specified by the arguments *ipv6-prefix/ prefixlength* , *gateway,* and *interface* . |
| **Example with ifconfig** tru64#**route delete -inet6 3ffe:b00:ffff::/48 -I fe80::260:3eff:fe47:1533** | The static IPv6 route 3ffe:b00:ffff::/48 is removed from the IPv6 routing table. |
| **ping and traceroute** | |
| tru64#**ping www.6bone.net** | Pings the destination www.6bone.net using IPv6. |
| tru64#**ping -I ln0 fe80::260:3eff:fe47:1533** | Pings the link-local address fe80::260:3eff:fe47:1533 using the network interface ln0. The **-I** keyword must be used to specify an interface when this is a link-local address. |
| tru64#**traceroute www.6bone.net** | Traces the route to the destination www.6bone.net using IPv6. |

NOTE          Additional information about the **ifconfig**, **netstat**, **route**, **ping**, and **traceroute** commands
with IPv6 support is available in the Tru64 documentation.

## Defining a Configured Tunnel on Tru64

Tru64 supports the configured tunnel as a transition and coexistence mechanism to deliver IPv6
packets over existing IPv4 networks. This section shows how you can establish a configured
tunnel between a Tru64 node and a Cisco router. Figure 6-13 shows a basic topology in which
Tru64 dual-stack node I has established a configured tunnel to Cisco dual-stack Router R9. The
IPv4 address assigned to the configured tunnel interface tunnel0 on Router R9 is 206.123.31.40,
and its IPv6 address is 3ffe:b00:ffff:b::1/64. On Tru64 node I, the IPv4 address 132.214.40.1
and the IPv6 address 3ffe:b00:ffff:b::2 define the configured tunnel on the interface ipt0.

**Figure 6-13** *Establishing a Configured Tunnel Between Tru64 and a Cisco Router*

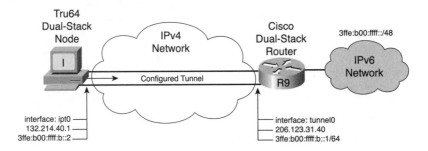

Example 6-39 is based on Figure 6-13. It shows the configuration applied on Cisco Router R9
to define the configured tunnel to Tru64 node I. The IPv6 source address of the tunnel0 interface
is assigned using the **ipv6 address 3ffe:b00:ffff:b::1/64** command on the Cisco router. Then
the **tunnel source 206.123.31.40** and **tunnel destination 132.214.40.1** commands define the
source and destination IPv4 addresses for this configured tunnel. Finally, **tunnel mode ipv6ip**
defines the type of tunneling as configured tunnel.

**Example 6-39** *Setting a Configured Tunnel on Cisco Router R9*

```
RouterR9(config)#int tunnel0
RouterR9(config-if)#ipv6 address 3ffe:b00:ffff:b::1/64
RouterR9(config-if)#tunnel source 206.123.31.40
RouterR9(config-if)#tunnel destination 132.214.40.1
RouterR9(config-if)#tunnel mode ipv6ip
RouterR9(config-if)#exit
```

The following section presents the counterpart of the tunnel configuration applied on the Tru64 node.

The pseudo-interfaces used as configured tunnel interfaces on Tru64 are called the *ipt interfaces*. Tru64 with IPv6 support is designed to handle multiple ipt interfaces simultaneously. The ipt interface used to establish a configured tunnel carrying IPv6 packets over IPv4 can be defined on Tru64 using a script or through manual configuration. Both methods are discussed here.

## Defining a Configured Tunnel Using a Script

To enable an IPv6-over-IPv4 configured tunnel on Tru64, follow this procedure:

**Step 1**  Run the /usr/sbin/ip6_setup script.

**Step 2**  Enter **yes** to enable inet services.

**Step 3**  Enter an IPv6 LAN interface.

**Step 4**  Enter **yes** to define IPv6-over-IPv4 configured tunnels.

**Step 5**  Enter the tunnel's destination IPv4 address.

**Step 6**  Enter the tunnel's source IPv4 address.

**Step 7**  Enter an IPv6 prefix to use on the tunnel interface (unless the router at the other end is advertising a prefix).

**Step 8**  Enter **yes** to start IPv6.

Each tunnel interface (ipt0, ipt1, ...) has its own line in the /etc/rc.config file (IPTUNNEL_x) containing the arguments to be passed to the **iptunnel** command for the source and destination addresses.

## Defining a Configured Tunnel Manually

Example 6-40 is based on Figure 6-13. It shows the manual configuration applied on Tru64 node I to enable a configured tunnel to Cisco Router R9. First, the **iptunnel create 206.123.31.40 132.214.40.1** command creates the configured interface on Tru64. Note that the destination IPv4 address of this tunnel is the first argument provided in the command. Then the interface ipt0 is enabled on Tru64 using the **ifconfig ipt0 ipv6 up** command. The **ifconfig ipt0 inet6 ip6prefix 3ffe:b00:ffff:b::/64** command assigns an IPv6 address to the ipt0 interface of Tru64 node I. This command appends the source IPv4 address 132.214.40.1 (converted into hexadecimal) of this tunnel interface to the prefix given as an argument. Finally, the **route add -inet6 default 3ffe:b00:ffff:b::2 -I ipt0** command adds a default IPv6 route that points to the tunnel interface ipt0.

**Example 6-40** *Defining a Configured Tunnel ipt0 Interface on Tru64 Using the* **iptunnel** *and* **ifconfig** *Commands*

```
tru64#iptunnel create 206.123.31.40 132.214.40.1
tru64#ifconfig ipt0 ipv6 up
tru64#ifconfig ipt0 inet6 ip6prefix 3ffe:b00:ffff:b::/64
tru64#route add -inet6 default 3ffe:b00:ffff:b::1 -I ipt0
```

As soon as this configuration is successfully applied, it can be displayed on Tru64 using the commands **ifconfig ipt0** and **netstat -f inet6 -rn**. To validate this setup with the Cisco router, you can ping the IPv6 address 3ffe:b00:ffff:b::1 of the router from this node.

# Other Host Implementations That Support IPv6

This chapter covered only the Microsoft, Solaris, FreeBSD, Linux, and Tru64 implementations, but IPv6 support is available on plenty of other host implementations such as BSDI, AIX, HP-UX, Novell, SGI, MAC OS X, and IBM zSeries. You can get information about these at www.ipv6.org/impl/index.html and playground.sun.com/pub/ipng/html/ipng-implementations.html.

# Summary

This chapter examined IPv6 support on some of the most common host operating systems such as Microsoft, Solaris, FreeBSD, Linux, and Tru64. The discussion covered lists of applications, utilities, tools, and open software applications that are already available with IPv6 support on these platforms.

More specifically, you learned to install, enable IPv6 support on, and activate stateless autoconfiguration on Windows NT, Windows 2000, Windows XP, Solaris 8, FreeBSD 4.x, Linux RedHat, and Tru64. Then you learned how to manage IPv6 addresses and routes on these operating systems using the IPv6-enabled tools.

You also examined the transition and coexistence mechanisms that are supported on Microsoft, Solaris, FreeBSD, Linux, and Tru64 such as configured tunnel and 6to4. You saw the basic configuration commands and steps to establish configured tunnels between Microsoft, Solaris, FreeBSD, Linux, Tru64, and Cisco routers. Then you learned how to enable and configure the 6to4 mechanism on Microsoft, FreeBSD, and Linux platforms to interact with Cisco routers.

Throughout this chapter, you have seen examples of router configurations (Cisco IOS Software commands) applied on Cisco routers to enable stateless autoconfiguration, configured tunnel, and 6to4. Now that you understand IPv6 support on Microsoft, Solaris, FreeBSD, Linux, and Tru64, you can deploy and manage IPv6 networks based on Cisco routers and these hosts as nodes.

# Case Study: Internetworking IPv6 Hosts with Cisco

Complete the following exercises to practice the skills you learned in this chapter. You will configure Solaris, Windows, and FreeBSD with IPv6 support to interact with a Cisco router.

## Objectives

In the following exercises, you will complete these tasks:

- Enabling IPv6 and stateless autoconfiguration on the network interfaces on Cisco

- Assigning static IPv6 addresses to interfaces of a Cisco router

- Turning off router advertisement on Cisco

- Adding a default IPv6 route on Cisco

- Enabling stateless autoconfiguration on Solaris

- Assigning a static IPv6 address to an interface and adding a default IPv6 router on Solaris

- Enabling and setting a configured tunnel interface on Cisco

- Enabling and setting 6to4 support on Cisco

- Adding a static IPv6 route for 6to4 on Cisco

- Enabling the 6to4 mechanism on Windows XP

- Establishing a configured tunnel on FreeBSD

- Verifying interfaces, addresses, and routes on Cisco, Solaris, Windows, and FreeBSD

## Commands List

You will use the Cisco IOS Software commands shown in Table 6-8 in the exercises.

**Table 6-8**    *Commands List*

| Command | Description |
| --- | --- |
| **copy run start** | Saves the current configuration to NVRAM. |
| **ipv6 unicast-routing** | Enables IPv6 traffic forwarding. |
| **ipv6 address 2001:410:ffff:0::1/64** | Configures a static IPv6 address. |
| **ipv6 address 2001:410:ffff:1::1/64** | Configures a static IPv6 address. |
| **ipv6 address 2001:410:ffff:2::1/64** | Configures a static IPv6 address. |

*continues*

**Table 6-8**   *Commands List (Continued)*

| Command | Description |
| --- | --- |
| **ipv6 address 2001:410:ffff:9::1/64** | Configures a static IPv6 address. |
| **ipv6 address 2002:ce7b:1f02:1::1/64** | Configures a static IPv6 address. |
| **ipv6 unnumbered ethernet0** | Instructs an interface to use the IPv6 address of another interface as a source address. |
| **ipv6 route 2002::/16 tunnel5** | Configures a static IPv6 route that points to the tunnel5 interface. |
| **ipv6 route::/0 2001:410:ffff:0::2** | Configures a default IPv6 route. |
| **ipv6 nd suppress-ra** | Suppresses router advertisement. |
| **show ip interface ethernet0** | Displays the IPv4 configuration applied to an interface. |
| **show ipv6 interface ethernet1** | Displays the IPv6 configuration applied to an interface. |
| **show ipv6 interface fastEthernet 0/0** | Displays the IPv6 configuration applied to an interface. |
| **show ipv6 interface fastethernet 0/1** | Displays the IPv6 configuration applied to an interface. |
| **show ipv6 route** | Displays the IPv6 routing table. |
| **tunnel mode ipv6ip** | Defines the tunnel interface as a configured tunnel. |
| **tunnel mode 6to4** | Defines the tunnel interface as the 6to4 tunnel. |
| **tunnel source ethernet0** | Specifies an interface with an IPv4 address assigned. |
| **tunnel source 206.123.31.3** | Assigns the IPv4 source address to a configured tunnel interface. |
| **tunnel destination 67.68.100.43** | Assigns the IPv4 destination address to a configured tunnel interface. |

## Network Architecture for the Configuration Exercise

Figure 6-14 shows the network architecture used in this case study. Your internal network contains Solaris, Windows 2000, and Windows XP nodes enabled with IPv6. They receive their IPv6 addresses from Router R1 on interface FE0/0 through stateless autoconfiguration. You must enable IPv6 on the hme0 interface of Solaris node A to perform stateless autoconfiguration on this node.

On interface FE0/1 of Router R1, a node based on Solaris with IPv6 support acts as an IPv6 web server. Because router advertisement is turned off on interface FE0/0, you will assign a static IPv6 address to Solaris's qfe0 interface.

**Figure 6-14**  *Adding Static IPv6 Routes on a Router*

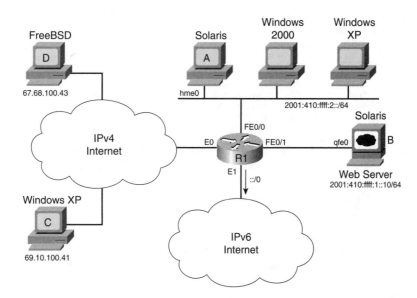

Router R1 of your network is also connected to the IPv4 Internet and the IPv6 Internet using interfaces E0 and E1, respectively. You will enable and configure 6to4 support on the Windows XP node C, and then you will establish a configured tunnel between the FreeBSD node D and Router R1.

# Task 1: Configure Network Interfaces on Router R1

To perform Task 1, use Table 6-9. It shows the assignment of addresses on network interfaces E0, E1, FE0/0, and FE0/1 for Router R1. The field RA represents the activation of router advertisement on the given interface. If the RA field is set to Y, be sure to turn on the given prefixes.

**Table 6-9**    *Assignment of Addresses and Parameters for Router R1's Network Interfaces*

| Interface | IPv4 Address | IPv6 Address | RA | Prefix Advertised |
|-----------|--------------|--------------|----|-------------------|
| E0 | 206.123.31.2/24 | None | N | None |
| E1 | None | 2001:410:ffff:0::1/64 | Y | 2001:410:ffff:0::/64 |
| FE0/0 | None | 2001:410:ffff:2::1/64 | Y | 2001:410:ffff:2::/64 |
| FE0/1 | None | 2001:410:ffff:1::1/64 | N | None |

Complete the following steps:

**Step 1**   Based on Table 6-9, assign the static IPv4 address 206.123.31.2/24 to interface E0 of Router R1. Following this task, add a default IPv4 route pointing to the next-hop IPv4 address 206.123.31.1 (the IPv4 Internet domain).

```
RouterR1(config)#interface ethernet0
RouterR1(config-if)#ip address 206.123.31.2 255.255.255.0
RouterR1(config-if)#exit
RouterR1(config)#ip route 0.0.0.0 0.0.0.0 206.123.31.1
RouterR1(config-if)#exit
```

**Step 2**   Enter the command to enable IPv6 traffic forwarding on Router R1 to forward unicast IPv6 packets between all interfaces. What command will you use?

```
RouterR1#conf t
RouterR1(config)#ipv6 unicast-routing
RouterR1(config)#exit
```

**Step 3**   Enable IPv6, assign the static IPv6 address 2001:410:ffff:0::1/64 to interface E1 of Router R1, and advertise the prefix 2001:410:ffff:0::/64 on the link. What command performs all these tasks?

```
RouterR1#conf t
RouterR1(config)#int ethernet1
RouterR1(config-if)#ipv6 address 2001:410:ffff:0::1/64
RouterR1(config-if)#exit
```

**Step 4**   On interface FE0/0 of Router R1, enable IPv6, assign the static IPv6 address 2001:410:ffff:2::1/64, and advertise the prefix 2001:410:ffff:2::/64.

```
RouterR1#conf t
RouterR1(config)#int fastethernet 0/0
RouterR1(config-if)#ipv6 address 2001:410:ffff:2::1/64
RouterR1(config-if)#exit
```

**Step 5**   Assign the IPv6 address 2001:410:ffff:1::1/64 to interface FE0/1 of Router R1. Then add the command to suppress the advertisement of the prefix 2001:410:ffff:1::/64 on interface FE0/1. Which commands will you use?

```
RouterR1#conf t
RouterR1(config)#int fastEthernet 0/1
RouterR1(config-if)#ipv6 address 2001:410:ffff:1::1/64
RouterR1(config-if)#ipv6 nd suppress-ra
RouterR1(config-if)#exit
```

**Step 6**   Verify the IPv4 and IPv6 addresses assigned on each interface. What are the commands used to display IPv4 and IPv6 addresses assigned on interfaces?

```
RouterR1#show ip interface ethernet0
RouterR1#show ipv6 interface ethernet1
RouterR1#show ipv6 interface fastEthernet 0/0
RouterR1#show ipv6 interface fastEthernet 0/1
```

**Step 7**    Configure a default IPv6 route pointing to the next-hop link-local address
fe80::1001 (the IPv6 Internet). Which command will you use?

```
RouterR1#conf t
RouterR1(config)#ipv6 route ::/0 ethernet1 fe80::1001
RouterR1(config)#exit
```

**Step 8**    Examine the current IPv6 routing table in Router R1 and verify the IPv6
routes. You should see a default IPv6 route. What is the command used to
display the IPv6 routes?

```
RouterR1#show ipv6 route
```

**Step 9**    Save the current configuration to NVRAM.

```
RouterR1#copy run start
Destination filename [startup-config]?
Building configuration...
[OK]
```

# Task 2: Enable Stateless Autoconfiguration and Assign a Static IPv6 Address on Solaris

Complete the following steps:

**Step 1**    Enable stateless autoconfiguration on the hme0 interface of Solaris node A as
shown in Figure 6-14.

```
Solaris-nodeA#touch /etc/hostname6.hme0
Solaris-nodeA#reboot
```

**Step 2**    After Solaris node A has rebooted, verify whether hme0 got one IPv6 address
through stateless autoconfiguration. What command verifies the IPv6
addresses assigned to a specific interface on Solaris?

```
Solaris-nodeA#ifconfig hme0 inet6
```

**Step 3**    Solaris node B, as shown in Figure 6-14, is acting as an IPv6 web server, and
it needs a permanent IPv6 address. Therefore, on Solaris node B, assign the
static IPv6 address 2001:410:ffff:1::10/64 to interface qfe0. Which command
will you use to perform this task?

```
Solaris-nodeB#touch /etc/hostname6.hme0
Solaris-nodeB#reboot
...
Solaris-nodeB#ifconfig qfe0 inet6 addif 2001:410:ffff:1::10/64 up
```

**Step 4**    Configure a default IPv6 route pointing to the next-hop IPv6 address
2001:410:ffff:1::1 (interface FE0/1 of Router R1). Which command will
you use?

```
Solaris-nodeB#route add -inet6 default 2001:410:ffff:1::1
```

**Step 5**    Verify the static IPv6 address assigned on the qfe0 interface and the default IPv6 route added. What commands are used?

```
Solaris-nodeB#ifconfig qfe0 inet6
Solaris-nodeB#netstat -rn
```

# Task 3: Configure Tunnel Interfaces on Router R1

To perform Task 3, use Table 6-10. It shows the assignment of addresses for the tunnel interfaces on Router R1.

**Table 6-10**    *Assignment of Addresses for the Tunnel Interfaces on Router R1*

| Interface | Type | Source IPv4 Address | Destination IPv4 Address | Source IPv6 Address | Destination IPv6 address |
|-----------|------|---------------------|--------------------------|---------------------|--------------------------|
| Tunnel2 | Configured tunnel | 206.123.31.3 | 67.68.100.43 | 2001:410:ffff:9::1/64 | 2001:410:ffff:9::2/64 |
| Tunnel5 | 6to4 | E0 | None | 2002:ce7b:1f02:1::1/64 | None |

Complete the following steps:

**Step 1**    Enable and set a configured tunnel with FreeBSD node D on the tunnel2 interface of Router R1. Use 206.123.31.3 as the source IPv4 address and 67.68.100.43 as the destination IPv4 address for the tunnel. Then assign 2001:410:ffff:9::1/64 as the source IPv6 address.

```
RouterR1#conf t
RouterR1(config)#interface tunnel2
RouterR1(config-if)#tunnel source 206.123.31.3
RouterR1(config-if)#tunnel destination 67.68.100.43
RouterR1(config-if)#ipv6 address 2001:410:ffff:9::1/64
RouterR1(config-if)#tunnel mode ipv6ip
RouterR1(config-if)#exit
RouterR1(config)#exit
```

**Step 2**    Enable the 6to4 mechanism on Router R1. Begin with the assignment of the static IPv6 address 2002:ce7b:1f02:1::1/64 to the E0 interface. This address is within the 6to4 prefix 2002:ce7b:1f02::/48. The 6to4 prefix has been calculated using the public IPv4 address 206.123.31.2 of interface E0.

```
RouterR1#conf t
RouterR1(config)#int ethernet0
RouterR1(config-if)#ipv6 address 2002:ce7b:1f02:1::1/64
RouterR1(config-if)#exit
```

**Step 3**  Enter the command to suppress the advertisement of the prefix
2002:ce7b:1f02:1::/64 on interface E0, because there is no reason to
send router advertisement messages on this router's public interface.

```
RouterR1#conf t
RouterR1(config)#int ethernet0
RouterR1(config-if)#ipv6 nd suppress-ra
RouterR1(config-if)#exit
```

**Step 4**  Enable the 6to4 router using the tunnel5 interface. Use the IPv4 and IPv6
addresses assigned to interface E0 as addresses for the 6to4 mechanism.
What commands are used to enable 6to4 on a Cisco router?

```
RouterR1#conf t
RouterR1(config)#int tunnel5
RouterR1(config-if)#no ip address
RouterR1(config-if)#ipv6 unnumbered ethernet0
RouterR1(config-if)#tunnel source ethernet0
RouterR1(config-if)#tunnel mode ipv6ip 6to4
RouterR1(config-if)#exit
```

**Step 5**  Because the 6to4 sites on the IPv4 Internet can be reached through the
tunnel5 interface, add a route for the destination prefix 2002::/16 in Router
R1 pointing out the interface tunnel5. What command will you use?

```
RouterR1#conf t
RouterR1(config)#ipv6 route 2002::/16 tunnel5
RouterR1(config)#exit
```

**Step 6**  Verify the tunnel2 and tunnel5 interfaces on Router R1. What commands are
used to display tunnel interface configurations?

```
RouterR1#show ipv6 interface tunnel2
RouterR1#show ipv6 interface tunnel5
```

**Step 7**  Save the current configuration to NVRAM.

```
RouterR1#copy run start
Destination filename [startup-config]?
Building configuration...
```

# Task 4: Enable 6to4 on Microsoft Windows XP

Complete the following steps:

**Step 1**  On Windows XP, the interface assigned to the 6to4 mechanism is pseudo-
interface 3. Enable the 6to4 mechanism on pseudo-interface 3 of Windows
XP node C, as shown in Figure 6-14. For this task, the IPv4 address
69.10.100.41 is assigned to Windows XP node C. Assign the static IPv6
address 2002:450a:6429:1::1 to pseudo-interface 3.

```
C:\ipv6.exe rtu 2002::/16 3
C:\ipv6.exe adu 3/2002:450a:6429:1::1
```

**Step 2** Display the pseudo-interfaces list on Windows XP node C and verify the pseudo-interface 3 configuration. What command is used to display pseudo-interface lists?

```
C:\ipv6.exe if
```

## Task 5: Define a Configured Tunnel on FreeBSD

Complete the following steps:

**Step 1** Start the configuration by enabling the configured interface gif0 on FreeBSD node D as shown in Figure 6-14.

```
FreeBSD-nodeD#ifconfig gif0 create
```

**Step 2** After the configured interface is created, assign the source and destination IPv4 addresses to establish the tunnel. Use 67.68.100.43 as the source and 206.123.31.3 as the destination.

```
FreeBSD-nodeD#gifconfig gif0 67.68.100.43 206.123.31.3
```

**Step 3** Assign the static IPv6 addresses 2001:410:ffff:9::2 and 2001:410:ffff:9::1 to the endpoints of the configured tunnel. The address 2001:410:ffff:9::2 is the source address of FreeBSD node D.

```
FreeBSD-nodeD#ifconfig gif0 inet6 2001:410:ffff:9::2 2001:410:ffff:9::1
    prefixlen 128 alias
```

**Step 4** Configure a default IPv6 route pointing to the next-hop IPv6 address 2001:410:ffff:9::1 (the tunnel endpoint). What command will you use?

```
FreeBSD-nodeD#route add -inet6 default 2001:410:ffff:9::1
```

**Step 5** Verify the IPv4 and IPv6 addresses assigned on the gif0 interface and the default IPv6 route. What commands are used?

```
FreeBSD-nodeD#ifconfig gif0
FreeBSD-nodeD#netstat -f inet6 -rn
```

# Review Questions

Answer the following questions, and then refer to Appendix B, "Answers to Review Questions," for the answers.

**1** What command enables IPv6 on Windows XP?

**2** What command lists all the pseudo-interfaces on Windows 2000 and Windows NT?

**3** For the Microsoft Windows platforms listed in the following table, specify the pseudo-interface numbers defined for each type of interface.

| Type of Interface | Windows XP | Windows 2000 | Windows NT |
|---|---|---|---|
| Loopback | | | |
| Configured tunnel | | | |
| 6to4 | | | |

**4** What command assigns the static IPv6 address fec0:0:0:1::1 to pseudo-interface 4 on Microsoft Windows XP?

**5** What do you do on Solaris 8 to enable IPv6 on interfaces hme0 and hme1?

**6** What command in Solaris 8 assigns the static IPv6 address fec0:0:0:1::1/64 to the hme0 interface?

**7** What pseudo-interface is assigned as the configured tunnel interface on Solaris 8?

**8** Based on the following table, what commands in Solaris 8 establish a configured tunnel? (Your node must use the source addresses.)

| | IPv4 | IPv6 |
|---|---|---|
| **Source addresses** | 10.100.50.20 | fec0:0:0:1000::2/128 |
| **Destination addresses** | 192.168.1.50 | fec0:0:0:1000::1 |

**9** What FreeBSD parameter enables stateless autoconfiguration on all interfaces?

**10** What command in FreeBSD enables the configured interface gif15?

**11** What interface name is defined on FreeBSD for the 6to4 mechanism?

**12** For each description in the following table, specify the command that is used in FreeBSD.

| Description | Command |
|---|---|
| Displays the IPv6 routing table | |
| Displays IPv6 information about the fxp1 interface | |
| Adds a default IPv6 route via gateway fec0::1:0:0:0:1 | |
| Assigns the static IPv6 address 2001:410:ffff:2::2/64 on fxp0 | |

**13** What do you do in Linux to enable stateless autoconfiguration on the eth2 interface at the boot of the Linux node?

**14** What command in Linux assigns the static IPv6 address fec0:0:1000:1::a/64 to the eth0 interface?

**15**  What pseudo-interface is assigned as the configured tunnel interface on Linux?

**16**  What Linux command creates the configured interface sit3?

**17**  For each description in the following table, specify the command that is used in Linux.

| Description | Command |
|---|---|
| Displays the IPv6 routing table | |
| Displays IPv6 information about the eth0 interface | |
| Adds a default IPv6 route via gateway fec0::1:0:0:0:1 | |
| Assigns the static IPv6 address 2001:410:ffff:2::2/64 on eth0 | |

**18**  What command enables stateless autoconfiguration in Tru64?

**19**  What command creates a configured interface in Tru64?

**20**  What pseudo-interface is assigned as the configured tunnel interface on Tru64?

# References

RFC 3041, *Privacy Extensions for Stateless Address Autoconfiguration in IPv6,* T. Narten, R. Draves, IETF, www.ietf.org/rfc/rfc3041.txt, January 2001

RFC 3068, *An Anycast Prefix for 6to4 Relay Routers,* C. Huitema, IETF, www.ietf.org/rfc/rfc3068.txt, June 2001

Microsoft IPv6 Technology Preview For Windows 2000, msdn.microsoft.com/downloads/sdks/platform/tpipv6.asp

Microsoft Research, research.microsoft.com/msrIPv6/msripv6.htm

Microsoft Windows IPv6, www.microsoft.com/ipv6

Solaris IPv6, www.sun.com/software/solaris/ipv6/

FreeBSD IPv6, www.freebsd.org/doc/en_US.ISO8859-1/books/developers-handbook/ipv6.html

FreeBSD IPv6 Ports, www.freebsd.org/ports/ipv6.html

KAME Project, www.kame.net

INRIA, www.inria.fr

Linux IPv6 HOWTO, www.tldp.org/HOWTO/Linux+IPv6-HOWTO/

Compaq Tru64 UNIX, h18000.www1.hp.com/ipv6/Tru64UNIX.html

IPng Implementations, playground.sun.com/pub/ipng/html/ipng-implementations.html

# PART IV

# The IPv6 Backbone

After you have seen in the previous parts the IPv6 design and the coexistence and integration mechanisms in the IPv6 protocol, Part IV presents the 6bone's architecture, allocation policy, and routing policy. Then it describes the criteria to become an IPv6 ISP on the IPv6 Internet, how production IPv6 address spaces are allocated by regional Internet registries (RIRs) to Tier-1 providers, and how IPv6 addresses are reassigned to customers. Finally, this part discusses industry support and trends for IPv6.

The following chapter comprises this part of the book:

Chapter 7     Connecting to the IPv6 Internet

"IPv4 works fine, and I have plenty of IPv4 addresses in my IP space for my company, so we don't need to upgrade to IPv6."

Anonymous person living in North America

# Connecting to the IPv6 Internet

The IPv6 Internet is currently in deployment worldwide. This chapter describes how the IPv6 Internet is built and how to connect to it. After reading this chapter, you will be able to describe the 6bone, its purposes, its architecture, and its addressing. You also will understand how your organization can become a pseudo-TLA on the 6bone, and you will learn the routing policy on the 6bone.

You will also understand policy allocation and how addresses are allocated on the production IPv6 Internet by the regional Internet registries (RIRs) to providers. This chapter discusses the criteria to become an IPv6 Tier-1 provider and the address allocation and reassignment of addresses to customers.

Later, you will learn how Internet service providers (ISPs) can become IPv6 providers and how they can deploy IPv6 connectivity to customer networks (end sites). This section basically describes the responsibilities of IPv6 providers, the exchange of IPv6 traffic through network access points (NAPs), examples of address space reassignments to customers, routing, and route aggregation by IPv6 providers.

Finally, this chapter discusses the industry support and trends for IPv6 such as the IPv6 Forum, the 3G (Third Generation), and some regional initiatives supported by governments in Asia, Europe, and North America.

## 6bone

6bone stands for "IPv6 backbone." The 6bone is a test-bed network that was created in 1996 by the IETF next-generation transition from IPv4 to IPv6 (NGtrans) working group to validate the new standards related to the IPv6 protocol. Another goal of the 6bone was to test the IPv6 implementations and network services to provide feedback to developers and protocol designers. Then, the 6bone was used to validate operational procedures and test transition and coexistence mechanisms.

The 6bone is informally operated by the IETF NGtrans working group, and it is managed on a collaborative, best-effort basis by its worldwide users. In 2002 (based on the 6bone registry database), more than 1100 sites located in 57 countries were connected to and participating on the 6bone. Because registration of IPv6 sites connected to this test-bed network in the 6bone registry database has never been mandatory (but was strongly recommended), the number of sites actually connected to the 6bone might be higher than 1100.

**NOTE**     The computing department of Lancaster University in the U.K. provides different statistics
about and views of countries and sites connected to the 6bone. You can find information about
sites connected to the 6bone at www.cs-ipv6.lancs.ac.uk/ipv6/6Bone/Whois/bycountry.html.

However, these statistics represent only sites that are fully registered in the 6bone registry
database, which you can find at www.6bone.net.

The 6bone is a network of IPv6 networks. The links between the IPv6 networks on the 6bone
are made using IPv6. The IPv6 protocol is carried over WANs, over LANs in exchange points,
and over IPv4 tunnels such as configured tunnels and 6to4 tunnels through the current IPv4
Internet.

**NOTE**     For more information about configured tunnels, see Chapter 5, "IPv6 Integration and
Coexistence Strategies."

In 1996, the 6bone started as a virtual network over the IPv4 Internet using IPv6-over-IPv4
tunnels to enable easy IPv6 connectivity and peering between IPv6 networks. Later, native IPv6
links were deployed between IPv6 networks. Past experience on the IPv4 Internet such as with
the Mbone (multicast datagrams over the IPv4 Internet) suggested the deployment of IPv6-
over-IPv4 tunnels until all links are converted to native IPv6 links.

**NOTE**     When network administrators of IPv6 networks such as ISPs, organizations, and companies,
agree to exchange their IPv6 traffic for free, this is called *peering*. Administrators also define
how the routes are advertised.

The 6bone is now a network made up of native IPv6 and tunneled links. New 6bone links are
mostly native, and old tunneled links are gradually being replaced by native IPv6 links.

**NOTE**     The 6bone is not a production network with 24/7 support. 6bone operation is best-effort.

The following sections present 6bone's topology, architecture, addressing, connection, and
routing policy.

## 6bone Topology

The 6bone topology is a hierarchy of providers. As illustrated in Figure 7-1, the first level of the hierarchy consists of 6bone's backbone nodes, representing the pseudo-Top-Level Aggregators (pTLAs).

**Figure 7-1**    *Hierarchical Topology of the 6bone, with pTLAs, Providers, and Sites*

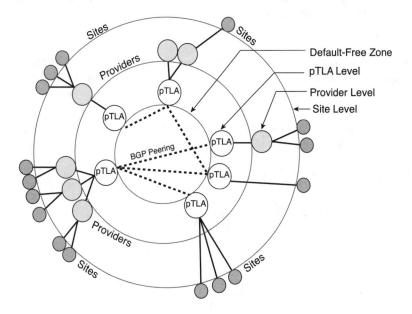

**NOTE**    These backbone nodes are called *pseudo* because the 6bone is a test-bed backbone simulating production service providers. On the production IPv4 Internet, these first-level nodes are called *Tier-1 providers (Tier-1 ISPs)*.

The pTLAs connect with other pTLAs in the default-free zone, where no default IPv6 route is advertised.

**NOTE**    The *default-free zone* is the place in the network where ISPs and other large networks use the global IPv6 routing table to exchange traffic. Within the global IPv6 routing table, no default route exists, and only aggregated IPv6 routes are present. The IPv4 Internet has the same topology, but routes are not fully aggregated as with IPv6.

These first-level nodes (pTLAs) are called *aggregators* because they must aggregate the IPv6 traffic of all their downstream customers and announce only a few IPv6 prefixes on the 6bone. As discussed in Chapter 1, "Introduction to IPv6," the aggregation of routes in IPv6 promotes efficient and scalable routing to the IPv6 Internet. Figure 7-1 shows that each pTLA on the 6bone provides IPv6 connectivity and IPv6 spaces to its downstream providers and sites.

The pTLAs peer with other pTLAs using BGP4+ to exchange their IPv6 routes. The peering between the pTLAs on the 6bone may be done over native IPv6 links or IPv6-over-IPv4 tunnels.

---

**NOTE**     BGP4+ is also called BGP4 with multiprotocol extension. BGP4+ supports IPv6. Refer to Chapter 4, "Routing on IPv6," for detailed information about the BGP4+ routing protocol.

---

Figure 7-2 shows the real peering between the pTLAs on the 6bone. This representation comes from the 6bone registry database and reflects only the peering information registered.

**Figure 7-2**     *Peering Between pTLAs on the 6bone*

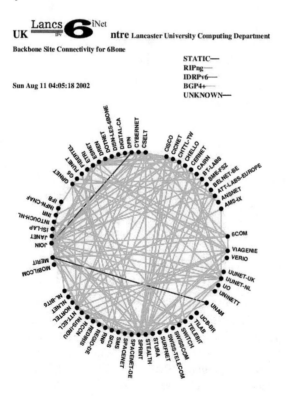

Source: IPv6 Resource Centre of the Lancaster University Computing Department in the U.K., www.cs-ipv6.lancs.ac.uk/ftp-archive/6Bone/Maps/backbone.gif

## 6bone Architecture

The 6bone topology is the conceptual view of this backbone, but the architecture of the 6bone has been made over time with a diversity of links. Moreover, as mentioned in the preceding section, the pTLAs on the 6bone are connected using a mix of native IPv6 links and tunnels over the IPv4 Internet.

Figure 7-3 shows the different types of links used between the pTLAs of the 6bone. pTLAs A, B, C, and D are connected through a native IPv6 NAP using native IPv6 links and pTLAs D and F have native IPv6 links to pTLA E. Finally, pTLAs F and G are connected to pTLA D using IPv6-over-IPv4 tunnels through the IPv4 Internet. These IPv6-over-IPv4 tunnels are simply acting as point-to-point links.

**Figure 7-3**    *Native IPv6 Links and IPv6-Over-IPv4 Tunnels Used Between pTLAs on the 6bone*

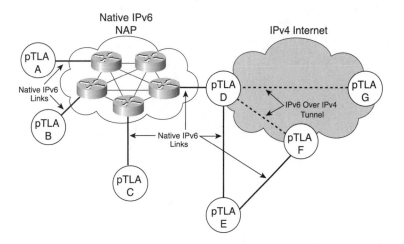

Thus, adjacent pTLAs in Figure 7-3 can enable BGP4+ peering between them to exchange IPv6 traffic by announcing and receiving IPv6 routes through their peering. Therefore, all these connected pTLAs form the worldwide IPv6 network called the 6bone.

A pTLA on the 6bone can provide addressing and connectivity to any provider, intermediate provider, or site directly connected to the pTLA.

In Figure 7-4, the pTLA at the top provides connectivity and addressing space to a first-level provider, intermediary provider, and site. Then, the provider can allocate address prefixes to the sites directly connected while the intermediary provider allocates address prefixes to another level of downstream providers.

As shown in Figure 7-4, prefixes are allocated from the pTLA to the end sites via different levels of providers. In the other direction, upstream providers aggregate the end sites' traffic and address prefixes. Therefore, upstream providers announce only one (or a few) aggregated prefixes directly to the pTLA or through another level of upstream provider.

**Figure 7-4** *Prefix Allocation and Aggregation Between the pTLA and Downstream Providers*

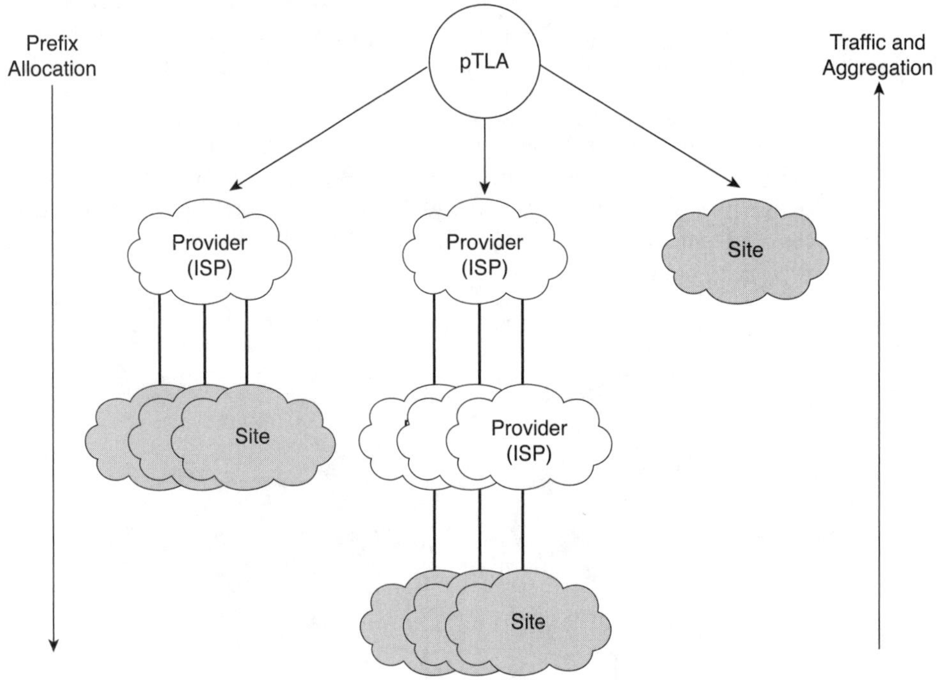

# IPv6 Addressing on the 6bone

As described in RFC 2471, *IPv6 Testing Address Allocation,* the aggregatable global unicast IPv6 address space assigned by the IANA for the 6bone is the 3ffe::/16 prefix. The 3ffe::/16 prefix is for experimental purposes only. This address space can be reclaimed in the future, forcing pTLAs, providers, and sites to renumber their networks.

RFC 2921, *6Bone pTLA and pNLA Formats (pTLA),* defines the 6bone's address allocation policy. The 6bone policy has evolved over time:

- **First allocation policy (1996 to 1999)**—6bone's first address space allocation started at 3ffe:0000::/24 and ended at 3ffe:3900::/24. Each pTLA received one /24 prefix. A total of 58 pTLAs received one /24 prefix. This policy allowed a maximum of 256 pTLAs on the 6bone.

- **Second allocation policy (1999 to 2002)**—The second address space allocation changed to allow a larger number of pTLAs on the 6bone. Each pTLA received one /28 prefix. The allocation started at 3ffe:8000::/28 and ended at 3ffe:8370::/28. A total of 56 pTLAs received one /28 prefix. This policy allowed a maximum of 4096 pTLAs on the 6bone.

- **Current allocation policy**—In March 2002, the address space allocation changed again to increase the maximum number of pTLAs on the 6bone. With this policy, each pTLA can receive one /32 prefix. The allocation starts at 3ffe:4000::/32, and the last prefix available for the policy is 3ffe:7fff::/32. The new policy, coupled with the /24 and /28 prefixes assigned to pTLAs in the past, allows a maximum of 16,384 pTLAs on the 6bone.

**NOTE**    Additional information about address space allocations already done on the 6bone can be found at www.6bone.net/6bone_pTLA_list.html.

The address allocation policy also defines the prefix lengths of subnets and end sites on the 6bone:

- **Site prefix**—The policy defines that each end site on the 6bone receives one /48 prefix from its upstream provider. The /48 is the minimum required for a site on the 6bone.

- **Subnet prefix**—The policy defines that each subnet within a site receives one /64 prefix within the site prefix. The allocation of the /64 prefix to the subnet is important for enabling the stateless autoconfiguration mechanism on networks.

**NOTE**    In theory, one /48 prefix allows a site to have up to 65,536 /64 prefixes. However, as discussed in Chapter 1, IP's address space IPv4 and IPv6, like any other addressing scheme, is not optimal. Therefore, the 65,536 /64 prefixes within one /48 is only a theoretical number.

Figure 7-5 shows the hierarchical allocation of prefixes between the 6bone prefix 3ffe::/16 to the subnet prefix in sites. The first level is the 16-bit prefix of the 6bone, followed by the pTLA allocation, which is based on 32-bit prefixes. Then comes the provider level, which can allow one to several providers in a hierarchy between the pTLA and a site. 16 bits are available for the provider level. Finally, Figure 7-5 illustrates the /48 allocated to sites and /64 prefixes assigned to subnets within sites.

**Figure 7-5**   *Hierarchical Allocations Within the 6bone Prefix 3ffe::/16*

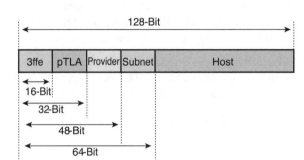

## Becoming a pTLA on the 6bone

It is possible for providers and ISPs to qualify as pTLAs on the 6bone. RFC 2772, *6bone Backbone Routing Guidelines,* defines the rules, criteria, and policy for becoming a pTLA on the 6bone:

- To become a pTLA, the applicant must have a minimum of three months of qualifying experience as a 6bone end site. During the requested period, the applicant must have done the following:

  — Registered its site in the 6bone registry database. A web interface of the 6bone registry database is available at www.viagenie.qc.ca/en/ipv6/registry/index.shtml

  — Maintained BGP4+ peering and connectivity between the applicant's boundary router and an appropriate connection point into the 6bone (a pTLA)

  — Maintained AAAA and PTR records for its border router in a local DNS server

  — Maintained an IPv6-accessible system providing at least one web page or more of information

- The applicant must have the ability and the intent to provide "production-quality" 6bone backbone service. More specifically, the applicant must claim to have the support staff and tools to operate as a pTLA.

- The applicant must have potential end users who would be served by it as a pTLA.

- The applicant must conform to the 6bone's routing policy by doing the following:

  — Announcing permitted IPv6 routes within the 6bone address space, production of IPv6 Internet address space, and 6to4 address space

— Announcing legal prefix lengths allocated over time on the 6bone and on the IPv6 Internet

— Not announcing prohibited routes

• The applicant must send its request to a steering committee for review purposes.

---

**NOTE**    Detailed information about rules, criteria, and policies with regard to becoming a pTLA on the 6bone can be found in RFC 2772. An overview of this RFC is presented in the next section.

---

## Routing Policy on the 6bone

The routing policy for the 6bone is described in RFC 2772. This policy was defined and designed to maintain the stability of routing on the 6bone by having a common set of rules and guidelines.

The routing policy has to be applied by 6bone providers and by all pTLAs. The routing policy contains the following rules:

• **Prohibited address ranges**—Specific ranges of addresses such as link-local, site-local, multicast, and loopback, of the whole IPv6 space must not be advertised by pTLAs on the 6bone. The "Prohibited Announcements" section details the prohibited address ranges on the 6bone.

• **Legal prefix lengths**—Allocation of prefixes to pTLAs on the 6bone changed over time. The policy defines the maximum length of prefixes announced on the 6bone. The prefix lengths vary from /24 through /32. The "Legal Prefix Lengths" section details the prohibited address ranges on the 6bone.

• **Guidelines for the 6bone route registry**—These are the guidelines that document the allocation of addresses and the connected sites in the 6bone route registry. The "6bone Route Registry" section provides an overview of the 6bone route registry.

• **Guidelines for enforcement**—These are the guidelines for the enforcement of the routing policy. Organizations connected on the 6bone commit to implement the 6bone's rules and policies, they should report any issues and problems detected to the 6bone Operations Group, and they are responsible for working toward the problem's resolution. See RFC 2772 for more information about this rule.

• **Guidelines for DNS**—These are the guidelines for maintaining DNS records (AAAA) and reverse (ip6.int) entries for the organization's router and at least one host system. See RFC 2772 for more information about this rule.

## Permitted Announcements

This section describes the IPv6 address spaces that are permitted to be advertised on the 6bone by the pTLAs:

- **6bone address space**—The 3ffe::/16 prefix that is assigned by the IANA for the 6bone operation is permitted. This means that any prefixes assigned to the pTLA within 3ffe::/16 may be advertised by pTLAs on the 6bone.

- **Production IPv6 Internet address space**—The 2001::/16 prefix that is assigned by the IANA for the production of IPv6 Internet operation is permitted. Prefixes assigned to ISPs within the 2001::/16 prefix may be advertised on the 6bone. More information about the IPv6 Internet address space is presented later in this chapter.

- **6to4 address space**—The 2002::/16 prefix that is assigned by the IANA for the 6to4 operation is permitted. Because the pTLA may implement a 6to4 relay in its network, it may advertise its 6to4 prefix to the 6bone. However, a pTLA announcing its 6to4 prefix on the 6bone must enable a 6to4 relay. The prefix of the 6to4 relay is based on the 6to4 router's globally unique unicast IPv4 address.

## Legal Prefix Lengths

Because route aggregation is enforced on the 6bone and on the IPv6 Internet, 6bone has a strict policy of announcing only aggregated routes. For each IPv6 address space permitted in the preceding section, the pTLAs on the 6bone should announce only the following legal prefix lengths:

- **6bone**—The allocation policy evolved over time. Therefore, the following prefix lengths are legal on the 6bone:

  - 3ffe:0000::/24 through 3ffe:3f00::/24

  - 3ffe:8000::/28 through 3ffe:83f0::/28

  - 3ffe:4000::/32 through 3ffe:7fff::/32

- **Production IPv6 Internet**—RIRs such as American Registry for Internet Numbers (ARIN), Asia Pacific Network Information Center (APNIC), and Réseaux IP Européens Network Coordination Center (RIPE NCC) started in 1999 with the assignment of /35 prefixes to ISPs. As with the 6bone, the allocation policy evolved over time. In 2002, registries started to assign /32 prefixes to ISPs instead of /35. Therefore, the following prefix lengths are legal on the 6bone:

  - 2001:0000::/35 through 2001:ffff::/35

  - 2001:0000::/32 through 2001:ffff::/32

- **6to4**—Because the IPv6 prefix of a 6to4 relay is based on the 2002::/16 prefix followed by the globally unique unicast IPv4 address of the 6to4 router in hexadecimal representation, the 2002:*xxxx*:*xxxx*::/48 prefixes are the only legal length permitted on the 6bone.

## Prohibited Announcements

Based on the 6bone's routing policy, the pTLAs on the 6bone must not advertise the following address ranges:

- **Link-local prefix (FE80::/10)**—Because the link-local prefix is for a local scope purpose only, it must not be advertised on the 6bone by pTLAs.

- **Site-local prefix (FEC0::/10)**—Because the site-local prefix is for a site local scope purpose only, it must not be advertised on the 6bone by pTLAs.

- **Multicast prefix (FF00::/8)**—Because the multicast prefix is used only in a multicast context, multicast addresses must not be advertised by pTLAs in a unicast IPv6 routing domain (6bone).

- **Loopback and unspecified**—The 1/128 (::1) and ::0/128 (::) prefixes must not be advertised on the 6bone.

- **IPv4-compatible prefix (::/96)**—The IPv4-compatible prefix is for automatic tunneling. It has no need to change the IPv6 routing domain (6bone), so it must not be advertised on the 6bone.

- **IPv4-mapped prefix (::FFFF:d.d.d.d/96)**—Because the IPv4-mapped prefix is used internally in the applications, there is no need to change the IPv6 routing. Thus, the IPv4-mapped prefix must not be advertised on the 6bone.

- **Default route**—Because a pTLA must be default-free, the default route must not be advertised on the 6bone by any pTLA.

- **Other unicast prefixes**—Any other unicast prefixes from undefined or unallocated prefixes by ARIN or RIRs that are not defined in the permitted announcement must not be advertised on the 6bone.

| | |
|---|---|
| **NOTE** | Chapter 2, "IPv6 Addressing," contains additional information about link-local, site-local, multicast, loopback, unspecified, IPv4-compatible, and IPv4-mapped addresses. |

## 6bone Route Registry

On the IPv4 Internet, a route registry is useful for sharing network prefix information and identifying the usage of address prefixes. The route registry does the following:

- Allows providers, ISPs, and registries to view the IPv6 address allocations.

- Identifies people who can be contacted for information and debugging purposes.

- Generates route filters by extracting all the routes in the registry. Thus, any pTLA can configure routing filters on its routers. The route registry can automate the process of route filtering required by the peering policy.

The 6bone route registry is available at www.6bone.net. All sites, providers, and pTLAs connected on the 6bone should register their sites in this IPv6 route registry.

# IPv6 Internet

As discussed, the 6bone is an IPv6 backbone used for testing purposes. The 6bone runs using the IPv6 test address space 3ffe::/16, and its operation is based on best effort.

However, to build and deploy a reliable production IPv6 Internet around the world, the IPv6 must be able to provide production IPv6 address spaces to ISPs. Since 1999, RIRs have been allocating IPv6 production prefixes to ISPs.

This section provides information about production IPv6 address allocation policy, criteria to become an IPv6 Tier-1 provider, and address space reassignment to customers.

## Regional Internet Registries

The IANA initially allocated the aggregatable global unicast IPv6 address space 2001::/16 for the production purposes of the IPv6 Internet.

As with IPv4, this IPv6 production address space is managed by the three RIRs located in different regions of the world:

- **APNIC**—Asia Pacific Network Information Center. Covers Asia and Australia.

- **ARIN**—American Registry for Internet Numbers. Covers North America, Central America, and South America.

- **RIPE NCC**—Réseaux IP Européens Network Coordination Center. Covers Europe and the Middle East.

ISPs can receive upon request their IPv6 production space from those registries. The addresses are free, but the registries generally charge a price for the service.

# The Registries' IPv6 Address Allocation Policy

As with the 6bone, the production IPv6 address allocation policy has evolved over time. The allocation policy is identical for all registries except for the prices and management. The policy was reviewed by the IETF and by a public consultation process. Prefixes are allocated only to ISPs, not to enterprises.

The initial address allocation of production IPv6 prefixes began in July 1999, and the current allocation policy was adopted in July 2002.

## Initial 1999 Allocation Policy

The initial allocation policy of production IPv6 addresses was adopted in July 1999. The initial policy was based on a slow-start process in which regional Internet registries allocated /35 prefixes to ISPs. By allocating smaller address space to new ISPs, this slow-start process allowed registries to conserve IPv6 address space.

A bootstrap procedure was defined to help new ISPs meet the initial criteria of this allocation policy. The criteria were based on past experience of ISPs with IPv4. Therefore, the policy helped groups of ISPs deploy IPv6 before enforcing permanent rules.

In 2001, work started to review the initial allocation policy toward the development of a general allocation policy that all RIRs can apply. The initial allocation policy is now outdated with the enforcement of the new policy in July 2002.

---

**NOTE**    An archived copy of the initial allocation policy can be found on the RIPE FTP site at ftp://ftp.ripe.net/ripe/docs/ripe-196.txt.

---

## Current Allocation Policy

The current allocation policy for production IPv6 addresses is defined in the document "IPv6 Address Allocation and Assignment Policy." It can be found on the APNIC, ARIN, and RIPE NCC web sites using these links:

- **APNIC**—ftp.apnic.net/apnic/docs/ipv6-address-policy

- **ARIN**—www.arin.net/policy/ipv6_policy.html

- **RIPE NCC**—www.ripe.net/ripe/docs/ipv6policy.html

The current policy contains the following initial criteria:

- **Be a Local Internet Registry (LIR)**—A LIR is an Internet registry that primarily assigns address space to the users of the network services it provides. LIRs are generally ISPs whose customers are primarily end users and possibly other ISPs.

- **Do not be an end site**—An end site is an end user (subscriber) who has a business relationship with an ISP.

- **Plan to provide IPv6 connectivity to organizations**—The provider should assign at least one /48 prefix per organization.

- **Plan to assign 200 /48 prefixes within two years**—The /48 prefixes should be assigned to organizations (end sites) within two years.

Then, the address allocation policy states that organizations (ISPs) that meet the initial criteria are eligible to receive a minimum allocation of /32. Organizations that hold a /35 prefix received from the initial allocation policy are automatically entitled to receive a /32 prefix. The /32 prefix contains the /35 prefix that was already allocated.

According to this allocation policy, it is possible for a provider to qualify for an initial allocation greater than /32 by submitting justifications. In this case, the allocation of addresses is based on the number of existing users and the extent of the organization's infrastructure.

It is also possible for a provider to request additional address space. Subsequent allocation criteria have been defined for this purpose. These criteria are based on the use of the /48 assignments realized by the providers. The HD ratio (as presented in RFC 3194, *The Host-Density Ratio for Address Assignment Efficiency: An update on the H ratio*) is used to determine which threshold justifies the additional address space required.

## Address Space Reassignment to Customers

The allocation policy also defines rules for the reassignment of address space to customers. These rules are based on the guidelines defined in RFC 3177, *IAB/IESG Recommendations on IPv6 Address Allocations to Sites,* and in the document "IPv6 Initial Request for IP Address Space." The allocation policy contains the following rules:

- **Customer prefix length**—In general, the IPv6 prefix assigned to a customer (end site) by a provider should be a /48. However, larger prefixes may be assigned to very large subscribers.

- **Subnet prefix length**—One /64 prefix may be assigned to a subnet only when it is known that one and only one subnet is needed in the design. Home networks and small networks designed with only one subnet are examples of /64 prefix assignments.

- **Device prefix length**—One /128 prefix may be assigned to a device only when it is absolutely known that one and only one device is connecting. A single PC, PDA, or cell phone that dials up from a remote location and uses a PPP connection are examples of /128 prefix assignments.

**NOTE**    Detailed information about the document "IPv6 Initial Request for IP Address Space" can be found on the ARIN web site at www.arin.net/library/guidelines/ipv6_initial.html.

## Address Allocation

As with the 6bone, boundaries are defined in the address allocation policy within the production aggregatable global unicast IPv6 prefix 2001::/16. Figure 7-6 illustrates the assignments between the prefix 2001::/16 and the end sites. The first level shown is the prefix of the production IPv6 address space assigned by IANA. It is followed by the RIR allocation. 16 bits are available for the RIR level, so RIRs can allocate the initial /32 prefix to each ISP. Finally, ISPs assign /48 prefixes to each customer (end site).

**Figure 7-6**    *Hierarchical Allocations Within the Production IPv6 Address Space 2001::/16*

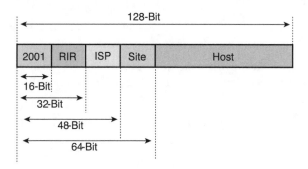

Figure 7-7 shows a hierarchical view of the address allocation. On the RIR level, APNIC receives the prefixes 2001:02xx::/23 and 2001:0cxx::/23, ARIN receives the 2001:04xx::/23 prefix and RIPE NCC receives 2001:06xx::/23. On the next level, /32 prefixes of the address spaces received by RIRs are allocated to ISPs and then /48 prefixes are assigned to sites (customers).

**Figure 7-7** *Hierarchical View of Allocations Within the Production IPv6 Address Space 2001::/16*

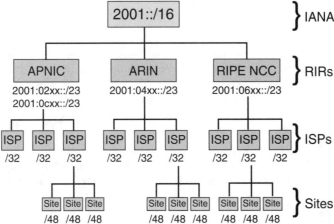

# Connecting to the Production IPv6 Internet

As mentioned, the deployment of the production IPv6 Internet started in July 1999 when the RIRs allocated production IPv6 spaces to very large providers.

The core of the production IPv6 Internet already exists. It is small compared to the current IPv4 Internet, but it has been growing steadily. The production IPv6 Internet is very similar to its equivalent in IPv4.

IPv6 ISPs exchange traffic in the NAPs such as in IPv4, and they provide connectivity to customers.

The following sections briefly cover these topics:

- Basic steps to become an IPv6 provider on the production IPv6 Internet

- IPv6 support needed in NAP for the exchange of routes by IPv6 providers

- Things customers should understand when they get IPv6 connectivity from an IPv6 provider

- Examples of IPv6 address space reassignment to customers by IPv6 providers

- Route aggregation by IPv6 providers

- How transition and coexistence mechanisms can be used in specific circumstances to provide IPv6 connectivity

## Becoming an IPv6 Provider

As with IPv4, ISPs are the core of the IPv6 Internet. They have multiple responsibilities to assume to provide efficient and reliable IPv6 connectivity to their customers. These responsibilities are very similar to those in IPv4 and include the following:

- **Obtaining IPv6 space**—One of the first steps of becoming a commercial IPv6 ISP is getting IPv6 space. For Tier-1 and very large providers, the IPv6 address space must be requested from one of the three RIRs. Then, intermediate IPv6 providers such as Tier-2 and Tier-3 providers should request their IPv6 address spaces from Tier-1 providers. The number of intermediate levels is not fixed.

- **Peering**—After the ISPs receive their IPv6 address spaces, they have to establish peering between them through neutral places such as NAPs. BGP4+ is the *de facto* EGP routing protocol used between ISPs to perform peering for IPv6.

- **Address space reassignment**—Customers and enterprises want addresses and IPv6 connectivity, but they cannot request IPv6 space from RIRs. Therefore, ISPs must reassign IPv6 address space to their customers. The reassignment of the address space has one consequence for the customers. If a customer changes IPv6 providers, it must renumber its site because of IPv6's strict aggregation policy. Moreover, IPv6 does not support the concept of portable address space. However, IPv6 has mechanisms to facilitate network renumbering in a site.

- **Route aggregation**—In IPv6, it is mandatory for ISPs to aggregate the routing entries from their customers. In practice, only the prefixes allocated by the registry to the ISP must be announced in the global IPv6 routing table. The strict aggregation should limit the number of entries in the global IPv6 routing table.

## Exchanging Traffic in NAPs

Network access points (NAPs) are neutral places where providers can exchange traffic and routes. NAPs generally have high-speed network infrastructures to interconnect the providers' links and routers.

If you are operating an IPv6 ISP, you probably need to be connected to an IPv6 NAP to exchange traffic with other peers. ISPs within NAPs exchange routes, but no default route is announced. Many advanced NAPs offer route servers to optimize peering and enforce route policing.

Because NAPs are generally based on Layer 2, it is possible for them to enable native IPv6 on their infrastructure with minimal effort. With IPv6, the agreements between the peers and the NAPs should not need to be modified because the IPv6 protocol does not introduce new issues. However, if a route server is present in the NAP, it must be enabled to IPv6 to be exploited by the IPv6 peers.

NAPs that support IPv6 are emerging around the world. In January 2003, 13 native IPv6 NAPs were operational and offering services to IPv6 Tier-1 providers—six in the U.S., two in Japan, two in the U.K., one in Germany, one in the Netherlands, and one in South Korea.

---

**NOTE**     You can find a list of the operational IPv6 NAPs at www.v6nap.net/

---

### Scenarios for Establishing IPv6 Peering

The following are scenarios for establishing peering between the IPv6 ISPs in a NAP:

- **Using link-local address for BGP4+**—IPv6 ISPs within a NAP might not want to use the IPv6 prefix from other IPv6 ISPs to configure their router's interfaces. By configuring IPv6 link-local addresses in their BGP4+ configurations, the IPv6 ISPs do not need a specific IPv6 prefix. This scenario appears as neutral for establishing peering between the IPv6 ISPs. However, the use of a link-local address in BGP4+ mandates a specific configuration. Refer to the section "Configuring BGP4+ for IPv6 Using Link-Local Addresses" in Chapter 4 to get detailed information about this specific configuration.

- **Using the aggregatable global unicast prefix registered by the NAP**—APNIC, ARIN, and RIPE NCC assigned /48 and /64 prefixes to NAPs to establish peering between the IPv6 ISPs. This scenario can also appear as neutral for the establishment of peering between the IPv6 ISPs. Refer to www.ripe.net/cgi-bin/ipv6allocs to see the list of aggregatable global unicast prefixes assigned to NAPs.

- **Sharing prefixes between IPv6 ISPs**—Another conventional scenario is the sharing of prefixes between IPv6 ISPs connected in the NAP, especially if the NAP does not provide IPv6 connectivity or aggregatable global unicast prefixes to IPv6 ISPs.

### Coexistence and Transition Strategies

With the transition from IPv4 to IPv6, some NAPs might offer coexistence and transition mechanisms such as 6to4 relay and tunnel server services. Chapter 5 has detailed information about the 6to4 relay and tunnel server.

## Connecting Customer Networks to IPv6 Providers

Assume that a customer wants IPv6 addresses and connectivity. The first step for the customer to get addresses and connectivity consists in finding a commercial IPv6 ISP. Because IPv6 can coexist concurrently on IPv4 infrastructures, it is highly possible that your IPv4 provider is already offering IPv6 connectivity through coexistence or transition mechanisms. Otherwise, the customer needs to interconnect its network to an IPv6 provider.

Following the agreement with the IPv6 provider, the customer should receive at least one /48 prefix and possibly more depending of its needs.

After the customer receives its IPv6 address space from the provider, it should design an IPv6 addressing plan using these two rules:

- Determine the number of current and future subnets within its sites

- Assign one /64 prefix to each subnet (not working with different netmask values as with IPv4)

Figure 7-8 shows prefix allocations within a customer site. First, an IPv6 provider allocates the 2001:420:0100::/48 prefix to the customer. Then the customer assigns one /64 prefix to each subnet within the network. The subnet between routers R1 and R2 is 2001:420:0100:1::/64, the subnet between routers R1 and R3 is 2001:420:0100:2::/64, and so on.

**Figure 7-8**   *Allocations of /64 Prefixes Within a Customer's Network*

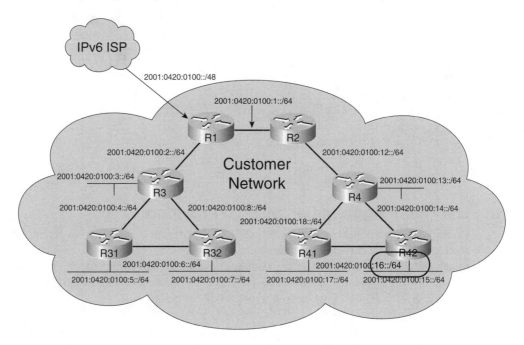

There are no clear guidelines for the reassignment of IPv6 prefixes within a site. However, an IETF informational document proposes an efficient method to help people making their addressing plans for IPv6. This IETF Internet draft can be found at www.ietf.org/internet-drafts/draft-ietf-ipv6-ipaddressassign-06.txt.

## Address Space Reassignment by IPv6 Providers

Figure 7-9 shows an aggregatable global unicast IPv6 address space allocated to four customers by two providers. The ISP NY gets the prefix 2001:0400::/32 from its RIR. Then it assigns 2001:0400:45::/48 to customer LGA and 2001:0400:b10::/48 to customer JFK. The second ISP UK gets the prefix 2001:0600::/32 from its RIR. Then it assigns 2001:0600:a1::/48 to customer LHR and 2001:0600:a2::/48 to customer YXU.

**Figure 7-9** *Allocations of /48 Prefixes by ISPs to Customers*

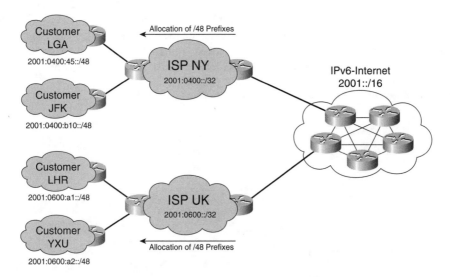

## Routing and Route Aggregation by IPv6 Providers

Figure 7-10 shows typical routing for the two ISPs and the four customers' sites connected. The routing table in ISP NY shows that the route 2001:0400:45::/48 points out customer LGA's router, and the route 2001:0400:b10::/48 points out router R2 of customer JFK. The routing table in ISP UK shows that the route 2001:0600:a1::/48 points out customer LHR's router, and the route 2001:0600:a2::/48 points out router R4 of customer YXU.

**Figure 7-10**  *Route Aggregation by ISPs*

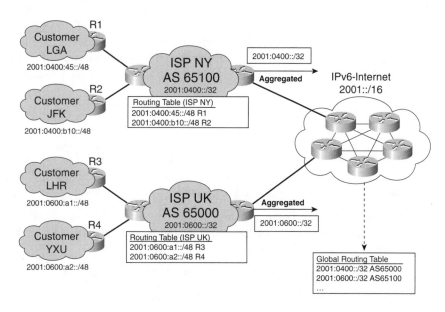

Both ISPs aggregate routes of their customers and announce only one route each to the IPv6 Internet. Therefore, the IPv6 Internet global routing table contains only the aggregated routes of these providers.

## Connecting as Host Using Transition and Coexistence Mechanisms

Hosts located on the current IPv4 Internet can link to the IPv6 Internet using transition and coexistence mechanisms. As mentioned in Chapter 5, the configured tunnel and the 6to4 mechanism can be used to connect a single host with dual-stack support to an IPv6 network over the IPv4 Internet.

The provider can also deploy a tunnel server or a router acting as a 6to4 site on the IPv4 Internet to provide IPv6 connectivity to its clients through the current IPv4 infrastructure.

# Industry Support and Trends

IPv6 is not just a new technology to replace the existing IPv4 protocol or simply a new trend developed by engineers around the world. IPv6 represents the normal evolution of the Internet for the next decades. In the long term, the main goal of IPv6 is to provide a global standard allowing electronic communication networks and devices such as computers, PDAs, cell phones, televisions, satellites, industrial machines, and so on to be interconnected within the same global digital network.

The work to achieve that goal is currently huge and difficult to figure out. The deployment of IPv6 around the world requires the full support of and efficient collaboration between research, industry, governments, standards bodies, and local and international IPv6 leaders. This section discusses industry support and trends for IPv6. IPv6 is promoted and driven by the IPv6 Forum, 3G industry, and several regional initiatives supported by governments, such as 6NET, the European IPv6 Task Force, the Japan IPv6 Promotion Council, and the North American IPv6 Task Force.

# IPv6 Forum

The IPv6 Forum is an international consortium of leading industries and research and educational networks. More than 100 members are involved in the IPv6 Forum, representing industries such as manufacturers, providers, and end users.

The main goal of the IPv6 Forum is to promote IPv6 by improving market and user awareness of IPv6. The IPv6 Forum does not design any standards or specifications for IPv6 because that responsibility is assumed by the IETF.

The IPv6 Forum has formed alliances with other international consortia:

- ETSI, the European Telecommunications Standards Institute (www.etsi.org/)

- UMTS Forum (www.umts-forum.org)

- 3GPP Project (www.3gpp.org/)

- Wireless Communications Association International (www.wcai.com/)

---

**NOTE**      More information about the IPv6 Forum can be found at www.ipv6forum.com

---

# 6NET

*6NET* is a European project launched to demonstrate that the continued growth of the Internet can be sustained on a very large scale using the new IPv6 protocol. The 6NET project aims to make European research and industry the world leader in the development of the networking technologies' next generation. More specifically, the main objectives of the 6NET project are the following:

- Deploying an international pilot IPv6 network based on 155 Mbps and increasing to 2.5 Gbps with static and mobile components to gain expertise on IPv6 deployment issues

- Testing migration strategies for IPv6 networks with the existing IPv4 infrastructure

- Introducing new IPv6 services and applications

- Collaborating with standardization bodies (IETF, 3GPP, ITU) and promoting the IPv6 technology

| NOTE | More information about 6NET can be found at www.6net.org. |
|------|----------------------------------------------------------|

## European IPv6 Task Force

The European IPv6 Task Force was launched in 2001 by the European Commission. The European IPv6 Task Force currently is in its second phase. The first phase allowed the task force to gain expertise in and awareness of IPv6. The task force's main objectives are the following:

- Promoting the development of applications that will make a real business case for IPv6. The home service and transportation industries are targeted.

- Promoting IPv6 for European research and industry and meeting European industry leaders and government officials.

- Increasing support for IPv6 in public networks and services.

- Organizing educational activities about IPv6.

- Integrating IPv6 in all strategic plans regarding new Internet services to be offered in Europe.

- Collaborating with standardization and Internet governance bodies such as ISOC, IETF, ICANN, ITU, RIPE NCC, 3GPP, ETSI, IPv6 Forum, ETNO, UMTS Forum, and GSM Europe.

| NOTE | More information about the European IPv6 Task Force can be found at www.ipv6tf.org. |
|------|------------------------------------------------------------------------------------|

## Japan IPv6 Promotion Council

The e-Japan Priority Policy Program, established in 2001, states that Japan will realize an Internet environment equipped with IPv6 by 2005. Everyone in Japan will be able to receive, share, and transmit information securely, promptly, and easily over IPv6 regardless of location. The Japan IPv6 Promotion Council is an initiative launched by the Japanese government to facilitate IPv6 cooperation with nongovernment organizations in Japan. The main objectives of the Japan IPv6 Promotion Council are as follows:

- Gathering wide-range intelligence from enterprises, government bodies, organizations, and personal users

- Assuming international leadership within the field of Internet deployment

- Developing human resources to maintain and develop an advanced information and telecommunications network society in Japan

- Creating and supporting new businesses related to hardware and software associated with networks and terminals

- Promoting IPv6 for Japanese research and industry

---

**NOTE**    More information on the Japan IPv6 Promotion Council can be found at www.v6pc.jp/en/

---

## North America IPv6 Task Force

When you look at the number of aggregatable global unicast IPv6 prefixes registered by the RIRs in Asia, Europe, and the U.S., you can see that North American research and industry are far behind Asia and Europe in the number of organizations that have received an IPv6 address space. This is why Asia and Europe have begun the early adoption of IPv6 and have initiated IPv6 task forces to deploy, test, and promote IPv6 and add new IPv6 services before North America.

In North America, people are probably less aware of IPv6 simply because the IPv4 shortage has not yet begun. This is not the case in Asia and Europe, where getting IPv4 address space is difficult and costly in several countries.

In 2002, the North American IPv6 Task Force was launched to be the North American counterpart of the Asian and European IPv6 task forces. The main objectives of the North American IPv6 Task Force are as follows:

- Writing Best Current Practice documentation for the deployment of IPv6 in North America

- Testing and evaluating migration strategies for IPv6 networks within Enterprise networks

- Developing next-generation applications

- Working on wireless and broadband deployments within North America

- Organizing IPv6 training and seminars

- Collaborating with standardization bodies (IETF, 3GPP, ITU) and promoting IPv6 for the North American military and research industries

---

**NOTE**    More information about North American IPv6 Task Force can be found at www.nav6tf.org

---

# 3G

3G stands for the third generation of wireless communication technology. The 3G aims to standardize wireless platforms, allowing the integration of voice calls, fax, e-mail, videoconferencing, radio, mapping, and so on in a global roaming environment in full interaction with the Internet. The 3G technology should allow data rates up to 2 Mbps for any mobile device, compared to 144 Kbps with the 2.5G (GPRS) or 10 Kbps with the 2G (GSM).

**NOTE**    GPRS stands for General Packet Radio Service, and GSM stands for Global System for Mobile communications. Both standards are related to cellular technology.

Obviously, the wireless devices for the 3G are based on an IP stack. Because the number of 3G devices to be manufactured in the next years is so huge (several billions of devices), the 3G standards bodies adopted IPv6 as the de facto IP stack for the 3G technology:

- **UMTS (Universal Mobile Telecommunications System)**—UMTS is the European brand name for the 3G. It bases its architecture on IPv6. The 3GPP is the body responsible for the evolution of the current GSM systems into 3G (UMTS). 3GPP coordinates with the IETF.

- **CDMA-2000 (Code Division Multiple Access)**—CDMA-2000 is the North American brand name for the 3G. It bases its architecture on IPv6—more specifically, on Mobile IPv6. The 3GPP2 is the body responsible for the evolution of CDMA One systems into 3G (CDMA-2000). 3GPP2 coordinates with the IETF.

IPv6 also received a clear commitment from wireless vendors such as Ericsson, Motorola, Nokia, and NTT.

People in the industry have to change their minds about IP, because the IPv6 protocol is not only designed to provide addresses and standards to computers on networks. The applicability of IPv6 is global to any electronic device. It is not limited to computers.

As discussed in this section, the 3G is another important driver for IPv6.

**NOTE**    More information about 3G, 3GPP, and 3GPP2 can be found at www.3gpp.org/ and www.3gpp2.org/

## Mobile Wireless Internet Forum (MWIF)

The Mobile Wireless Internet Forum (MWIF) was founded in 2000 to drive acceptance and adoption of mobile wireless and Internet architectures. The MWIF works on 3GPP and 3GPP2 architectures that are based on the IPv6 protocol. Here are the main objectives of the MWIF:

- Publishing studies, discoveries, and conclusions about mobile technologies.

- Working to harmonize between 3GPP and 3GPP2's core network architecture. The core network of both architectures is specifically based on IPv6.

- Promoting the vision of influencing global wireless industry standards that improve interoperability of mobile technologies.

| | |
|---|---|
| **NOTE** | More information about MWIF can be found at www.mwif.org |

## Governments

IPv6 is an emerging standard at an early stage of commercial deployment. For some countries, IPv6 represents an opportunity to place their industries at the forefront of this market.

More specifically, the Japanese government introduced tax incentives for IPv6 in its 2002 budget. The Japanese government is interested in attracting manufacturers and enterprises that will develop new technologies to be compatible with IPv6.

The European Commission made a clear commitment to IPv6 by providing funding and by recommending that the European industry base its new generation of products and technologies on IPv6.

In North America, an IPv6 task force that includes the U.S., Canada, and Mexico has been launched to encourage the use of IPv6 in the industry as much as possible. The U.S. military is one of the leading organizations participating in this task force.

# Summary

This chapter examined the 6bone, including its architecture, which is based on the pseudo-TLA, providers, and end sites. It also looked at assigning address spaces to pTLA within the 3ffe::/16 prefix allocated by the IANA, the steps to become a pTLA, and the routing policy enforced in the 6bone.

This chapter also examined the former and current policy allocation of IPv6 address spaces to providers on the production IPv6 Internet. Address spaces are allocated by regional Internet registries. You also reviewed the criteria for becoming an IPv6 Tier-1 provider on the IPv6 Internet and reassigning IPv6 addresses to customers.

This chapter also discussed how providers can deploy IPv6 connectivity to customer networks (end sites) and how providers can exchange and establish peering with other providers using native IPv6 network access points. Examples of address space reassignment, routing, and route aggregation by providers were also presented.

Finally, this chapter discussed industry support and trends for IPv6.

# Review Questions

Answer the following questions, and then refer to Appendix B, "Answers to Review Questions," for the answers.

1  What is the 6bone?

2  What name is assigned to backbone nodes physically and logically connected on the 6bone that exchange routes?

3  What is *not* advertised by the pTLAs on the 6bone?

4  What aggregatable global unicast IPv6 address space is assigned by the IANA for 6bone operation?

5  In the following table, specify whether the prefixes are allowed or prohibited on the 6bone according to the 6bone's routing policy.

| Prefix | Allowed or Prohibited? |
|---|---|
| 3ffe:3000::/24 | |
| Fec0:2100::/24 | |
| 3ffe:82e0::/28 | |
| 2001:04e0::/32 | |
| 2003:410::/32 | |
| 3ffe:b00:c18::/48 | |
| Fec0::/16 | |
| 3ffe:400a::/32 | |
| Fec0:3100::2:8/126 | |
| ::/0 | |
| ::1 | |
| ::0 | |
| Fe02::/16 | |

*continues*

| Prefix | Allowed or Prohibited? |
| --- | --- |
| 2001:0648::/35 | |
| Fe80::/16 | |
| 2001:350:1::/48 | |

**6** Which RIRs allocate IPv6 address space to providers?

**7** Which aggregatable global unicast prefix did the IANA allocate for the production of the IPv6 Internet?

**8** What IPv6 prefix length was allocated during the initial allocation policy by the RIRs in 1999?

**9** What are the main criteria to get IPv6 address space in the current allocation policy?

**10** List the rules for the reassignment of address spaces to customers by the providers.

**11** What are the basic steps for an ISP to become an IPv6 provider?

**12** List the two neutral scenarios presented in this chapter to establish IPv6 peering between the IPv6 ISPs in a NAP.

**13** Does the IPv6 Forum design standards and specifications for IPv6?

**14** List the main regional IPv6 initiatives/projects for Asia, Europe, and North America. Then list two international organizations that are considered important drivers for IPv6.

**15** What is the main long-term goal of IPv6?

# References

RFC 2471, *IPv6 Testing Address Allocation,* R. Hinden, R. Fink, J. Postel, IETF, www.ietf.org/rfc/rfc2471.txt, December 1998

RFC 2772, *6Bone Backbone Routing Guidelines,* R. Rockwell, R. Fink, IETF, www.ietf.org/rfc/rfc2772.txt, February 2000

RFC 2921, *6Bone pTLA and pNLA Formats (pTLA),* R. Fink, IETF, www.ietf.org/rfc/rfc2921.txt, September 2000

RFC 3177, *IAB/IESG Recommendations on IPv6 Address Allocations to Sites,* IAB, IETF, www.ietf.org/rfc/rfc3177.txt, September 2001

RFC 3194, *The Host-Density Ratio for Address Assignment Efficiency: An update on the H ratio,* C. Huitema, A. Durand, IETF, www.ietf.org/rfc/rfc3194.txt, November 2001

3GPP, www.3gpp.org

3GPP2, www.3gpp2.org

6bone, www.6bone.net

6NET, www.6net.org

European IPv6 Task Force, www.ipv6tf.org

IPv6 Forum, www.ipv6forum.com

Japan IPv6 Promotion Council, www.v6pc.jp/en/

Mobile Wireless Internet Forum, www.mwif.org

North American IPv6 Task Force, www.nav6tf.org

Operational IPv6 NAP, www.v6nap.net

# PART V

# Appendixes

The appendixes at the end of this book represent a summary of the Cisco IOS Software IPv6 commands presented in this book, the answers to the review questions in each chapter, and a list of RFCs related to IPv6. In addition, the glossary defines the new terms introduced for the IPv6 protocol.

# Cisco IOS Software IPv6 Commands

This appendix gathers, defines, and groups all the IPv6 Cisco IOS Software commands presented in this book. These commands are also referenced by the chapter in which they appear.

**Table A-1** *Enabling IPv6 on Cisco IOS Software Technology*

| Command | Description | Type | Reference |
|---|---|---|---|
| `ipv6 unicast-routing` | Enables the forwarding of unicast IPv6 packets on the router. | Global | Chapter 2 |

**Table A-2** *Assigning an IPv6 Address and Parameters on an Interface*

| Command | Description | Type | Reference |
|---|---|---|---|
| `ipv6 address` `ipv6-address/` `prefix-length` `[link-local]` `[eui-64]` | Specifies an IPv6 address and a prefix length to be assigned to the network interface. By default, when a site-local or aggregatable global unicast address is specified with this command, the link-local address is automatically configured. The **link-local** parameter is an optional argument used when the IPv6 address to assign is a link-local address. **eui-64** is another optional parameter that may be used to automatically complete the low-order 64-bit of the IPv6 address. | Interface | Chapter 2 |
| `ipv6 enable` | Enables IPv6 on an interface and automatically configures the link-local address. | Interface | Chapter 2 |
| `ipv6 unnumbered` `interface` | Forces an interface to use the site-local or aggregatable global Interface unicast address of another interface as the source address for packet originating. | Interface | Chapter 2 |
| `ipv6 mtu bytes` | Configures an MTU value on a network interface. | Interface | Chapter 2 |
| `show ipv6 mtu` | Displays the path MTU cache per destination. | EXEC mode | Chapter 3 |
| `show ipv6 interface` `interface` | Displays parameters related to the IPv6 configuration applied to a specific interface. | EXEC mode | Chapter 2 |

**Table A-3**    *Replacing ARP and Prefix Advertisement (Neighbor Discovery Protocol)*

| Command | Description | Type | Reference |
|---|---|---|---|
| `show ipv6 neighbors` *ipv6-address-or-name* \| *interface_type interface_number* | Displays neighbor entries of the neighbor discovery table. | EXEC mode | Chapter 3 |
| `ipv6 neighbor` *ipv6-address interface hw-address* | Adds a static entry to the neighbor discovery table. Both the network interface and the hardware address must be specified. | Global | Chapter 3 |
| `clear ipv6 neighbors` | Removes all entries of the neighbor discovery table. | Global | Chapter 3 |
| `ipv6 nd ns-interval` *milliseconds* | Specifies a new neighbor solicitation time interval. | Interface | Chapter 3 |
| `ipv6 nd reachable-time` *milliseconds* | Specifies a new neighbor discovery reachable-time interval for the detection of dead neighbors in the neighbor discovery table. | Interface | Chapter 3 |
| `ipv6 nd prefix` *ipv6-prefix/ prefix-length* \| `default` [[*valid-lifetime preferred-lifetime*] \| [`at` *valid-date preferred-date*] [`off-link`] [`no-autoconfig`] [`no-advertise`]] | Defines parameters of a prefix advertised on a network interface. | Interface | Chapter 3 |
| `no ipv6 nd prefix` *ipv6-prefix* | Removes an advertised IPv6 prefix. | Interface | Chapter 3 |
| `ipv6 nd suppress-ra` | Suppresses router advertisement on an interface. | Interface | Chapter 3 |
| `no ipv6 nd suppress-ra` | Cancels the suppression of router advertisements. | Interface | Chapter 3 |
| `ipv6 nd ra-lifetime` *seconds* | Defines the lifetime of router advertisement messages. The minimum value is 0, and the maximum value is 9000 seconds. | Interface | Chapter 3 |
| `ipv6 nd ra-interval` *seconds* | Defines the interval between consecutive router advertisement messages. The minimum value is 3 seconds, and the maximum value is 1800 seconds. | Interface | Chapter 3 |

**Table A-3**    *Replacing ARP and Prefix Advertisement (Neighbor Discovery Protocol) (Continued)*

| Command | Description | Type | Reference |
|---|---|---|---|
| `ipv6 nd managed-config-flag` | If this flag is set, the nodes should use a stateful autoconfiguration mechanism (but not stateless autoconfiguration). By default, this flag is turned off. | Interface | Chapter 3 |
| `ipv6 nd other-config-flag` | If this flag is set, the nodes using a stateful autoconfiguration mechanism can configure parameters other than the IPv6 address. By default, this flag is turned off. | Interface | Chapter 3 |
| `ipv6 nd dad attempts` *number* | Defines the number of router solicitation messages for duplicate address detection (DAD) to send on the link before considering an IPv6 address unique. The value 0 disables the DAD mechanism. | Interface | Chapter 3 |
| `show ipv6 interface` *interface* `prefix` | Displays parameters of the prefix advertised on an interface. | EXEC mode | Chapter 3 |
| `show ipv6 routers` | Displays router advertisement information received from other routers. | EXEC mode | Chapter 3 |
| `debug ipv6 nd` | Enables debugging for neighbor discovery messages. | EXEC mode | Chapter 3 |

**Table A-4**    *ICMPv6 and Route Redirection*

| Command | Description | Type | Reference |
|---|---|---|---|
| `ipv6 icmp error-interval` *msec* | Defines the minimum interval in milliseconds between ICMPv6 error messages. | Global | Chapter 3 |
| `debug ipv6 icmp` | Enables debugging for ICMPv6 messages. Logs are printed on the console port. | EXEC mode | Chapter 3 |
| `undebug ipv6 icmp` | Deactivates debugging mode for ICMPv6 messages. | EXEC mode | Chapter 3 |

*continues*

**Table A-4**    *ICMPv6 and Route Redirection (Continued)*

| Command | Description | Type | Reference |
|---|---|---|---|
| `no ipv6 redirects` | Disables the sending of ICMPv6 redirect messages. | Interface | Chapter 3 |
| `ipv6 redirects` | Enables the sending of ICMPv6 redirect messages. By default, ICMPv6 redirect is enabled on all interfaces. | Interface | Chapter 3 |

**Table A-5**    *IPv6 Access Control List*

| Command | Description | Type | Reference |
|---|---|---|---|
| `ipv6 access-list access-list-name` | Defines the name of a standard or extended IPv6 access control list. *access-list-name* is the name of the ACL. | Global | Chapter 3 |
| `ipv6 traffic-filter access-list-name {in \| out}` | Applies an IPv6 access control list to an interface. *access-list-name* is the name of the ACL. The IPv6 ACL may be used to filter incoming (**in**) or outgoing (**out**) traffic. | Interface | Chapter 3 |
| `ipv6 access-list access-list-name {permit \| deny} {source-ipv6-prefix/prefix-length \| any \| host host-ipv6-address} {destination-ipv6-prefix/prefix-length \| any \| host host-ipv6-address} [log \| log-input]` | Defines a statement to create a standard IPv6 access control list. *access-list-name* is the name of the ACL. The **permit** and **deny** actions specify the condition to be applied. The source may be *source-ipv6-prefix/prefix-length* or **any** addresses or a single IPv6 address (**host** *host-ipv6-address* ). The destination address may be *destination-ipv6-prefix/prefix-length* or **any** addresses or a single IPv6 address (**host** *host-ipv6-address*). The **log** keyword enables the logging of events. **log-input** includes the input interface and the source MAC address where applicable for the logging. | Global | Chapter 3 |

**Table A-5**    *IPv6 Access Control List (Continued)*

| Command | Description | Type | Reference |
|---|---|---|---|
| `ipv6 access-list` *access-list-name* {**permit** \| **deny**} [*protocol*] {*source-ipv6-prefix/prefix-length* \| **any** \| **host** *host-ipv6-address*} [**eq** \| **neq** \| **lt** \| **gt** \| **range** *source-port(s)*] {*destination-ipv6-prefix/prefix-length* \| **any** \| **host** *host-ipv6-address*} [**eq** \| **neq** \| **lt** \| **gt** \| **range** *destination-port(s)*] [**dscp** *value*] [**flow-label** *value*] [**fragments**] [**routing**] [**undetermined-transport**] [[**reflect** *reflexive-access-list-name*] [**timeout** *value*]] [**time-range** *time-range-name*] [**log** \| **log-input**] [**sequence** *value*] | Defines a statement to create an extended IPv6 access control list. *access-list-name* is the name of the ACL. The **permit** and **deny** actions specify the condition to be applied. The optional keyword *protocol* identifies the upper-layer protocols (icmp,tcp,udp,..). The source may be *source-ipv6-prefix/prefix-length* or **any** addresses or a single IPv6 address (**host** *host-ipv6-address*). Operators such as **eq, neq, lt, gt** and **range** may be specified for the source. The destination address may be *destination-ipv6-prefix/prefix-length* or **any** addresses or a single IPv6 address (**host** *host-ipv6-address*). The operators for the source are also available for the destination. New optional keywords such as **dscp, flow-label, fragments, routing**, and **undetermined-transport** may be applied. The **reflect** keyword applies a reflexive IPv6 access control list. The **time-range** keyword enables a time-based IPv6 access control list. The **log** keyword enables the logging of events. **log-input** includes the input interface and the source MAC address where applicable for the logging. | Global | Chapter 3 |
| `show ipv6 access-list` [*access-list-name*] | Displays the IPv6 access control list defined in the router. The number of matches against each statement is displayed. The entries can be cleared using the **clear ipv6 access-list** command. | EXEC mode | Chapter 3 |

*continues*

**Table A-5** *IPv6 Access Control List (Continued)*

| Command | Description | Type | Reference |
|---|---|---|---|
| `clear ipv6 access-list` [*access-list-name*] | Clears the IPv6 access control list hit counters. | EXEC mode | Chapter 3 |
| `debug ipv6 packet` [`access-list` *access-list-name*] [`detail`] | Enables IPv6 packet-level debugging. You can specify an IPv6 access control list name using the *access-list-name* parameter. | EXEC mode | Chapter 3 |

**Table A-6** *DNS*

| Command | Description | Type | Reference |
|---|---|---|---|
| `ipv6 host` *name* [*port*] *ipv6-address* [*ipv6-address* ...] | Defines a static host name-to-IPv6 address mapping. | Global | Chapter 3 |
| `ip name-server` *ipv6-address* | Configures the IPv6 address of a native IPv6 DNS server that the router can query over IPv6. The router may accept up to six different name servers. | Global | Chapter 3 |
| `ip domain-lookup` | Enables the domain lookup on the router. | Global | Chapter 3 |

**Table A-7** *IOS IPv6 Tools*

| Command | Description | Type | Reference |
|---|---|---|---|
| `ping ipv6` *ipv6-address* | Sends ICMPv6 echo request messages to an IPv6 destination address. | EXEC mode | Chapter 3 |
| `telnet` *ipv6-address* | Initiates a Telnet session to an IPv6-enabled destination Telnet server. | EXEC mode | Chapter 3 |
| `ip http server` | Enables the HTTP server on the router. The HTTP server is enabled for both IPv4 and IPv6. | Global | Chapter 3 |

**Table A-7**    *IOS IPv6 Tools (Continued)*

| Command | Description | Type | Reference |
|---|---|---|---|
| `traceroute ipv6` *ipv6-address* | Traces the route to reach an IPv6 destination. | EXEC mode | Chapter 3 |
| `ssh` [`-l` *userid*] [`-c` {**des** \| **3des**}] [`-o` **numberofpasswdprompts** *n*] [`-p` *portnum*] {*ipv6-address* \| *hostname*} [**command**] | Initiates an SSH session to an IPv6-enabled destination SSH server. An optional *userid* argument may be specified as the login. A crypto algorithm such as **des** or **3des** must be specified. Optionally, the number of tries may be specified for the SSH session using the **numberofpasswdprompts** keyword. You can use a destination port number other than 22 by specifying the **-p** keyword. The destination SSH server is entered using either a valid IPv6 address (*ipv6-address*) or a *hostname* corresponding to an IPv6 address. | EXEC mode | Chapter 3 |

**Table A-8**    *Configuring and Displaying Static IPv6 Routes*

| Command | Description | Type | Reference |
|---|---|---|---|
| `ipv6 route` *ipv6-prefix/prefix-length* {*next-hop* \| *interface*} [*distance*] | Defines a static IPv6 route on the router. The *ipv6-prefix* parameter is the destination IPv6 network in the IPv6 address format. *prefix-length* is the length of the IPv6 prefix given. *next-hop* is an IPv6 address used to reach the destination IPv6 network. *interface* can be used to direct the static route out of the interface, such as serial links or tunnels. *distance* is an optional parameter that sets the administrative distance. By default, the administrative distance of a static route is 1. | Global | Chapter 4 |

*continues*

**Table A-8** *Configuring and Displaying Static IPv6 Routes (Continued)*

| Command | Description | Type | Reference |
|---|---|---|---|
| `ipv6 route` *ipv6-prefix/prefix-length* `interface` *link-local-address* [*distance*] | Defines a static IPv6 route using a link-local address as the next-hop argument. When the next-hop address has to be a link-local address, this definition is mandatory to identify the corresponding network interface on the router. | Global | Chapter 4 |
| `ipv6 route ::/0` *interface next-hop* [*distance*] | Defines a default IPv6 route on the router. The destination IPv6 network **::/0** means any IPv6 address. | Global | Chapter 4 |
| `show ipv6 route` [*ipv6-prefix/prefix-length* \| *ipv6-address* \| `connected` \| `local` \| `static` \| `rip` \| `bgp` \| `isis` \| `ospf`] | Displays the router's current IPv6 routing table. The optional argument *ipv6-prefix/prefix-length* may be used to display routing information for a single IPv6 route. The optional argument *ipv6-address* may be used to display routing information for a single IPv6 address. Routing information regarding a specific routing protocol may be displayed using the optional keywords **connected**, **local**, **static**, **rip**, **bgp**, **isis**, and **ospf**. | EXEC mode | Chapter 4 |
| `show ipv6 protocols` [`summary`] | Displays the parameters and current state of the active IPv6 routing protocol process, including the redistribution between the protocols. | EXEC mode | Chapter 4 |

**Table A-9**     *BGP4+*

| Command | Description | Type | Reference |
|---|---|---|---|
| `router bgp autonomous-system` | Enables a BGP process on the router and specifies the local autonomous system. This is the same command as in IPv4. | Global | Chapter 4 |
| `no bgp default ipv4-unicast` | By default, the advertisement of routing information for the IPv4 address family is activated automatically for each BGP session using the **neighbor [..]remote-as** command. If you use the **no bgp default ipv4-unicast** command, only the IPv6 address family is advertised in BGP updates. | BGP4+ subcommand mode | Chapter 4 |
| `bgp router-id ipv4-address` | Defines the local router ID parameter for the BGP process. The local router ID parameter for BGP has the same size and format for both IPv4 and IPv6. The local router ID is a 32-bit number written as four octets separated by periods (dotted-decimal format). When no IPv4 is set on the router (an IPv6-only router), the local router ID parameter must be defined. You can use any IPv4 address as a value for the **router-id** parameter. | BGP4+ subcommand mode | Chapter 4 |
| `neighbor ipv6-address remote-as autonomous-system` | Defines a BGP neighbor. *ipv6-address* is the BGP neighbor's next-hop IPv6 address. This command defines either the IBGP or EBGP neighbor. | BGP4+ subcommand mode | Chapter 4 |
| `neighbor ipv6-address peer-group peer-group-name` | Assigns an IPv6 address of a BGP neighbor to a peer group. | BGP+4 subcommand mode | Chapter 4 |
| `address-family ipv6 [unicast]` | Places the router in the address family IPv6 configuration submode. The **unicast** keyword is optional. By default, the router is placed in the unicast address family IPv6. | BGP4+ subcommand mode | Chapter 4 |

*continues*

**Table A-9** *BGP4+ (Continued)*

| Command | Description | Type | Reference |
|---|---|---|---|
| `exit-address-family` | Leaves address family configuration mode and returns to BGP subcommand mode. | BGP4+ subcommand mode | Chapter 4 |
| `neighbor {ip-address | peer-group-name | ipv6-address} activate` | Enables the exchange of information with the BGP neighbor. The BGP neighbor can be an IPv4 address, the name of a BGP peer group, or an IPv6 address. By default, the exchange of information with BGP neighbors is enabled for the IPv4 address family only. However, when the neighbor is an IPv6 address, this command must be used to activate the IPv6 BGP peer. | address-family subcommand mode | Chapter 4 |
| `network ipv6-prefix/prefix-length` | Specifies an IPv6 prefix to announce via BGP4+ for this AS. The IPv6 prefix is entered into the BGP4+ routing table. | address-family subcommand mode | Chapter 4 |
| `neighbor {peer-group-name | ipv6-address} prefix-list prefix-list-name {in | out}` | Applies an IPv6 prefix list to a BGP neighbor to filter input or output route announcements. The *ipv6-address* argument is the neighbor's next-hop IPv6 address. Optionally, the IPv6 address can be a *peer-group-name* instead. The *prefix-list-name* argument following the **prefix-list** keyword is the name of the IPv6 prefix list. The **in** and **out** keywords applied on the prefix list are to inbound or outbound update messages. | address-family subcommand mode | Chapter 4 |

**Table A-9**    *BGP4+ (Continued)*

| Command | Description | Type | Reference |
|---|---|---|---|
| neighbor {peer-group-name \| ipv6-address} **route-map** map-tag {**in** \| **out**} | Applies an IPv6 prefix list to a BGP neighbor to modify the input or output route attributes. The *ipv6-address* argument is the neighbor's next-hop IPv6 address. Optionally, the IPv6 address can be a *peer-group-name* instead. The *map-tag* argument following the **route-map** keyword is the name of the route map. The **in** and **out** keywords applied on the route map are to inbound or outbound update messages. | address-family subcommand mode | Chapter 4 |
| neighbor link-local-address **remote-as** autonomous-system | Defines a BGP neighbor using its link-local address instead of an aggregatable global unicast address. The *link-local-address* argument is the link-local address of the BGP neighbor. | BGP4+ subcommand mode | Chapter 4 |
| neighbor link-local-address **update-source** interface | Identifies the network interface corresponding to the neighbor's link-local address. | BGP4+ subcommand mode | Chapter 4 |
| neighbor {peer-group-name \| ipv6-address} **soft-reconfiguration inbound** | Asks the local router to store BGP updates received from members of the BGP peer group or from an *ipv6-address* without modifying them. | address-family subcommand mode | Chapter 4 |
| neighbor {ipv6-address \| peer-group-name} **password 5** password-string | Protects BGP IPv6 sessions via the TCP MD5 signature option. The *ipv6-address* argument is the BGP neighbor's IPv6 address. *peer-group-name* is the name of the BGP peer group. The **password** keyword enables authentication on the TCP connection between BGP neighbors. The number **5** stands for MD5. *password-string* is the shared secret password used on both BGP IPv6 peers. | address-family subcommand mode | Chapter 4 |

*continues*

**Table A-9**    *BGP4+ (Continued)*

| Command | Description | Type | Reference |
|---|---|---|---|
| `redistribute {bgp | connected | isis | ospf | rip | static}` | Redistributes routes learned from other protocols, such as **bgp, connected, isis, ospf, rip**, and **static**, into BGP4+. Refer to Chapter 4 for detailed information about route redistribution with BGP4+. | address-family subcommand mode | Chapter 4 |
| `show bgp ipv6 [ipv6-prefix/0-128 | community | community-list | dampened-paths | filter-list | flap-statistics | inconsistent-as | neighbors | quote-regexp | regexp | summary]` | Displays the IPv6 BGP table. See the following commands for detailed information about the keywords. | EXEC mode | Chapter 4 |
| `show bgp ipv6 ipv6-prefix/0-128` | Displays all the path information related to the IPv6 prefix and the prefix length given as an argument. | EXEC mode | Chapter 4 |
| `show bgp ipv6 community` | Displays information on the routes matching IPv6 BGP communities. | EXEC mode | Chapter 4 |
| `show bgp ipv6 community-list` | Displays information on the routes matching the IPv6 BGP community list. | EXEC mode | Chapter 4 |
| `show bgp ipv6 dampened-paths` | Displays information on the IPv6 paths suppressed due to dampening. | EXEC mode | Chapter 4 |
| `show bgp ipv6 filter-list` | Displays routes conforming to the filter list. | EXEC mode | Chapter 4 |
| `show bgp ipv6 flap-statistics` | Displays information on the flap statistics of IPv6 BGP neighbors. | EXEC mode | Chapter 4 |
| `show bgp ipv6 inconsistent-as` | Displays information on routes with inconsistent origin ASs. | EXEC mode | Chapter 4 |
| `show bgp ipv6 neighbors` | Displays information on the state of IPv6 BGP neighbors. | EXEC mode | Chapter 4 |
| `show bgp ipv6 quote-regexp` | Displays IPv6 BGP routes that match the autonomous system path regular expression as a quoted string of characters. | EXEC mode | Chapter 4 |
| `show bgp ipv6 regexp` | Displays IPv6 BGP routes that match the autonomous system path regular expression. | EXEC mode | Chapter 4 |

**Table A-9**    *BGP4+ (Continued)*

| Command | Description | Type | Reference |
|---|---|---|---|
| `show bgp summary` | Displays summary information on the state of IPv6 BGP neighbors. | EXEC mode | Chapter 4 |
| `clear bgp ipv6 *` | Resets all IPv6 BGP neighbors. | EXEC mode | Chapter 4 |
| `clear bgp ipv6 autonomous-system` | Resets all IPv6 BGP neighbors with the AS number given as an argument. | EXEC mode | Chapter 4 |
| `clear bgp ipv6 ipv6-address` | Resets the TCP connection to the BGP neighbor specified and removes from the BGP table all the routes that have been learned from this session. | EXEC mode | Chapter 4 |
| `clear bgp ipv6 dampening` | Resets all flap dampening information relating to IPv6 BGP neighbors. | EXEC mode | Chapter 4 |
| `clear bgp ipv6 external` | Resets all external IPv6 peers. | EXEC mode | Chapter 4 |
| `clear bgp ipv6 flap-statistics` | Clears all route flap statistics relating to IPv6 BGP neighbors. | EXEC mode | Chapter 4 |
| `clear bgp ipv6 peer-group peer-group-name` | Resets the TCP connection to this peer group name and removes from the BGP table all routes that have been learned from this session. | EXEC mode | Chapter 4 |
| `debug bgp ipv6 dampening` | Enables BGP routing protocol debugging for IPv6. Displays messages related to dampening. | EXEC mode | Chapter 4 |
| `debug bgp ipv6 updates` | Enables BGP routing protocol debugging for IPv6. Displays BGP4+ update messages. | EXEC mode | Chapter 4 |

**Table A-10**    *RIPng*

| Command | Description | Type | Reference |
|---|---|---|---|
| `ipv6 router rip tag` | Defines a RIPng process on the router. The *tag* argument identifies a unique process. | Global | Chapter 4 |
| `ipv6 rip tag enable` | Enables a RIPng process on an interface. | Interface | Chapter 4 |

*continues*

**Table A-10**    *RIPng (Continued)*

| Command | Description | Type | Reference |
|---------|-------------|------|-----------|
| `ipv6 rip` *tag* `default-information originate` | Generates a default IPv6 route (::/0) into a RIPng process and sends it in RIP updates. | Interface | Chapter 4 |
| `ipv6 rip` *tag* `default-information only` | Generates a default IPv6 route (::/0) into a RIPng process. However, this command suppresses the sending of any other IPv6 routes except the default IPv6 route. | Interface | Chapter 4 |
| `ipv6 rip` *tag* `summary-address` *ipv6-prefix/prefix-length* | Summarizes the IPv6 routes. When the first *prefix-length* bits of a route match the statement, the statement's prefix is advertised instead. In this case, multiple routes are replaced by a single route whose metric is the lowest metric of the multiple routes. This command may be used multiple times. | Interface | Chapter 4 |
| `distance` *distance* | Defines the administrative distance for a RIPng process. If two RIP processes attempt to insert the same IPv6 route into the same routing table, the route with the lower administrative distance takes precedence. The default value is 120. | RIPng subcommand mode | Chapter 4 |
| `distribute-list prefix-list` *prefix-list-name* `{in | out}` `[`*interface*`]` | Applies an IPv6 access list to RIPng routing updates received or sent on an interface. If no interface is specified, the IPv6 access list is applied to all interfaces on the router. | RIPng subcommand mode | Chapter 4 |
| `metric-offset` *number* | Sets the increment to a new value between 1 and 16. By default, the RIPng metric is incremented by 1 before being entered in the routing table. | RIPng subcommand mode | Chapter 4 |

**Table A-10**   *RIPng (Continued)*

| Command | Description | Type | Reference |
|---|---|---|---|
| `poison-reverse` | Performs poison-reverse processing of updates. Poison reverse causes the advertisement of an unreachable metric when RIPng advertises network IPv6 prefixes on interfaces from which it learned them. If both split horizon and poison reverse are enabled, only split horizon processing is done. Poison reverse is turned off by default. | RIPng subcommand mode | Chapter 4 |
| `split-horizon` | Performs split-horizon processing of updates. Split horizon suppresses the advertisement of network IPv6 prefixes on interfaces from which RIPng learned them. | RIPng subcommand mode | Chapter 4 |
| `port` *udp-port* `multicast-group` *multicast-address* | Defines a different UDP port number and multicast address than the default values. By default, the standardized UDP port 521 and the multicast address FF02::9 of RIPng are used by the RIPng processes. | RIPng subcommand mode | Chapter 4 |
| `timers` *update expire holddown garbage-collect* | Configures the RIPng routing timers. The *update* argument defines the periodic updates interval. The default *update* value is 30 seconds. The *expire* argument is a timeout parameter used to mark as unreachable the network prefixes that aren't heard after *n* seconds. The default *expire* value is 180 seconds. Information about unreachable network prefixes is ignored for a further *holddown* seconds. The default *holddown* value is 0. The *garbage-collect* argument deletes an expired entry in the RIPng routing table. The removal is done *garbage-collect* seconds after either the expiration or holddown termination. The default *garbage-collect* value is 120. | RIPng subcommand mode | Chapter 4 |

*continues*

**Table A-10**   *RIPng (Continued)*

| Command | Description | Type | Reference |
|---|---|---|---|
| `redistribute {bgp | connected | isis | ospf | rip | static} [metric metric-value] [level-1 | level-1-2 | level-2] [route-map map-tag]` | Redistributes routes learned from other protocols, such as **bgp**, **connected**, **isis**, **ospf**, **rip**, and **static**, into RIPng. Refer to Chapter 4 for detailed information about route redistribution with RIPng. | RIPng subcommand mode | Chapter 4 |
| `exit` | Exits RIPng configuration mode. | RIPng subcommand mode | Chapter 4 |
| `show ipv6 rip` | Displays the status of the various RIPng processes. | EXEC mode | Chapter 4 |
| `show ipv6 rip database` | Displays the RIPng database. | EXEC mode | Chapter 4 |
| `show ipv6 rip next-hops` | Displays the RIPng next hops. | EXEC mode | Chapter 4 |
| `clear ipv6 rip [name]` | Clears the RIPng database. | EXEC mode | Chapter 4 |
| `debug ipv6 rip` | Enables RIPng routing protocol debugging and displays RIPng packets sent and received on all interfaces where RIPng is enabled. | EXEC mode | Chapter 4 |
| `debug ipv6 rip interface` | Enables RIPng routing protocol debugging and displays RIPng packets sent and received on a specific interface. | EXEC mode | Chapter 4 |

**Table A-11**   *IS-IS for IPv6*

| Command | Description | Type | Reference |
|---|---|---|---|
| `router isis [tag]` | Defines the IS-IS process on the router. The *tag* parameter specifies a name for a process. | Global | Chapter 4 |
| `address-family ipv6 [unicast]` | Places the router in the address-family ipv6 configuration sub-mode. The **unicast** keyword is optional. By default, the router is placed in the unicast address-family ipv6. | IS-IS for IPv6 subcommand mode | Chapter 4 |

**Table A-11**    *IS-IS for IPv6 (Continued)*

| Command | Description | Type | Reference |
|---|---|---|---|
| `net network-entity-title` | Assigns an IS-IS NET address to the routing process. | IS-IS for IPv6 subcommand mode | Chapter 4 |
| `distance 1-254` | The default administrative distance for IS-IS is 115. However, this command sets a new administrative distance for IS-IS. | address-family subcommand mode | Chapter 4 |
| `default-information originate [route-map map-tag]` | Generates a default IPv6 route (::/0) into IS-IS for IPv6. Optionally, a route map may be used with this command. This command is the same as the **default-information** command in IPv4. | address-family subcommand mode | Chapter 4 |
| `maximum-paths 1-4` | Defines the maximum number of paths allowed for an IPv6 route learned through IS-IS. | address-family subcommand mode | Chapter 4 |
| `redistribute {bgp | ospf | rip | static} [metric metric-value] [metric-type {internal | external}] [level-1 | level-1-2 | level-2] [route-map map-tag]` | Redistributes IPv6 routes learned from other IPv6 routing protocols, such as **bgp**, **ospf**, **rip**, and **static**, into IS-IS for IPv6. A route map may be applied to this command to filter attributes of the incoming routes.<br><br>This command is the same as the **redistribute** command in IPv4. Refer to Chapter 4 for detailed information about route redistribution with IS-IS for IPv6. | address-family subcommand mode | Chapter 4 |
| `redistribute isis {level-1 | level-2} into {level-1 | level-2} distribute-list prefix-list-name` | Redistributes the IPv6 routes of the IS-IS routing table between the IS-IS areas. An IPv6 prefix list can be applied to filter the IPv6 routes to be redistributed between the areas. This command is the same as the **redistribute isis [...] into [...]** command in IPv4. Refer to Chapter 4 for detailed information about route redistribution with IS-IS for IPv6. | address-family subcommand mode | Chapter 4 |

*continues*

**Table A-11** *IS-IS for IPv6 (Continued)*

| Command | Description | Type | Reference |
|---|---|---|---|
| `no adjacency-check` | During the transition from IPv4-only IS-IS routers to IPv4-IPv6 IS-IS routers in a network, this command maintains the adjacencies between IS-IS routers using different protocol sets. This command prevents the IS-IS routers using different protocol sets from performing the hello check and dropping the adjacencies. This command must be used only during the transition. After the transition, when all IS-IS routers support both IPv4 and IPv6, this command can be removed. | address-family subcommand mode | Chapter 4 |
| `summary-prefix` *ipv6-prefix*/*prefix-length* [`level-1` \| `level-2` \| `level-1-2`] | Configures IPv6 summary prefixes. The summary IPv6 prefix, the prefix length, and the IS-IS level must be specified as parameters. | address-family subcommand mode | Chapter 4 |
| `exit-address-family` | Leaves address-family configuration mode and returns to IS-IS router configuration mode. | address-family subcommand mode | Chapter 4 |
| `ipv6 router isis` | Starts the IS-IS for IPv6 routing process on an interface. | Interface | Chapter 4 |
| `isis circuit-type` {`level-1` \| `level-1-2` \| `level-2-only`} | Configures the type of adjacency on an interface. This is the same command as in IPv4. | Interface | Chapter 4 |
| `show isis database` [`detail` \| `level-1` \| `level-2`] | Displays the contents of the IS-IS link-state database. This is the same command as in IPv4. | EXEC mode | Chapter 4 |
| `show isis topology` | Lists all connected routers in all IS-IS areas. This is the same command as in IPv4. | EXEC mode | Chapter 4 |
| `show isis route` | Displays the IS-IS level-1 routing table only. This is the same command as in IPv4. | EXEC mode | Chapter 4 |

**Table A-11**    *IS-IS for IPv6 (Continued)*

| Command | Description | Type | Reference |
|---|---|---|---|
| `show ipv6 protocols [summary]` | Shows the parameters and current state of the IPv6 routing protocol. | EXEC mode | Chapter 4 |
| `show ipv6 route is-is` | Shows only the IPv6 IS-IS routes. | EXEC mode | Chapter 4 |
| `clear isis *` | Refreshes the link-state database and recalculates all routes. | EXEC mode | Chapter 4 |
| `clear isis [tag]` | Refreshes the link-state database and recalculates all routes related to the IS-IS tag specified. | EXEC mode | Chapter 4 |
| `debug isis adj-packets` | Displays the events related to the adjacency packets. | EXEC mode | Chapter 4 |
| `debug isis update-packets` | Displays the events related to the IS-IS update packets. | EXEC mode | Chapter 4 |

**Table A-12**    *OSPFv3*

| Command | Description | Type | Reference |
|---|---|---|---|
| `ipv6 router ospf process-id` | Enables an OSPFv3 process on the router. The *process-id* parameter identifies a unique OSPFv3 process. This command is used on a global basis. | Global | Chapter 4 |
| `router-id ipv4-address` | For an IPv6-only OSPF router, a **router-id** parameter must be defined in the OSPFv3 configuration as an IPv4 address using this command. You can use any IPv4 address as a value for the local **router-id** parameter. | OSPFv3 subcommand mode | Chapter 4 |
| `area area-id range ipv6-prefix/prefix-length` | Summarizes IPv6 routes that match the *ipv6-prefix/prefix-length* parameters. | OSPFv3 subcommand mode | Chapter 4 |
| `ipv6 ospf process-id area area-id` | Identifies the IPv6 prefix assigned to this interface as part of the OSPFv3 network. This command replaces the **network area** command used with OSPFv2. | Interface | Chapter 4 |

*continues*

**Table A-12** *OSPFv3 (Continued)*

| Command | Description | Type | Reference |
|---|---|---|---|
| `redistribute {bgp | isis | rip | static}` | Redistributes IPv6 routes learned from other IPv6 routing protocols, such as **bgp**, **isis**, **rip**, and **static**, into OSPFv3. This command is the same as the **redistribute** command in IPv4. Refer to Chapter 4 for a summary of route redistribution with OSPFv3. | OSPFv3 subcommand mode | Chapter 4 |
| `show ipv6 ospf [process-id]` | Displays information about an OSPFv3 process configured on the router. | EXEC mode | Chapter 4 |
| `show ipv6 ospf database` | Displays the contents of the topological database maintained by the router. | EXEC mode | Chapter 4 |
| `show ipv6 ospf [process-id] database link` | Displays the new Link-LSA type added in OSPFv3. | EXEC mode | Chapter 4 |
| `show ipv6 ospf [process-id] database prefix` | Displays the new Intra-Area-Prefix-LSA type added in OSPFv3. | EXEC mode | Chapter 4 |
| `show ipv6 route ospf` | Displays all IPv6 routes learned by the router through OSPFv3. | EXEC mode | Chapter 4 |
| `clear ipv6 ospf [process-id]` | Clears the IPv6 OSPF database. | EXEC mode | Chapter 4 |

**Table A-13** *IPv6 Prefix List*

| Command | Description | Type | Reference |
|---|---|---|---|
| `ipv6 prefix-list name [seq seq-value] permit | deny ipv6-prefix/prefix-length [ge min-value] [le max-value]` | Defines an IPv6 prefix list. The *name* argument is the name of the prefix list. The parameter *seq-value* is a sequence number used with the keyword **seq** to determine the order in which the statements are used during the filtering. **deny** and **permit** are the action parameters. *ipv6-prefix/prefix-length* are the IPv6 prefix and the length of the prefix to be matched. *min-value* and *max-value* define ranges of prefix length to be matched for prefixes that are more specific than the *ipv6-prefix/prefix-length* values. The operator **ge** means greater than or equal to, and the operator **le** means less than or equal to. | Global | Chapter 4 |
| `show ipv6 prefix-list [summary | detail] name` | Displays a summary of or details about an IPv6 prefix list given as an argument. | EXEC mode | Chapter 4 |

**Table A-14**    *Route Map with IPv6*

| Command | Description | Type | Reference |
|---|---|---|---|
| `route-map` *map-tag* [`permit` \| `deny`] [*sequence-number*] | Defines a route map. *map-tag* is the route map name. **permit** and **deny** are optional action keywords to be performed if the route map match conditions are met. *sequence-number* is another optional argument that defines the position of a new **route-map** statement. This is the same command as in IPv4. | Global | Chapter 4 |
| `match ipv6 {ipv6-address` \| `next-hop` \| `route-source} prefix-list` [*prefix-list-name*] | Defines the conditions to match with IPv6. These conditions can be a route's matching IPv6 address, a route's next-hop IPv6 address, or a route's advertised IPv6 source address. A *prefix-list-name* must be specified following the **prefix-list** keyword in the matching condition. | route-map subcommand mode | Chapter 4 |
| `set ipv6 next-hop` [*ipv6-address*] [*link-local-address*] | Defines the next-hop IPv6 address of a BGP neighbor and defines the action to be carried out on a match condition. The action allowed is the specification of a route's **next-hop** IPv6 address. The **next-hop** argument for IPv6 may be an aggregatable global unicast address or a link-local address of an adjacency BGP neighbor. | route-map subcommand mode | Chapter 4 |

**Table A-15**   *Cisco Express Forwarding IPv6 (CEFv6)*

| Command | Description | Type | Reference |
|---|---|---|---|
| `ipv6 cef` | Enables the central CEFv6 mode on the router. IPv4 CEF must also be enabled using the **ip cef** command. | Global | Chapters 2, 4 |
| `ipv6 cef distributed` | Enables distributed CEFv6 mode on the router. IPv4 dCEF must also be enabled using the **ip cef distributed** command. | Global | Chapter 4 |
| `show ipv6 cef` *ipv6-prefix* `[detail]` | Shows IPv6 CEF information for the given IPv6 prefix. | EXEC mode | Chapter 4 |
| `show ipv6 cef` *interface* `[detail]` | Shows all IPv6 prefixes using the interface specified. | EXEC mode | Chapter 4 |
| `show ipv6 cef adjacency` *adjacency* | Shows all IPv6 prefixes resolved through the specified adjacency. | EXEC mode | Chapter 4 |
| `show ipv6 cef non-recursive` `[detail]` | Shows nonrecursive prefixes. | EXEC mode | Chapter 4 |
| `show ipv6 cef summary` | Shows IPv6 CEF table summary information. | EXEC mode | Chapter 4 |
| `show ipv6 cef traffic prefix-length` | Shows per-prefix length accounting statistics. | EXEC mode | Chapter 4 |
| `show ipv6 cef unresolved` | Shows unresolved prefixes. | EXEC mode | Chapter 4 |
| `show cef drop` | Shows a counter of IPv6 and IPv4 packets dropped. | EXEC mode | Chapter 4 |
| `show cef interface [detail]` `[statistics]` *interface* | Shows CEF interface status and configuration. | EXEC mode | Chapter 4 |
| `show cef linecard [detail]` `[statistics]` *slot* | Shows CEF information related to linecards. | EXEC mode | Chapter 4 |
| `show cef not-cef-switched` | Shows counters of IPv6 and IPv4 packets passed on to the next switching layer. | EXEC mode | Chapter 4 |
| `debug ipv6 cef drops` | Enables debugging of packets dropped by CEFv6 switching. | EXEC mode | Chapter 4 |
| `debug ipv6 cef events` | Enables the debugging of control plane events for CEFv6. | EXEC mode | Chapter 4 |
| `debug ipv6 cef hash` | Enables the debugging of load-balancing hash setup events for CEFv6. | EXEC mode | Chapter 4 |

**Table A-15**    *Cisco Express Forwarding IPv6 (CEFv6) (Continued)*

| Command | Description | Type | Reference |
|---|---|---|---|
| `debug ipv6 cef receive` | Enables the debugging of packets passed to IPv6 process-level switching. | EXEC mode | Chapter 4 |
| `debug ipv6 cef table` | Enables the debugging of CEFv6 table modification events. | EXEC mode | Chapter 4 |

**Table A-16**    *IPv6 Integration and Coexistence Strategy Commands: Configured Tunnel*

| Command | Description | Type | Reference |
|---|---|---|---|
| `interface` *tunnel-interface-number* | Specifies a tunnel interface number to enable a configured tunnel. | Global | Chapter 5 |
| `ipv6 address` *ipv6-address/ prefix-length* | Statically assigns an IPv6 address and a prefix length to the tunnel interface. | Interface | Chapter 5 |
| `tunnel source` *ipv4-address* | Defines the local IPv4 address used as a source address for the tunnel interface. | Interface | Chapter 5 |
| `tunnel destination` *ipv4-address* | Defines the destination IPv4 address of the tunnel endpoint. The destination IPv4 address is the far end of the tunnel. | Interface | Chapter 5 |
| `tunnel mode ipv6ip` | Defines the type of tunnel interface as a configured tunnel. | Interface | Chapter 5 |
| `show ipv6 interface` *tunnel-interface-number* | Displays information about the tunnel interface on the router. | EXEC mode | Chapter 5 |
| `ipv6 route` *ipv6-prefix/prefix-length interface-type interface-number* | A static route may be used to forward matching IPv6 packets to the configured tunnel interface. | Global | Chapters 4, 5 |

**Table A-17**    *IPv6 Integration and Coexistence Strategy Commands:*    *6to4 Tunnel*

| Command | Description | Type | Reference |
|---|---|---|---|
| `interface interface-number` | Specifies a physical or logical interface on the router for the 6to4 operation. It may be a loop-back or network interface on the router. | Global | Chapter 5 |
| `ip address ipv4-address netmask` | Assigns an IPv4 address to the given interface. This address is used as the source IPv4 address for the IPv6 packets to be tunneled over IPv4. This IPv4 address also determines the 6to4 site's prefix. | Interface | Chapter 5 |
| `interface interface-type interface-number` | Specifies a network interface on the router to enable the 6to4 router. | Global | Chapter 5 |
| `ipv6 address ipv6-address/ prefix-length` | Assigns an IPv6 address to a network interface inside the 6to4 site. The IPv6 address assigned is based on the concatenation of the IPv6 prefix 2002::/16 and the IPv4 address of the 6to4 router. The IPv4 address must be represented in hexadecimal. | Interface | Chapter 5 |
| `interface tunnel-interface- number` | Specifies a tunnel interface number to enable the 6to4 router. | Interface | Chapter 5 |
| `no ip address` | In 6to4 operation, there is no IPv4 or IPv6 address to assign to the tunnel interface. The tunnel inter-face uses the addresses of other interfaces instead. Therefore, the **no ip address** command must be used. | Interface | Chapter 5 |
| `ipv6 unnumbered interface-type interface-number` | Specifies the *interface-type* and *interface-number* used by the tunnel interface for the 6to4 operation (the network interface must have an IPv6 address). | Interface | Chapter 5 |

**Table A-17**    *IPv6 Integration and Coexistence Strategy Commands:*    *6to4 Tunnel (Continued)*

| Command | Description | Type | Reference |
|---|---|---|---|
| `tunnel source` *interface-type* *interface-number* | Specifies an interface where an IPv4 address has been assigned for the 6to4 operation. This interface's IPv4 address is used to determine the 6to4 prefix (/48). | Interface | Chapter 5 |
| `tunnel mode ipv6ip 6to4` | Defines the type of tunnel interface used for the 6to4 operation. | Interface | Chapter 5 |
| `ipv6 address 2002:c058:6301::/` `128 anycast` | Lets the router act as a 6to4 relay. This command is applied on the tunnel interface of a 6to4 router. | Interface | Chapter 5 |
| `ipv6 route 2002::/16` *interface-type interface-number* | Defines a static route to forward all IPv6 packets matching the 2002::/16 prefix through the 6to4 tunnel interface. | Global | Chapter 5 |

**Table A-18**    *IPv6 Integration and Coexistence Strategy Commands:*    *IPv6-Over-GRE Tunnel*

| Command | Description | Type | Reference |
|---|---|---|---|
| `interface` *tunnel-interface-number* | Specifies the tunnel interface number to enable a GRE tunnel. | Global | Chapter 5 |
| `ipv6 address` *ipv6-address/ prefix-length* | Statically assigns an IPv6 address and a prefix length to the tunnel interface. | Interface | Chapter 5 |
| `tunnel source` *ipv4-address* | Defines the IPv4 address used as the source address for the tunnel interface. | Interface | Chapter 5 |
| `tunnel destination` *ipv4-address* | Identifies the destination IPv4 address of the tunnel endpoint. The destination IPv4 address is the far end of the tunnel. | Interface | Chapter 5 |
| `tunnel mode gre ipv6` | Defines the tunnel interface as the GRE tunnel for IPv6. | Interface | Chapter 5 |

**Table A-19**   *IPv6 Integration and Coexistence Strategy Commands:*      *ISATAP*

| Command | Description | Type | Reference |
|---------|-------------|------|-----------|
| `interface interface-type interface-number` | Specifies a network interface for the ISATAP operation. | Global | Chapter 5 |
| `ip address ipv4-address netmask` | Assigns an IPv4 address to the network interface. This address is used as the source IPv4 address for the IPv6 packets to be tunneled. This IPv4 address also determines the IPv6 ISATAP address of the ISATAP router. | Interface | Chapter 5 |
| `interface tunnel-interface-number` | Specifies a tunnel interface number to enable the ISATAP mechanism on the router. | Interface | Chapter 5 |
| `tunnel source interface-type interface-number` | Must point to a network interface where an IPv4 address has been configured. The IPv4 address on this network interface defines the low-order 32-bit of the ISATAP address assigned to the router. | Interface | Chapter 5 |
| `tunnel mode ipv6ip isatap` | Defines the type of tunnel interface as ISATAP. | Interface | Chapter 5 |
| `no ipv6 nd suppress-ra` | By default in Cisco IOS Software technology, router advertisement is disabled on the tunnel interface. This command enables router advertisement on the tunnel interface. Router advertisement must be enabled on the tunnel interface for ISATAP. | Interface | Chapter 5 |
| `ipv6 address ipv6-address/ prefix-length` **eui-64** | The ISATAP IPv6 address has to be configured using EUI-64 format because the low-order 32-bit of the address is based on the IPv4 address. This command also enables the advertisement of the prefix on the tunnel interface. The prefix defined here must be the ISATAP prefix assigned to the site. | Interface | Chapter 5 |

**Table A-20**    *IPv6 Integration and Coexistence Strategy Commands:    Enabling NAT-PT*

| Command | Description | Type | Reference |
|---|---|---|---|
| `interface interface-type interface-number` | Specifies a first network interface to enable the NAT-PT mechanism. | Global | Chapter 5 |
| `ipv6 nat` | Enables the NAT-PT mechanism on this interface. This command is enabled on an interface basis. | Interface | Chapter 5 |
| `interface interface-type interface-number` | Determines a second interface to enable the NAT-PT mechanism. | Global | Chapter 5 |
| `ipv6 nat` | Enables the NAT-PT mechanism on this interface. This command is enabled on an interface basis. | Interface | Chapter 5 |
| `ipv6 nat prefix ipv6-prefix` | Defines the IPv6 prefix used as a NAT-PT prefix for the site. | Global | Chapter 5 |

**Table A-21**    *IPv6 Integration and Coexistence Strategy Commands:    Static NAT-PT*

| Command | Description | Type | Reference |
|---|---|---|---|
| `ipv6 nat v6v4 source ipv6-address ipv4-address` | Forces outbound IPv6 packets using the source ipv6 address (originating from an IPv6-only host) identified in the command to be translated into an IPv4 packet. The IPv4 packet uses the IPv4 source address specified in the command to reach the destination IPv4 host. | Global | Chapter 5 |
| `ipv6 nat v4v6 source ipv4-address ipv6-address` | Forces inbound IPv4 packets using the source IPv4 address identified in the command to be translated into an IPv6 packet. The IPv4 address is the destination host on the IPv4-only network. The IPv6 address is the corresponding destination IPv6 address to reach the destination host on the IPv4-only network. | Global | Chapter 5 |
| `show ipv6 nat translations` | Displays the NAT-PT translation table. | EXEC mode | Chapter 5 |

*continues*

**Table A-21**    *IPv6 Integration and Coexistence Strategy Commands:    Static NAT-PT (Continued)*

| Command | Description | Type | Reference |
|---|---|---|---|
| `clear ipv6 nat translation *` | Clears the NAT-PT translation table. | EXEC mode | Chapter 5 |
| `show ipv6 nat statistics` | Displays statistics about the translation. | EXEC mode | Chapter 5 |
| `debug ipv6 nat [detailed]` | Enables debugging mode for NAT-PT. The debug output shows all translation events. | EXEC mode | Chapter 5 |

**Table A-22**    *IPv6 Integration and Coexistence Strategy Commands:    Dynamic NAT-PT*

| Command | Description | Type | Reference |
|---|---|---|---|
| `ipv6 access-list` *name* `permit` *source-ipv6-prefix/prefix-length destination-ipv6-prefix/ prefix-length* | Defines the range of IPv6 addresses within the IPv6-only network allowed to be translated into IPv4 addresses and configures a standard IPv6 access control list for this task. | Global | Chapter 5 |
| `ipv6 nat v6v4 pool` *natpt-pool-name start-ipv4 end-ipv4* `prefix-length` *prefix-length* | Defines a pool of source IPv4 addresses used during the translation. The *natpt-pool-name* argument defines the name of this pool. The pool's first and last IPv4 addresses, represented by the *start-ipv4* and *end-ipv4* arguments, must be specified as well with the prefix length of the IPv4 pool. | Global | Chapter 5 |
| `ipv6 nat v6v4 source {list \| route-map}` *{list-name \| map-name}* `pool` *natpt-pool-name* | Configures dynamic NAT-PT mapping. The **list** keyword used with the *list-name* argument specifies a standard IPv6 ACL to define the range of IPv6 addresses. The **route-map** keyword with the *map-name* argument may be used instead. The **pool** keyword with the *natpt-pool-name* argument defines the pool of source IPv4 addresses. | Global | Chapter 5 |
| `ipv6 nat translation max-entries` *number* | Limits the number of concurrent translations handled by NAT-PT. By default, there is no limit. | Global | Chapter 5 |

**Table A-22**    *IPv6 Integration and Coexistence Strategy Commands:*    *Dynamic NAT-PT (Continued)*

| Command | Description | Type | Reference |
|---|---|---|---|
| `ipv6 nat translation timeout` *seconds* | Defines a global translation timeout for dynamic translations. By default, the timeout is 86,400 seconds. | Global | Chapter 5 |
| `ipv6 nat translation tcp-timeout` *seconds* | Defines the translation time out for TCP. By default, the timeout is 86,400 seconds. | Global | Chapter 5 |
| `ipv6 nat translation finrst-timeout` *seconds* | Defines the translation time out for FIN and RST. By default, the timeout is 60 seconds. | Global | Chapter 5 |
| `ipv6 nat translation icmp-timeout` *seconds* | Defines the translation time out for ICMP. By default, the timeout is 86,400 seconds. | Global | Chapter 5 |
| `ipv6 nat translation udp-timeout` *seconds* | Defines the translation time out for UDP. By default, the timeout is 300 seconds. | Global | Chapter 5 |
| `ipv6 nat translation dns-timeout` *seconds* | Defines the translation time out for DNS sessions. By default, the timeout is 60 seconds. | Global | Chapter 5 |

# Answers to Review Questions

Appendix B contains the answers to each chapter's "Review Questions". For some questions, there might be more than one possible answer. In those cases, the author provided the best answer.

## Chapter 1

**1** What is the size in bits of the IPv4 address scheme?

**Answer: IPv4 is based on a 32-bit address scheme.**

**2** Which classes of IPv4 addresses are not considered globally unique unicast IP addresses?

**Answer: Class D (multicast) and Class E (experimental) are not used as globally unique unicast IP addresses by hosts and routers on the Internet. Although the private addresses are within the range of unicast addresses, they must not be considered globally unique, because many organizations use them inside their network only.**

**3** What is the main rationale behind IPv6?

**Answer:**

**The IPv4 address scheme is limited by being 32-bit.**

**Some parts of the address scheme cannot be used as globally unique unicast addresses (Class D, Class E, loopback, 0.0.0.0, private addresses).**

**Very large blocks of addresses are assigned to organizations.**

**The size of the global Internet routing table is huge.**

**NAT is deployed everywhere. It saves globally unique unicast addresses but breaks IP's end-to-end model.**

**The Internet is still growing.**

**Address exhaustion is projected to occur during the current decade.**

**There is enough time to design an update of the current protocol.**

**4** Explain the consequences of the exhaustion of the IPv4 address space.

**Answer:**

**New IPv4 address space will be impossible to get.**

**There are not enough globally unique unicast addresses for every device, but the number of new devices requiring IP addresses (such as PDAs and cell phones) is increasing.**

**5** Describe the short history of IPv6 from 1993 to 2000.

**Answer:**

**1993: IETF IPng working group.**

**1995: First specifications for IPv6.**

**1996: 6bone is started using prefix 3ffe::/16.**

**1997: Provider-based address format.**

**1998: First IPv6 exchange is deployed.**

**1999: ARIN, RIPE, and APNIC are assigned IPv6 spaces to Tier-1 providers using 2001::/16.**

**1999: IPv6 Forum is founded.**

**2000: Cisco announces support for IPv6 in its IOS.**

**6** Name some limitations of NAT.

**Answer:**

**It breaks the end-to-end model of IP.**

**The network must handle connections and state.**

**It causes problems for networks with fast rerouting, links, and route redundancy.**

**It hinders network performance.**

**Keeping records of all connections becomes mandatory for providers and organizations that must have records for security reasons.**

**NAT modifies the IP header. This affects end-to-end security protocols such as IPSec AH.**

**Applications that are not NAT-friendly cannot pass through NAT.**

**Address space collisions are frequent when organizations merge networks. Private addressing is recommended behind NAT.**

**7**  Describe some of the features added by IPv6.

**Answer:**

**Plenty of IP addresses are available for the next decades.**

**Multiple levels of hierarchy provide efficient and scalable routing to the Internet.**

**Multihoming with route aggregation.**

**Autoconfiguration allows nodes to configure their IPv6 addresses.**

**A renumbering mechanism provides transparency when customers change IPv6 providers.**

**ARP broadcast is replaced by multicast.**

**The IPv6 header is more efficient than IPv4**

**Fewer fields**

**A Flow Label field for traffic differentiation**

**New extension headers replace IPv4's Options field**

**Mobility and security mechanisms are built into IPv6.**

**Transition mechanisms help networks move from IPv4 to IPv6.**

**8**  What is the size in bits of an IPv6 address?

**Answer: An IPv6 address has 128 bits. This is 4 times more bits than in IPv4 addresses.**

**9**  Comparing the OSI reference model of IPv4 to that of IPv6, which layer is updated?

**Answer: IPv6 has a change at Layer 3 (the network layer). Upper and lower layers are lightly modified to handle IPv6.**

**10**  With plenty of IP addresses with IPv6, what is not desirable to have?

**Answer: NAT is undesirable in IPv6.**

**11**  Define aggregation.

**Answer: Aggregation is a synonym for route summarization, which is a consolidation of routes in a routing table. The main benefit of aggregation is the reduction of routes in a routing table.**

**12**  What happens when a customer changes IPv6 providers?

**Answer: IPv6 space allocated to a customer is part of the ISP's IPv6 space. To keep a strict aggregation in IPv6, which is desirable for the Internet global routing table, the customer must change its IPv6 prefixes each time it changes providers.**

**13** Why is multihoming more interesting with IPv6 than with IPv4?

**Answer: Multihoming is possible in both IPv4 and IPv6. But in IPv6, multihoming is made possible by keeping strict route aggregation in the Internet global routing table.**

**14** Explain autoconfiguration.

**Answer: A router on the local link sends network information to all nodes. Nodes listen to this information and can configure their own IPv6 addresses.**

**15** Besides autoconfiguration, name the other methods used to configure IPv6 addresses on nodes.

**Answer:**

**Static configuration (manually), DHCPv6, using random interface identifiers**

**16** Describe the disadvantages of ARP broadcast in IPv4.

**Answer: ARP broadcast requests cause many interrupts in every node connected on a local link. An ARP broadcast is sent to the IP stack through the interface and the operating system.**

**17** List the main change in the IPv6 header compared to IPv4.

**Answer:**

**The IPv4 packet length is 20 bytes compared to 40 bytes for IPv6.**

**Fewer fields are present in the IPv6 header.**

**The IPv4 Header Checksum field is removed.**

**Fragmentation is handled differently in IPv6, so fields related to the fragmentation are either gone or are replaced by extension headers.**

**The Flow Label field is added for traffic differentiation.**

**The IPv4 header Options field is replaced by several extension headers.**

**18** What is the purpose of an extension header?

**Answer: It provides better efficiency in the options processing, because each extension header ensures that routers and nodes compute only headers targeted for them.**

**19** List and define two mechanisms that are embedded in the IPv6 protocol but that are considered add-ons with IPv4.

**Answer:**

**Mobile IP lets nodes move from one IP network to another while keeping the same IP addresses.**

**IPSec enables end-to-end security over IP networks.**

**20** How is the migration from IPv4 to IPv6 different from the Y2K bug?

**Answer: The Y2K bug was a major shift scheduled for a specific date. The migration from IPv4 to IPv6 will be a smooth transition over several years.**

# Chapter 2

**1** For each of the fields in the following table, give the field's length and indicate whether it is used in the IPv4 header or IPv6 header.

**Answer:**

| Field | Length in Bits | IPv4 Header | IPv6 Header |
|---|---|---|---|
| Type of Service | 8 | X | |
| Identification | 16 | X | |
| Version | 4 | X | X |
| Time to live | 8 | X | |
| Header checksum | 16 | X | |
| Header length | 4 | X | |
| Traffic Class | 8 | | X |
| Total Length | 16 | X | |
| Flow Label | 20 | | X |
| Flags | 3 | X | |
| Padding | Variable | X | |
| Extension header | Variable | | X |
| Payload Length | 16 | | X |
| Protocol Number | 8 | X | |
| Hop Limit | 8 | | X |
| Source Address | 32, 128 | X | X |
| Destination Address | 32, 128 | X | X |
| Options | Variable | X | |
| Next Header | 8 | | X |
| Fragment Offset | 13 | X | |

**2** List the fields removed from the IPv4 header.

**Answer: Header length, Identification, Flags, Fragment Offset, Header checksum, Options, Padding**

**3** What new field is added in the IPv6 header?

**Answer: Flow Label**

**4** Describe the use of the Next Header field in the IPv6 header.

**Answer: The Next Header field defines the type of information following the basic IPv6 header. The type of information can be a transport-layer protocol such as TCP or UDP, or it can be an extension header.**

**5** List the extension headers that may be placed after the basic IPv6 header, and place them in the order they must appear.

**Answer:**

**IPv6 header**

**Hop-by-Hop Options header**

**Destination Options header (if the Routing header is used)**

**Routing header**

**Fragment header**

**Authentication header**

**Encapsulating Security Payload header**

**Destination Options header**

**Upper-layer header (TCP, UDP, ICMPv6, ...)**

**6** What is mandatory with UDP when used over IPv6?

**Answer: The UDP Checksum field within the UDP packet is mandatory with IPv6. This field was optional in IPv4.**

**7** What is recommended as a mechanism for nodes in IPv6 to avoid fragmentation?

**Answer: The path MTU discovery (PMTUD) mechanism**

**8** What are IPv6's minimum MTU and recommended minimum MTU?

**Answer: The minimum MTU in IPv6 is 1280 octets, and the recommended minimum MTU is 1500 octets.**

**9**  What are the three representations of IPv6 addresses?

**Answer:**

**Preferred representation (always a series of eight 16-bit hexadecimal fields)**

**Compressed representation (successive 16-bit fields made up of 0s are replaced by a double colon; leading 0s in 16-bit fields are removed)**

**IPv6 address with an embedded IPv4 address (used by transition mechanisms)**

**10**  Compress the following IPv6 addresses into the shortest form possible.

**Answer:**

| Preferred Representation | Compressed Representation |
|---|---|
| A0B0:10F0:A110:1001:5000:0000:0000:0001 | A0B0:10F0:A110:1001:5000::1 |
| 0000:0000:0000:0000:0000:0000:0000:0001 | ::1 |
| 2001:0000:0000:1234:0000:0000:0000:45FF | 2001::1234:0:0:0:45FF |
| 3ffe:0000:0010:0000:1010:2a2a:0000:1001 | 3ffe:0:10:0:1010:2a2a:0:1001 |
| 3FFE:0B00:0C18:0001:0000:1234:AB34:0002 | 3ffe:b00:c18:1:0:1234:ab34:2 |
| FEC0:0000:0000:1000:1000:0000:0000:0009 | FEC0::1000:1000:0:0:9 |
| FF80:0000:0000:0000:0250:FFFF:FFFF:FFFF | FE80::250:FFFF:FFFF:FFFF |

**11**  Describe the IPv6 address representation for URL.

**Answer: Because the colon specifies an optional port number in a URL, the IPv6 address must be enclosed in brackets.**

**12**  List the three kinds of addresses in the IPv6 addressing architecture.

**Answer: Multicast, unicast, anycast**

**13**  For each of the following address types, find the IPv6 prefix and write the address in the compressed representation.

**Answer:**

**Unspecified—::**

**Loopback—::1**

**IPv4-compatible IPv6—::/96**

**Link-local—FE80::/10**

**Site-local—FEC0::/10**

**Multicast—FF00::/8**

**Solicited-node multicast—FF02::1:FF00:0000/104**

**Aggregatable global unicast—2000::/3**

**14** What is a link-local address?

**Answer: Link-local addresses are used by nodes on a local link scope only. These addresses cannot be routed between segments. Each IPv6 node by default owns one link-local address per network interface.**

**15** What is similar to the site-local address in IPv4?

**Answer: Site-local addresses are similar to the private addressing space in IPv4, such as 10.0.0.0/8, 172.16.0.0/12, and 192.168.0.0/16. Site-local addresses must not be routed to the IPv6 Internet.**

**16** In the following table, list the solicited-node multicast address that corresponds to each unicast address.

**Answer:**

| Unicast Address | Solicited-Node Multicast Address |
|---|---|
| A0B0:10F0:A110:1001:5000:0000:0000:0001 | FF02::1:FF00:0001 |
| 2001:0000:0000:1234:0000:0000:0000:45FF | FF02::1:FF00:45FF |
| 3ffe:0000:0010:0000:1010:2a2a:0000:1001 | FF02::1:FF00:1001 |
| 3FFE:0B00:0C18:0001:0000:1234:AB34:0002 | FF02::1:FF34:0002 |
| FEC0:0000:0000:1000:1000:0000:0000:0009 | FF02::1:FF00:0009 |

**17** Give the length in bits of the host and site parts of an aggregatable global unicast IPv6 address.

**Answer:**

**Host—64-bit**

**Site—16-bit**

**18** What three prefixes are assigned by IANA and are available as public addresses in IPv6?

**Answer:**

**2001::/16—IPv6 Internet**

**2002::/16—6to4 transition mechanism**

**3ffe::/16—6bone**

**19** What is the Cisco IOS Software command to enable IPv6 on a Cisco router?

**Answer: ipv6 unicast-routing**

**20** What protocol ID is used for IPv6 in Ethernet frames?

**Answer: 0x86DD**

**21**  Explain how IPv6 multicast addresses are mapped over Ethernet.

**Answer: Multicast mapping over Ethernet uses the multicast Ethernet prefix to which the low-order 32-bit of the IPv6 addresses is appended.**

**22**  Generate IPv6 interface IDs (in EUI-64 format) from the following Ethernet link-layer addresses.

**Answer:**

| Ethernet Link-Layer Address | EUI-64 Format |
|---|---|
| 00:90:27:3a:9e:9a | 02:90:27:FF:FE:3a:9e:9a |
| 00:90:27:3a:8d:c3 | 02:90:27:FF:FE:3a:8d:c3 |
| 00:00:86:4b:fe:ce | 02:00:86:FF:FE:4b:fe:ce |

**23**  What command assigns one IPv6 address to an interface using EUI-64 format?

**Answer: ipv6 address *ipv6-address/prefix-length* eui-64**

**24**  What is the goal of the path MTU discovery mechanism?

**Answer: The main goal of the path MTU discovery mechanism is to find out the maximum MTU value along a path when a packet is sent.**

# Chapter 3

**1**  Complete the following table by specifying the name of each ICMPv6 message type.

**Answer:**

| ICMPv6 Type | Name of Message |
|---|---|
| Type 133 | Router solicitation |
| Type 134 | Router advertisement |
| Type 135 | Neighbor solicitation |
| Type 136 | Neighbor advertisement |
| Type 137 | Redirect message |

**2** Fill in the following table by specifying which ICMPv6 message types are used for each NDP mechanism.

**Answer:**

| Mechanism | Type 133 | Type 134 | Type 135 | Type 136 | Type 137 |
|---|---|---|---|---|---|
| **Replacement of ARP** | | | X | X | |
| **Prefix advertisement** | X | X | | | |
| **DAD** | | | X | | |
| **Prefix renumbering** | X | X | | | |
| **Router redirection** | | | | | X |

**3** What is the goal of stateless autoconfiguration?

**Answer: Stateless autoconfiguration allows nodes on a local link to assign their IPv6 addresses by themselves. Network information is advertised by a router on the local link.**

**4** List the main information carried by the router advertisement message when a prefix is advertised.

**Answer:**

**IPv6 prefix**

**Valid and preferred lifetimes**

**Default router information**

**Flags/options**

**5** What command displays the prefix advertisement parameters on an interface?

**Answer: show ipv6 interface** *interface* **prefix**

**6** What command overrides the default prefix advertisement parameters on an interface?

**Answer: ipv6 nd prefix**

**7** What is duplicate address detection (DAD)?

**Answer: Before assigning an IPv6 address to an interface, each node must verify that the address it wants to use is unique and is not already in use by another node.**

**8** Fill in the following table with the type of multicast address used for each NDP mechanism listed.

**Answer:**

| Mechanism | Multicast Address |
|---|---|
| Replacement of ARP | All-nodes multicast (ff02::1) |
| | Solicited-node multicast (ff02::1:ffxx:xxxx) |
| Prefix advertisement | All-nodes multicast (ff02::1) |
| | All-routers multicast (ff02::2) |
| DAD | Solicited-node multicast (ff02::1:ffxx:xxxx) |
| Prefix renumbering | All-nodes multicast (ff02::1) |
| | All-routers multicast (ff02::2) |
| Router redirection | — |

**9** What new DNS record was added for IPv6?

**Answer: AAAA**

**10** What are the implicit rules in an extended IPv6 ACL?

**Answer:**

**permit icmp any any nd-ns**

**permit icmp any any nd-na**

**deny ipv6 any any**

**11** What commands and tools are available in IOS IPv6 to diagnose problems and manage a router?

**Answer: Commands available are ping and traceroute. Tools are Telnet, SSH, TFTP, and HTTP. All of them include IPv6 support.**

# Chapter 4

**1** What command displays the whole IPv6 routing table?

**Answer: The command show ipv6 route displays the current IPv6 routes of the IPv6 routing table.**

**2** Using the following table, specify the commands used to add the static IPv6 routes in the router for each destination IPv6 network given.

| Destination IPv6 Network | Next Hop | Corresponding Interface |
|---|---|---|
| 3ffe::/16 | fe80::260:3eff:fe58:2644 | ethernet0 |
| 2002::/16 | — | Tunnel0 |
| 2001:410:ffff::/48 | fe80::260:3eff:fec5:8888 | ethernet1 |
| Default IPv6 route | fe80::260:3eff:fe69:3322 | fastethernet0/0 |

**Answer:**

| Destination IPv6 Network | Command Used in the Cisco IOS Software |
|---|---|
| **3ffe::/16** | **ipv6 route 3ffe::/16 ethernet0 fe80::260:3eff:fe58:2644** |
| **2002::/16** | **ipv6 route 2002::/16 Tunnel0** |
| **2001:410:ffff::/48** | **ipv6 route 2001:410:ffff::/48 ethernet1 fe80::260:3eff:fec5:8888** |
| **Default IPv6 route** | **ipv6 route ::/0 fastethernet0/0 fe80::260:3eff:fe69:3322** |

**3** What changes were made to BGP4+ for IPv6 support?

**Answer:**

**The NEXT_HOP attribute can be expressed as an IPv6 address. Also, this attribute can contain both a global and link-local IPv6 address.**

**The NLRI can be expressed as an IPv6 prefix.**

**4** What command is used in the BGP router subcommand mode to disable the advertisement of routing information for the IPv4 address family?

**Answer: The no bgp default ipv4-unicast command disables the advertisement of IPv4 information by BGP4+.**

**5** How should an IPv6 prefix list be applied in a BGP4+ configuration?

**Answer: An IPv6 prefix list is applied to a BGP neighbor in the address-family ipv6 router subcommand mode.**

**6**  List the IPv6 commands that are equivalent to the well-known IPv4 commands listed in the following table.

**Answer:**

| IPv4 Command | Equivalent Command in IPv6 |
|---|---|
| show ip route | show ipv6 route |
| router bgp | router bgp |
| ip prefix-list | ipv6 prefix-list |
| route-map | route-map |
| show ip bgp | show bgp ipv6 |
| clear bgp | clear bgp ipv6 |
| debug bgp | debug bgp ipv6 |
| show ip prefix-list | show ipv6 prefix-list |

**7**  What destination address is used by RIPng in IPv6 to send updates?

**Answer: The destination address is the multicast address FF02::9. This multicast address is an all-rip-routers multicast address on the link-local scope.**

**8**  Which command enables RIPng on an interface?

**Answer: ipv6 rip *tag* enable**

**9**  What are the new TLVs and the values they add in the IS-IS specification to support IPv6?

**Answer:**

**IPv6 reachability—236 (hex 0xEC)**

**IPv6 interface address—232 (hex 0xE8)**

**10**  What NLPID value is defined in IS-IS for IPv6 support?

**Answer: 142 (hex 0x8E)**

**11**  Which command starts IS-IS for IPv6 on an interface?

**Answer: ipv6 router isis**

**12**  Which RFC describes the OSPFv3 specification?

**Answer: RFC 2740, *OSPF for IPv6***

**13**  Which command enables an OSPFv3 process on the router?

**Answer: ipv6 router ospf**

**14** What replaces the network area command in OSPFv3?

**Answer: This command is replaced by a new way to identify an IPv6 network. The command ipv6 ospf *process-id* area *area-id* is now used on an interface basis to perform this task.**

# Chapter 5

**1** List the three classes of integration and coexistence strategies presented in this chapter.

**Answer: Dual stack, tunneling, protocol translation mechanism**

**2** Describe the dual-stack approach.

**Answer: Dual stack is a way for nodes on a network to handle and use the IPv4 and IPv6 protocols simultaneously.**

**3** What type of Ethernet frame is made by IPv6-only applications on nodes?

**Answer: The Ethernet frame used is 0x86DD in the protocol-ID field instead of 0x0800 for IPv4.**

**4** How do IPv4- and IPv6-enabled applications choose the IP stack when both IPv6 and IPv4 stacks are available?

**Answer:**

**The end user can enter either the IPv4 or IPv6 address.**

**The node can use the naming service (DNS) to select the stack.**

**5** Which type of address is preferred by IPv4- and IPv6-enabled applications when the naming service provides both IPv4 (A-record) and IPv6 (AAAA-record) address types?

**Answer: The IPv6 address is preferred by IPv4 and IPv6-enabled applications.**

**6** When should you consider using integration and coexistence mechanisms?

**Answer: Integration and coexistence mechanisms should be considered as an alternative only when getting native IPv6 connectivity on networks and links is not possible.**

**7** What is the protocol number defined for the encapsulation of IPv6 packets in IPv4?

**Answer: Protocol number 41**

**8** List the three scenarios presented in this chapter in which the tunneling of IPv6 packets in IPv4 is possible.

**Answer: Host to host, host to router, router to router**

**9** What is the main requirement of tunneling?

**Answer: Tunneling is possible on nodes that have dual-stack support.**

**10** List all the tunneling techniques presented in this chapter.

**Answer: Configured tunnel, tunnel broker (based on configured tunnel), tunnel server (based on configured tunnel), 6to4, GRE tunnel, ISATAP, automatic IPv4-compatible tunnel**

**11** What is the main characteristic of a configured tunnel?

**Answer: It is configured manually on the dual-stack node.**

**12** What is the purpose of the tunnel broker and the tunnel server?

**Answer: Tunnel broker and tunnel server are mechanisms that automate the deployment and configuration of configured tunnels.**

**13** Describe how the prefix to a 6to4 site is assigned.

**Answer: The prefix of a 6to4 site is made by appending the IPv4 address of the 6to4 router to prefix 2002::/16. The IPv4 address of the 6to4 router is converted to hexadecimal. The final representation is 2002:*ipv4-address*::/48.**

**14** What is the purpose of the 6to4 relay?

**Answer: Basically, 6to4 sites can route traffic within the 2002::/16 prefix only. The 6to4 relay is a gateway between the IPv4 Internet and the IPv6 Internet. Therefore, 6to4 sites on the IPv4 Internet can exchange IPv6 traffic with the IPv6 Internet through a 6to4 relay.**

**15** Define the ISATAP address format.

**Answer: The ISATAP address format is created from the concatenation of a prefix and the interface ID in ISATAP format. The link-local prefix of an ISATAP address is FE80::/10. One aggregatable global unicast prefix must be dedicated to the ISATAP operation within a domain (all ISATAP devices must use the same prefix). The interface ID (low-order 64-bit) in the ISATAP format is made by appending the IPv4 address of the ISATAP host or ISATAP router to the hexadecimal value 0000:5EFE. The final representation of an ISATAP address is *prefix*:0000:5EFE:*ipv4-address*.**

**16** Describe how the ISATAP unicast prefix is advertised to the ISATAP host by an ISATAP router.

**Answer: The ISATAP host starts by sending a router solicitation to an ISATAP router through an ISATAP tunnel (over IPv4). After receiving the router solicitation, the ISATAP router sends a router advertisement containing the ISATAP unicast prefix to the ISATAP host through an ISATAP tunnel (over IPv4). Finally, the ISATAP host uses the aggregatable global unicast prefix received to autoconfigure its unicast IPv6 address.**

**17**  Does the IPv4-compatible tunnel mechanism provide a solution to the IPv4 address space exhaustion?

**Answer: Because the IPv4-compatible tunnel mechanism is based on the global unicast IPv4 addresses, this mechanism does not offer a solution to the IPv4 address space exhaustion.**

**18**  List the two methods that allow IPv6-only nodes in an IPv6-only network to communicate with IPv4-only nodes in an IPv4-only network.

**Answer: Application-Level Gateway (ALG), NAT-PT**

**19**  List the different types of operations defined for the NAT-PT mechanism.

**Answer: Static NAT-PT, dynamic NAT-PT, NAPT-PT, NAT-PT DNS ALG**

**20**  What is the purpose of the 96-bit prefix for the NAT-PT mechanism?

**Answer: A /96 prefix must be reserved in an IPv6 domain for the NAT-PT operation. All IPv6 packets addressed to the /96 prefix must be routed to the NAT-PT device. Then the NAT-PT device translates IPv6 addresses into IPv4 addresses according to its mapping rules.**

# Chapter 6

**1**  What command enables IPv6 on Windows XP?

**Answer: The command ipv6 install in the DOS shell enables IPv6 on Windows XP. The netsh interface ipv6 install command may also be applied on Windows XP.**

**2**  What command lists all the pseudo-interfaces on Windows 2000 and Windows NT?

**Answer: ipv6 if**

**3**  For the Microsoft Windows platforms listed in the following table, specify the pseudo-interface numbers defined for each type of interface.

**Answer:**

| Type of Interface | Windows XP | Windows 2000 | Windows NT |
|---|---|---|---|
| Loopback | 1 | 1 | 1 |
| Configured tunnel | Variable | 2 | 2 |
| 6to4 | 3 | 2 | 2 |

**4**  What command assigns the static IPv6 address fec0:0:0:1::1 to pseudo-interface 4 on Microsoft Windows XP?

**Answer:**

**ipv6 adu 4/fec0:0:0:1::1**

**or**

**netsh interface ipv6 add address 4 fec0:0:0:1::1**

**5**  What do you do on Solaris 8 to enable IPv6 on interfaces hme0 and hme1?

**Answer: Creating /etc/hostname6.hme0 and /etc/hostname6.hme1 files and then rebooting the computer enables IPv6 on interfaces hme0 and hme1.**

**6**  What command in Solaris 8 assigns the static IPv6 address fec0:0:0:1::1/64 to the hme0 interface?

**Answer: #ifconfig hme0 inet6 addif fec0:0:0:1::1/64 up**

**7**  What pseudo-interface is assigned as the configured tunnel interface on Solaris 8?

**Answer: The logical interface ip.tun0**

**8**  Based on the following table, what commands in Solaris 8 establish a configured tunnel? (Your node must use the source addresses.)

|                        | IPv4          | IPv6                 |
|------------------------|---------------|----------------------|
| Source addresses       | 10.100.50.20  | fec0:0:0:1000::2/128 |
| Destination addresses  | 192.168.1.50  | fec0:0:0:1000::1     |

**Answer:**

**#ifconfig ip.tun0 inet6 plumb**

**#ifconfig ip.tun0 inet6 tsrc 10.100.50.20 tdst 192.168.1.50 up**

**#ifconfig ip.tun0 inet6 addif fec0:0:0:1000::2/128 fec0:0:0:1000::1 up**

**9**  What FreeBSD parameter enables stateless autoconfiguration on all interfaces?

**Answer: Adding the line ipv6_enable="YES" in the /etc/rc.conf file enables stateless autoconfiguration on FreeBSD.**

**10**  What command in FreeBSD enables the configured interface gif15?

**Answer: #ifconfig gif15 create**

**11**  What interface name is defined on FreeBSD for the 6to4 mechanism?

**Answer: The stf0 interface is used on FreeBSD for the 6to4 mechanism.**

**12** For each description in the following table, specify the command that is used in FreeBSD.

**Answer:**

| Description | Command |
|---|---|
| **Displays the IPv6 routing table** | **#netstat -f inet6 -rn** |
| **Displays IPv6 information about the fxp1 interface** | **#ifconfig fxp1 inet6** |
| **Adds a default IPv6 route via gateway fec0::1:0:0:0:1** | **#route add -inet6 default fec0::1:0:0:0:1** |
| **Assigns the static IPv6 address 2001:410:ffff:2::2/64 on fxp0** | **#ifconfig fxp0 inet6 2001:410:ffff:2::2 prefixlen 64** |

**13** What do you do in Linux to enable stateless autoconfiguration on the eth2 interface at the boot of the Linux node?

**Answer:**

**Add the line NETWORKING_IPV6=YES to the /etc/sysconfig/network file.**

**Add the line IPV6INT=yes to the /etc/sysconfig/network-scripts/ifcfg-eth2 file.**

**14** What command in Linux assigns the static IPv6 address fec0:0:1000:1::a/64 to the eth0 interface?

**Answer:**

**#ifconfig eth0 inet6 add fec0:0:1000:1::a/64**

**or**

**#ip -f inet6 addr add fec0:0:1000:1::a/64 dev eth0**

**15** What pseudo-interface is assigned as the configured tunnel interface on Linux?

**Answer: The logical interface sit**

**16** What Linux command creates the configured interface sit3?

**Answer:**

**#iptunnel add sit3 remote *destination-ipv4-address* mode sit ttl *ttl-value***

**or**

**#ip tunnel add sit3 mode sit ttl *ttl-value* remote *destination-ipv4-address* local *source-ipv4-address***

**17** For each description in the following table, specify the command that is used in Linux.

**Answer:**

| Description | Command |
|---|---|
| **Displays the IPv6 routing table** | **#route -A inet6**<br><br>or<br><br>**#ip -f inet6 route show**<br><br>or<br><br>**#netstat -A inet6 -rn** |
| **Displays IPv6 information about the eth0 interface** | **#ifconfig eth0**<br><br>or<br><br>**#ip -f inet6 addr show dev eth0** |
| **Adds a default IPv6 route via gateway fec0::1:0:0:0:1** | **#route -A inet6 add ::/0 gw fec0::1:0:0:0:1**<br><br>or<br><br>**#ip -f inet6 route add ::/0 via fec0::1:0:0:0:1** |
| **Assigns the static IPv6 address 2001:410:ffff:2::2/64 on eth0** | **#ifconfig *eth0* inet6 add *2001:410:ffff:2::2/64***<br><br>or<br><br>**#ip -f inet6 addr add *2001:410:ffff:2::2/64* dev *eth0*** |

**18** What command enables stateless autoconfiguration in Tru64 ?

**Answer: Run the /usr/sbin/ip6_setup script**

**19** What command creates a configured interface in Tru64?

**Answer:**

**Run the /usr/sbin/ip6_setup script**

**or**

**iptunnel create *destination-ipv4-address source-ipv4-address***

**20** What pseudo-interface is assigned as the configured tunnel interface on Tru64 ?

**Answer: The logical interface ipt**

# Chapter 7

**1** What is the 6bone?

**Answer: The 6bone is a test-bed network that was created to validate the new standards related to the IPv6 protocol, to test the IPv6 implementations and network services, to provide feedback to developers and protocol designers, and to validate operational procedures.**

**2** What name is assigned to backbone nodes physically and logically connected on the 6bone that exchange routes?

**Answer: Backbone nodes on the 6bone that exchange IPv6 routes are called pseudo-TLAs.**

**3** What is *not* advertised by the pTLAs on the 6bone?

**Answer: Because the pTLAs connect with each other in the default-free zone, no default IPv6 route is advertised on the 6bone.**

**4** What aggregatable global unicast IPv6 address space is assigned by the IANA for 6bone operation?

**Answer: The IANA assigns the 3ffe::/16 prefix to the 6bone.**

**5** In the following table, specify whether the prefixes are allowed or prohibited on the 6bone according to the 6bone's routing policy.

**Answer:**

| Prefix | Allowed or Prohibited? |
|---|---|
| 3ffe:3000::/24 | Allowed |
| Fec0:2100::/24 | Prohibited |
| 3ffe:82e0::/28 | Allowed |
| 2001:04e0::/32 | Allowed |
| 2003:410::/32 | Prohibited |
| 3ffe:b00:c18::/48 | Prohibited |
| Fec0::/16 | Prohibited |
| 3ffe:400a::/32 | Allowed |
| Fec0:3100::2:8/126 | Prohibited |
| ::/0 | Prohibited |
| ::1 | Prohibited |
| ::0 | Prohibited |
| Fe02::/16 | Prohibited |

| Prefix | Allowed or Prohibited? |
|--------|------------------------|
| 2001:0648::/35 | Allowed |
| Fe80::/16 | Prohibited |
| 2001:350:1::/48 | Prohibited |

**6** Which RIRs allocate IPv6 address space to providers?

**Answer: APNIC, ARIN, RIPE NCC**

**7** Which aggregatable global unicast prefix did the IANA allocate for the production of the IPv6 Internet?

**Answer: The IANA allocated the 2001::/16 prefix.**

**8** What IPv6 prefix length was allocated during the initial allocation policy by the RIRs in 1999?

**Answer: The RIRs allocated /35 prefixes.**

**9** What are the main criteria to get IPv6 address space in the current allocation policy?

**Answer:**

**Be a local Internet registry**

**Do not be an end site**

**Plan to provide IPv6 connectivity**

**Plan to assign 200 /48 prefixes within two years**

**10** List the rules for the reassignment of address spaces to customers by the providers.

**Answer:**

**Prefixes assigned to customers should be a /48**

**/64 prefixes may be assigned to subnets**

**/128 prefixes may be assigned to a device**

**11** What are the basic steps for an ISP to become an IPv6 provider?

**Answer:**

**Obtain address space for an RIR**

**Peer with other TLAs**

**Allocate prefixes to customers**

**Aggregate route entries from the customers**

**12**  List the two neutral scenarios presented in this chapter to establish IPv6 peering between the IPv6 ISPs in a NAP.

**Answer:**

**Using link-local addresses for BGP4+**

**Using the aggregatable global unicast prefix registered by the NAP**

**13**  Does the IPv6 Forum design standards and specifications for IPv6?

**Answer: No. The IETF is responsible for designing standards and specifications for the IPv6 protocol.**

**14**  List the main regional IPv6 initiatives/projects for Asia, Europe, and North America. Then list two international organizations that are considered important drivers for IPv6.

**Answer:**

**Asia—Japan IPv6 Promotion Council**

**Europe—European IPv6 Task Force, 6NET**

**North America—North American IPv6 Task Force**

**International organizations: IPv6 Forum and 3G**

**15**  What is the main long-term goal of IPv6?

**Answer: IPv6 provides a global standard allowing electronic communication networks and devices such as computers, PDAs, cell phones, televisions, satellites, and industrial machines to be interconnected within the same global digital network.**

# RFCs Related to IPv6

This appendix provides an exhaustive list of the RFCs defined by the IETF and related to the IPv6 protocol. These RFCs are grouped by category.

## Rationale for IPv6

RFC 2775, *Internet Transparency,* B. Carpenter, IETF, www.ietf.org/rfc/rfc2775.txt, February 2000

RFC 2993, *Architectural Implications of NAT,* T. Hain, IETF, www.normos.org/rfc/rfc2993.txt, November 2000

RFC 3194, *The Host-Density Ratio for Address Assignment Efficiency: An update on the H ratio,* C. Huitema, A. Durand, IETF, www.ietf.org/rfc/rfc3194.txt, November 2001

## Protocol Specifications

RFC 2460, *Internet Protocol, Version 6 (IPv6) Specification,* S. Deering, R. Hinden, IETF, www.ietf.org/rfc/rfc2460.txt, December 1998

RFC 2463, *Internet Control Message Protocol (ICMPv6) for the Internet Protocol version 6 (IPv6),* A. Conta, S. Deering, IETF, www.ietf.org/rfc/rfc2463.txt, December 1998

## Addressing

RFC 2373, *IP Version 6 Addressing Architecture,* R. Hinden, S. Deering, IETF, www.ietf.org/rfc/rfc2373.txt, July 1998

RFC 2374, *An IPv6 Aggregatable Global Unicast Address Format,* R. Hinden, S. Deering, M. O'Dell, IETF, www.ietf.org/rfc/rfc2374.txt, July 1998

RFC 2375, *IPv6 Multicast Address Assignments,* R. Hinden, S. Deering, www.ietf.org/rfc/rfc2375.txt, July 1998

RFC 2450, *Proposed TLA and NLA Assignment Rules,* R. Hinden, IETF, www.ietf.org/rfc/rfc2450.txt, December 1998

RFC 2526, *Reserved IPv6 Subnet Anycast Addresses,* D. Johnson, S. Deering, IETF, www.ietf.org/rfc/rfc2526.txt, March 1999

RFC 2732, *Format for Literal IPv6 Addresses in URL's,* R. Hinden, B. Carpenter, L. Masinter, IETF, www.ietf.org/rfc/rfc2732.txt, December 1999

RFC 2928, *Initial IPv6 Sub-TLA ID Assignments,* R. Hinden et al., IETF, www.ietf.org/rfc/rfc2928.txt, September 2000

# Neighbor Discovery Protocol: Advertisement, Stateless Autoconfiguration, and Replacement of ARP

RFC 2461, *Neighbor Discovery for IP Version 6 (IPv6),* T. Narten, E. Normark, W. Simpson, IETF, www.ietf.org/rfc/rfc2461.txt, December 1998

RFC 2462, *IPv6 Stateless Address Autoconfiguration,* S. Thomson, T. Narten, IETF, www.ietf.org/rfc/rfc2462.txt, December 1998

RFC 3041, *Privacy Extensions for Stateless Address Autoconfiguration in IPv6,* T. Narten, R. Draves, IETF, www.ietf.org/rfc/rfc3041.txt, January 2001

RFC 3122, *Extension to IPv6 Neighbor Discovery for Inverse Discovery Specification,* A. Conta, IETF, www.ietf.org/rfc/rfc3122.txt, June 2001

# Link Layer Technologies

RFC 2464, *Transmission of IPv6 Packets over Ethernet Networks,* M. Crawford, IETF, www.ietf.org/rfc/rfc2464.txt, December 1998

RFC 2467, *Transmission of IPv6 Packets over FDDI Networks,* M. Crawford, IETF, www.ietf.org/rfc/rfc2467.txt, December 1998

RFC 2470, *Transmission of IPv6 Packets over Token Ring Networks,* M. Crawford, T. Narten, S. Thomas, IETF, www.ietf.org/rfc/rfc2470.txt, December 1998

RFC 2472, *IP Version 6 over PPP,* D. Haskin, E. Allen, IETF, www.ietf.org/rfc/rfc2472.txt, December 1998

RFC 2473, *Generic Packet Tunneling in IPv6 Specification,* A. Conta, S. Deering., IETF, www.ietf.org/rfc/rfc2473.txt, December 1998

RFC 2491, *IPv6 over Non-Broadcast Multiple Access (NBMA) Networks,* G. Armitage et al., IETF, www.ietf.org/rfc/rfc2491.txt, January 1999

RFC 2492, *IPv6 over ATM Networks,* G. Armitage, P. Schulter, M. Jork, IETF, www.ietf.org/rfc/rfc2492.txt, January 1999

RFC 2497, *Transmission of IPv6 Packets over ARCnet Networks,* I. Souvatzis, IETF, www.ietf.org/rfc/rfc2497.txt, January 1999

RFC 2529, *Transmission of IPv6 over IPv4 Domains without Explicit Tunnels,* B. Carpenter, C. Jung, IETF, www.ietf.org/rfc/rfc2529.txt, March 1999

RFC 2590, *Transmission of IPv6 Packets over Frame Relay Networks Specification,* A. Conta, A. Malis, M. Mueller, IETF, www.ietf.org/rfc/rfc2590.txt, May 1999

RFC 3146, *Transmission of IPv6 Packets over IEEE 1394 Networks,* K. Fujisawa, A. Onoe, IETF, www.ietf.org/rfc/rfc3146.txt, October 2001

# Routing Protocols

RFC 2080, *RIPng for IPv6,* G. Malkin, R. Minnear, IETF, www.ietf.org/rfc/rfc2080.txt, January 1997

RFC 2545, *Use of BGP-4 Multiprotocol Extensions for IPv6 Inter-Domain Routing,* P. Marques, F. Dupont, IETF, www.ietf.org/rfc/rfc2545.txt, March 1999

RFC 2740, *OSPF for IPv6,* R. Coltun, D. Ferguson, J. Moy, IETF, www.ietf.org/rfc/rfc2740.txt, December 1999

RFC 2858, *Multiprotocol Extensions for BGP-4,* T. Bates et al., IETF, www.ietf.org/rfc/rfc2858.txt, June 2000

# DNS

RFC 1886, *DNS Extensions to support IP version 6,* S. Thomson, C. Huitema, IETF, www.ietf.org/rfc/rfc1886.txt, December 1995

RFC 2673, *Binary Labels in the Domain Name System,* M. Crawford, IETF, www.ietf.org/rfc/rfc2673.txt, August 1999

RFC 2874, *DNS Extensions to Support IPv6 Address Aggregation and Renumbering,* M. Crawford, C. Huitema, IETF, www.ietf.org/rfc/rfc2874.txt, July 2000

RFC 3152, *Delegation of IP6.ARPA,* R. Bush, IETF, www.ietf.org/rfc/rfc3152.txt, August 2001

RFC 3363, *Representing Internet Protocol version 6 (IPv6) Addresses in the Domain Name System (DNS),* R. Bush et al., IETF, www.ietf.org/rfc/rfc3363.txt, August 2002

RFC 3364, *Tradeoffs in Domain Name System (DNS) Support for Internet Protocol version 6 (IPv6),* R. Austein, Bourgeois Dilettant, IETF, www.ietf.org/rfc/rfc3364.txt, August 2002

# 6bone

RFC 2471, *IPv6 Testing Address Allocation,* R. Hinden, R. Fink, J. Postel, IETF, www.ietf.org/rfc/rfc2471.txt, December 1998

RFC 2772, *6Bone Backbone Routing Guidelines,* R. Rockwell, R. Fink, IETF, www.ietf.org/rfc/rfc2772.txt, February 2000

RFC 2921, *6Bone pTLA and pNLA Formats (pTLA),* R. Fink, IETF, www.ietf.org/rfc/rfc2921.txt, September 2000

# Production IPv6 Internet

RFC 3177, *IAB/IESG Recommendations on IPv6 Address Allocations to Sites,* IAB, IETF, www.ietf.org/rfc/rfc3177.txt, September 2001

# Transition and Coexistence Mechanisms

RFC 2529, *Transmission of IPv6 over IPv4 Domains without Explicit Tunnels,* B. Carpenter, C. Jung, IETF, www.ietf.org/rfc/rfc2529.txt, March 1999

RFC 2765, *Stateless IP/ICMP Translation Algorithm (SIIT),* E. Nordmark, IETF, www.ietf.org/rfc/rfc2765.txt, February 2000

RFC 2766, *Network Address Translation Protocol Translation,* G. Tsirtsis, P. Srisuresh., IETF, www.ietf.org/rfc/rfc2766.txt, February 2000

RFC 2767, *Dual Stack Hosts using the "Bump-In-the-Stack" Technique (BIS),* K. Tsuchiya, H. Higuchi, Y. Atarashi, IETF, www.ietf.org/rfc/rfc2767.txt, February 2000

RFC 2893, *Transition Mechanisms for IPv6 Hosts and Routers,* R. Gilligan, E. Nordmark, IETF, www.ietf.org/rfc/rfc2893.txt, August 2000

RFC 3053, *IPv6 Tunnel Broker,* A. Durand et al., IETF, www.ietf.org/rfc/rfc3053.txt, January 2001

RFC 3056, *Connection of IPv6 Domains via IPv4 Clouds,* B. Carpenter, K. Moore, IETF, www.ietf.org/rfc/rfc3056.txt, February 2001

RFC 3068, *An Anycast Prefix for 6to4 Relay Routers,* C. Huitema, IETF, www.ietf.org/rfc/rfc3068.txt, June 2001

RFC 3089, *A SOCKS-based IPv6/IPv4 Gateway Mechanism,* H. Kitamura, IETF, www.ietf.org/rfc/rfc3089.txt, April 2001

RFC 3142, *An IPv6-to-IPv4 Transport Relay Translator,* J. Hagino, K. Yamamoto, IETF, www.ietf.org/rfc/rfc3142.txt, June 2001

# Multicast

RFC 2710, *Multicast Listener Discovery (MLD) for IPv6,* S. Deering, W. Fenner, B. Haberman, IETF, www.ietf.org/rfc/rfc2710.txt, October 1999

RFC 3019, *IP Version 6 Management Information Base for The Multicast Listener Discovery Protocol,* B. Haberman, R. Worzella, IETF, www.ietf.org/rfc/rfc3019.txt, January 2001

RFC 3306, *Unicast-Prefix-based IPv6 Multicast Addresses,* B. Haberman, D. Thaler, IETF, www.ietf.org/rfc/rfc3306.txt, August 2002

RFC 3307, *Allocation Guidelines for IPv6 Multicast Addresses,* B. Haberman, IETF, www.ietf.org/rfc/rfc3307.txt, August 2002

# API

RFC 2292, *Advanced Sockets API for IPv6,* W. Stevens, M. Thomas, IETF, www.ietf.org/rfc/rfc2292.txt, February 1998

RFC 2553, *Basic Socket Interface Extensions for IPv6,* R. Gilligan et al., IETF, www.ietf.org/rfc/rfc2553.txt, March 1999

# Miscellaneous

RFC 1981, *Path MTU Discovery for IP version 6,* J. McCann et al., IETF, www.ietf.org/rfc/rfc1981.txt, August 1996

RFC 2428, *FTP Extensions for IPv6 and NATs,* M. Allman, IETF, www.ietf.org/rfc/rfc2428.txt, September 1998

RFC 2675, *IPv6 Jumbograms,* D. Borman, S. Deering, R. Hinden IETF, www.ietf.org/rfc/rfc2675.txt, August 1999

RFC 2711, *IPv6 Router Alert Option,* C. Partridge, A. Jackson, IETF, www.ietf.org/rfc/rfc2711.txt, October 1999

RFC 2894, *Router Renumbering for IPv6,* M. Crawford, IETF, www.ietf.org/rfc/rfc2894.txt, August 2000

RFC 3111, *Service Location Protocol Modifications for IPv6,* E. Guttman, IETF, www.ietf.org/rfc/rfc3111.txt, May 2001

RFC 3162, *RADIUS and IPv6,* B. Aboba, G. Zorn, D. Mitton, www.ietf.org/rfc/rfc3162.txt, August 2001

RFC 3178, *IPv6 Multihoming Support at Site Exit Routers,* J. Hagino, H. Snyder, IETF, www.ietf.org/rfc/rfc3178.txt, October 2001

RFC 3266, *Support for IPv6 in Session Description Protocol (SDP),* S. Olson et al., IETF, www.ietf.org/rfc/rfc3266.txt, June 2002

# MIB

RFC 2452, *IP Version 6 Management Information Base for the Transmission Control Protocol,* M. Daniele, IETF, www.ietf.org/rfc/rfc2452.txt, December 1998

RFC 2454, *IP Version 6 Management Information Base for the User Datagram Protocol,* IETF, www.ietf.org/rfc/rfc2454.txt, December 1998

RFC 2465, *Management Information Base for IP Version 6: Textual Conventions and General Group,* D. Haskin, S. Onishi, IETF, www.ietf.org/rfc/rfc2465.txt, December 1998

RFC 2466, *Management Information Base for IP Version 6: ICMPv6 Group,* D. Haskin, S. Onishi, IETF, www.ietf.org/rfc/rfc2466.txt, December 1998

# History

RFC 1550, *IP: Next Generation (IPng) White Paper Solicitation,* S. Bradner, A. Mankin, IETF, www.ietf.org/rfc/rfc1550.txt, December 1993

RFC 1752, *The Recommendation for the IP Next Generation Protocol,* S. Bradner, A. Mankin, IETF, www.ietf.org/rfc/rfc1752.txt, January 1995

# GLOSSARY

# NUMBERS

---

**2001::/16.** The address space assigned by the IANA for the production IPv6 Internet.

**2002::/16.** The address space assigned by the IANA for the 6to4 mechanism.

**3ffe::/16.** The address space assigned by the IANA for the 6bone.

**6bone.** A virtual IPv6 backbone made of native IPv6 links and IPv6-over-IPv4 tunnels. The 6bone is a test-bed network used to validate standards, test IPv6 implementations, experiment with network IPv6 services, provide feedback to protocol designers, and validate operational procedures. See *RFCs 2471, 2772,* and *2921.*

**6to4.** Involves automatic tunneling of IPv6 packets over IPv4 (a point-to-point link) between 6to4 routers. 6to4 is a transition and coexistence mechanism that provides a /48 prefix to a 6to4 site within the 2002::/16 address space. The 6to4 prefix is based on the 6to4 router's unicast IPv4 address. Tunnels are established dynamically. See *RFC 3056.*

**6to4 relay.** A 6to4 router acting as gateway between the IPv4 Internet and the IPv6 Internet. The 6to4 relay provides traffic forwarding to the IPv6 Internet for 6to4 routers on the IPv4 Internet.

**6to4 router.** A routing device on which the 6to4 mechanism is enabled. A 6to4 router is dual-stack.

# A

---

**advertisement.** Routing or service updates sent by a router at specified intervals so that other routers and hosts on the link-local network can get information such as the network prefix, default router, and so on. See *router advertisement.*

**aggregatable global unicast address.** A unicast IPv6 address used for the generic IPv6 traffic on the IPv6 Internet. Represents the most important part of the whole IPv6 address space. Aggregatable global unicast address enables strict aggregation of routing prefixes to limit the size of the global Internet routing table.

**aggregation.** The process by which many long IPv6 prefixes are summarized to form a shorter IPv6 prefix. Therefore, instead of having multiple long IPv6 prefixes in the global Internet routing table, there are only few short IPv6 prefixes.

**anycast.** A source node sends a single packet to the nearest destination. Like multicast, anycast implies the concept of a group.

**APNIC.** Asia Pacific Network Information Center. One of the three regional Internet registries in the world that can allocate production IPv6 address spaces to ISPs. APNIC covers Asia and Australia.

**ARIN.** American Registry for Internet Numbers. One of the three regional Internet registries in the world that can allocate production IPv6 address spaces to ISPs. ARIN covers the Americas.

**ARP.** Address Resolution Protocol. An Internet protocol used to map an IPv4 address to a MAC address. See *RFC 826*.

**autoconfiguration.** See *stateless autoconfiguration*.

# B - F

**BGP4+.** Also known as Multiprotocol Extensions for BGP4. BGP4+ is an enhanced version of BGP4 that supports IPv6. BGP4+ is an EGP protocol. See *RFCs 2858* and *2545*.

**CIDR.** Classless Interdomain Routing. A technique supported by BGP4 and based on route aggregation. CIDR allows routers to group routes to cut down on the quantity of routing information carried by the core routers. With CIDR, several networks appear to networks outside the group as a single, larger entity.

**configured tunnel.** An IPv6-over-IPv4 tunnel (a point-to-point link) defined statically between dual-stack nodes. Configured tunnel is a transition and coexistence mechanism that allows the tunneling of IPv6 packets over IPv4 networks.

**dual stack.** Hosts, servers, and routers that have one IPv4 stack and one IPv6 stack enabled simultaneously. Dual stack is a transition and coexistence strategy that allows nodes to receive and send both IPv4 and IPv6 traffic.

**duplicate address detection (DAD).** An IPv6 mechanism that verifies the existence of an IPv6 address on the local link before configuring an IPv6 address on a network interface.

**EUI-64.** Extended Unique Identifier 64-bit. Related to network interface link-layer addresses. The EUI-64 format is defined by the IEEE as a combination of the 24-bit manufacturer ID assigned by IEEE and a 40-bit value assigned by the manufacturer. Link-local addresses assigned at bootup by IPv6 nodes and stateless autoconfiguration mechanisms use the EUI-64 format.

**extension header.** Optional headers defined for IPv6 that may follow the basic IPv6 header. These optional headers are described in RFC 2460. The extension headers include the authentication header, encapsulation security payload header, destination option header, fragment header, hop-by-hop option header, and routing header.

**flow label.** A field of the basic IPv6 header used to tag a flow for IPv6 packets.

# H - J

**IANA.** Internet Assigned Numbers Authority. An organization operated under the auspices of ISOC as a part of IAB. IANA delegates authority for IPv4 and IPv6 address space allocations. IANA also maintains a database of assigned protocol identifiers used in the TCP/IP stack, including autonomous system numbers.

**IETF.** Internet Engineering Task Force. A task force consisting of more than 100 working groups responsible for developing Internet standards. The IETF operates under the auspices of ISOC.

**IPng.** IP next generation. The former name of the IETF working group that designed the technical specifications for IPv6. This IETF working group was renamed IPv6 in 2001. IPng is also the former name of the IPv6 protocol.

**IPv4.** Internet Protocol version 4. A network layer protocol in the TCP/IP stack offering a connectionless internetwork service. IP provides features for addressing, type-of-service specification, fragmentation and reassembly, and security. IPv4 is based on a 32-bit address scheme. IPv4 is documented in RFC 791.

**IPv4-compatible IPv6 address.** A special unicast IPv6 address used by IPv6 transition and coexistence mechanisms. An IPv4-compatible IPv6 address is represented by the prefix ::/96.

**IPv4 Internet.** The current production unicast IPv4 Internet. The IPv4 Internet is also known by non-IPv6 users as the Internet.

**IPv4-only node.** A node that runs only an IPv4 stack.

**IPv6.** Internet Protocol version 6. Introduced by the IETF in 1992, IPv6 appears to be a fundamental and well-engineered solution to the IPv4 addressing space shortage. IPv6 is significantly more efficient than IPv4. IPv6 is based on a 128-bit address scheme. IPv6 provides nodes with multiple types of addresses and has a basic header of 40 octets and several optional extension headers and mechanisms.

**IPv6 Internet.** The growing production unicast IPv6 Internet, which includes the 6bone.

**IPv6-only node.** A node that runs only an IPv6 stack.

**ISATAP.** Intrasite Automatic Tunnel Addressing Protocol. A transition and coexistence mechanism that tunnels IPv6 packets in IPv4 within an administrative domain to create one virtual IPv6 network over an IPv4 network. See *draft-ietf-ngtrans-isatap-12.txt*.

**IS-IS.** A routing protocol based on the OSI routing protocol IS-IS, but with support for IPv4, IPv6, and other protocols. Integrated IS-IS is an IGP protocol. See *draft-ietf-isis-ipv6-05.txt*.

**ISP.** Internet service provider. A company that provides Internet connectivity and IPv6 address space to other companies, organizations, and individuals.

# L - M

**link-local address.** A unicast IPv6 address that can be used only on the local link scope. Link-local addresses are based on the IPv6 prefix fe80::/10. Several IPv6 mechanisms, such as prefix advertisement and duplicate address detection, use link-local addresses for their operations.

**Mobile IPv6.** An IPv6 version of the Mobile IPv4 protocol designed to allow computers to maintain their IP connectivity with remote nodes while moving from one point of attachment to another. Mobile IPv6 is much more efficient than Mobile IPv4.

**multicast.** A source node sends a single packet to multiple destinations (one-to-many). Multicast implies the concept of a group. IPv6 uses multicast addresses in several of its mechanisms on the link-layer scope. Multicast addresses in IPv6 are based on the prefix FF00::/8.

**multicast assigned address.** A multicast IPv6 address reserved within the multicast scope for the operation of the protocol. FF01::1, FF01::2, FF02::1, FF02::2, and FF05::2 are examples of reserved IPv6 addresses. See *RFC 2373*.

**multicast mapping over Ethernet.** A special mapping of multicast addresses to Ethernet link-layer addresses for IPv6. Mapping consists of appending the low-order 32-bit of an IPv6 multicast address to the prefix 33:33.

# N - P

**NAP.** Network Access Point. A neutral place where ISPs can interconnect and exchange IPv6 routes and traffic.

**NAT.** Network Address Translation. A mechanism that typically translates IPv4 packets from networks based on private addressing to the IPv4-Internet or to other private networks. See *RFCs 1631* and *1918*.

**NAT-PT.** Network Address Translation Protocol Translation. NAT-PT translates IPv6 addresses into IPv4 addresses and vice versa. The NAT-PT is a transition and coexistence mechanism that allows IPv6-only nodes to communicate with IPv4-only nodes. See *RFC 2766*.

**neighbor advertisement (NA).** An ICMPv6 type 136 message is the response sent by an IPv6 node that has received a neighbor solicitation message from another IPv6 node. Neighbor solicitation replaces ARP.

**Neighbor Discovery Protocol (NDP).** A protocol that defines several mechanisms that are built into IPv6, such as prefix advertisement, duplicate address detection, ARP replacement, and router redirection. NDP uses ICMPv6 message types 133 through 137. See *RFC 2461*.

**neighbor solicitation (NS).** An ICMPv6 type 135 message sent by an IPv6 source node to solicit another IPv6 node on the local link. Neighbor solicitation is used to replace ARP and for duplicate address detection.

**NGtrans.** An IETF working group that has designed tools, protocols, and strategies allowing the transition of IPv4 networks to IPv6.

**OSPFv3.** Open Shortest Path First version 3. The IPv6 counterpart of OSPFv2. OSPFv3 is an IGP. See *RFC 2740*.

**path MTU discovery (PMTUD).** A mechanism that allows a source node to detect the largest MTU value along a delivery path to a destination node.

**pseudo-TLA (pTLA).** On the 6bone, the pseudo-TLAs are the backbone providers that are connected to each other. pTLAs are equivalent to the Tier-1 providers on the IPv4-Internet.

# Q - Z

**RFC.** Request For Comments. A document series that is the primary means of communicating information about the Internet. Some RFCs are designated by the IAB as Internet standards. Most RFCs document protocol specifications.

**RIPE NCC.** Réseaux IP Européens Network Coordination Center. One of the three regional Internet registries in the world that can allocate production IPv6 spaces to ISPs. RIPE NCC covers Europe and the Middle East.

**RIPng.** Routing Information Protocol next generation. An enhanced version of RIP that supports IPv6. RIPng is an IGP. See *RFC 2080*.

**router advertisement (RA).** An ICMPv6 type 134 message sent periodically on the local link by an IPv6 router or upon request of a router solicitation message. The router advertisement message in IPv6 contains the IPv6 prefixes, valid and preferred lifetimes of prefixes, default router information, and some flags and options for nodes.

**router solicitation (RS).** An ICMPv6 type 133 message used by an IPv6 node to request the sending of router advertisement messages by an IPv6 router.

**site-local address.** A unicast IPv6 address that can be used only within a site scope. Site-local addresses are based on the IPv6 prefix fec0::/10. Site-local address are similar to private address space in IPv4.

**solicited-node multicast address.** A multicast IPv6 address within the multicast scope that is automatically enabled on the interface for each unicast and anycast address assigned. Solicited-node multicast addresses are used in IPv6 to replace ARP and in duplicate address detection. Solicited-node multicast addresses in IPv6 are based on the prefix FF02::1:FF00:0000/104.

**stateless autoconfiguration.** An IPv6 mechanism that allows nodes to configure their IPv6 addresses by themselves using router advertisement messages received.

**traffic class.** A field of the basic IPv6 header that is similar to the Type of Service field in the IPv4 header.

**unspecified address.** A unicast IPv6 address that is not assigned to any interface. The unspecified address in IPv6 is represented by ::0/128 and indicates the absence of an IPv6 address. Unspecified addresses are used by some IPv6 mechanisms.

# INDEX

## Symbols

%zoneid argument, 298

## Numerics

3G, 379
6bone (IPv6 backbone), 12, 355–356
    addresses, 360–361
    architecture, 359
    BGP4+, 163
    qualifying as pTLAs, 362–363
    route registry, 366
    routing policies, 363–365
    topology, 357–358
6NET, 376
6to4 mechanisms
    deploying, 245–248
    enabling, 248–251
    relays, 251
    tunnels
        FreeBSD, 319–321
        Linux, 332
        Microsoft Windows, 301–305

## A

a/127 IPv6 prefixes, assigning to point-to-point links, 239
A6 resource records, 129
access
    NAPs, 371–372
    NSAP, 11, 78
ACLs (access control lists), 129
    applying, 130
    creating, 130
    defining, 130–133
    extended ACLs
        defining, 133–140
    managing, 140

activation of IPv6, 79
adding static neighbor entries, 110
Address Resolution Protocol (ARP), 24
addresses, 41, 53, 77–78
    6bone, 360–361
    AAAA records, 127–129
    aggregatable global unicast, 173
    allocation, 369
        policies, 367–369
        providers, 374
    anycast, 72, 73
    autoconfiguration, 21–22
    DAD, 121–123, 239
    DHCP, 144
    IPv4
        exhaustion of, 9–11
        growth, 8–9
        IANA allocation, 8
        space, 6–8
    IPv4-compatible IPv6, 74
    ISATAP, 256
    link-layer, 21–23
    link-local, 160, 173
    loopback, 74
    MAC, 22
    Microsoft Windows, 296
    NAT, 13–15, 236
    NAT-PT, 264–273
    NET, 198
    next-hop, 160, 192
    NSAP, 11
    private, 247
    querying, 230
    representation of, 54–61
    required IPv6, 76
    space, 16
        aggregatable global unicast, 67
        automatic IPv4-compatible tunnels, 261
        reassignment of, 368
    static
        configuration, 83
        FreeBSD, 315–316
        Linux, 326–328
        Solaris, 308–309
        Tru64 UNIX, 336

# B

# C

# D

## E

# G

# H

# J

# K

# L

# O

# P

# S

# T

# U

CISCO SYSTEMS

**Cisco Press**

## NETWORKING TECHNOLOGY GUIDES
### MASTER THE NETWORK

Turn to Networking Technology Guides whenever you need **in-depth knowledge of complex networking technologies**. Written by leading networking authorities, these guides offer theoretical and practical knowledge for **real-world networking applications and solutions**.

**Look for Networking Technology Guides
at your favorite bookseller**

**Cisco CallManager Best Practices:
A Cisco AVVID Solution**
ISBN: 1-58705-139-7

**Cisco IP Telephony: Planning, Design,
Implementation, Operation, and Optimization**
ISBN: 1-58705-157-5

**Cisco PIX Firewall and ASA Handbook**
ISBN: 1-58705-158-3

**Cisco Wireless LAN Security**
ISBN: 1-58705-154-0

**End-to-End QoS Network Design:
Quality of Service in LANs, WANs, and VPNs**
ISBN: 1-58705-176-1

**Network Security Architectures**
ISBN: 1-58705-115-X

**Optimal Routing Design**
ISBN: 1-58705-187-7

**Top-Down Network Design**, Second Edition
ISBN: 1-58705-152-4

Visit **www.ciscopress.com/series** for details about Networking Technology Guides and a complete list of titles.

Learning is serious business.
**Invest wisely.**

# SEARCH THOUSANDS OF BOOKS FROM LEADING PUBLISHERS

Safari® Bookshelf is a searchable electronic reference library for IT professionals that features thousands of titles from technical publishers, including Cisco Press.

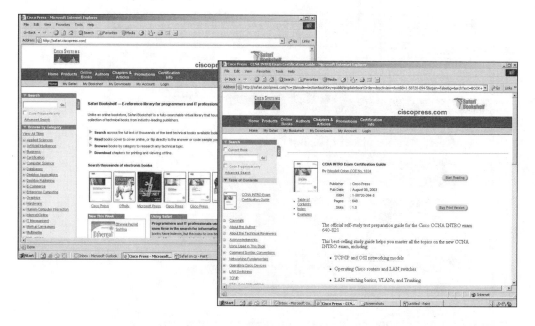

With Safari Bookshelf you can

- **Search** the full text of thousands of technical books, including more than 130 Cisco Press titles from authors such as Wendell Odom, Jeff Doyle, Bill Parkhurst, Sam Halabi, and Dave Hucaby.

- **Read** the books on My Bookshelf from cover to cover, or just flip to the information you need.

- **Browse** books by category to research any technical topic.

- **Download** chapters for printing and viewing offline.

With a customized library, you'll have access to your books when and where you need them—and all you need is a user name and password.